Economic Analysis for Management Decisions

THE IRWIN SERIES IN ECONOMICS

Consulting Editor   LLOYD G. REYNOLDS   *Yale University*

To—
Jim, Mary F., and Marilyn

Economic Analysis for Management Decisions

JAN WALTER ELLIOTT
The University of Wisconsin—Milwaukee

1973

Richard D. Irwin, Inc., *Homewood, Illinois 60430*
IRWIN–DORSEY INTERNATONAL *London, England WC2H 9NJ*
IRWIN–DORSEY LIMITED *Georgetown, Ontario L7G 4B3*

First printing, January 1973
Second printing, May 1974

ISBN 0-256-01430-2

Library of Congress Catalog Card No. 72-90773

Printed in the United States of America

PREFACE

Courses in the economics of the firm and its markets have been part of university business administration programs for some time. Since Joel Dean's pathbreaking *Managerial Economics* over two decades ago, these courses have been concerned with exploring real-world business applications of the logical structure of microeconomics. That objective is as pertinent today as it was then. Indeed, perhaps more so. Corporate economic problems have grown in size as corporations have grown. More is at stake in pricing, production, and resource allocation decisions than ever before. This makes careful analysis of economic problems increasingly a practical necessity for corporate prosperity. In addition, economists have by now learned more about the implications of existing theory. Moreover, new inquiry has been undertaken in several directions, some of which are highly pertinent to modern corporate management. But, most importantly, in my view, the field of econometrics has made significant advancements in the last two decades in dealing with the question of measuring economic relationships. Our understanding of the strengths and weaknesses of regression and regression-related models for measuring time-series relationships among economic variables has doubled and redoubled over the past 20 years.

This growth in knowledge of econometrics has important implications for the pursuit of real-world applications of conceptual economic schemes. It means we are closer now than ever to getting the demand curves, production functions, cost curves, and other apparatus of microeconomic theory down from the blackboard of the classroom and into the quantifiable form necessary to use this apparatus for creation of information useful in management decision making. For the major problem in applying economic concepts to specific management decisions is quantitative measurement of the important relationships involved. Do returns to labor diminish over a particular operating region of the production function? Is demand price-elastic over a given range? Are there economies of scale in enlarging the plant? These are questions involving measurement. To obtain concrete answers to questions such as these, we must come to grips with explicit measurement of the theoretical functions involved. This means an interest in real-world economic applicatons as of 1973 quite reasonably includes an interest in the measurement methods of econometrics as well as the conceptual apparatus of economic theory. If we can knit together the tools of econometrics and the ideas of microeconomic theory, we shall succeed in putting these two areas of inquiry to work in the development of concrete information useful in management decision making. In doing this, we shall have moved a step beyond the qualitative level of analysis which characterizes the previous study of managerial economics.

Because of their pivotal role in later analysis, model building and the tools of econometrics are the subject of Part I of the book. The survey of economic measurement occupies Chapters 2 to 4 and is written strictly with the user in mind. Only an introductory preparation in statistical inference and regression methods is assumed. In Part II the major areas of microeconomics are taken up, building upon the ideas of Part I. Specific applications to management decision issues are discussed and developed through logical analysis, illustrations, and case studies in which the student is asked to perform his own analyses. The major areas included are demand analysis, Chapter 5, business forecasting, Chapter 6, production and cost analysis, Chapters 7 to 9, and market price behavior, Chapters 10 and 11. A principles-level microeconomics course is helpful but I judge not required background for the material in this part.

Part III surveys areas outside the traditional scope of microeconomics but highly pertinent to managers of modern corporations. In Chapters 12 and 13, a series of models and methods for analyzing major economic problems in corporations is introduced, including behavioral approaches, industrial dynamics, programming, simulation, and econometric models. Finally, the last two chapters of the book provide an outline of a contemporary model of financial resource allocation in the modern corporation. This model emphasizes the role in overall corporate financial performance of investment strategy, debt policy, and dividend policy as well as the interactions between these decision areas.

This book has been greatly improved by the unselfish ideas of many colleagues, students, and friends. Particular thanks go to Professor Richard B. Westin who read and reread the entire manuscript and provided hundreds of useful suggestions. Also, Lloyd Reynolds, Myron Gordon, Clarke Johnson, and J. Robert Moore made numerous helpful comments on parts of the work. Thanks go to many former students who used parts of the book in the MBA course in Managerial Economics at the University of Wisconsin—Milwaukee and provided important feedback during its preparation. As with all authorships, these acknowledgments do not relieve me from the burden of responsibility for such errors and lapses from truth as may remain in the work.

Milwaukee, Wisconsin   J. WALTER ELLIOTT
December 1972

CONTENTS

PART III
ANALYZING ECONOMIC BEHAVIOR OF FIRMS

PART I

Tools for Measuring Economic Relationships

An interest in applying the logic of economic theory to specific management problems in more than a qualitative way leads immediately and necessarily to a concern with methods and tools for measuring relationships among economic variables. If we can mingle adequate measurement methods with theory, we may be able to translate blackboard solutions into specific answers to specific questions. Part I considers the tools of statistics and econometrics that directly address this measurement question.

Chapter 1

ECONOMIC ANALYSIS, MODELS, AND MANAGEMEMT DECISIONS

This book deals with measuring economic relationships, analyzing market behavior, and examining some major economic decisions in the business firm. The firm is primarily an economic institution in a market system. It organizes the production of goods and services, and marshals the resources required in this production process. The firm in a market economy is the driving force behind the continual improvement and development of the quality and character of goods and services that measure the material progress of a society.

In directing our analysis to the economic dimension of the business enterprise, we are focusing directly upon the institutional roots of the firm. Accordingly, in a study of the economic character of a distinctly economic institution, we should expect to deal with some of the major decisions made within that institution. To a large extent, this is indeed our goal. We shall be concerned with the economics of pricing decisions in the firm. Attention will be paid to the problem of forecasting in firms. We shall consider the determination of how much and what kind of resources the firm employs in its production process. We shall devote attention to the analysis of cost-output relationships in the firm. We shall consider the selection of the firm's marketing, capital, and research and development budget, and the decision to employ both internal and external funds in the expansion of the firm's operations. We will review methods by which firms may analyze and evaluate their own economic behavior and performance.

Although the business enterprise in a market economy is a distinctly economic institution, the decisions made by those to whom the resources of the enterprise are entrusted are not all, or perhaps not even pre-dominantly economic in terms of the factors that dominate the decision. Relationships with suppliers and labor unions, with stockholders and sub-ordinates, all have economic factors that enter into decisions. Yet many strategic decisions that mold these relationships are not primarily economic. This is important. It means this treatise on economic decision making does not deal with all the mainstream issues in the firm. Because

3

of this limitation, we cannot profess to offer a general model of decision making in the firm.

Even with regard to the distinctly economic decisions with which we are concerned, we cannot assure ourselves that our optimal solutions are truly optimal if noneconomic factors are introduced into our analysis. We should begin by recognizing this limitation.

Our analysis typically focuses upon the economic factors in economic decisions to the exclusion of the impact of noneconomic factors, and to the exclusion of the interaction effect of other noneconomic decisions. By this omission, we are not implying that noneconomic dimensions of the firm are of little importance in economic decision making, for that is clearly not the case. Instead, we find ourselves in the position of the small boy faced with a seemingly giant birthday cake flanked on one side by a mountainous dish of ice cream and on the other by a virtual pyramid of cookies. Both this treatise and the small boy have their capacities. We shall have reached ours in this work if we can effectively analyze the economic dimension. As in the case of the small boy, the cookies will have to wait.

SOME COMMON DENOMINATORS IN ECONOMIC ANALYSIS

Several important areas of economic analysis employ common methods in arriving at their conclusions. Two ideas that appear frequently in various areas of economic analysis are the techniques of marginal analysis and the notion of opportunity costs.

Marginal Analysis

Marginal analysis focuses primarily upon changes in economic variables and secondarily upon the values of the variables. It deals with changes in costs, outlays, or forfeitures of resources as compared with revenues, benefits, or receipts of resources. If we are given a state of affairs, which may be a level of output, a set of purchase decisions, a combination of labor and capital goods, or in general any baseline, marginal analysis can be applied to consider the impact of a change in the state of affairs. We investigate the benefits associated only with the change, and the costs associated only with the change. In looking at these differences, we are investigating the value of benefits and costs "at the margin." If the benefits exceed the costs for a particular hypothesized change, where both benefits and costs are measured in terms of the objective towards which we are striving, then making the hypothesized change will contribute positively towards the objective. After the change, the marginal values of both benefits and costs will likely have changed. A reappraisal of the new marginal benefits and costs is now appropriate.

In those cases wherein it is reasonable to specify certain likely properties to the marginal benefit function and the marginal cost function,
we may be able to state conditions for maximum attainment of our objective in terms of the marginal functions. For example, suppose we are
comparing the change in sales revenues associated with selling a hypothesized increase in output with the change in costs associated with producing the increased increment of output. If it can be assumed that marginal
revenues will remain constant with successive increments of output (that
is, that additional units can be sold at a constant price) while marginal
costs will constantly rise, then we can stipulate the profit-maximizing
point as the point at which the rising marginal costs are equated with
the constant marginal revenues. At this point, all available additions to
profits have been taken. That is, all units of output were produced
wherein marginal revenues exceeded marginal costs.

The marginal idea shows up in other forms. Consider the consumer
who is dividing his income between product A and product B. If his
marginal satisfaction from A, per dollar spent on A, exceeds his marginal
satisfaction from B per dollar spent on B, then lowering his consumption
of B by spending less on B would represent a forfeiture of the lower
B satisfaction. But this would be more than offset by the increase in
satisfaction that would result from his increasing his consumption of A
by reallocating funds to A with the resources freed by the decrease
in his B consumption. Such an argument for switching his purchases
would continue to exist until the purchase of A had shoved the marginal
satisfaction per dollar of that product down to a level equal to the rising
marginal satisfaction of B per dollar.[1]

Another example of marginal analysis can be found in the model for
profit-maximizing levels of factor use. Using labor as an example, additional units of this factor should be employed as long as the marginal
productivity of that labor, measured in the dollar value of the output
produced by an additional labor unit, exceeds the dollar cost per unit
of labor.

Opportunity Costs

A second notion which reappears in economic analysis is that of opportunity costs. Opportunity costs become relevant when a new or continued
commitment of resources is being considered and an alternative resource
commitment exists and is known. Opportunity costs are defined in such
a situation as the loss of benefits resulting from not committing available
resources to their best alternative use. In the case of several alternatives,

---

[1] This assumes that more of the product will result in a falling marginal satisfaction; i.e., that the tenth unit of product A, while perhaps adding to satisfaction,
would add less than that added by the ninth unit, and so forth.

opportunity costs would be the benefit associated with the most attractive alternative. The *cost* part of the term refers to the classification of the profit associated with an alternative resource commitment as a cost of accepting another resource commitment. When such a cost is added to the explicit costs associated with the resource commitment, if profits are positive, then the resource commitment is not only profitable but more profitable than other alternatives. If profits including opportunity costs are negative, then a better alternative is available for resources and it should be prosecuted.

Consider, for example, the classic example of the self-employed businessman who adds up costs and revenues at the end of a month and declares that he has made a profit of $300 on his operation. If he has alternative employment opportunities that will pay $400, then this opportunity cost causes his profit to be indeed a $100 loss in terms of realizing his best economic opportunity. While he may be perfectly willing to forfeit the $100 in order to run his own business, he should recognize the forfeiture he is engaging in to obtain this satisfaction. The term "opportunity cost" is a convenient way to analyze this dimension of resource allocation.

A second example of the use of opportunity costs can be illustrated by considering the use of floor space in a shop in which all floor space is utilized. The shopkeeper can be assumed to carry a number of products, each of which contributes something towards paying his fixed costs and his profits (which we will assume include opportunity costs). He also presumably has a number of products not now on his floor that he could introduce at the expense of other products. Then, the best profit contribution item per square foot of floor space required among the group not now being carried establishes the opportunity cost for the items now being carried. Any item in stock that does not contribute this opportunity cost or better per square foot of floor space required should be replaced by the item not in stock.

There are numerous examples of cases like the two discussed where opportunity costs are unambiguously defined. In these cases, their application is clear. However, they can also be applied in situations where their apparent simple clarity masks deeper difficulties. An illustration of such an application is contained in the *1968 Economic Report of the President.*[2] The following is taken from that report:

The large recent gains in output reflect the fact that overall demand has caught up and kept up with the economy's rising productive capacity. In the late 1950's and early 1960's the Nation was sacrificing the opportunity to consume and invest a substantial amount of the output it was capable of producing. Potentially productive men and machines were idle because

---

[2] *Economic Report of the President, 1968* (Washington, D.C.: United States Government Printing Office, 1968).

of inadequate demand for their services. At the recession trough in the first quarter of 1961, actual GNP was $50 billion below the estimated potential output of the economy at a 4 percent unemployment rate.[3]

This discussion of output sacrificed because of less-than-full employment of the labor force states in different terms that the opportunity cost of engaging in public policies not designed to move the economy towards full employment is the lost output associated with those less-than-full employment production levels. If it is true that this lost output is an opportunity cost, then clearly the benefit associated with engaging in less-than-full employment public policies must more than offset these costs if we are to logically maintain such policies.

But what are the benefits associated with not engaging in full employment policies? Unfortunately, they are not defined in the *Economic Report* along with the opportunity costs. We may speculate that the benefits might be represented by tolerable levels of general price rises. And what of the opportunity costs? Can we be assured that any set of public policies we could devise would deliver the alternative of full employment? In other words, can we be assured the alternative is attainable? Then how can we compare the GNP-measured opportunity cost with the price-level-measured alternative? And what of the measure of potential that establishes opportunity costs in this case? It has been defined in terms of a 4 percent labor force unemployment rate. What if this rate corresponds with 150 percent of available physical plant capacity?

These are not simple questions. However, they illustrate a simple point. To apply opportunity costs implies we know enough about the related economic measures to operationally specify the alternatives. In complicated cases, specifying such alternatives may involve subtle but often crucial problems of statistical measurements, a general topic that will occupy our attention in Chapters 2–4.

MODELS AND MODEL BUILDING

Marginal analysis and opportunity costs are two common tools that reappear in the apparatus of economics. A third common denominator that pervades the systems of reasoning in economics is the use of conceptual models. Therefore, a consideration of some general characteristics of economic models and model building will sharpen our understanding of the nature of the reasoning process that will commonly be employed.

Composition of Models

In general, a model consists of structural components and rules of relationship that bind the structural components together. The relative

---
[3] Ibid., p. 60.

importance of these two ingredients is highly variable in different kinds of models. In an engineer's wind tunnel model of a proposed new aircraft, the structural components include such parts as wings, fuselage, and empennage; while the rules of relationship simply state that wings bear a fixed relationship to the fuselage, as do the tail section and other parts. In abstract models not involving physical components, but only mathematical components, the rules of relationship may be overriding in significance when compared to the structural elements, which may be in some cases equally as trivial as the rules of relationship seem in the case of an aircraft wind tunnel model. We may define a model by defining the nature of these two ingredients.

Models as Functional Representations

Any model serves as a *functional representation* of the physical or abstract system with which it is concerned. This statement imputes a powerful property to a model. To be functionally representative, the model must behave essentially the way its subject system functions. The word *essentially* is key here. For the model to function in essence the way the system functions does not require that the model behave exactly the way the system behaves. It does require that elements of systematic behavior critical to analysis are reflected in the model. In attempts to model large-scale or highly complex systems, this representative functioning is of overwhelming importance. For, in such models, the omission of certain actual characteristics of the real system is an absolute necessity due to unmanagably complex relationships among large sets of variables. Moreover, in this process of abstraction a separation must be made between essential and nonessential, and herein lies a major portion of the problem of model building.

For example, in efforts to model complex socioeconomic systems, the feasible subset of variables included in the model usually represents a small fraction of all possible variables. Specifying this subset typically relies as much on qualitative factors as upon quantitative procedures. Rigorous and totally relevant tests do not yet exist to classify and evaluate potential models. The same quality is present with respect to the rules of relationship. They may naturally exist in ways that defy direct observation. Their quantitative reflection in such cases involves the formulation of statistical hypotheses regarding relationships among variables, testable only by reference to performance over a past period.

In turn, reference to a past time period as a means to develop judgments about the worthiness of model structure creates the possibility that two or more models, possessing different structural components and different rules of relationship, may both be consistent with a past period of data. Indeed, many fundamental conflicts in economic theory have resulted from the situation where two or more models of differing composition can both successfully represent past data.

APPLICATIONS OF MODELS

Models in general have a variety of applications. In the world of the physical sciences a dramatic illustration of the use of a model has been given in connection with Sir Isaac Newton's "Law of Gravitation," which proposed that the force of gravity between two objects is proportional to the product of the two masses and inversely proportional to the square of the distance between them. The mathematical model is:

$$F = k(mN)/d^2$$

This model, whose components are the two bodies and their proximities in space, had significant predicting ability. The relationship among the components so proposed did, in fact, seem to be a useful functional representation of various physical systems.

One use of the model was to trace planet motion. In using the model in this regard early in the 19th century, it was observed that Uranus was not following its calculated orbit. Using later data, the orbit was recalculated and for a few years the planet's movements seemed to conform to the new calculations. However deviations were again observed. Was Newton's model faulty? There was so very much evidence supporting Newton that this possibility was not forcefully argued. It was then hypothesized by a few scientists that the deviation could be caused by another and undiscovered planet influencing Uranus. If this were so, the mass and location of the unknown planet could be calculated using Newton's model.

One proponent of this hypothesis was U. Leverrier, who developed the calculated orbital structure given the assumed new planet. In his final research paper, he announced the position of the hypothesized planet at particular points in time. He arranged for a high-powered telescope, and on December 23, 1846, directed the telescope to be pointed to a particular point in the sky according to his calculations, whereupon the planet Neptune was discovered with clear recognition. Leverrier's hypothesis had been dramatically and conclusively proven.

This illustration deals with the use of a model, formulated and tested over a certain range of data, to predict *beyond* that data. In other words, having formulated the model partly on the basis of the observations available, and tested it in terms of these observations, scientists then used it to make strong inferences about the nature of further observations.

In moving from an example drawn from the "exact" sciences to one from the "inexact," namely economics, the ability to exhibit the drama of pointing the telescope at a point in the sky and announcing that a planet will appear on such-and-such a date is perhaps lost. For example, it would be of substantial benefit if the researcher in economics could appeal to his model and deliver the following conclusion with respect to, say, a proposed 10 percent income tax hike and a $6 billion spending cut. "The proposal will result in 6 percent unemployment, a $10 billion rise in inventory accumulation, and a $4 billion decline in business fixed investment." Unfortunately, he can only make such a statement accompanied by appropriate terms and conditions regarding the impact of all other forces and the assumed values of economic unknowns such as military requirements. Of course, he could always say that the results would be his if only those other things did not enter and confuse the picture. But alas, they do.

The major variables in an economic system, unlike the masses of planets and their physical correspondence to each other, are undergoing constant and partially unsystematic change. With this premise, one may ask, why attempt to model such systems, if the results are only of hypothetical use? Such a question would confuse inexactness with the state of being hypothetical. Although the results of an economic model can only be used inexactly, and although their verification is difficult and sometimes impossible, they still have value in (1) analysis and decisionmaking, and (2) as means for understanding.

Several points are contained in this last statement. First, the subject of verification in economics represents a special problem, which can be focused upon by reference to the Neptune example. In that discovery, a peek in the telescope constituted a conclusive test of the hypothesis proposed by Leverrier. In economics, two analysts can peer through the same telescope of data at the economic system and each see sharply different hypotheses conclusively proven. This unfortunate fact must be accepted as part of the inexact but permanent landscape of economics. Furthermore, that landscape consists of macro and micro systems involving many highly subtle relationships—some interacting, others running in one direction, others interacting after a time lag, still others jointly determined—with change in the system's variables measured imperfectly at discrete intervals when certain data "boils to the surface," usually, containing measurement errors. It is thus hardly surprising that academic sifting and winnowing into economic issues often produces inconclusive results.

This inconclusive character does not mean lack of conclusions altogether, for in that case, model building in economics would be of little use. It rather means that the nature of the conclusions formed as a result of model building come about in the form of implications, a point to which we shall return. The general ideas discussed so far can be advanced in a concrete fashion by using an illustration to focus the discussion, which will also bring out the major elements in the process of model building.

AN ILLUSTRATIVE MODEL

Take the situation of a market arena in which two groups inter-act—suppliers and demanders. For purposes of illustration, consider the stock market as the system under consideration. Focus now upon the market for a single stock, the XYZ company. The "product" here is homogeneous in the sense that all shares of the company are indistinguishable. Also, within a short period of time (say one trading day) a large percentage of suppliers and demanders of this stock are aware and constantly updated as to changes in the price of this stock in the market place. Also, the group of suppliers and demanders is quite large, implying the shares are widely held. This means that the actions of a single demander or supplier are relatively unimportant when compared to the action of the system. The individual is then a relatively powerless component in the operation of an impersonal market. There are no deals to buy stock at anything other than the going market price. Finally, the mechanics of the market arena operate in such a way that the market is cleared on an approximately continual basis. This means that if there are more suppliers in the arena trying to sell at the going rate than there are buyers attempting to buy at the going rate, the result will be a drop in the going rate to a level that will motivate more buyers to buy and discourage some sellers from selling. The resulting price will continually fluctuate up and down, approximately equating suppliers and demanders of stock at any point in time.

Though a formal model of the market of XYZ stock has not yet been presented, a number of key observations have been made (about product homogeneity, flow of information, market power of individuals, functioning of the market mechanism) that will significantly affect the rules of relationship and the structure of the model that does result. So, in essence, these perceived terms and conditions of the model, the assumptions, are an underlying task in the construction of the model itself. They build a bridge between the real system under study and the abstract model that will attempt to represent that system.

Specifying Model Structure

Having delineated the assumptions, we turn in the analysis to the specification of the structure and rules of relationship that define the model. Let us begin by attempting to represent functionally the quantity demanded per unit of time—say in a one-month period. There are a discouragingly large number of factors having a possible impact on the quantity of XYZ company stock demanded in a month. The first problem is selecting a set of variables that represent major underlying forces. Such a selection is in the form of a hypothesis, which remains to be tested.

Let us go further and report the results of such an analysis, the identification of three such forces, as follows: Let $EPrf_{t+1}$ stand for the profit per share expected in the next month by a potential investor in the firm's stock. Let *Stk* stand for an index of general stock market performance, such as the Standard and Poors index or the Dow Jones Industrial Average. Let *P* stand for the average price of the stock during the month. It may be reasonable to further stipulate in the model the direction of these relationships. We might be prepared to propose that as $EPrf_{t+1}$ goes up, so should the demand for stock, *ceteris paribus*. The same may be said of the relationship between the demand for stock and the market index. So a positive relationship may be postulated between $EPrf_{t+1}$, *Stk*, and the demand for stock. In the case of *P*, a negative relationship seems most reasonable. As the price of the stock gets higher, its yield goes down, and its capital appreciation potential becomes less attractive, *ceteris paribus*.

Specifying the direction of the relationship is only part of the specification of the model. We also need to consider the mathematical way in which the positive and negative influences upon the demand for stock exert themselves. This requires that the earlier hypothesis be further refined. In this case, it may be reasonable to assume that a 100-unit increase in $EPrf_{t+1}$ in a given time period may exert approximately twice the effect that a 50-unit increase would, but that a 200-unit increase would likely not exert double the influence of a 100-unit increase. If this is the case, the marginal impact of this variable is subject to decay at higher levels. An exponential relationship is suggested. On the other hand, if a marginal decay of this type is not envisioned by the model builder, then such a structural form can be dispensed with in favor of a simple linear form.

Having dealt with this question with respect to each of the variables in the model, we need to specify the way in which the linear, exponential, and other influences are jointly exerted. The simplest possibility is that they are additive, that is, the effect of each can be added to the effect of the others, summing up to the total effect. Another possibility is that the effect of one is multiplied by the effect of another. Still another possibility is that a variable relates after the fashion of the exponent in an exponential. The specific possibilities are large in number.

Resolving this question involves an analysis of the way in which the selected components in the model interrelate. For example, the model builder in our case must consider whether it is reasonable to hypothesize that $EPrf_{t+1}$ and *Stk* play independent or interdependent roles in influencing the demand for stock. If it is reasonable to assume their influences are independent, then possibly structuring their impact as additive is appropriate. If an interaction between the two is logical, then perhaps their effects should be multiplied, or a term added to the additive expression containing the product of the two. These possibilities can be expressed as follows:

$$Y = aEPrf_{t+1} + bStk$$
$$Y = a(EPrf_{t+1})(Stk)$$
$$Y = aEPrf_{t+1} + bStk + c(EPrf_{t+1})(Stk)$$

where a, b, c represent the constants or parameters of the equations.

Choosing among Structural Forms

The choice among alternative structural forms will have a marked impact on the way the model performs. In our example, the question of which form is more functionally representative might be considered by the following kind of exercise. Let $a = 5$, $b = 2$, $c = 4$, $EPrf_{t+1} = X$, $Stk = Z$. Then,

$$(1) \quad Y = 5X + 2Z$$
$$(2) \quad Y = 5XZ$$
$$(3) \quad Y = 5X + 2Z + 4XZ$$

Now, take (1) and consider the effect on Y of increasing X by 100 percent; that is, doubling X. The impact can be traced through as follows:

$$Y = 5X + 2Z$$
$$Y' = 5(2X) + 2Z \qquad \text{substituting } 2X \text{ for } X$$
$$Y' = 5X + 2Z + 5X \qquad \text{algebraically rearranging,}$$
$$\text{since } 10X = 5X + 5X$$
$$Y' = Y + 5X \qquad \text{substituting the original } Y$$
$$\text{back in}$$

This shows that in the case of the first structural form, doubling the value of X will have the effect of increasing Y by an amount of $5X$, and that the response will be of this nature for any and all increases in X. As X is increased the *percentage response* in Y will decline, since the progression is linear. In other words, an equal arithmetic increase in Y of $5X$ each time X is doubled will result in smaller and smaller percentage increases in Y, the base having been enlarged each time.

In the case of (2) the analysis is as follows:

$$Y = 5XZ$$
$$Y' = 5(2X)Z, \text{ inserting } 2X$$
$$Y' = (2)5XZ, \text{ rearranging}$$
$$Y' = (2)Y, \qquad \text{reinserting } Y$$

In contrast with the case shown in (1), this exercise shows that doubling X will result in doubling Y, that the response of Y to changes in X is proportional, or constant in percentage terms. It further indicates the relationship embodied in the expression is not constant in arithmetic terms.

In the case of (3) the analysis is as follows:

$$
\begin{aligned}
Y &= 5X + 2Z + 4XZ \\
Y' &= 5(2X) + 2Z + 4(2X)Z \\
Y' &= (2)5X + 2Z + (2)4XZ, \text{ rearranging} \\
Y' + 2Z &= (2)5X + 4Z + (2)4XZ, \text{ adding } 2Z \text{ to both sides} \\
Y' + 2Z &= (2)(5X + 2Z + 4XZ), \text{ rearranging} \\
Y' &= (2)Y - 2Z, \qquad\quad \text{substituting } Y \text{ and rearranging}
\end{aligned}
$$

Notice that in this case the effect of a change in X on Y will be modified by the value of X, and that as Z becomes larger the effect of X on Y declines in its impact in percentage terms.

In the stock market example, the problem is now to select the form that best represents the hypothesis. This is a matter of the intuition of the model builder. Of course, such a specific hypothesis would be shaped by reference to the data and by statistical tests of goodness of fit. Assume in our example the quantity of stock demanded in a given month will be affected linearly by the factors mentioned above, and in a simple additive fashion. Thus, we can write the following for the quantity of stock demanded (Q_d):

$$
Q_d = -aP + bEPrf_{t+1} + cStk
$$

where again the values of a, b, and c are constants, but are constrained by the sign designations discussed earlier in the analysis.

We now need to consider the other side of the market, the suppliers of stock. Assume that some of the factors affecting the demand for stock will affect the supply of stock. Let us again report the results of an analysis of supply conditions in the form of a hypothesized expression for the supply of stock in a given month (Q_s):

$$
Q_s = dP - eEPrf_{t+1} - fStk - gPrf_t
$$

In this case, higher expected profits would lower the supply of stock on the market, since holders upgrade their evaluations of the worth of their holdings and accordingly demand a higher price to part with the same quantity of stock, *ceteris paribus*. The effect of the stock index is similar. A rising stock index, in attracting more demand, would likely reduce the supply, *ceteris paribus*. This reflects the notion that the same group is alternatively on the demand side and the supply side, so that shifts in the behavior of this group have an effect on both sides of the market.

The final term, the current level of profits, appears in the expression for supply of but not demand for stock. This expresses the hypothesis that the actual level of profits is not a quantitatively significant factor in determining the demand for stock (which is influenced by profit expectations), but only affects the market price of stock by affecting the supply. This stipulation denotes that the quantitative impact of this variable per se is small enough to be effectively dispensed with.

Conditions for Equilibrium Solution

Having now defined conceptual demand and supply expressions, we may stipulate the conditions for operation of the market in which they interact by imposing the equilibrium condition that $Q_d = Q_s$ in any month. This indicates that the prevailing price will equate quantity demand with quantity supplied. Noting that P in Q_d had a negative sign and P in Q_s had a positive sign, we can clearly see that a freely fluctuating price can achieve this result in each month. The expression for Q_d, in equilibrium, is equal to the expression for Q_s, and so an expression can be derived for the equilibrium price, as follows:

$$Q_d = Q_s \text{ at equilibrium}$$
$$-aP + bEPrf_{t+1} + cStk = dP - eEPrf_{t+1} - fStk - gPrf_t$$
$$-aP - dP = -EPrf_{t+1}(e + b) - Stk(f + c) - gPrf_t$$
$$-P(a + d) = -(EPrf_{t+1}(e + b) + Stk(f + c) + gPrf_t)$$
$$P = \frac{Eprf_{t+1}(e + b) + Stk(f + c) + gPrf_t}{(a + d)}$$

In this case, the reader should note that all factors that appeared in either the demand or supply expression influence the price, quantitatively depending on the values of the coefficients a through g. Obtaining values for the coefficients is the next problem of our model builder. Estimating the coefficients in economic models is a primary concern of the discipline of econometrics. Chapters 2–4 are concerned with this problem in some detail. Therefore, we shall defer consideration of the statistical processes leading to estimates of a through g, and for now assume such estimates have been made, and result in: $a = 3$, $b = 10$, $c = 0.7$, $d = 4$, $e = 5$, $f = 1.3$, $g = 5$. Then:

$$Q_d = -3P + 10EPrf_{t+1} + 0.7Stk$$
$$Q_s = 4P - 5EPrf_{t+1} - 1.3Stk - 5Prf_t$$
$$P = \frac{15}{7} EPrf_{t+1} + \frac{2}{7} Stk + \frac{5}{7} Prf_t$$

For now, we only suggest that the problems in reliably producing such parameter estimates are usually quite significant. Given a set of values of $EPrf_{t+1}$, Prf_ts, and of Stk, we can now translate the composite of these three values into the corresponding equilibrium stock price. A hypothetical set of data is presented in Table 1–1 along with the resulting computed values of the price of XYZ stock.

TABLE 1–1

Period	Expected profit	Profit	Stk	Price	Modified price
0........	8	8	100	51.4	51.4
1........	8	8	100	51.4	51.4
2........	8	8	110	54.3	57.8
3........	10	8	120	61.4	65.1
4........	12	12	130	71.4-HI	75.9-HI
5........	12	12	120	68.6	63.8
6........	8	12	110	57.4	52.6
7........	6	6	110	48.6	47.5
8........	6	6	100	45.7-LO	42.5-LO
9........	8	6	90	47.1	45.7
10........	10	10	90	54.3	56.6
11........	10	10	100	57.4	60.0
12........	11	10	110	62.1	65.5
13........	10	10	90	54.3	45.7

Model Development

After comparison with the actual pattern of XYZ stock price variation, changes in the model may be indicated. For example, inspection may reveal that the peaks and troughs in system and model coincide, but amplitude of variation does not. It may also be evident that when XYZ stock is going up rapidly, it is in disproportionately heavy demand and short supply. This leads to the hypothesis that the *change* in the overall market index as well as the *value* of the index (already included in the model) is a factor in determining the price. For example, when the market is rapidly rising, an effect may be induced to the demand and supply of XYZ stock independently from the now-represented effect of the *level* of the market index. The model could be modified in several ways to simulate these further refinements.

A simple but not necessarily most satisfactory way of accomplishing this is as follows: First, to the expression for Qd, add $+ h(Stk - Stk_{t-1}) + i(P - P_{t-1})$; and to the expression for Q_s, add $+ j(Stk_{t-1} - Skt) + k(P_{t-1} - P)$. This will result in additional demand for stock, resulting specifically from the upward movement in the price of the stock over its value in the last period. This additional demand would have the effect of pushing up the equilibrium price of the stock. On the other hand, demand would decrease when the price of stock was falling period to period. This would accelerate the decline in the price. A rise in the market index would have a similar effect, increasing the demand for the stock because of a rising market and decreasing demand because of a falling market.

In the expression for supply, the opposite is true. A rising price would have the effect of reducing the supply of stock, thereby further adding to the upward price pressures. Also, a rising market would per se reduce the supply of stock. Of course, one would expect that such speculative effects would eventually reverse themselves. After the price of the stock became too high, the expectation of still higher prices that stands behind our assumption of the price-change behavior would disappear and such a speculative effect would likely be not only eliminated but reversed. The same is true of the speculative effect we have ascribed to the market index. A more complicated model structure could be formed to account for the diminution and reversal of the effect we have added.

The solved form, or reduced form expression, for the price must now be recomputed with the addition of the new factors, as follows:

$$P = \frac{EPrf_{t+1}\,(b+e) + Stk(c+h+f+j) - Stk_{t-1}(h+j) - P_{t-1}(i+k) + gPrf_t}{(a - i + d - k)}$$

where values for the additional parameters are: $h = 0.7$, $i = 0.9$, $j = 0.8$, $k = 0.6$. A new pattern of price movement results which exhibits the additional speculative behavior we have described. The result is shown under the *modified price* column in Table 1–1.

In comparing the two prices in the table, we can clearly see that the modification has the net effect of accentuating movements in price (which is not startling). Also note that the high and low values occur in the same time period in both cases. Thus, we have modified the way the model behaves in response to a given set of inputs. Such a modification would normally be made to cause the model to more nearly behave as the system behaves. Let us now assume that after this modification and several more like it the pattern of the stock price, in response to actual historical values of the three independent variables, shows a high correspondence with the actual stock price. What then? Can we say that we have a predictive model of stock price behavior?

Inferential Reasoning from Models

The answer to this question unfortunately is not totally clear, for it evokes the more general question of what should be expected from a model in economics. For example, is it a sufficient criterion that our model can generate a series of stock prices over a past period that closely approximates the actual prices? If we answer yes, then we must stand ready to defend a second model that contained, as independent variables, the age of our stockbroker, the population of Switzerland, and the current rice yield per acre in Indonesia (rather than expected XYZ profits, and so forth), if that model had a strong past correspondence with price movement. Are we to employ two such models interchangeably for prediction?

Applying the singular criterion of past predictive correspondence between model and system, we have to say yes again. But what of the reliability of the two models looking forward to the forecast period? Establishing a level of confidence in the resulting prediction can hardly be kept separate from the model user's intuitive perception of the model he is employing. More confidence would logically reside in a model whose composition was defensible on economic as well as statistical grounds. This notion indicates the need for an additional dimension in our criteria for judging an economic model.

In addition to predictive correspondence, the components and relationships in the model must possess two characteristics.[4] First, they must establish logical connections between input variables and output variables. Second, these logical connections must have empirical relevance with respect to the system. In our example, if the choice of the independent variables was judged to have a priori economic relevance, and if the way in which these variables affected the model also contained these properties, then this model could be assigned a high reliability with respect to the prospect that its past predictive correspondence will carry into the future.

The two dimensions, predictive correspondence and reliability, have an important relationship with time. At a point in time, we can only establish the predictive correspondence of a given model with reference to the past—to a set of historical data. On the other hand, our assignment of reliability must be based on the confidence we have that this correspondence will persist into the future. That assessment, we have proposed, must depend upon the logic and relevance of the components and relationships in the model itself.

GENERALIZATIONS ON MODELS

At this point in the discussion of models, it is perhaps useful to formalize and categorize some of the concepts introduced informally. Drawing a distinction between the system and the model of the system defines a relationship between these two that deserves some additional discussion. Following M. B. Hesse, we can describe three kinds of analogies between the model and the system.[5] First, a negative analogy refers to those prop-

---

[4] For a contrary view on this subject, see Milton Friedman, *Essays in Positive Economics* (Chicago: University of Chicago Press, 1953).

[5] M. B. Hesse, *Models and Analogies in Science* (Notre Dame, Ind.: University of Notre Dame Press, 1966), p. 8.

erties of the system that are not contained in the model. A positive analogy is defined as the properties of the system that are also properties of the model. Neutral analogies are properties of the model about which correspondence to the system is unknown.

The need for abstraction in large economic systems implies that most economic models will be characterized by a number of negative analogies. As indicated earlier, the successful abstraction will have retained those negative analogies that are quantitatively insignificant. Referring to the earlier discussion, the model will have abstracted from those aspects of the system that do not affect the essential functioning of the system. The reader will recall the stock market example, in which all factors affecting price were abstracted from except three. The number of negative analogies was therefore quite large.

A useful model will obviously contain a sufficient number of positive analogies to capture the quantitatively critical aspects of the system. In our stock market example, if a given movement of the general price index over time evokes a certain quantitatively significant reaction in the price of XYZ stock, *ceteris paribus*, then this analogy must be made in the model. If it is not, the resulting negative analogy, being quantitatively significant, represents an error of omission in the model.

The effect of a neutral analogy is to alter the way in which the model behaves in response to at least one or more sets of input data. This alteration is a potential error of commission when the data set is employed for which the analogy is made. In the stock market example, let us in Table 1–2 trace through the effect on the model price of the stock in response to a set of input data wherein profits are doubled, where expected profits are doubled one period before actual profits double, i.e., they are correctly anticipated to have doubled, and where the market index is constant. Notice that the price of the stock moves to a higher value and then goes through a damped cyclical movement. Determining whether or not the actual price of the stock would undergo such a cyclical movement is a matter of actually obtaining the set of input data described in Table 1–2, or an analogous set of data, then inspecting the

TABLE 1–2

Period	EPrf	Prf	Stk	Price
0.........	10	10	100	57.1
1.........	20	10	100	84.4
2.........	20	20	100	86.1
3.........	20	20	100	85.6
4.........	20	20	100	85.8
5.........	20	20	100	85.7
6.........	20	20	100	85.7

corresponding stock price. In the absence of such data, we cannot say with certainty that the effect our model has imputed to the system is an actual characteristic of that system, or whether we have generated a property that incorrectly represents the system in this circumstance. The existence of the cyclical property in the model represents a neutral analogy in the absence of evidence from the system.

Static and Dynamic Models

A distinction of importance in economic model building is between static and dynamic models. The definitional split between these two varies among those who use the concepts, but the general sense of the distinction may be stated as follows. The output of a static model in period x is determined entirely as a function of the value of parameters and variables in period x. What occurred in period $x - 1$ has no relevance to the value of any system variables in period x. Each period can be thought of as a separate compartment containing sufficient data and relationships to determine all model output. This quality is not true of dynamic models. Dynamic models have a specific structural link between the position of the system in period x and the position of the system in $x - 1$. The past, in other words, has a specific impact on the present, and the present on the future.

Referring back to the example, the original model of XYZ stock price was static. Both the quantity demanded and supplied were hypothesized to be functions of variables occurring in the current period. The expected profit in the next period is a useful example of this quality. Although this variable refers to a future period, it has been defined as the profits expected in the future period, *as of the present time.* When the model was modified to represent speculative effects, the addition of the change in the price of the stock period to period and the change in the overall market index transformed the model from static to dynamic. In the modified model, the value of the stock price in the previous period and the value of the market index in the previous period have an impact on the current price. The current period value of the variables in the modified model are now coupled with the previous status of the model in determining the present status of the model.

The two effects on the model are illustrated in the data of Table 1–1. Note that the set of input data for period 10 is identical with that of period 13. Now notice the static model has generated identical estimates of the equilibrium price in both periods. Not so in the modified case. When the dynamic model approached period 10, the values of the three independent variables indicating an upward movement was appropriate. The equilibrium price was 56.6. The second time the same values of the independent variables occurred, in period 13, the market index was falling and the profit picture was weakening. The resulting equilibrium price was now 45.7. In the modified case, the price was determined not only by where the independent variables indicated the model price should be, but from where the model had come.

Deterministic and Probabilistic

Models may be classified as either deterministic or probabilistic. A deterministic model is one in which the functional relationships are expressed in a fixed way. When a given set of initial conditions and previous conditions prevails, a deterministic model will produce the same output. Both the original and modified stock market examples are deterministic. Presented with the same set of initial conditions, i.e., previous price, and the same set of independent variables over time, both models will generate identical stock prices each quarter. This is not true of a probabilistic model. Such a model allows for stochastic variation in the way in which the variables in the model relate to each other. At all points in the model where such variation is hypothesized to be a significant factor, it is entered into the model functional relationships. In the original stock market example, the first equation representing the demand for stock would yield a specific quantity demanded when the price was 50, the expected earnings were 8, and the market index was 100. The estimate would be the same every time these three numbers occurred.

In the probabilistic model, the model builder would be interested in representing the uncertainty in this functional relationship. Such uncertainty could be a result of the factors omitted from the model in the process of abstraction. As these omitted forces fluctuate, they would tend to cause some (hopefully minor) effect on the demand for stock resulting from a given set of included independent variables. That effect would cause the amount to be either larger or smaller than that produced by a deterministic equation. No systematic pattern would occur in this effect. The quantitative extent of this random fluctuation could be measured by statistical methods. It could then be included in the equation for the demand for stock by the addition of a factor.

This factor would typically be computed by employing a statistical probability distribution with a zero central tendency, and a standard deviation equal to the quantitatively measured extent of uncertainty in the relationship. Draws would be made randomly from this distribution, and the resulting quantity added or subtracted from the otherwise computed value. Such a mechanism would be added to each point in the model where the effect of random variation is hypothesized to be significant. A probabilistic model of stock prices would give different results on successive trials for the same set of input data. The resulting array of answers would aid the model builder in establishing a range within which the system output is predicted to fall. In the stock market example, let us suppose that a stochastic element was included in both the demand and supply functions. Then, let us suppose that the equilibrium price was computed 100 times with the random factors present. The range of prices that would result sets up a confidence band for the actual price. The average price of the 100 trials should approximate the price produced by our deterministic model, and become a better approximation as the number of trials becomes larger.

Normative and Positive Models

A final classification of models is that of normative or positive. A normative model prescribes a set of outputs that is optimal in terms of some objective. Given a set of inputs, such a model delivers optimal values for related variables. For example, consider the familiar classical model for pricing and output determination. Given a production function, factor costs, fixed costs, and information on demand, the model stipulates the profit-maximizing level of output. The classical model is not directly dealing with the most probable level of output by a given producer faced with a given set of inputs, but that producer's best output level for profit maximization. Of course, if it is assumed that a producer is conducting his business to maximize profits, then the model would correspond to his output decision.

In contrast with the optimal results of a normative model, a positive model is concerned with constructing a representation of a system as is, to the end of being able to demonstrate a correspondence between model output and system output in response to a given set of inputs. Our stock market example is an illustration of a positive model, as it was our intent to construct a model of the movement of actual stock prices. In contrast, a normative model of stock prices would be concerned with defining equilibrium prices that correspond to optimal values of an objective function based on some criterion (say a criterion of social justice or equality).

Normative models can provide an optimal baseline against which to compare results. They can provide a guide to action. Positive models are most useful in predicting the actual outcome of the system, regardless of whether or not that outcome is optimal. Positive models can represent a planning tool for evaluating the impact on a system of proposed changes in its operations. For example, if a positive model of the communication system in a firm were available, then proposed changes in that system could be evaluated on the model and implications drawn as to the probable effect on the system.

DISCUSSION QUESTIONS

1. A small firm has a capacity of 900 units of output per month when working regular shifts. If they work overtime excluding Sundays, they may add another 200 units. If Sundays are also worked, they can add 100 more units. Past experience shows the out-of-pocket (direct) costs under these three circumstances to be as follows:

Regular production	$45.10/unit
Overtime (except Sunday)	54.20/unit
Sunday	65.50/unit

   The firm has a regular market for 900 units per month at $65.00 per unit. It also has received three tentative orders, which it may decide or not decide to fill. They are as follows:

   a) offer to buy 100 units at $60.00
   b) offer to buy 100 units at $55.00
   c) offer to buy 100 units at $50.00

   Which, if any, orders should the firm accept and why? What is the principle?

2. Formulate a measure of the opportunity cost associated with studying the remainder of these discussion questions.

3. A man quits his $15,000-a-year junior executive job to go into cattle ranching in Arizona, staking himself with $10,000 of personal savings plus a $90,000 bank loan at 6 percent. The first year of operation he turns a profit of $20,000 before interest and taxes. Exactly where and how do opportunity costs enter this picture? Making such assumptions as are necessary, do you find the man has made a profit in the economic sense?

4. Why are tests of economic models inexact by nature?

5. What is meant by equilibrium solution of an economic model?

6. Point out unique uses for positive economic models relative to normative models and vice versa.

Chapter 2

STATISTICAL MEASUREMENT IN SIMPLE ECONOMIC MODELS

Economic models generally share the property of formulating relationships among variables, and exploring the implications of these relationships. Quantitative measurement of economic relationships is the concern of the field of econometrics. In this chapter and the two to follow, we shall explore some ideas from this field. The objective will be to enable the reader to more critically review the empirical studies and findings reported on in later sections of this book, as well as to provide an introduction to the problems of measurement in economic relationships.

MEASUREMENT AND MODEL BUILDING

Associated patterns of fluctuation among groups of variables are not uncommon in macro- and microeconomic systems. In a broad sense, the task of measuring such economic relationships is essentially one of discovering associated patterns of change among variables, and reducing these patterns to visible form through the use of specific mathematical structures that approximate the observed covariant patterns. Such approximations are bound to be inexact. Patterns of associated change in economic systems simply do not adhere precisely to underlying "true" mathematically structured approximations of actual unstructured covariant patterns. A second primary task of measurement is to formulate and interpret estimates of the unknown parameters of this approximating structure. We shall consider both these aspects of the measurement problem, beginning with the formulation of approximating mathematical structures.

In selecting an appropriate mathematical approximation for an economic relationship, we may obtain at best only rough suggestions by direct observation of the data in even the simplest of cases.

The choice among alternatives is basically a matter of exploring the relative statistical properties of various structural hypotheses, and selecting that which best represents the observed data. For example, consider the simple pattern of data in Figure 2-1, which plots the relationship between X and Y in a scatter diagram. At least two possible structural hypotheses are suggested:

$$Y = a + bX + \mu \tag{2-1}$$
$$Y = a + bX + cX^2 + \mu \tag{2-2}$$

where μ represents an unexplained variation in Y. It is not clear on observation which of the two theses about the way Y and X relate is more correct, given that they both are approximations of a true unknown and unstructured relationship. In fact, the two alternatives listed are only the simplest suggested by Figure 2-1, the number of conceivable alterna-

FIGURE 2-1

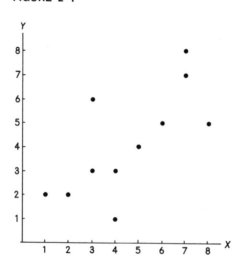

tives being quite large. Selection of the optimal structural approximation in any specific case is a matter of choosing from among limited alternatives on the basis of statistical comparison. Fortunately, researchers studying particular economic relationships can usually limit the number of alternatives considered by formulating a priori hypotheses about the nature of the relationships to be studied. These hypotheses lead to selection of a limited number of structures that upon measurement tend either to confirm or not confirm the a priori notions. In many applications and investigations, the simplest linear approximating structure is assumed. Indeed, most of the empirical results considered in this book rely upon linear assumptions. This practice undoubtedly occurs partly because of the computational ease that occurs in the linear case. Also, if the range of X and Y values over which the relationship is measured is quite restricted, then a linear approximation can be a reasonable representation of a wide variety of actual mathematical relationships. If variables comprising an economic relationship comprise a time series, as is often the case in actual applications, then restricting X within a narrow range often means dealing with a short period of time. Thus, linear approximations often become better representations of a variety of alternative relationships in time series as the time period over which the relationship applies is shortened. This is further justification for extensive use of linear statistical techniques in short-run circumstances. In the discussion that follows, little indication will be given as to the nature of the problem of estimating and evaluating nonlinear models. We shall focus attention upon linear systems in which the techniques of econometrics have been extensively developed.

ESTIMATING COEFFICIENTS IN SINGLE-EQUATION MODELS

The simplest starting point for considering the problem of estimating coefficients is a linear model of the (2–1) type, which is repeated here:

$$Y = a + bX + \mu \tag{2-1}$$

where Y is a dependent variable, X is a predetermined variable, and μ is an unexplained portion of Y assumed to have no systematic relationship with Y. Estimating the coefficients a and b of this equation is a matter of fitting the best line through a series of points such as those in Figure 2–1. Although a danger is always present in setting forth a criterion by which something can be judged best, a commonly accepted criterion for the best-fitting line is that it minimizes the sum of the squared deviation from individual points to the line, measured in the vertical direction. This is illustrated in Figure 2–2. The parameters of a function $Y_c = a + bX$ can be selected in such a way to minimize (in a mathematical sense) this sum-squared deviation.[1] Parameters estimated in this way are called least-squares estimates. The reader unfamiliar with the techniques involved in computing least-squares parameter estimates is invited to consult an elementary statistics text for details.[2]

Under some circumstances, least-squares estimating techniques have highly desirable statistical properties.[3] Among these properties, that of unbiasedness is of major importance. An unbiased estimate is one whose expected value (or average value over the whole population of estimates) equals the true value of the parameter being estimated. This means if

---

[1] When the expression for sum-squared deviation is put in the form $SS = (Y - a - bX)^2$ and partial derivations are taken on a and b, and minimums are found by setting the two equations equal to zero and solving simultaneously, the resulting minimum yield least-square estimates for a and b.

[2] For example, T. Yamane, *Statistics*, 2d ed. (New York: Harper and Row, 1967), Chapter 14.

[3] See, for a discussion of relevant properties, J. Johnston, *Econometric Methods* (New York: McGraw-Hill, 1960), pp. 9–20.

FIGURE 2–2

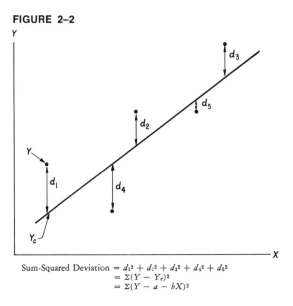

$$\text{Sum-Squared Deviation} = d_1{}^2 + d_2{}^2 + d_3{}^2 + d_4{}^2 + d_5{}^2$$
$$= \Sigma(Y - Y_c)^2$$
$$= \Sigma(Y - a - bX)^2$$

a frequency distribution of unbiased estimates was formed (computed) from all possible varying samples in a given population, its mean would equal the true parameter being estimated. A biased estimate, on the other hand, would not have this property. The mean of the sampling distribution would not be equal to the true value. For least squares to be a useful estimating technique, it is important that it produce unbiased estimates of equation coefficients. It has been shown that this property of unbiasedness will be present in least squares only if the independent variables (X) are, in fact, predetermined outside the scope of the general system of influence that produced the dependent variable Y.[4] In other words, the X or right-hand side variable (s) must be truly independent of Y, the left-side variable, for their value, while Y in turn is assumed to be dependent upon X but incapable of exerting any influence upon the value of that variable in the same sample observation. The path of statistical association must run only one way.

The consumption function of aggregate economics is a notable violation of this assumption, an extremely simple version of which is as follows:

$$C_t = a + bY_t + \mu_t$$

where C_t = consumption expenditures, Y_t = aggregate income, and μ_t an error term.

---

[4] The original article is T. Haavelmo, "The Statistical Implications of a Systems of Simultaneous Equations," *Econometrica* (Vol. 11, 1943), pp. 1–12.

It is clear from consideration of national income accounting and aggregate economic relationships that C_t influences Y_t concurrently as Y_t influences C_t, which produces the aggregate multiplier. In this case, least squares will produce biased estimates of coefficients such as a and b. A study by Wagner is representative of a number of works that illustrate the quantitative magnitude of the bias can be quite significant.[5] We shall return to this problem in Chapter 4.

Thus, underlying our entire discussion of the analysis and evaluation of single-equation systems is the premise that the independent variables are predetermined and not simultaneously influenced by the dependent.

Estimating parameters by the methods of least-squares involves certain other inherent limitations that should be taken into account when interpreting the results of such estimates. Most of the peculiar characteristics of least-squares methods result from the effect of extreme values on the estimates. Since the vertical distance from line to point is squared, largely deviant observations tend to disproportionately pull the line in their direction. For example, several small positive squared deviations trade off favorably in reducing a large negative deviation, thereby skewing the line. This is illustrated in Figure 2–3. In panel (a), six points from the function $Y = 2 + x$ are plotted. Since there are no deviant points, the least-squares estimates reproduce these parameters and fit a line exactly through the points, giving minimum sum-squared deviation at zero where each $Y = Y_c$ and $(Y - Y_c) = 0$. Panel (b) shows the effects on the parameter estimates of adding two highly deviant observations in opposite corners of the scatter. The effect has been to pivot the line toward the two deviant points, reducing the two large sum-squared components while producing six smaller components.

If both deviant points are on the same side of the line, as in Panel (c), the effect on the parameter estimates is seen to be a pivoting about the intercept, with the slope of the line larger than in panel (b) and the intercept smaller than (b). If the points in panels (b) and (c) are in some way unrepresentative of the true relationship between Y and X, it is clear that their inclusion works a drastic effect on the parameter estimates. With six of the eight points being products of the equation $Y = 2 + X$, the calculated values, $Y_c = 6.3 + .12X$ and $Y_c = 4.7 + .19X$, are rather badly skewed by the two deviant points. If the systematic points were larger in number, the Y_c line would not be pulled as far off the mark, although the effect would continue to persist. Figure 2–3 tempts one to discard data such as the two deviant points of panels (b) and (c), which would return the fit to perfect in these two hypothetical cases. Indeed, in instances where the point can be judged deviant for sound reasons in terms of the specific meaning

[5] H. Wagner, "A Monte Carlo Study of Estimates of Simultaneous Linear Structural Equations," *Econometrica* (Vol. 26, 1958), pp. 117–33.

FIGURE 2–3

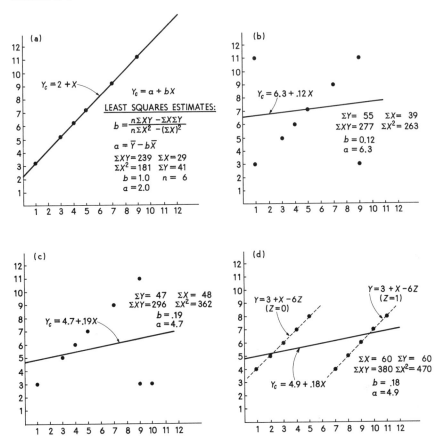

that attaches to the data, this is a recommended procedure when fitting equations via least-squares. We must, on the other hand, be careful not to pervert this notion to the extreme of discarding data that does not support the analyst's hypothesis. For example, we could probably display some dramatic least-squares fits if we discarded data greater than 5 percent away from an arbitrarily drawn line through a scatter. As in most endeavors, judgment must be applied as to the use of the least-squares line when deciding upon the classification of data as unrepresentative of a sought-after relationship. Unfortunately as we have shown, least-squares techniques are rather sensitive to the product of this judgment, particularly for small sample sizes.

A second facet of least-squares estimates relates to the effects of omitted variables. If we fit an equation to data in which the effects of an influential variable have been omitted, the effects of the included variables reflected in the coefficient estimates will not be measured faithfully by least squares. This problem is illustrated in panel (d) of Figure 2–3, where a shift in the relationship between X and Y due to the effects of a third omitted variable Z has produced data in two distinct arrays in the XY dimension.

If the least-squares line is fit through these data, a very poor fit occurs because no vehicle is present in the equation to measure the shift. If the Z variable were explicitly introduced into the curve fitting (a multivariate least-squares fit) with a value of zero for $X = 1 - 5$ and one for $X = 6 - 10$, then the correct parameters would be reproduced in the least-squares estimate. The error in parameter estimates resulting from failure to include the effects of Z in estimating the parameters of the XY relationship is called a *specification error*. By omitting Z, the model being estimated has not been specified correctly, since an important variable influencing Y is missing. Panel (d) suggests the effects of such specification errors can be dramatic upon the misspecified parameter estimates.

Unfortunately, in parameter estimates of complex economic models, the analyst is never sure that his parameter values are free of specification error because he has no true value as a baseline. Thus, he lives with the continual possibility that the measured relationships in his model are statistical mutations resulting from ignorance as to the influential effects of some yet undiscovered variable. We shall return to this point later in our discussion.

The techniques of least squares, and the inherent characteristics of these techniques that have been illustrated, are not confined to simple, single independent variable relationships of the $Y = a + bX$ variety. The same technique of fitting the best line through a two-dimensional array of points applies in the case of three-, four-, or more dimensional arrays. In the case of two independent variables, $Y = a + bX + cZ$, the problem becomes one of minimizing the sum-squared deviation of the XYZ measured points from a plane representing Y_c. Highly deviant observations on the independent variables will, as before, substantially alter the location of the least-squares plane, as will specification errors. Students are again referred to a statistics text for computational details.[6]

STATISTICAL PROPERTIES OF SINGLE-EQUATION MODELS

Assume a particular pattern of statistical association can be approximated by the following "true" regression equation:

$$Y = a + bX + cZ + \mu$$

[6] See T. Yamane, *Statistics*, Chapter 22, and Mordecai Ezekiel and Karl A. Fox, *Methods of Correlation and Regression Analysis* (New York: Wiley, 1959), Chapters 10–13.

In this equation, $a + bX + cZ$ represents the portion of the value of Y that is systematically and linearly associated with fluctuations in X and Z. The remaining portion of the value of Y is assumed to vary unsystematically, for reasons not accounted for by variables included in the model. We shall call this unexplained or residual portion μ.

If we apply least-squares formulae to calculate estimates of the parameters a, b, and c (call these the least-squares estimates a^*, b^*, and c^*), the resulting estimated equation yields a calculated value of Y (call it Y_c) for each observed X and Z combination:

$$Y_c = a^* + b^*X + c^*Z$$

In addition, an estimate μ^* of the true residual error term μ results. As mentioned earlier, it can be shown that the estimates a^*, b^*, and c^* calculated by least squares are unbiased estimates of the true a, b, and c, i.e.:

$$E[a^*] = a$$
$$E[b^*] = b$$
$$E[c^*] = c$$

where E refers to the expected value of the estimate.

These three expressions mean that if all possible differing samples were formed for a particular sample size and estimates a^*, b^*, and c^* computed for each sample, the expected or mean value of this entire population of estimates would equal the true values a, b, and c underlying the data.

This property of unbiasedness in calculated least-squares coefficients offers no assurances that these estimates will be useful in analysis or prediction of fluctuations in economic systems. The a^*, b^*, and c^* will only measure whatever relationships are observable in the data. Such measured relationships may be of little or no statistical significance, or they may be of considerable importance. It is to a consideration of this question that our attention now turns.

Tests of Significance

Judging the quantitative significance of an equation estimated by least squares, and of its individual variables, can be accomplished by applying statistical tests of significance such as F-tests and t-tests, if certain statistical assumptions are approximately met. These assumptions all relate to the inherent inexact property of economic relationships embodied in the residual error term μ associated with a regression equation. Specifically, if we may approximately assume:

1. μ is a stochastic variable normally distributed with a zero mean and a constant variance σ_μ^2, i.e., $\mu = N(0,\sigma_\mu)$; $\sigma_\mu = k$

2. μ is not in any way serially correlated, i.e., $r_{\mu_j \mu_k} = 0$ for all $j \neq k$[7]
3. μ is not correlated with any of the independent variables, i.e.,

$$r_{x_i \mu_i} = 0 \text{ for all } x$$

then we may apply forceful tests of significance of particular equations and variables. Before discussing significance tests, we will discuss the meaning of these assumptions.

The first assumption indicates that the unexplained portion of Y will be essentially noise (having an expected value of zero), will be positive as frequently as negative, and will fluctuate approximately according to a normal distribution whose variance will be a constant, regardless of the value of the independent variables involved in the calculation of Y_c and therefore μ.

The second assumption states that no discernible pattern will be evident in μ chronologically as the sample occurs. Thus, in inspecting μ, we should not observe strings of positive or negative μ that seriously violate our random assumption. This assumption should be distinguished from the first assumption of normality, as it would be possible to obtain a series of μ that were normally distributed over the entire sample, but where the entire positive half of the distribution occurred first and the negative half of the distribution last.

The third assumption indicates that the magnitude of the error term is not affected by the size of any of the independent variables. We expect the same general magnitude for μ when X takes on its maximum sample value as when it assumes its smallest value.

IMPORTANCE OF A GIVEN LEAST-SQUARES FIT

With these assumptions about the error term, we may discuss tests of the significance of obtained regression results. In this, we shall proceed from the following guiding principle:

Empirically significant equations will have large fractions of the value of Y explained by linear combinations of the values of included independent variables, leaving small fractions unexplained.

We now turn to the application of this principle in testing the overall significance of the fit represented by a specific regression equation. Two highly similar tests are available for making direct inferences about overall goodness-of-fit, an F-test and a significance test of the multiple correlation coefficient. We shall focus most of our attention on the latter of these tests, due to the greater intuitive familiarity and ease in interpretation that accompanies its use.

---

[7] $r_{\mu_j \mu_k}$ denotes the correlation between the jth and kth error terms for all values of j and k where $j \neq k$.

The Multiple Correlation Coefficient

A common way to evaluate the significance of a regression equation is to test the multiple correlation coefficient R. Although the test we shall describe is made using R, its squared value R^2, called the coefficient of multiple determination, has the clearest interpretation. We shall therefore describe R^2 even though R is used for the significance test. R^2 can be expressed as a ratio of explained variation to total variation, which makes it a measure of the fraction of the total variation in Y explained by the regression equation. The definition involves specific formulations for explained and unexplained deviation in the dependent variable. They are:

$$SS_E = \Sigma (Y_c - \bar{Y})^2 \quad \text{Explained variation}$$
$$SS_U = \Sigma (Y - Y_c)^2 \quad \text{Unexplained variation}$$

in which the summations cover the entire sample.

SS_E and SS_U have been labeled *explained* and *unexplained* variation, respectively. Figure 2–4 helps show graphically the logic behind this

FIGURE 2–4

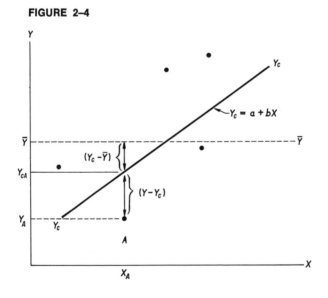

classification. The line $\bar{Y}\bar{Y}$ is the simple arithmetic mean of Y; it is obviously not affected by changes in X and so appears on the XY scatter as a horizontal line. The $Y_c Y_c$ line is a plot of the regression equation. One particular component in the SS_E sum is now seen to be the squared distance between the mean of Y and a particular regression estimate of Y. This component is explained variance in the sense that the regression equation explains a fraction of the value of Y over and above that explained by the average value of that variable in this instance. In other words, the $\bar{Y}$ value is the best single point estimate of Y in the absence of any knowledge of the value of related variables.

When X is known and a regression line given, then Y_c is the best point estimate of Y. For example, point A in Figure 2–4 corresponds to an actual value of Y_A when X was equal to X_A. The best single estimate of this value when X is ignored is $\bar{Y}$, which is higher than the true value. Knowledge of the regression line and that X is equal to X_A causes the best estimate to be lowered to Y_{cA}. It is in this sense that the value $(Y_c - \bar{Y})$ represents the Y variation uniquely explained by X. The more quantitative difference X makes upon the best estimate of Y, the greater will be the total value of SS_E.

The SS_U value measures the total variation in Y left unexplained by the regression equation. In the simple linear case where the true regression equation is

$$Y = a + bX + \mu$$

the calculated value of Y, taken as the average Y given X, is:

$$Y_c = a^* + b^*X.$$

The total squared variation in Y, $SS_T = \Sigma(Y - \bar{Y})^2$, is either explained or unexplained, i.e.,

$$SS_T = SS_E + SS_U$$

Thus, R^2 may be expressed as:

$$R^2 = \frac{SS_E}{SS_T} = \frac{SS_T - SS_U}{SS_T} = 1 - \frac{SS_U}{SS_T}$$

The latter version expresses R^2 as the complement of the fraction of total variation left unexplained, SS_U/SS_T. R^2 becomes larger because the regression equation accounts for a larger fraction of the total variation inherent in Y. In fact, if every observed Y value fell on the regression line, $SS_U = 0$, $SS_E = SS_T$, and $R^2 = 1.0$, which would mean the regression equation accounted for all the fluctuation in Y. At the other extreme, where the value of X in the expression $Y = a + bX$ made absolutely no quantitative difference in the determination of Y, the best estimate of the parameter b would be $b = 0$. Then, the value of a would be given by:

$$a = \bar{Y} - b\bar{X} = \bar{Y}$$

so that

$$Y_c = \bar{Y} \text{ regardless of } X.$$

This would produce

$$SS_E = \Sigma(\bar{Y} - \bar{Y})^2 = 0$$
$$SS_U = \Sigma(Y - \bar{Y})^2 = SS_T$$

Therefore

$$R^2 = 1 - \frac{S_U}{S_T} = 1 - \frac{S_T}{S_T} = 0$$

and no fraction of the variation inherent in Y is attributable to the equation.

In testing for the significance of obtained sample R^2 values, an adjustment is necessary to account for statistical bias arising from using sample estimates to measure underlying population characteristics. The adjusted value of R^2 is:

$$R_a{}^2 = 1 - \frac{SS_U}{SS_T}\left[\frac{n-1}{n-k-1}\right]$$

where, as before, n = sample size and k = number *of* independent variables.

In the significance test, we are interested in determining whether an obtained R_a (unsquared) value is large enough to be judged to have arisen from an underlying population with a non zero correlation.[8] The conclusion that the true R_a value is non zero implies that the regression relationship involved is significant.

A convenient hypothesis for this test is:

$$H_o: R_p = 0$$

where R_p is the true underlying population correlation coefficient. Obtained R_a values different enough from zero will cause rejection of H_o and acceptance of the alternative that

$$H_1: R_p \neq 0$$

Wallace and Snedecor have tabled critical sample R_a values for various sample sizes and number of variables drawn from populations where $R_p = 0$. These critical R_a values represent points in the distribution of sample R_a values that would be exceeded in only 5 percent and 1 percent of all possible samples drawn from populations where $R_p = 0$. Thus, obtained R_a values less than these critical values could reasonably have come from populations with $R_p = 0$ while obtained values greater than,

---

[8] Strictly speaking, the variables involved in computing R^2 are assumed to have arisen from a bivariate normal distribution, i.e., each variable is normally distributed with regards to the other. Since R^2 can be interpreted as the simple coefficient of determination between Y and Y_c, this means that we assume Y and the X that linearly determine Y_c are bivariate normal variates for purposes of the significance tests.

say, the 5 percent critical value could only be expected less than one in 20 times when $R_p = 0$.

Table 1 in the appendix contains a table of critical R_a values at 5 percent and 1 percent levels of significance. The critical R_a value is affected by the number of variables and the sample size. The table is entered across the top at the number of coefficients in the equation (usually the number of independent variables plus one, for the constant, $(k + 1)$, and down the side by the value $n - k - 1$. The entry is the critical value of R_a when $R_p = 0$.

For example, in an equation with four independent variables established on the basis of 30 observations, the obtained $R_a = .60$. This means that $(.60)^2 = .36$, or 36 percent of the variation in Y in the sample is accounted for by the four independent variables. The critical values of R_a from the table at $k + 1 = 5$ and $n - k - 1 = 25$ are

$$R_{.05} = .553 \qquad R_{.01} = .633$$

We thus expect values as great as the .600 obtained fewer than 5 percent of the time but more frequently than 1 percent of the time when the true $R_p = 0$. This means the obtained R value is significantly different from zero at the 5 percent level of significance but not at the 1 percent level, since we expect to obtain R_a values as high as .633 as often as one in 100 samples when the true $R_p = 0$. Thus, the $R_a = .600$ represents positive evidence of a significant underlying regression relationship.

F-Statistic

An alternative test of the overall significance of a regression equation is the F-test. As with the test on R_a, the F-test deals with a comparison of the relative magnitudes of explained vs. unexplained variation in the equation. Specifically, in the F-test it is hypothesized that all the regression coefficients in a multiple regression equation are zero, i.e.:

$$H_o: \beta_1 = \beta_2 = \cdots = \beta_m = 0 \text{ for an } m\text{-variable equation}$$

vs. the alternative hypothesis that some β_i are not zero. If the null hypothesis (H_o) is true, then the unexplained variation in the equation SS_u will approximately equal the total variation SS_T. Little variation will be explained by the equation, i.e., $SS_E \cong 0$.

To test H_o, an F-statistic may be formed by comparing the explained variation to the unexplained variation:

$$F = \frac{SS_E/df_1}{SS_u/df_2}$$

where df_1 and df_2 are the degrees of freedom for the numerator and denominator.

Under the null hypothesis, the numerator will be close to zero and thus F will be very small. Calculated values of F that depart substantially from zero indicate large magnitudes of explained variation relative to unexplained, and imply that significant explanatory value attaches to the equation. In other words, when the level of explanation is significant, the ratio of explained to unexplained variance will no longer follow an F-distribution.

We may refer to a table of the critical value of F to decide whether an obtained F-value deviates significantly from values consistent with the null hypothesis.

Table 3 in the appendix shows critical values of the F-distribution. These values depend upon two degrees-of-freedom measures, one for the numerator and one for the denominator. In the numerator, the degrees of freedom are equal to the number of independent variables while in the denominator they are equal to the sample size minus the number of independent variables minus one. That is, the critical $F = F_{n_1, n_2}$ where $n_1 = m$ and $n_2 = N - m - 1$ for $N =$ number of observations and $m =$ number of independent variables.

For example, consider the following results:

$$F_{\text{obtained}} = 14.73$$
$$N = 35 \text{ observations}$$
$$m = 4 \text{ independent variables in equation.}$$

This gives $n_1 = 4$, $n_2 = 30$. Table 3 shows the critical value to be:

$$F_{4,30} = 2.69 \text{ at five percent significance level}$$
$$= 4.02 \text{ at one percent significance level}$$

Since the obtained value is greater than even the one percent value, we may conclude the explanatory significance of the equation to be substantial. We should thus reject the null hypothesis.[9]

Other Indications of Goodness-of-Fit

While the coefficient of determination is often a convenient figure of merit in assessing the goodness-of-fit of a particular equation to a set of data, occasions arise where an even more direct measure of ex-

---

[9] It was earlier noted that the test of significance performed on the multiple correlation coefficient depended upon the independent variables having arisen from a bivariate normal distribution. In some applications the independent variables in regression models will not be stochastic in nature, but will occur in a deterministic fashion. In these cases, the R_a test described earlier is not strictly correct, since it is tied to the bivariate normal assumption. The F-test is not so restricted, however, and remains strictly applicable. Where the bivariate normal assumption is met, both tests can be shown to produce the same results.

plained and unexplained variation can be helpful. The standard deviation of the error term μ is such a measure, as is the average absolute error.

The standard deviation of μ, σ_μ, is the root mean square value of the error term

$$\sigma_\mu = \sqrt{E(\mu^2)}$$

where E denotes the expected value of the error term. For finite populations of size n, σ_μ is usually considered to be given by:

$$\sigma_\mu = \sqrt{\sum_{i=1}^{n} \frac{\mu_i^2}{n}}$$

Defined this way, σ_μ can be interpreted as a measure of the effective standard deviation of Y, once knowledge of the independent variables and the equation parameters has been used to compute Y_c, i.e., once we have explained a portion of the inherent variation in Y through use of the regression equation.

As indicated earlier, we usually do not know the true value of μ since that rests on knowledge of the true coefficients of the approximating regression equation. Estimating the regression coefficients from a sample of data produces a similar estimate of μ, earlier designated μ^*. In the (normal) case where only μ^* is available, we similarly cannot calculate σ_μ, but only an estimate of it S_μ. This estimate differs only by the denominator, which is $n\text{-}2$ rather than n. With this adjustment, S_μ can be shown to be an unbiased estimate of σ_μ:

$$S_\mu = \sqrt{\frac{\sum_{i=1}^{n} \mu_i^{*2}}{n-2}}$$

$$E(S_\mu) = \sigma_\mu.$$

Confidence Intervals

The similarity of S_μ and σ_μ to estimated and actual simple standard deviations makes it tempting to suggest their use in constructing confidence intervals about calculated values of Y for particular values of the independent variables. In the case of perfect knowledge of the regression equation, i.e., σ_μ, this is both possible and convenient. Our earlier assumption that $\mu = (Y - Y_c)$ was a stochastic variable approximately normally distributed with zero mean is the key. The normality of μ is equivalent to saying that Y is approximately normally distributed around Y_c for any group of X. This is illustrated in Figure 2–5 for the simple case of two variables. Our earlier expression for σ_μ showed this statistic to be the standard error of μ; therefore, it is now seen as the standard deviation

FIGURE 2–5

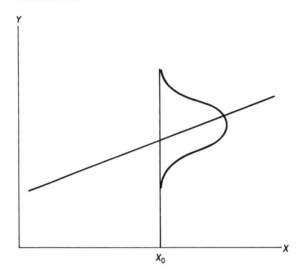

of this conditional distribution of Y given X. With the true regression line known, the uncertainty represented by this conditional distribution is the only source of inexactness present in the calculation of Y from X. Therefore, we may construct intervals employing such conditional distributions and expect particular computed Y values to fall within the intervals with known frequency as in classic hypothesis testing. For example, say the true regression equation:

$$Y = a + bX + \mu; \; \mu = N(0,\sigma_\mu)$$

is evaluated at $X = X_0$, resulting in:

$$Y_0 = a + bX_0$$

We compute the interval:

$$Y_0 \pm \sigma_\mu Z_{.025},$$

where $Z_{.025}$ is the standard normal deviate associated with the number of standard deviations from the mean, containing 95 percent of all values from the underlying normally distributed stochastic process. Then, the computed interval contains 95 percent of all values of Y that occur when X equals X_0. Therefore, this interval shows the extent of uncertainty inherent in the best conditional point estimate of Y, Y_0.

As just described, computation of this interval rests upon knowledge of the true regression coefficients, implying the entire data population is known. This characteristic does not often occur in practical research. Under the more usual circumstances where the regression coefficients must be established on the basis of a sample of data from a larger population (as with most time series), additional uncertainty is present besides that associated with μ. This additional uncertainty relates to the inexactness in calculating Y values based on estimated regression coefficients as opposed to actual coefficients. Specifically, for a true regression equation:

$$Y = a + bX + \mu$$

estimated by

$$Y = a^* + b^*X + \mu^*$$

The obtained estimates of a^* and b^* are point estimates of a and b obtained from a particular sample. If a second differing sample was drawn from the same underlying population characterized by a and b differing estimates $a^{*\prime}$ and $b^{*\prime}$ would result. In fact, if every conceivable differing sample of a particular size was drawn, statistical distributions of a^* and b^* values would result, containing the entire population of possible estimates of a and b.

Such distributions are called sampling distributions, as they involve computed statistics as the stochastic variable rather than raw data. In regression analysis, the sampling distributions of a^* and b^* are useful in making inferences about the true underlying values of a and b. We shall return to that subject later in this chapter when we discuss tests of individual variables. For now, it suffices to recognize that individual coefficient estimates a^* and b^* in general will differ from the actual values a and b.

The difference $(a - a^*)$ and $(b - b^*)$ represents additional sources of error in confidence interval estimates. A correctly computed interval must take into account this additional source of variation.

In the case of simple two-variable regression models such as our illustration, this computation can be accomplished by summing the total variation associated with the sampling distribution of a and b estimates along with the error variance as follows:

$$S_T{}^2 = S_a{}^2 + (X_o - \bar{X})^2 S_b{}^2 + S_\mu{}^2$$

In this expression, the total estimated variance $S_T{}^2$ is the sum of the estimated variance of the sampling distribution of a^* ($S_a{}^2$), plus the variance of the sampling distribution of b^* ($S_b{}^2$), multiplied by the squared distance from the mean of X ($\bar{X}$) of the given X value (X_o), plus the variance of the error term ($S_\mu{}^2$). The middle term in this expression reveals that the further from the mean of X the given X is, the greater the contribution of the variance $S_b{}^2$ will be to the total. If X_o is in an extreme portion of its observed range (high or low), any sampling error present in b will have a magnified effect on Y_c. On the other hand, if $X_o = \bar{X}$, then the $S_b{}^2 (X_o - \bar{X})^2$ term exerts no influence on $S_T{}^2$. (The $\bar{X}$ point is the point around which the estimated regression line pivots from the original.) The square root of $S_T{}^2$:

$$S_T = \sqrt{S_a{}^2 + (X_o - \bar{X})^2 S_b{}^2 + S_\mu{}^2}$$

may be used in place of σ_μ to set up an interval around the estimated regression line. For example:

$$Y_c \pm t_{.025} S_T$$

is a correct 95 percent confidence interval for individual Y values given X. Note that the use of an estimate of σ_μ has also made the t distribution an appropriate substitute for the normal distribution. Predictions about Y made from information on X could be bounded by this interval with 95 percent confidence.

For estimated regression models containing more than a single independent variable, the same basic sources of error remain in making interval predictions about Y from a group of Xs. Now, the intercept estimate plus all the coefficient estimates plus the distances of all Xs from their means join the error variance in the formulation of $S_T{}^2$. However, computationally the task is considerably more involved than in the simple case. To deal with intervals for individual Y estimates in this case is beyond the scope of our effort.[10]

Other Figures of Merit

In explaining the results of a regression fit to a nonstatistician, it is sometimes useful to develop a measure of "how far off the equation is on the average." For this purpose, the estimated standard deviation of μ, S_μ, is too conservative since it gives undue weight to extreme deviations by squaring them before the square root is extracted. A better measure of how far we are off on the average is the mean absolute error:

$$E = \sum_{i=1}^{n} \frac{|Y - Y_c|_i}{n}$$

For example, if an equation for predicting sales has been developed producing E of 10.1 million, we may state that on the average, our equation missed the true past sales value by 10.1 million. While of no use in making inferences or constructing confidence intervals, E is often of considerable use in communication.

----

[10] The interested reader is directed to R. J. Wonnacott and T. H. Wonnacott, *Econometrics* (New York: John Wiley, 1970), pp. 259–61.

A percentage measure of average absolute error observed in the sample can be constructed from E as follows:

$$P = \frac{E}{\bar{Y}}$$

where $\bar{Y}$ is the mean value of Y. This shows the average percent error over the sample. P is often a highly communicable figure of merit to illustrate an obtained goodness-of-fit. For example, with $E = 10.1$, if $\bar{Y}$ is 882.0, then $P = 10.1/882.0 = 1.1\%$. On the average, the calculated Y deviated from the actual by 1.1 percent of the mean $\bar{Y}$.

In using P and E, we should guard against their misuse as limits of an interval for predicted Y. They have no statistical basis for this task, and are likely to lead to strained relations between statistical analysts and nonstatisticians if incorrectly interpreted in this manner.

TESTS OF INDIVIDUAL VARIABLES

Our second major interest in significance tests of regression relationships is in assessing the contribution of individual variables towards an equation's level of explanation. In testing hypotheses about economic relationships, we are often interested in evidence regarding the empirical significance of individual variables within equations representing a priori theories. The results of such inquiry are made more meaningful by the partial nature of regression coefficients in multivariate equations. In the equation $Y = a + bX + cZ + \mu$, the b and c values are basically weights that attach movements in the variables X and Z to movements in Y. In addition, the coefficients also implicitly translate between whatever units Y is expressed in and the units of X and Z respectively.[11]

In their role as weights, the regression coefficients measure the partial effect of individual independent variables on Y, where the effect of other variables has been held constant. To illustrate, the b coefficient measures the impact of X on Y, when the effects of Z on Y are held constant. Given the earlier statistical assumptions about μ, the partial nature of regression coefficients means that the quantitative effect of one influential variable upon Y can be isolated from the effects of others. In analyzing economic data, this partialing out of statistical effect can often allow the economist's famous stipulation of *ceteris paribus* (all other factors remaining constant) to be operationalized. Since our model stipulates that Y is jointly influenced by X and Z, the b coefficient measures the influence of X upon Y, *ceteris paribus*.

The significance test we now discuss is a test of this partial effect. It evolves from two thoughts discussed earlier, which we now collect

---

[11] In the case where all units are the same in the equation, then the b and c values are straightforward weights.

and extend. First, we earlier noted that the statistical variability associated with coefficient estimates a^*, b^*, and c^* gives rise to sampling distributions for each of these statistics. In addition, it has been stated that the means of these distributions $E(a^*)$, $E(b^*)$, $E(c^*)$ will equal the true values of the parameters being estimated (a,b,c) for all unbiased estimators such as least squares applied to single-equation models. In addition, our statistical procedures enable calculation of the estimated standard deviation of individual sampling distributions, designated S_a, S_b, S_c.[12] Furthermore, it can be shown that if our earlier assumptions about the error term hold, sampling distributions of coefficient estimates will follow a t distribution.

Thus, from this knowledge of the mean, variance, and distribution of particular coefficient estimates we may construct confidence intervals for true regression coefficients, and test hypotheses about true values of coefficients from obtained sample results.

We now turn to these specific tests, beginning with a test of the significance of an individual obtained regression coefficient. Beginning with calculated b^* and S_b values and knowledge that b^* is distributed according to t, a convenient way to proceed is via the hypothesis:

$$H_o: \quad b = 0$$

against the alternative:

$$H_1: \quad b \neq 0$$

If the obtained b^* value is close to zero, we shall accept H_o and conclude that our data demonstrates no important relationship running from X to Y. On the other hand, if b^* is significantly different from zero, we may accept H_1 and conclude that the true regression coefficient is importantly different from zero and that X exerts a significant influence upon Y in the data. The easiest way to test this hypothesis is to construct a normalized t statistic:

$$t = \frac{b^* - b}{S_b}$$

which for the hypothesis $b = 0$ becomes $t = \dfrac{b^*}{S_b}$. When b^* is drawn from a t distribution with b mean, the statistic t will measure the number of standard deviations away from b that a given b^* estimate represents.

Often in testing hypotheses about economic relationships, it will be more meaningful to test a hypothesis about the direction of the hypothesized relationship as well as its significance. That is, we will have an

---

[12] For computational formulas, see Yamane, *Statistics*, pp. 789–90. Most library-type computer programs for regression analysis include these S_a, S_b, and S_c estimates.

a priori thesis as to the expected direction of the relationship between two variables. Under these circumstances, the appropriate hypothesis is:

$$H_o: \quad b \leq 0 \text{ vs. } H_1: \quad b > 0$$
$$\text{or } H_o: \quad b \geq 0 \text{ vs. } H_1: \quad b < 0$$

which can be tested similarly to our original two-tail hypothesis.

Critical values of the t distribution are included in Table 1 of the appendix for five percent and one percent significance levels, and are dependent upon the degrees of freedom, $n - k - 1$ (k = the number of independent variables). For example, for 20 degrees of freedom, the critical t values are $t_{.05} = \pm 2.086$ and $t_{.01} = \pm 2.845$ (or $t_{.025} = +2.086$ and $t_{.005} = +2.845$ for a test of the null hypothesis that $b \leq 0$). This means in the two-tail test we expect occurrences greater than 2.086 standard deviations on either side of the mean in fewer than five percent of all cases, and greater than 2.845 standard deviations on either side of the mean in fewer than one percent of all cases, when b^* comes from a population with b mean. Thus, if a sample produces the following:

$$b^* = 34.5 \qquad t = \frac{34.5}{7.4} = 4.66$$
$$S_b = 7.4$$

we may conclude that the observed deviation of 4.66 standard deviations from the hypothesized $b = 0$ is too great to have occurred by chance alone, and would occur less than one time in 100 when in fact $b = 0$. Therefore, the $b = 0$ hypothesis is untenable at greater than one percent levels of significanc and a significantly nonzero b is inferred to exist in the population. Following classical hypothesis testing, we could alternatively construct a 95 percent confidence interval for b as follows:

$$b^* \pm t_{.05}S_b = 34.5 \pm (2.086)(7.4) = 19.1 - 49.9$$

This interval constructed around the estimated b^* value contains the true b value with 95 percent confidence. It thus illustrates the level of uncertainty contained in the estimate b^*. If the estimated interval spanned both positive and negative values, it would illustrate a high level of uncertainty as to the true value of the coefficient.

In empirical studies in economics and in several equations presented later in this book, it is conventional to present either the standard error of regression coefficients S_b, or the computed t value for the hypothesis $b = 0$ under the coefficient in parenthesis, as follows:

$$\text{(standard errors)} \qquad\qquad \text{(computed } t \text{ values)}$$
$$Y = -3.75 + 34.5X - 23.4Z \quad \text{or} \quad Y = -3.75 + 34.5X - 23.4Z$$
$$\qquad\quad (7.4) \quad (19.5) \qquad\qquad\qquad\quad (4.66) \quad (-1.20)$$

This enables some indication as to the role of specific variables to be seen rather quickly. For example, the coefficient on the Z variable does not provide evidence of being significantly different from zero at the five percent level, and could easily represent a sample statistic taken from a population having zero mean. We can conclude from a t value of 4.66 that X exerts a significant influence upon Y.

AN EXAMPLE

We have now discussed overall goodness-of-fit of a particular equation to a set of data and the goodness-of-fit of individual variables, defining R^2 and t tests for each. These ideas are now summarized by application to an illustrative situation. Assume the value of a particular dependent variable Y is determined as a linear combination of two independent variables, X and Z, plus an error term, as follows:

$$Y = bX + cZ + \mu$$

or specifically:

$$Y = 1.0X + 2.0Z + \mu \qquad (2\text{-}2)$$

where:

1) $\mu = N(\bar{\mu} = 0, \sigma = 10)$
2) μ has little or no serial correlation $r_{\mu_t \mu_{t-1}} = .014$
3) μ is not importantly correlated with X or Z, i.e.,
    $r_{X_t \mu_t} = .031,\ r_{Z_t \mu_t} = .062$

Also, X and Z are truly independent and not influenced by the value of Y, and in addition are independent of each other, i.e., $r_{X \cdot Z} = .051$.

In this equation, we thus have near-perfect conditions for the application of regression analysis. To illustrate our discussion, we calculated 20 observations on Y from our known equation (2-2) via simulation, starting with given values of X and Z, and applying the known coefficients and values of the error term drawn randomly from a normal distribution having the properties given above. This produced 20 observations on X, Z, and Y generated by the above known underlying equation.

Applying least squares to these simulated data yields the following estimates:

$$Y_c = 3.90 + .948X + 1.721Z$$
$$(2.94) \quad\ (3.07)$$

where numbers in parentheses are computed t values.

Other data obtained:

$$
\begin{array}{ll}
R = \quad .728 & S_b = .322 \\
R^2 = \quad .529 & S_c = .560 \\
S_\mu = 11.33 & n = \quad 20
\end{array}
$$

where:

$$\text{Critical } R_{.05} = .545$$
$$\text{Critical } R_{.01} = .647$$
$$\text{Critical } t_{.05} \text{ (degrees of freedom } 20 - 3 = 17) = 2.11$$
$$\text{Critical } t_{.01} = 2.90$$

From these results we may conclude:

1. Our equation explains close to 53 percent of the variation in Y through associated variation in X and Z.

2. The R value is significantly different from zero beyond the one percent level, indicating the equation is an important explanatory mechanism for fluctuations in Y.

3. Both coefficients are significantly nonzero beyond the one percent level, therefore X and Z are likely to be importantly related to Y on an individual basis.

4. We may predict the true b value will fall in the interval $.948 \pm (2.11)(.322) = .269 - 1.627$ with 95 percent confidence.

5. We may predict the true c value will fall in the interval $1.721 \pm (2.11)(.560) = .539 - 2.903$ with 95 percent confidence.

With our simulated data, we have the advantage of knowing the true coefficients of the equation which produced the Y data. Reference back to that true equation (2-2) reveals that the conclusions now listed are indeed correct when compared to the known true values.

Our ability to draw these and other similar conclusions rests on the properties of the error term, which we know to be ideal (due to the construction of the data) and the properties of independence among the X and Z variables.

If these ideal properties do not exist in the data, the reliability of obtained regression equations may be questionable. We turn in the next chapter to a series of questions relative to reliability and interpretation of obtained results under less than ideal conditions.

DISCUSSION QUESTIONS

1. In least-squares curve fitting, outlying observations have been seen to exert large effects upon estimated coefficient values. Under what circumstances do you think it is reasonable to exclude greatly deviant observations?

2. Given an estimated regression equation of the following form:

$$Y = a + bX + cZ + \mu$$

what would you make of the finding that:

$$E = b\bar{X} + c\bar{Z}$$

where E is the mean absolute error and $\bar{X}$, $\bar{Z}$ are mean values of X and Z respectively?

3. Where does the assumption of normality of the error term enter the regression model?

4. Point out a hypothetical but plausible situation in which a t-test of a regression coefficient would more logically be made in a two-tailed fashion than in a one-tailed fashion.

5. For a particular independent variable, is it possible to have both (a) a "computed t value" of 14.5 and (b) a 95 percent confidence interval for the regression coefficient (c) of:

$$-4.1 < c < 4.4$$

Why or why not?

6. In Chapter 2 the statement is made: Assume a particular pattern of statistical association can be approximated by the following "true" regression equation:

$$Y = a + bX + cZ + \mu$$

If this equation is the true regression equation, why is the term "approximated" used?

CASE 1—MIDWEST EQUIPMENT COMPANY (A)

Mr. Salnas leaned back in his chair and pondered the budget request for capital expenditures he was preparing to present at the board meeting. It was September, 1968, and a decision had to be reached concerning the proposed installation of two new aluminum casting machines by the end of the month. A much longer postponement would mean the machines would not be ready for utilization until after the peak production period this coming spring. If only Schwendinger, the marketing department manager, would produce some concrete figures for next year's forecast! As general manager of the Power Division of Midwest Equipment Co., Salnas was responsible for providing adequate output of his division's products at competitive prices.

The Midwest Equipment Co. was founded in Winaska Falls 62 years ago as a manufacturer of a limited line of hand garden tools. Today the company has two major divisions and produces a full line of lawn and garden equipment. The Power Division is responsible for the production and marketing of the company's full line of power lawn mowers, which comprise about 60 percent of the company's total sales. The 'Sprint' mower line ranges from a small one-horsepower unit to a riding mower with a full complement of attachments.

The new marketing department manager, Jim Schwendinger, had been assigned the task of providing such a forecast of the division's unit sales over the next two years. This forecast was of particular concern because a favorable return from installation of the new machines depended upon achieving a minimum sales volume. Schwendinger had previously been employed as an analyst by the Green Wonder Pickle Co. and had come to Midwest Equipment about four months ago. In hiring him, Mr. Salnas had been particularly impressed by Schwendinger's apparent knowledge of regression analysis in sales forecasting. Although Schwendinger's background in regression analysis had been mainly academic, he felt that a reliable model using this technique could be developed for the Midwest Equipment Co.

Jim Schwendinger sat at his desk and pondered the sales equation he had constructed. He had finally come up with predicted unit sales for the next two years. The process of trial and error in finding significant variables had been lengthy. Many combinations were tried, tests of significance were made, and those variables that didn't measure up were eliminated.

Schwendinger lamented that he must have run every bit of data in the *Industry Statistics* manual through his regression analysis. He had a pile of computer output 16 inches thick. The final equation contained three variables. Sales was a function of advertising (A), productivity index (PI), and housing starts (HS).

The equation and the various tests for significance are given below (20 years' data were used in fitting the equation).

$$S = 15.0 + 4.0A + .5PI - 2.2HS$$

(Standard errors)   (0.20)   (0.15)   (1.0)

$$\text{Average Sales} = \bar{S} = 4,010 \qquad \bar{S}_\mu = 43.8$$
$$R^2 = 89.4$$

Questions

1. Comment on the statistical worth of the equation, and of individual variables.
2. Note that advertising (A) was used as one of the independent variables. How does this affect the reliability of the forecast, if at all?
3. Is any statistical data missing that you would find useful in your evaluation of the model?
4. What do you think of Mr. Schwendinger's approach in general? How would you develop the equation for a sales forecast in the above case?

Chapter 3

JUDGING THE RELIABILITY
OF REGRESSION
CONCLUSIONS

In Chapter 2, we discussed the interpretation of regression results under conditions of perfect behavior of the error term. However, samples of economic data are largely drawn in time series, and predictive models are usually concerned with projections about future time-series values. This characteristic frequently introduces special patterns of behavior of the error term that limit our ability to reliably use the results of regression analysis. Other problems not directly connected with the error term also limit our ability to draw useful conclusions from regression results. In this chapter, we shall discuss these problems under the headings of autocorrelation, heteroscedasticity, multicollinearity, and others.

AUTOCORRELATION

One assumption about the error term was that no predictable pattern existed in the error term produced by a regression equation. Failure to meet this assumption, i.e., the existence of a significant pattern in the error term, is called *autocorrelation*. An autocorrelated error term contains a systematic trend such that knowledge of the value of μ_{t-1} will improve the ability to predict μ_t. For example, an error term corresponding to:

$$\mu_t = \alpha\mu_{t-1} + e_t$$

where e_t was nonsystematic in pattern would be autocorrelated to the extent α is significant. Two general types of patterns are possible, called *positive* and *negative* autocorrelation respectively. Positive autocorrelation results when the occurrence of a positive (negative) error term raises the probability above 0.5 that the next successive error term will have a positive (negative) value. In our example, α would be positive and significant. The condition is depicted graphically for the simple case of $Y = f(x)$ in panel (a) of Figure 3–1. Notice in this figure the observations

49

FIGURE 3–1

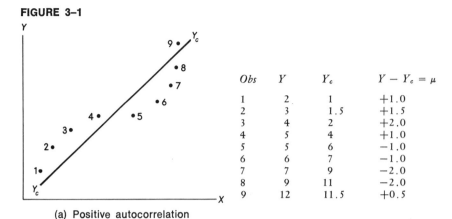

(a) Positive autocorrelation

Obs	Y	Y_c	$Y - Y_c = \mu$
1	2	1	+1.0
2	3	1.5	+1.5
3	4	2	+2.0
4	5	4	+1.0
5	5	6	−1.0
6	6	7	−1.0
7	7	9	−2.0
8	9	11	−2.0
9	12	11.5	+0.5

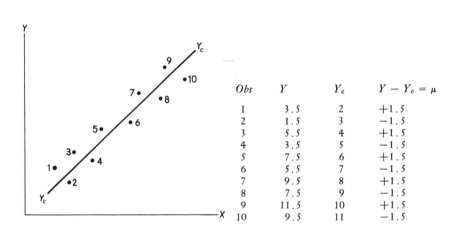

(b) Negative autocorrelation

Obs	Y	Y_c	$Y - Y_c = \mu$
1	3.5	2	+1.5
2	1.5	3	−1.5
3	5.5	4	+1.5
4	3.5	5	−1.5
5	7.5	6	+1.5
6	5.5	7	−1.5
7	9.5	8	+1.5
8	7.5	9	−1.5
9	11.5	10	+1.5
10	9.5	11	−1.5

in the scatter are numbered in the order of their occurrence. This is important in the evaluation of autocorrelation, since we are concerned with whether the order in which the sample points occurred influenced the value of the error term. Notice the error term has a positive value over the first four observations followed by a negative value over the next four. In the case shown, this patern results from fitting a linear function through data that is significantly nonlinear. The resulting autocorrelation is produced by this significant nonlinear trend.

Panel (b) of Figure 3–1 shows negative autocorrelation. Positive residuals are invariably followed by negative residuals, and so forth. In our earlier expression, α is negative and significant. In this case, the occurrence of a positive (negative) error term raises the probability above

0.5 that the next residual will be negative (positive). The pattern in panel (b) implies a kind of *sin* wave pattern in the data unaccounted for by movements in X.

If a variable that significantly influences Y and is not intercorrelated with other independent variables is omitted from a regression equation, the partial influence of this omitted variable may be revealed in the error term. Although we cannot depend on the property of autocorrelation to reveal all circumstances where a truly significant independent variable has been omitted from the equation, the existence of patterns in the error term should raise our suspicions that an influential explanatory variable has been overlooked in the equation.

Effects of Autocorrelation on Results

If autocorrelation is found to exist, its major impact upon regression analysis is to cause the calculated error measures to be unreliably estimated. Goodness-of-fit statistics such as R^2 may have more significant calculated values than may be warranted. This means we cannot rely on significant findings obtained from such values to buttress conclusions about the importance of economic relationships when significant autocorrelation is present. Also, the sample variances of individual regression coefficients will unreliably estimate the true values, causing t-tests to produce possibly spurious conclusions. Finally, serious autocorrelation may adversely affect the property of least-squares techniques to produce the best (minimum-variance) estimates. This means the computed least-squares line or plane that results will not have the desirable qualities we expect it to have, and conclusions drawn from R and t-tests are likely to be unreliable.

To illustrate these remarks, suppose we return to the simulated numerical example presented near the end of Chapter 2, in which:

$$Y_t = 1.0X_t + 2.0Z_t + \mu_t$$
$$\mu_t = N(0,10)$$

and now replace μ_t by v_t where

$$v_t = \mu_t + 0,4,8,4,0,-4,-8,-4,0, \ldots \text{ for } t = 1,2,3, \ldots \text{ etc.}$$

In other words, the new error term v_t now contains in addition to the normally distributed "ideal" μ_t component a systematic *sin*–wave–type pattern that is not attributable to either of the explanatory variables X or Z. As before, 20 observations of Y were simulated from data on X and Y by applying the "true coefficients" and the modified error term v. When we apply least-squares to calculate the coefficients in this modified data, we obtain:

$$Y = 29.13 + .346X + 1.389Z$$
$$(1.34) \quad (3.08)$$

$$R = .631 \qquad S_b = .259$$
$$R^2 = .398 \qquad S_c = .450$$
$$S_\mu = 9.11 \qquad n = 20$$

in which a 95 percent confidence interval for b is given by:

$$-.200 < b < .892$$

and for c by:

$$.440 < c < 2.339$$

Thus, our interval for b does not include the true value of 1.0, while the interval for c correctly does. Similarly, our estimates for b and c are considerably worsened from the earlier estimates of .948 and 1.721. The R^2 value has been reduced from .529 in the original case to .398, while the measured standard error of 9.11 is actually smaller than the

FIGURE 3–2
Effects of Autocorrelation

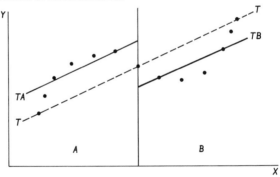

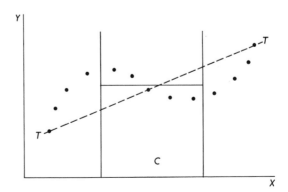

previous 11.33 (possibly due to a negative bias in the cyclical pattern).

These results tend to illustrate possible effects of autocorrelation on measured regression relationships. However, they may not be taken as general directional principles in the effects of autocorrelation. Figure 3–2 illustrates some reasons with a two-variable model. In the upper panel, the "true" regression line is given by *TT*. If the sample chosen covered only the first half of the data or only the second half, as illustrated by regions *A* and *B*, then the regression line would be positioned respectively too high and too low, as with *TA* and *TB*. However, the proximity of the incomplete sample points to *TA* or *TB* would likely cause the obtained goodness-of-fit measures for the equation and for the regression coefficient to appear to be more significant than warranted. On the other hand, if the sample data were chosen from region *C*, the result might be a very poorly estimated coefficient value and impredictable values for goodness-of-fit tests. Thus, our confidence in the meaning of obtained regression results is shaken when autocorrelation is present in obtained residuals. We now turn to a test for this condition.

Testing for Autocorrelation

The simplest way to examine statistical results for autocorrelation is to inspect the error term resulting from fitting the equation for runs of + or − values. A non-autocorrelated error term should have a patternless array of + or − values. As we have seen, autocorrelated error terms will have either heavy concentrated + or − zones, or alternating patterns.

A specific quantitative interpretation of the level of autocorrelation can be made by computing and interpreting the Durbin-Watson statistic, so named after its founders.[1] This statistic, *d* is defined as follows:

$$d = \frac{\sum_{t=2}^{n} (\hat{\mu}_t - \hat{\mu}_{t-1})^2}{\sum_{t=1}^{n} \hat{\mu}_t^2}$$

where $\hat{\mu}$ is the calculated error term resulting from the estimated regression equation and *n* is the sample size.

For positively autocorrelated $\hat{\mu}$ values, the numerator of *d* will be disproportionately small, since the runs of positive and negative $\hat{\mu}$ values

---

[1] The original article is J. Durbin and G. S. Watson, "Testing for Serial Correlation in Least-Squares Regression," *Biometrika*, Parts I and II, 1950 and 1951. An alternative test of the Durbin-Watson statistic is given by H. Theil and A. L. Nagar, "Testing the Independence of Regression Disturbances," *Journal of the American Statistical Association*, Vol. 56, 1961, pp. 793–806.

will cancel out in the computation of the squared successive differences. For example, for the positive autocorrelation shown in Figure 3–1, panel (a), $d = 0.69$. Negatively autocorrelated $\hat{\mu}$, on the other hand, will produce large d values, as the systematic sign changes will cause successive terms to add together rather than cancel out. In the negative autocorrelation of Figure 3–1, panel (b), $d = 3.57$.

The Durbin-Watson statistic has a value of approximately $2 \left[\dfrac{n-1}{n} \right]$ in the complete absence of autocorrelation. In testing the d statistic for significantly large or small values, the Durbin-Watson test either indicates the existence or nonexistence of significant autocorrelation, or produces an inconclusive result. The applicable regions are shown in Figure 3–3. Two critical values of the d statistic, d_l and d_u, are involved in applying the Durbin-Watson test. As seen from the figure, d_l and d_u describe the boundaries between the acceptance and rejection region for positive autocorrelation, thereby defining the inconclusive region.

FIGURE 3–3

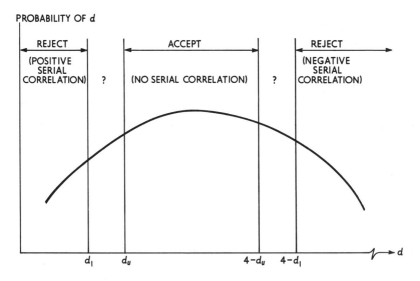

The corresponding right-tail boundaries, $4 - d_u$ and $4 - d_l$, define critical values for negative autocorrelation. Thus, if we apply a two-tail test, and formulate the hypothesis that no autocorrelation exists (that d is close to $2[n - 1/n]$), then the acceptance and rejection regions are:

$$\text{accept if } d_u < d < 4 - d_u$$
$$\text{reject if } d > 4 - d_l \text{ or } d < d_l$$

Otherwise, the test is inconclusive. Tables for the critical value of d_l and d_u are given in Table 2 of the appendix. Note that for a two-tail test, the significance levels relate to each tail so that their value is doubled, e.g., the correct five percent two-tail figures are given in the 2.5 percent table. The critical values d_l, d_u are a function of the number of independent variables, identified as k in the table, and the sample size n. For example, in our modified numerical example in which the error term was replaced by the known serially correlated error term v, the calculated $d = 0.94$. At the five percent level for $k = 2$ independent variables and $n = 20$:

$$d_u = 1.41 \qquad 4 - d_u = 2.59$$
$$d_l = 0.99 \qquad 4 - d_l = 3.01$$

Since $d < d_l$, we conclude at the five percent level that significant positive autocorrelation is present in the error term.

Dealing With Autocorrelation

We have defined autocorrelation, outlined its effects on regression results, and discussed a test for its presence. We shall now consider ways to correct for autocorrelation when it is found to be present.

An iterative procedure is available that repeatedly adjusts the variables for the autocorrelated movements. A regression is then computed based on the corrected Y value, the level of autocorrelation measured, and a new iteration undertaken if necessary.[2] This procedure involves an assumption about the form of the autocorrelation. For example, assume that the nonrandom pattern in the error term is of the following form:

$$\mu_t = \alpha \mu_{t-1} + e_t$$

The value of α could be estimated by first fitting the desired regression equation, then fitting a second regression equation on the original calculated residuals:

$$\mu_t = a \mu_{t-1} + v_t$$

This produces an estimate a for α, which is then used to compute transformed values of the variables $(Y_t - a Y_{t-1})$, $(X_t - a X_{t-1})$, $(Z_t - a Z_{t-1})$ for the original equation $Y_t = c_0 + c_1 X_t + c_2 Z_t$. If the transformed variables again produce an autocorrelated error term when least squares is applied, the transformation is repeated.

This iterative procedure offers a remedy for autocorrelation that involves an a priori assumption about the time-lagged structure, and an additional computational complexity. In cases where these are not obstacles, the technique is recommended by its simplicity.

More fundamentally, Figure 3–1 suggests that nonlinear relationships or omission of influential variables may produce autocorrelation. If nonlinearities are of a general geometric nature, the use of percent changes

---

[2] See J. Johnston, *Econometric Methods* (New York: McGraw-Hill Book Co., 1963), pp. 193–94.

in some or all the variables rather than the value of the variables may reduce the autocorrelation. Sometimes, raw changes will also reduce autocorrelation.

To see the reason for this, consider the following model:

$$Y_t = a + bX_t + \mu_t$$

in which μ_t is autocorrelated according to the following simple scheme:

$$\mu_t = \mu_{t-1} + e_t$$

where $e_t = N(O,\sigma)$.

If our model is lagged, we obtain:

$$Y_{t-1} = a + bX_{t-1} + \mu_{t-1}$$

Now, subtracting the lagged version from the original gives:

$$Y_t - Y_{t-1} = b[X_t - X_{t-1}] + \mu_t - \mu_{t-1}$$

Substituting our autocorrelated expression for μ_t gives:

$$\Delta Y_t = b[\Delta X_t] + \mu_{t-1} - \mu_{t-1} + e_t$$

or

$$\Delta Y_t = b[\Delta X_t] + e_t$$

which is free of autocorrelation. Of course, we may not safely presume the nature of actually observed autocorrelation will always follow our simple scheme. Thus, we cannot prescribe the use of differences as a general solution for autocorrelation. But the example has illustrated the general way in which differences operate on the error term, and in practice the effect of differing variables is often to reduce observed autocorrelation.

A final technique often used to reduce autocorrelation is to include a linear index in the equation. Certain of the effects of omitted variables and of trends in included variables will attach to such an index, which will often reduce autocorrelation.

Some Limitations in Testing for Autocorrelation

If the equation to be estimated contains the lagged value of the dependent variable Y_{t-1}, Durbin and Watson have cautioned that their statistic is biased towards accepting the hypothesis of no autocorrelation. This makes strict interpretation of d unreliable. The Durbin-Watson test also rests on the earlier-stated basic premise that independent variables in the equation are indeed predetermined, and are not jointly determined along with Y. If the latter is true, the d statistic will not strictly hold, although a modified test can be employed.[3]

---

[3] See J. Durbin, "Testing for Serial Correlation in Systems of Simultaneous Regression Equations," *Biometrika*, 44, Parts III and IV (December 1957), pp. 370–77.

HETEROSCEDASTICITY

Part of the second statistical assumption given earlier stipulated that the variance of the error term was constant across the sample. This property can be summarized by the unwieldy term *homoscedasticity*. The lack of this property is called *heteroscedasticity*, which occurs when the variance of the error term associated with the fit of an equation is not constant in size across observations. Various factors in economic time series can produce this condition in the variance of the error term, which we shall call $\text{var}(\mu)$. For example:

1. As certain patterns of economic behavior mature over time, they may become more systematic and predictable. This would cause the $\text{var}(\mu)$ to become smaller over the sample.
2. As techniques for collecting economic data improve over time, definitional errors and $\text{var}(\mu)$ are reduced.
3. As sales or assets grow, organizational and structural changes in firms may produce a trend towards more highly programmed behavior patterns that would reduce $\text{var}(\mu)$.

Heteroscedasticity distorts the measure of unexplained variation, thereby similarly distorting conclusions from R, and t-tests based on them. Essentially, the problem is that the true value of a heteroscedastic error term is dependent upon the related independent variable. This means that R and t-values become dependent on the range of the related independent variable. Consequently, obtained goodness-of-fit statistics will usually be misleading.

The error term and successive independent variables may be inspected to formulate a conclusion as to the extent to which the $\text{var}(\mu)$ is homoscedastic. Any systematic correspondence in the absolute size of the error term and the size of the independent variables indicates a heteroscedastic pattern.

For example, consider the following partial listing of results from a regression of X_1 and X_2 on Y:

Y	Y_c	μ	X_1	X_2
.	.	.	.	.
.	.	.	.	.
.	\.	.	.	.
200	190	10	38	120
230	245	−15	25	160
250	268	−18	29	185
280	245	35	28	300
240	260	−20	32	210
.	.	.	.	.
.	.	.	.	.
.	.	.	.	.

If the X_1 values are ranked in ascending order along with the absolute values of the error term, the following results:

X_1	μ
25	15
28	35
29	18
32	20
38	10
.	.
.	.
.	.

No particular trend is evident in the error term as X_1 is increased, therefore μ appears to be homoscedastic with regard to X_1. However, when X_2 values are ranked in ascending order along with the absolute values of the error term, as follows:

X_2	μ
120	10
160	15
185	18
210	20
300	35

a definite pattern emerges indicating the particular value of X_2 is likely to affect the size of the error term—which means the assumption of constant variance of μ does not hold and therefore μ is heteroscedastic.

Although a generally applicable and rigorous test for heteroscedasticity is not available, a test has been developed by Goldfield and Quandt that applies in certain cases where it is possible to designate a variable as a deflator variable used to construct a ratio-type model from a linear model.[4] We shall not discuss their test here due to the limited nature of its applicability, but instead shall confine our analysis to rank-ordering each independent variable and then inspecting the associated μ.

Certain types of heteroscedasticity can often be eliminated by deflating all variables by a common term, in cases where the error term is linearly related to the variance of that term. For example, consider the equation

$$M_t = aS_t + bCF_t + cSH_t + \mu$$

where M_t = marketing expenditures by a firm, S_t = sales, CF_t = cash flow, SH_t = market share, and μ = the error term. Now assume that the source of the heteroscedasticity is the relationship between σ_μ (standard deviation of the error term) and S, which takes the following form:

$$\sigma_{\mu_t} = dS_t$$

---

[4] S. M. Goldfield and R. E. Quandt, "Some Tests for Homoscedasticity," *Journal of the American Statistical Association* (June 1965).

If both sides are divided by S, the transformed homoscedastic value d results,

$$d = \sigma_{u_t}/S_t$$

which is now constant after transformation. This transformation may be accomplished by dividing the original expression by sales S_t, as follows:

$$\frac{M_t}{S_t} = a + b\frac{CF_t}{S_t} + c\frac{SH_t}{S_t} + \frac{\mu}{S_t}$$

Under the specific linear circumstances described, this procedure will produce a constant (homoscedastic) standard deviation of the error term d. Even where the nature of the heteroscedasticity is not linear, using a deflation procedure will often reduce the heteroscedasticity. However, it should be recognized that the specific hypothesis has been changed by the deflation. The dependent variable now measures intensity of marketing expenditures per dollar of sales, and the cash flow variable is similarly redefined. Such an alternative hypothesis must be defensible per se in terms of the altered definitions if this deflation procedure is to be useful.

MULTICOLLINEARITY

Although not in the category of the three statistical assumptions about the error term given earlier, a crucial property necessary in multivariate equations is independence in the influence of X and Z on Y in the model $Y = a + bX + cZ$. In other words, the correlation between X and Z is presumed low in the application of least squares in estimating a, b, and c, i.e., the effects of X and Z are assumed to be independent, linear, and additive. But what if this independence does not exist? For example, assume that the R^2 of X and Z has a value of 0.90. Movements in either variable account for 90 percent of movements in the other. Now, assume both importantly influence Y. (Obviously, if one was a significant influence, the other would necessarily be also.) The task of least-squares analysis is to assign a correct weighting to b and c. But if movements in X and Z are closely related, so that

$$X = c_0 + c_1 Z$$

is a significant relationship, it will not be possible to reliably assign a value for b and c. The statistical effects of X and Z on Y are so entangled that separation of the joint effect into separate coefficients is very unreliable. This high level of intercorrelation among the independent variables is called *multicollinearity*.

In one sense, multicollinearity is a data problem. For example, say that over a given sample period, general increases in X and in Z occurred continuously. A high R^2 between the two would result. If data were provided on the pattern of Z when X was declining or of X when Z was declining, a vastly different R^2 might result, along with greatly altered estimated regression coefficients. So, the lack of data on sufficiently differing combinations of X and Z may produce the problem. For example, consider the following model:

$$Y = a + bX + cZ$$

in which the value of X can take on only the values 1, 2, 3 and Z only the values 2, 4, 6. This means that $3 \times 3 = 9$ possible combinations of X and Z values may occur. If X and Z are independent, we would expect combinations to be scattered approximately evenly across the nine cells. This would be the best data configuration for reliable estimates of a, b, and c. However, if X and Z are related such that:

$$X = 1 \rightarrow Z = 2$$
$$X = 2 \rightarrow Z = 4$$
$$X = 3 \rightarrow Z = 6$$

then most of the data observed will be bundled in only three of the nine cells and the a, b, and c estimates are likely to be unreliable as they will be based on what amounts to inadequately fluctuating variables in the sample.

More fundamentally, two independent variables may in fact be highly correlated even if completely thorough data patterns were present in the sample. This would mean the two correlated independent variables were nearly identical and indistinguishable statistically, with neither providing unique explanations of Y movements not contained in the other.

Effects of Multicollinearity on Results

Although least squares will succeed in assigning numerical values to the coefficients of highly correlated independent variables, these coefficients will be highly unreliable in magnitude. They will also be highly volatile. If an observation or two is deleted or added to the sample in the case of significant multicollinearity, coefficient estimates for the variables involved are likely to change radically. The same volatile pattern will persist if variables are deleted from or added to the equation. Our earlier analysis of the significance of individual regression coefficients relied on use of a t-test formed by the ratio of a regression coefficient to its standard error. As multicollinearity damages the reliability of obtained regression coefficients, it also damages the ability to draw well-supported conclusions about the significance of individual variables from t-tests. We cannot reliably make inferences about the statistical importance of individual variables under these circumstances.

On the other hand, the value of the overall equation may not be impared by the existence of multicollinearity. If predicting the dependent variable is the sole purpose of the model and if whatever multicollinear pattern present in the data persists into the forecast period, then the equation may produce reasonable forecasts in spite of the somewhat arbitrary weighting attached to individual intercorrelated variables. However, if the pattern of multicollinearity shifts in the forecast period, the equation may be expected to produce bizarre results.

To illustrate the effects of multicollinearity, we return to our original numerical example:

$$Y = 1.0X + 2.0Z + \mu; \ \mu = N(0,10)$$

and now introduce a new variable Z' in place of Z, such that

$$Z' = 2X + e; \ e = N(0,2)$$

As before, we compute 20 observations of Y from this simulated system. The simple correlation between X and Z' for this modified data is 0.994, which suggests we have succeeded in producing data with a whopping case of multicollinearity between X and Z'. Estimating the coefficients by least squares gives:

$$Y_c = 1.991 - 1.717X + 3.283Z'$$
$$(-.58) \quad (2.31)$$

where:

$$R^2 = .939 \qquad S_b = 2.96$$
$$R = .969 \qquad S_c = 1.42$$
$$S_\mu = 11.15$$

and values in parentheses are computed t values.

As seen, the estimates of b and c are both poor. In fact, the b coefficient is measured to be negative rather than its actual value of $+1.0$. These results illustrate the unreliable character of obtained regression coefficients under such circumstances. Similarly, the computed t values lead to the incorrect conclusion that X exerts an insignificant influence on Y.

However, if we look at the combined influence of the two variables on Y, we find a different result. Substituting in the original expression our expression for Z' (at the means of the error terms e and μ) gives:

$$Y = 1.0X + 2.0(2X) = 5.0X$$

Our obtained result:

$$Y_c = 1.991 - 1.717X + 3.283(2X)$$
$$= 1.991 + 4.849X$$

is quite close to the true value, reflecting the continued usefulness of the combined result. This is borne out by the high R^2 values obtained and a standard error similar to that resulting in the original example. In fact, as long as our relationship

$$Z' = 2X + e$$

holds, our obtained equation will assign approximately the correct combined weight to fluctuations in X and Z' in influencing Y, and thus be a reasonable forecasting mechanism.

Indicators of Multicollinearity

Analysis of simple and partial correlation coefficients yields an indication as to the extent and location of intercorrelation among independent variables. The simplest indicator is the simple correlation between independent variables. This measures covariance in the raw data series. It does not, however, reveal the relationship between two variables in isolation. For this, the partial correlation is useful. The partial correlation coefficient measures the associated movement in two variables when the effects of all others have been held constant. Thus, high partial correlations between independent variables in a regression equation suggest the presence of multicollinearity in the equation.

Partial correlation coefficients are closely related to regression coefficients. Where the former is an index of association between two variables, the latter is a direct numerical weight that associates movements in the two variables. Unfortunately, this close relationship means that severe multicollinearity can damage the reliability of the measure of partial correlation. That is, partial correlation coefficients are aimed at defining the association of a particular variable with a second variable under conditions where *other influences have been held constant.* If variables cannot be statistically separated as to their influence upon Y, it will not be possible for partial correlations to reliably measure an association based on this separation. Thus, when the condition of multicollinearity is severe, the reliability of partial correlations as an indicator of the condition is damaged. Usually, the results of regression analysis contain sufficient indications of interrelationships through partial correlation data, so that this does not represent a severe limitation in assessing multicollinearity.

Formal statistical tests for multicollinearity have been proposed by Wilks and Bartlett which enable inferential statements about the significance of this condition.[5] We shall not discuss these tests here due to their

---

[5] For a discussion of these tests and of the general problem of multicollinearity, the reader may consult D. E. Farrar and R. R. Glauber, "Multicollinearity in Regression Analysis: The Problem Revisited," *Review of Economics and Statistics* (February 1967), pp. 92–107. The inferential tests are attributable to S. Wilks, "Certain Generalizations in the Analysis of Variance," *Biometrika*, Vol. 24 (1932), pp. 477–93, and M. S. Bartlett, "Tests of Significance in Factor Analysis," *British Journal of Psychology, Statistical Section*, Vol. 3 (1950), pp. 83–95.

reliance upon statistics which are computationally obscure and not available in most library-type computer programs.

Multicollinearity visits empirical research on single-equation models habitually, resulting in coefficient estimates and therefore t-test results that are quite unreliable. Upon detection, efforts can be made to eliminate common trends in the independent variables, since they can somewhat spuriously introduce the condition. Trends may be eliminated by dealing with differences in the raw data, or by deflating data by an appropriate trend variable. Differences or deflating will often reduce trend-related multicollinearity adequately. However, more fundamental multicollinearity requires the deletion of all the multicollinear influences except one. Since t-tests are of no use in this selection, it should be done on a priori grounds, based on the expected influences represented by included variables. Since by definition the explanatory properties of multicollinear variables are largely duplicated, this elimination will result in little statistical loss in terms of multiple R^2 values, but it will mean alterations in maintained hypotheses and model structure.

IMPACT OF OMITTING VARIABLES

As we have just indicated, multicollinearity invites the exclusion of variables from single-equation models. In general, when this is done, we must keep in mind the changing structure of our underlying model in order to correctly interpret the modified results. We may illustrate the change by an example. If Z is omitted in the expression

$$Y = a + bX + cZ + \mu$$

and the coefficients of modified expression estimated, the calculated b value will measure the joint effect of X and Z on Y, and no longer the impact of only X alone. This must be borne in mind when interpreting the value of obtained regression coefficients under such circumstances.

More generally, whenever truly influential variables have been omitted from a regression equation, their impact will be taken up by included variables to the extent of the correlation between those included and those excluded. This will influence the magnitudes of included regression coefficients and may lead to mistaken impressions as to the partial effects of included explanatory variables. On the other hand, if the excluded variables are independent of all included independent variables, they will merely result in a larger error term, thus preserving the partial character of included coefficients. This general effect may be illustrated by a further modification of our example:

$$Y' = 1.0X + 2.0Z + \mu; \ \mu = N(0,10)$$

in which

> $Y' = Y$ for the first 10 observations and
> $Y' = Y + 20 - \mu/5$ for the 11th through 20th observations.

In other words, an upward shift in the true regression plane occurred after the first 10 observations, which is unaccountable for directly by the model. This provides a simple case of a truly influential variable having been omitted from the model, i.e., an error in specification has occurred. The regression results for this modified data are:

$$Y_c = -8.224 + 1.152X + 2.984Z$$
$$(3.24) \qquad (4.84)$$

with

$$R^2 = .677 \qquad S_b = .355$$
$$R = .823 \qquad S_c = .617$$
$$S_\mu = 12.48 \qquad d = 1.127$$

Notice that the X coefficient is tolerably measured but that the Z coefficient is overestimated and the R^2 value is reduced while the S_μ value is increased. These results together reveal that the impact of the influence of the omitted variable has been shared by the coefficient on Z and by the error term. The reason the influence attaches primarily to Z is that this variable shows somewhat of an upward trend while X is virtually without trend. Thus, c now imperfectly measures the combined effect of Z and of the shift. If both X and Z had near-zero correlations with the shift variable, the result of its inclusion would have been only to enlarge the error term while leaving the estimates of the X and Z coefficients unaffected.

The obtained Durbin-Watson d statistic shows some evidence of autocorrelation (inconclusive at the five percent level) due to the specification error. This comes about because the best-fitting overall curve is consistently above the data during the 10 observations before the shift (8 of 10 values where $Y_c > Y$) and below the data after the shift (8 of 10 values where $Y_c < Y$). Thus, the suspicious level of autocorrelation provides a clue to the underlying specification error.

The enlarged Z coefficient and higher standard error in our example illustrate our earlier remarks as to the impact of specification errors upon obtained regression coefficients. We may see the effect further by "patching up" our omission with a new variable included to account for the shift. This shift or dummy variable D has a value of 0 during the 10 observations before the shift and a value of 1.0 after the shift. With D included, the new regression becomes:

$$Y_c = 1.826 + 1.088X + 1.525Z + 22.260D$$
$$(4.70) \qquad (3.05) \qquad (4.91)$$

with

$$R^2 = .871 \qquad S_b = .231$$
$$R = .933 \qquad S_c = .500$$
$$S_\mu = 8.13 \qquad S_D = 4.533$$
$$d = 1.78$$

Notice now that both b and c coefficient estimates have improved, the R^2 value has improved, and the d value no longer shows signs of autocorrelation (d shows insignificant autocorrelation at .05). In addition, the shift in Y of 20 units has approximately attached to D, thus producing an improved estimate of c.[6]

LAGGED VALUES OF THE DEPENDENT VARIABLE

It is sometimes useful for theoretical reasons to include the dependent variable lagged as an explanatory variable. The simplest possible equation of this kind is:

$$Y_t = a + bY_{t-1} + \mu_t$$

For equations of this type estimated by small samples of the magnitude usually encountered in econometric investigations (for example, less than 30), Hurwicz has demonstrated the existence of a negative bias in the least-square estimates of the b coefficient.[7] Although it is not possible to assign a specific quantitative value to the magnitude of this bias, a study by Orcutt and Cochrane indicates that, in conjunction with autocorrelated μ, it can produce seriously erroneous sample estimates of a and b for sample sizes of 20.[8] The basic reason for this estimation problem is a breakdown in the independence of the explanatory variable over the entire sample period, i.e., the error term becomes somewhat complex. Thus, we should downgrade the reliability of regression coefficients obtained from such models. As with multicollinearity, the equation may remain useful for predicting purposes.

NONLINEAR RELATIONSHIPS

So far in this and the previous chapter, we have considered the statistical estimation of relationships among variables under the assumption these

---

[6] Notice that actually too much effect has shifted to D and too little to c. This results from the same degree of covariance between Z and D (simple correlation = .596) that caused the specification error to earlier exert most of its influence upon Z.

[7] L. Hurwicz, "Least-Squares Bias in Time Series," in T. C. Koopmans (ed.) *Statistical Inference in Dynamic Economic Models*, Cowles Monograph 10, (New York: Wiley, 1950), pp. 365–83.

[8] See G. H. Orcutt and D. Cochrane, "A Sampling Study of the Merits of Autoregressive and Reduced Form Transformations in Regression Analysis," *Journal of the American Statistical Association* (Volume 44, 1949), pp. 356–72.

relationships were approximately linear. In some cases, this will be a poor assumption, resulting in unimpressive goodness-of-fit measures and often as not producing autocorrelation. Figure 3–4 illustrates why. In this figure, the relationship between X and Y is actually cubic in nature. Its representation by a linear function produces poor goodness-of-fit statistics (R^2, σ_μ) not because of the lack of a *systematic* relationship between X and Y, but because that relationship is not approximately *linear*.

FIGURE 3–4

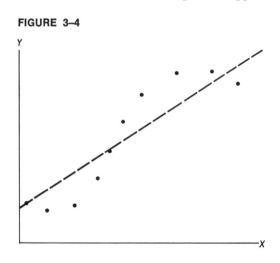

Thus, in such a case we may be led to inappropriately conclude that X and Y are not importantly related if we rely exclusively on linear analysis. In addition, our illustration suggests a possible signal of this condition may be found in the degree of autocorrelation found in the residuals. In the present case, high positive autocorrelation would be found due to "runs" of plus and minus residual values (assuming the data occurred from left to right in the figure, as with a growing time series). Although we shall not deal extensively with nonlinear analysis, important nonlinear cases may be handled comparatively easily by variants of the methods already discussed. We now consider these cases.

Nonlinearities in Variables but not Parameters

In many cases (including our example) nonlinear transformations of variables may be related in a linear way, even though the variables in raw form are not well related linearly. In Figure 3–4, the true relationship between X and Y is cubic as follows:

$$Y = a + bX + cX^2 + dX^3 + \mu$$

But if we let:

$$Z = X^2 \text{ and } M = X^3$$

we have:

$$Y = a + bX + cZ + dM + \mu$$

which structurally is a straightforward multivariate regression equation estimatable by least squares. At first glance, it may appear that the inclusion of X, X^2, and X^3 as explanatory variables in the same equation has assured a substantial case of multicollinearity, since all three variables are related by definition. However, when it is recalled that *linear* covariance among explanatory variables is the damaging condition, it is clear that we are not assured of high linear covariance between X, X^2, and X^3 just because of their power relationship. Whether they will show high correlations depends on the magnitude of fluctuation in X relative to its size, and as such ultimately upon whether or not a linear relationship

FIGURE 3–5

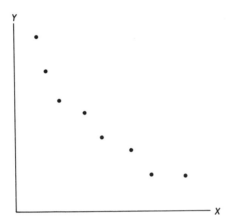

approximates the actual relationship well. This means that the existence of nonexistence of multicollinearity in such cases depends on the nature of the data.

As a second example, consider the relationship shown in Figure 3–5. This is typical of relationships often depicted in economies relative to consumer indifference curves and production isoquants. One likely functional representation of this data is as follows:

$$Y = \frac{c}{X}$$

In this expression, the specific curvature the function will display is determined by the value of c; the larger c, the flatter the curve and the smaller c, the more bent the curve. In statistically fitting a curve to the data of Figure 3–5, we would like to select c to best represent the data. This can be accomplished via least squares in the same way as our first example by letting:

$$Z = \frac{1}{X}$$

Then, we may estimate:

$$Y = b + cZ + \mu$$

by the methods discussed earlier, which gives:

$$Y = b + \frac{c}{X}$$

as our estimated function. As these two examples have perhaps suggested, the number of nonlinear transformations we may perform is large, encompassing a variety of algebraic, logarithmic, and trigonometric functions. As long as an approximately linear relationship exists between transformed variables, a range of nonlinear patterns may be successfully estimated by linear methods. However, in some cases, nonlinearities occur in the nature of the relationships themselves. We now turn to this case.

Relationships Nonlinear in the Parameters

Many nonlinear functions cannot conveniently be transformed into linear counterparts due to their basic structure. If such functions are known or thought to importantly characterize data, special estimating procedures are appropriate. To see the basic nature of these procedures, we now consider a specific example and a procedure tailored to its estimation. Consider the following function:

$$Y = a(b)^X + c(d)^X + \mu$$

where Y and X are variables and a, b, c, and d are coefficients to be estimated. From the beginning of Chapter 2 it will be recalled that the least-squares formulas were derived by constructing an algebraic expression for the sum-squared deviation between the regression plane and the observed data, and then minimizing the value of this expression through selection of the regression coefficients. We may follow the identical procedure in this case, i.e.:

Minimize

$$SS = \Sigma(Y - Y_c)^2.$$

Since

$$Y_c = a(b)^X + c(d)^X,$$
$$SS = \Sigma(Y - a(b)^X - c(d)^X)^2$$

Our objective is to make *SS* as small as possible by the selection of *a*, *b*, *c*, and *d*. Operationally, this is accomplished by taking partial derivatives of *SS* with respect to *a*, *b*, *c*, *d*, and setting equal to zero, as follows:

$$\frac{\partial SS}{\partial a} = \Sigma 2[Y - a(b)^X - c(d)^X][-b^X] = 0$$

$$\frac{\partial SS}{\partial b} = \Sigma 2[Y - a(b)^X - c(d)^X][-aX(b)^{X-1}] = 0$$

$$\frac{\partial SS}{\partial c} = \Sigma 2[Y - a(b)^X - c(d)^X][-d^X] = 0$$

$$\frac{\partial SS}{\partial d} = \Sigma 2[Y - a(b)^X - c(d)^X][-cX(d)^{X-1}] = 0$$

This system of equations involves four expressions in four unknowns. However, the relationships are nonlinear and for that reason are not as easily solved as their linear counterparts. Often in such cases, unique minimizing solutions cannot be found by other than trial-and-error methods.

Thus, while our least-squares concept remains logical regardless of the functional relationship involved, we often encounter computational barriers in deriving least-squares formulas for coefficients such as *a*, *b*, *c*, and *d* in nonlinear cases. Perhaps for this reason, little empirical research in economics employs models having relationships nonlinear in the parameters. On the other hand, the use of nonlinear transformations of the type discussed above is commonplace in empirical economic analysis, thus freeing the results of such analysis at least in part from the restrictions of linearity.

At the beginning of Chapter 2, it was stated that if some of the independent variables in single-equation models are in fact jointly determined with the dependent variable instead of independently determined, least squares will produce biased coefficient estimates. The bias is sufficiently large quantitatively to recommend the use of alternative estimating techniques under such circumstances. Our discussion in the next chapter turns to a consideration of the major problems involved in estimating the coefficients in simultaneous equation models.

DISCUSSION QUESTIONS

1. You have estimated the coefficients in a regression equation and found a high R^2, large *t* values for all variables, but substantial autocorrelation. Where and how does the autocorrelation affect your results? Suppose you want to use the equation only for forecasting. Should you be concerned about autocorrelation?

2. Where and how does multicollinearity affect the results of regression analysis? Suppose you have a forecasting equation in which an excellent

goodness-of-fit has been obtained but which has substantial multicollinearity. Would you still use it for forecasting?

3. What is a specification error? Where and how might it affect regression results?

4. Mr. Baker, manager of the budget planning department in a particular firm, has supervised the formulation of a forecasting equation for his direct production costs. The following equation resulted:

$$PC = 37.1 + 14.3 \ MTC + 0.7 \ HLC - 13.4 \ PRD$$
$$\quad\quad\quad (3.9) \quad\quad (3.7) \quad\quad (0.4)$$

where:

PC = total production costs		
MTC = materials costs per unit	R^2 = .98	
HLC = hourly labor costs	$D.W.$ = 2.01	
PRD = production level	n = 36	

and where numbers in parentheses are computed t values. "Ridiculous," said Baker as he looked at these results. "This minus 13.4 says that my total production costs decline as production rises." "Well," said his assistant, "at least the t value is small." "Great," replied Baker, "that means production levels don't really affect my costs." Baker was about to discard the equation as foolishness when the following forecasting results for the five periods beyond the data period were placed in front of him:

Actual PC	Predicted PC	Difference
374.1	373.0	1.1
392.3	394.2	−1.9
366.1	366.0	0.1
401.2	397.2	4.0
404.5	405.1	−0.6

Baker's eyes bulged. "Sweet mama," he said. "I don't come anywhere near this with my present methods." He tilted back in his chair. "But how can I justify a prediction based on a model that tells me total costs decline when production rises?" Can you help Baker?

5. If you are interested in fitting a regression equation primarily for the purpose of judging whether independent variable X_1 is more important than independent variable X_2 in influencing dependent variable Y, on what statistical data would you rely in drawing and supporting such a conclusion?

CASE 2—MGO CORPORATION

Tim Mason, production manager for the refim division of the MGO Corporation, has a rather poor record at predicting his operating costs. He has had a conversation with his boss Bob Barnard that ended with Barnard saying, "Dammit, Mason, I'm sick and tired of your fly-by-night guesses at your costs. If you don't give me better predicted costs, I'll find somebody for your spot who will."

Always sensitive to the subtle political realities of his job, Mason thought he detected in his boss's comment an undertone of hostility. He decided he had better finally do something about his cost estimating results before his boss became angry about the situation. Until now, he had simply been applying a rule-of-thumb technique that involved multiplying the scheduled direct labor hours by $6 ($3 of labor costs and $3 of other miscellaneous expenses). While in the general ballpark, this approach was erroneous enough on a regular basis to cause his boss some embarrassment.

Mason's actual operating costs are shown in Table 3–1.

TABLE 3–1
Operating Costs—Refim Division

	1968	1969	1970
January	80,310	79,210	96,005
February	84,950	90,110	95,420
March	87,010	93,100	99,250
April	91,610	100,040	103,925
May	100,990	121,700	107,900
June	91,870	125,500	95,005
July	81,680	122,660	98,200
August	71,110	126,342	94,210
September	70,700	124,900	92,900
October	68,420	111.010	93,510
November	69,720	98.050	107,410
December	72,310	87,120	117,618

Mason had the feeling that the biggest problem with his rule of thumb was the failure to account explicitly for fluctuations in nonlabor expense. For example, he normally ordered his copper tubing one month ahead. In turn, the suppliers of this tubing typically ordered raw copper a month or so ahead of his orders, and passed through any price changes that occurred in copper prices. This meant that copper prices two months earlier were the crucial factor in Mason's tubing costs. How those prices had gyrated lately is illustrated by Table 3–2. How the hell could Barnard blame him for those screwed-up copper prices that invariably became translated into price changes for the copper tubing used in Mason's operation?

And another thing, thought Mason, is the turnover rate in his hourly workers. When too many new people were coming on board, the production speeds had to be slowed down, and as a result operating expenses rose. Even though new people were given two weeks of off-line training and two weeks of warm-up by the training department at no cost to Mason, one month after new employees came on board they were delivered to Mason and put to work. As he pondered the hourly tunrover rates shown in Table 3–3, Mason felt it was hard to figure the cost of this factor.

TABLE 3–2
Copper Prices—Raw Copper (dollars)

	1967	1968	1969	1970
January	0.89	0.88	0.95	0.80
February	0.87	0.86	1.00	0.70
March	0.90	0.84	1.00	0.60
April	0.88	0.78	0.95	0.70
May	0.83	0.60	0.97	0.80
June	0.79	0.62	1.00	0.90
July	0.85	0.58	1.10	1.10
August	0.83	0.64	1.10	1.25
September	0.85	0.70	1.05	1.15
October	0.81	0.75	1.08	1.10
November	0.76	0.80	1.00	1.05
December	0.91	0.84	0.90	1.05

TABLE 3–3
Hourly Turnover Rates

	1967	1968	1969	1970
January	0.13	0.10	0.08	0.05
February	0.16	0.12	0.10	0.08
March	0.19	0.13	0.10	0.10
April	0.28	0.25	0.15	0.10
May	0.38	0.30	0.20	0.15
June	0.35	0.40	0.30	0.18
July	0.40	0.50	0.40	0.20
August	0.50	0.60	0.50	0.25
September	0.35	0.40	0.35	0.29
October	0.28	0.35	0.25	0.39
November	0.14	0.15	0.18	0.61
December	0.08	0.05	0.06	0.09

TABLE 3–4
Hourly Labor Use (man-months)

	1968	1969	1970
January	141.3	135.5	150.2
February	150.0	151.1	155.5
March	153.5	158.0	161.2
April	160.2	166.0	175.5
May	181.1	210.5	182.2
June	162.5	213.8	173.4
July	141.9	207.8	160.5
August	120.0	210.5	148.8
September	114.5	210.1	141.2
October	112.8	180.2	139.1
November	118.0	160.1	161.2
December	124.0	141.1	180.4

TABLE 3–5
Number of Production Line Stoppages

	1968	1969	1970
January	14	19	21
February	32	24	16
March	8	16	15
April	13	18	17
May	17	21	18
June	22	17	19
July	19	19	22
August	24	25	20
September	20	22	19
October	23	20	23
November	19	24	22
December	23	18	20

Mason's experience made him sure of one thing. His rule of thumb was essentially correct in assigning a major role to hourly labor use. Mason felt sure these fluctuations (shown in Table 3–4) must figure into the forecast. However, it was troublesome that hourly labor costs had risen from an average of 2.80 in 1968 to 2.94 in 1969 and 3.09 in 1970, typically in lumps at the start of each year according to the union contract.

There were other factors involved. One thing that seemed to always cost him money was the number of machine breakdowns and other production line stoppages, shown in Table 3–5. Although these usually resulted in costs of some kind, they did not always result in actual bills that had to be paid. In Tom's mind, this made their effect difficult to discern.

Another troubling factor was the cost of other materials besides the copper tubing. The production process required at least a half-dozen kinds of other materials, generally of the nonferrous metal variety. Mason had an index of selected nonferrous metal prices obtained from purchasing that might be useful in accounting for this factor (shown in Table 3–6).

TABLE 3–6
Selected Nonferrous Metal Prices (dollars)

	1968	1969	1970
January.................	0.45	0.47	0.39
February...............	0.43	0.50	0.36
March.................	0.42	0.51	0.31
April..................	0.39	0.48	0.34
May...................	0.32	0.48	0.40
June...................	0.31	0.49	0.44
July...................	0.29	0.55	0.44
August................	0.32	0.54	0.73
September.............	0.35	0.52	0.67
October...............	0.36	0.54	0.45
November.............	0.42	0.49	0.63
December.............	0.42	0.45	0.42

However, after reviewing the index, Mason could see no specific way to involve this information in his forecast.

Although this jumble of statistics turned his stomach, Mason nonetheless sensed the time was right for him to display his initiative by making a concerted effort to improve his forecasting record.

Questions

1. Build a regression model on the basis of the data through June, 1970 given in the case.
2. Evaluate the goodness-of-fit represented by this model, employing various statistical tests in your reasoning process.
3. Evaluate the reliability of the obtained results in terms of the statistical assumptions of the regression model.
4. Prepare a simulated forecast for the last six months of data not included in that used to fit the model.

Chapter 4

STATISTICAL MEASUREMENT
OF MULTI-EQUATION
MODELS

When the problem of estimating coefficients is expanded from a single equation to multiple equations, two new issues arise. The first of these relates to the mathematical and statistical properties of the equations and is called the identification problem. The second issue is concerned with estimating the coefficients of the equations in a reliable manner.

VARIABLES AND IDENTIFICATION

Multiple-equation models in economics consist of dependent or *endogenous* variables and independent or *exogenous* variables. Endogenous variables typically appear on the right-hand side of some equations and on the left-hand side of others, whereas exogenous variables only appear on the right-hand (explanatory) side. This forms the basis for the definitional division between the two: Exogenous variables help explain the endogenous variables in the model but are not explained by the model. Endogenous variables, on the other hand, are explained by the model. Endogenous variables can be viewed as the outputs of the model while exogenous variables are inputs. In essence, econometric models attempt to explain behavior of endogenous variables through behavior of exogenous variables and relationships among endogenous variables.

Obtaining reliable statistical estimates of the coefficients in multiple-equation systems of endogenous and exogenous variables involves most of the same data problems (e.g., autocorrelation, multicollinearity) encountered in the case of single-equation models. In addition, a separate problem uniquely visits multiple-equation systems, relating to the data and also to the particular variables incorporated into each equation. This is referred to as the *identification* problem. To help see the essence of identification, we formulate a very simple two-equation model consisting of Y_1 and Y_2 endogenous variables and X_1 and X_2 exogenous variables, structured as follows:

$$Y_1 = C_1 + C_2 Y_2 + C_3 X_1 + \mu_1$$
$$Y_2 = C_4 + C_5 Y_1 + C_6 X_2 + \mu_2$$

where μ_1 and μ_2 are normally distributed error terms with means of zero and constant variances.

This system will produce estimates or "solutions" for Y_1 and Y_2 given values of X_1 and X_2 and the coefficients $C_1 \ldots C_6$. Y_1 and Y_2 are jointly determined dependent variables in the system.

In computing estimates of $C_1 \ldots C_6$, ideally we would like to have a wide variety of X_1, X_2, Y_1, Y_2 data combinations, wherein each variable fluctuated widely over its range of possible values, pairing up with other widely ranging variables to produce a widely scattered dispersion of observed X_1, X_2, Y_1, Y_2 points. Such a condition is important in obtaining good estimates of the C_i because it is only through an adequate scatter of data combinations that we may fit reliable functions through the data. This is the aspect of coefficient estimation with which identification is concerned. To further see the basic idea, consider the case where X_1 in our example was for all practical purposes a constant over the period of the data. Lack of fluctuation in X_1 blots out a number of possible Y_1, Y_2, X_1, X_2, combinations, thus offering no statistical evidence on this dimension of the regression plane to be estimated. Estimates made under such circumstances will not be based on sufficient usable information to be judged reliable. The variable X_1 might as well have been omitted from the model as its contribution to the estimate is nil. More specifically, all the damage due to the constancy of X_1 will occur in the coefficient estimates C_4, C_5, C_6 of the *second equation*. For it is precisely a range of differing values of X_1 that causes an adequate dispersion of data relative to Y_1, Y_2 and X_2—the variables in the second equation. With X_1 fixed, many Y_1, Y_2 "solutions" to the model for various given X_2 are rendered unobservable. On the other hand, if X_2 fluctuates adequately, it will result in a similarly rich array of Y_1, Y_2 solutions to the model even if X_1 remains constant. The coefficients C_1, C_2, C_3 of the first equation should thus remain susceptible to reliable estimation.

In our example, if X_1 and X_2 both varied substantially and systematically with Y_1 and Y_2, but were highly correlated, the situation would be even worse, for X_1 and X_2 would be essentially the same variable for statistical purposes. Thus, a shifting pattern in X_1 would bring about systematic shifts in X_2, thus limiting the possible Y_1, Y_2 solutions to only a fraction of their possibilities, and similarly damaging the reliability of resulting statistical estimates.

The crucial property we may distill from this discussion can be described as statistical uniqueness of each equation. Each equation must possess an operative mechanism apart from those contained in other equations to produce independent shifts in the equation relative to other equations. If all equations have such uniqueness, the possible universe of data points can be represented in the observed data, and reasonable coefficient estimates may be expected, *ceteris paribus*. Equation systems or single equations not sufficiently unique in our sense are called *under-identified*. Those just adequately unique statistically are called *exactly identified*, while those with more than adequate uniqueness are called *over-identified*. The ideas now expressed can now be formalized into a specific rule for determining identification:

The number of predetermined and exogenous variables excluded from an equation must at least equal the number of endogenous variables included on the right-hand side of the equation for it to be identified.

To illustrate this definition, consider a second example:

$$DD:\quad Q = a + bP + \mu_1$$
$$SS:\quad Q = c + dP + eR + \mu_2$$
$$\text{In equilibrium, } DD = SS.$$

where Q is the quantity demanded and supplied of a particular product, P is the price, R is the rainfall (assumed to occur independently), and μ_i is the error term. In the model, P and Q are endogenous variables whose value is explained by the model, while R is an exogenous variable whose value is not affected by the model.[1]

In this simple system, the exogenous variable R is excluded from DD, making the number of excluded exogenous variables equal to the number of included endogenous variables (P). DD is therefore identified according to our formal definition. However, in the second equation, no exogenous variables are excluded from SS but P is included. SS is therefore not identified according to our definition. Since one of its equations is under-identified, the model is similarly under-identified.

The meaning contained in this definition of identification can be examined graphically for our DD-SS model. The two equations are depicted in Figure 4–1, along with an illustrative combination of equilibrium price-quantity combinations once a random error term is included. For convenience, three different general levels of rainfall are assumed to have characterized the data, causing the supply curve to be positioned at three general locations, and generating a general trace of points along the unfluctuating demand function. The inclusion of R as an influential variable

---

[1] The endogenous nature of P and Q is perhaps best seen by an alternative algebraic expression of the model, as follows:

$$DD:\quad P = a' + b'Q + \mu_1'$$
$$SS:\quad Q = c + dP + eR + \mu_2$$

In the original case, application of the equilibrium condition $DD = SS$ produces a solution for both P and Q jointly.

FIGURE 4-1

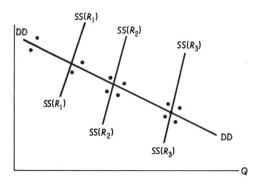

in SS had caused three different regions of DD to be measured, leading to a reasonable estimate of the coefficients a and b of that curve. But for SS, the evidence upon which to estimate c, d, and e is meager. Points have not been observed in sufficiently diverse regions of SS to support the reliable estimation of c, d, and e. The cause is the lack of a unique source of fluctuation in DD sufficient to create adequate observations along the family of SS curves. What is needed is a source of fluctuation in DD that is excluded from the right-hand side of SS—exactly the property our definition requires. The situation of Figure 4–1 would not be improved if the model were altered as follows:

$$DDA: \quad Q = a + bP + cR + \mu_1$$
$$SS: \quad Q = d + eP + fR + \mu_2$$
$$DDA = SS$$

In this case, both equations contain exactly the same variables, so that according to our definition, neither equation is identified. Indeed, it is statistically impossible to distinguish them. The situation is graphically depicted in Figure 4–2. Since the shifts in the two functions are perfectly correlated, the system fails to produce sound evidence on the shapes of either. Fitting DDA and/or SS through these data would result in an equation similar to Q_cQ_c, which would have little meaning relative to either of the two equations of interest.

As suggested earlier, to identify the original model it is necessary for demand DD to be significantly influenced by a variable other than R in order to produce observed evidence at a representative number of locations along the supply function. The following is now exactly identified:

$$DDB: \quad Q = a + bP + cY + \mu_1$$
$$SS: \quad Q = d + eP + fR + \mu_2$$
$$DDB = SS$$

FIGURE 4–2

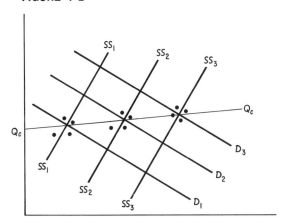

where Y is income. Graphically, the system looks similar to Figure 4–2. However, one crucial difference now exists. The factor causing DDB to shift is independent of the factor causing SS to shift. Therefore, the effects of DD and SS are statistically separable, since the data contains evidence at various locations along the supply and demand curves. We may obtain reasonable statistical estimates of both.

If an equation contains more than a minimum number of unique variables, it usually produces over-identification in the model, as DDC in the following:

$$DDC: \quad Q = a + bP + cY + dPR + \mu_1$$
$$SS: \quad Q = e + fP + gR + \mu_2$$
$$DDC = SS$$

where PR is the price of related goods, an exogenous variable. DDC contains both Y and PR as instruments to identify SS. According to our definition, DDC remains exactly identified because one of the three exogenous variables is excluded while one endogenous variable is included on the right-hand side of the equation. However, in SS, two variables (Y,PR) are now excluded from the equation while only one endogenous variable is included on the right-hand side. Thus, in SS, more exogenous variables are excluded than necessary for minimum identification. The equation is thus over-identified. If an equation is over-identified, the system is over-identified. DDC now is affected by two separate independent influences. Over-identification does not damage our ability to obtain estimates of the coefficients of this sytem, but it does limit our choice of statistical estimating methods, as will be discussed below under that topic.

So far, we have discussed the inclusion or exclusion of variables in equations in a predetermined sense. But often an a priori decision to include a variable in an equation will prove to be unsupported by the data, as the coefficient will be insignificantly different from zero on the basis of a t-test, or will have an unsupportable sign.[2] In the former case, the indication is that the variable does not play a significant role in producing shifts in the dependent variable for the observed data. In such a case, it will not in fact contribute to the identification of the equation. Inadequate amounts of fluctuation in Y are attributable to the variable. For all it contributes statistically, the variable might as well be excluded. In the second case, the explanatory role of the variable itself is out of accord with a priori hypotheses. For example, if Y, the variable added to DDA to produce DDB, is found upon examination of the statistical results to be insignificant in the equation, then it does not in fact aid in identifying SS since it has not produced the necessary significant fluctuations in Y. SS would remain unidentified and parameter estimates of DDB and SS would still not be useful. Thus, the property of identification is one that must hold a priori and also stand up to statistical tests of significance of the individual variables in the system. One therefore cannot be sure a system is identified until the statistical results are in, verifying the a priori hypotheses about significant included variables.

A similar argument applies to excluded variables. If, a priori, a variable has been excluded from an equation, thus enabling its identification according to our definitions, this hypothesis must be confirmed in the data for the obtained coefficient estimates to be useful. In the example involving DDB and SS, if Y is truly an influential variable in SS, then this source of fluctuation in DDB is highly correlated with shifts in SS. The unique information about the shape of SS is thus lost, as shifts in DDB will be accompanied by shifts in SS. In this case, SS reverts to again being under-identified.

ESTIMATION OF SIMULTANEOUS SYSTEMS

In Chapters 2 and 3, the applicability of least-squares estimating techniques was limited to models with one-way influence channels, in which all the right-hand side variables were predetermined outside the system that produced the dependent variable. It was pointed out that in multiple equation models where some of the right-hand side variables were jointly determined with the dependent, least-squares techniques yielded biased estimates of equation coefficients. We shall now consider further the

---

[2] In our discussion of simultaneous-equation models, we shall refer occasionally to t-tests in the same manner as discussed in Chapter 2. This is often done in simultaneous systems but is not technically correct. The sampling distributions of estimated coefficients in simultaneous systems approach normality as the sample size increases, but do not generally correspond to the t-distribution. Thus, a normal-test statistic becomes a somewhat better approximation than a t-test statistic for simultaneous systems.

nature of this bias, and offer an alternative estimating technique that has more desirable statistical properties.

Least-Squares Bias

Consider the following highly simplified two-sector aggregate model:

$$C_t = a + bY_t + \mu_t \tag{4-1}$$
$$I_t = \text{Exogenous} \tag{4-2}$$
$$C_t + I_t = Y_t \text{ (Identity)}$$

where C is consumption expenditure, Y is national income, and I is investment expenditure, considered to be predetermined or exogenous, and not influenced by current levels of Y or C. The error term μ_t is assumed to follow the assumptions of Chapter 2. Applying the definition of identification, it is clear that the model is exactly identified a priori, as one exogenous variable (I) is excluded from $(4-1)$ while one endogenous variable (Y) is included on the right-hand side.

Furthermore, the structure of the model contains in $(4-1)$ the simultaneity between C and Y that produces the Keynesian multiplier. Let us consider the result if least squares were applied to the consumption function $(4-1)$. To do this, assume that I has varied continuously and evenly from I_0 at the start of the sample period to I_1 at the end of sample period $(I_1 > I_0)$. This means equilibrium income and consumption expenditure would have fluctuated similarly. This situation is illustrated graphically in Figure 4–3. In the figure, the vertical axis is the level of consumption expenditure, while the horizontal axis is the level of consumption plus investment expenditure. If I were zero, $C = C + I = Y$

FIGURE 4–3

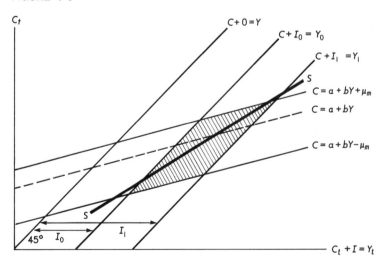

and a $45°$ line through the origin depicts the total aggregate expenditure function. For positive levels of investment, the aggregate expenditure function is represented by an outward shift in the function. The starting point of the sample period where $I = I_0$ and the ending point where $I = I_1$ are shown in the figure. The dotted line is the expected consumption function, when the error term μ equals zero. The two parallel lines on either side represent the position of the consumption function when the error term assumes its maximum value $a + bY + \mu_m$ (upper line) and its minimum value $a + bY - \mu_m$ (lower line). Over the course of the sample period, the systematic movement in I and I_0 to I_1, coupled with the continuously random movements of the consumption function within the range shown, would produce a scatter of points dispersed across the bounding parallelogram shown as the shaded area.

If the error term were indeed random and rectangularly distributed, we would expect this scatter to approximately evenly cover the area. Accordingly, it can be shown that with these data, applying least squares to fit (4–1) will result in the heavy line *LS*, which is substantially different from the desired dotted line $C = a + bY$.[3] In fact, in this case it would produce an estimate of b that is too large, or biased positively; furthermore, as more sample data is added within the shaded area, the estimate of b will come closer and closer to the biased *LS* line rather than the true line. This characteristic of the estimate is called *inconsistent*. For an estimator to be consistent, it must produce estimates that approach the true value of the parameter as the sample size becomes larger. Consistency in this sense is a desirable quality for estimators. Least-squares estimates, while consistent when the equation contains only predetermined variables, are inconsistent when variables are jointly determined.

Further inspection of Figure 4–3 reveals that it is the joint interaction of C and Y that causes the shaded data area to be skewed up to the right, and in turn that causes the best-fitting line to be biased and inconsistent. If C did not affect Y jointly as Y affects C, then the $45°$ lines bounding the shaded area would be vertical and the least-squares line would fall on the true line if data were complete in the shaded area.

This biased and inconsistent result in general occurs whenever least squares is applied to equations involving jointly determined dependent and independent variables.[4] It indicates the need for alternative estimating

---

[3] If the error term is distributed normally rather than rectangularly as assumed here, the effect would not be as pronounced since points would be more intensely arrayed closer to the true line than farther away. It would still remain, however, due to the skewed nature of the shaded sample area.

[4] This was originally discussed in a landmark article by T. Haavelno, "The Statistical Implications of a System of Simultaneous Equations," *Econometrica* (Vol. 11, 1943), pp. 1–12, and is sometimes called Haavelno bias. For a mathematical discussion, see J. Johnston, *Econometric Methods* (New York: McGraw-Hill Book Co., 1963), pp. 231–33.

techniques that do not share these properties. We now consider some of the techniques that have been developed to meet this need.

REDUCED-FORM ESTIMATES

One way to deal with the simultaneous estimation problem without really solving it is to transpose the model algebraically such that the joint relationships no longer appear in the transposed equations. These equations are known as the reduced-form equations. When the model is exactly identified, least squares can be used on the reduced form and the original structural coefficients obtained by algebraic solution in a consistent although still biased manner.[5]

One may ask, why trade off ordinary least squares for another biased estimator. The answer is (a) the bias is usually less than the least-squares bias, and (b) the reduced-form process, being consistent, at least becomes less biased as the sample size is enlarged. Having estimated the coefficients of the reduced-form, it is possible in the exactly identified case to use these reduced form coefficients to solve backwards for the original coefficients. Our example will illustrate this technique. To repeat, with the time period subscript deleted for convenience,

$$C = a + bY + \mu \qquad (4\text{--}1)$$
$$I = I_a = \text{exogenous} \qquad (4\text{--}2)$$
$$C + I = Y$$

Now, inserting (4–1) and (4–2) into the identity gives:

$$a + bY + \mu + I_a = Y$$

Collecting Y terms on the left-hand side

$$Y - bY = a + I_a + \mu$$

and

$$Y(1 - b) = a + I_a + \mu$$
$$Y = \frac{(a)}{1 - b} + \frac{(1)}{1 - b} I_a + \frac{(\mu)}{1 - b}$$

Now we define:

$$K_1 = \frac{(a)}{1 - b}$$

$$K_2 = \frac{(1)}{1 - b}$$

$$\mu^* = \frac{(\mu)}{1 - b}$$

---

[5] For a mathematical demonstration of the consistency and bias associated with this estimator, see Johnston, *Econometric Methods*, pp. 234–36.

which gives:

$$Y = K_1 + K_2(I_a) + \mu^* \qquad (4\text{–}3)$$

the reduced-form equation involving only the predetermined I_a value. The new error term μ^* is a simple multiple $(1/1 - b)$ of the original, so that it should share the properties that we assume μ to possess, which are the assumptions of Chapter 2. Now we may fit (4–3) with least squares and obtain values of K_1 and K_2 that are unbiased and consistent.[6]

In circumstances where we are interested only in predicting Y with our model and have faith in the worthiness of the basic model structure contained in (4–1) and (4–2), the reduced form is all that is needed. However, if we are concerned with (1) trying to measure specific behavioral relationships such as the marginal propensity to consume (b) in our consumption function, or (2) examining the empirical significance of our assumptions about the model structure, or (3) employing our model in a simulation sense to explore the impact of autonomous shifts in structural equations, then we shall need to estimate the basic structural coefficients a and b. In this case, we know that:

$$K_2(1 - b) = 1$$

and therefore

$$b = 1 - \frac{1}{K_2} \qquad (4\text{–}4)$$

We also know:

$$K_1(1 - b) = a$$

and therefore

$$a = \frac{K_1}{K_2} \qquad (4\text{–}5)$$

Thus, in our example we can solve algebraically for our original parameters a and b from obtained estimates K_1 and K_2. But this will not generally be the case for all models. It will depend upon the number of original parameters and the number of K-type coefficients resulting from the reduced form. This in turn depends upon the identification status of the model. If the model is under-identified, a solution for all the parameters is not possible. We will have more structural parameters than K expressions. If it is exactly identified as in our case, we will have as many original structural parameters as K expressions, and will have a unique algebraic solution for the structural parameters. However, in the case of an over-identified model, we will have fewer original coefficients than K expressions and thus will not have a unique solution for the original parameters. For example, consider this modification of the original model:

---

[6] See Johnston, *Econometric Methods*, p. 234, for a demonstration of this property.

$$C = a + bY + cL + dS_{-1}$$
$$I = e + fY + gSTK$$
$$L = L_a$$
$$STK = STA_a$$
$$C + I = Y$$

where L is liquidity of business (exogenous), S_{-1} is lagged consumer savings (predetermined), and STK is security prices (exogenous). Endogenous variables are C, I, and Y. The C equation excludes STK and includes Y, and is thus exactly identified. However, the I equation excludes S_{-1} and L, while including Y and is over-identified, thus imparting this characteristic to the model. The reduced form now involves equations for at least two of the three endogenous variables (the identity accounting for the third). We arbitrarily choose Y and I, giving:[7]

$$Y = \left(\frac{a+e}{1-b-f}\right) + \left(\frac{c}{1-b-f}\right)L$$
$$+ \left(\frac{d}{1-b-f}\right)S_{-1} + \left(\frac{g}{1-b-f}\right)STK$$

$Y =$	K_1	$+$	$K_2 L$	$+$	$K_3 S_{-1}$	$+$	$K_4 STK$
$I =$	$e + fK_1 + fK_2 L$			$+$	$fK_3 S_{-1} + (fK_4 + g)STK$		
$I = \cdot$	K_5	$+$	$K_6 L$	$+$	$K_7 S_{-1}$	$+$	$K_8 STK$

Fitting reduced-form equations for Y and I now yields estimates of K_1, K_2, . . . K_8. With seven structural parameters a, b, . . . g, these eight expressions would not yield a unique solution for the parameters. This directly results from the over-identified status of the modified model, i.e., more structural coefficients are present than necessary to identify the system. The conclusion is that estimates of the original structural coefficients can be recovered through a reduced-form solution only in the case of an exactly-identified model. In such cases, it can be shown that the resulting estimates of coefficients such as a and b are biased but are at least consistent.

An Example

We have discussed the biased and inconsistent nature of least squares when applied to the coefficients of jointly determined models. We then offered an improved solution to the estimation problem in the exactly

---

[7] In general, the reduced form will have equations for each of the jointly determined variables, each of which will involve all the independent variables. In this case, this reason for choosing Y over C as the second reduced-form expression is only consistency with the earlier discussion. We could as well have formed expressions for C and I in a similar way.

identified case that involved computing and solving the reduced form, and working back to the original parameters. Consider the following data on aggregate expenditures and income:

Period	Ia	C	Y
1	50	465	515
2	60	515	575
3	70	575	645
4	60	475	535
5	50	505	555
6	60	435	495
7	70	555	625
8	80	510	590
9	90	485	575
10	100	765	865

that was produced by the following numerical version of our original exactly identified aggregate model:

$$C = 50 + .8Y + \mu \qquad (4\text{--}1)a$$
$$I = Ia, \text{ given as shown}$$
$$C + I = Y$$

Values of the error term were simulated from a normally distributed population with mean $= 0$ and standard deviation $= 10$. With the normally unattainable advantage of knowing the true value of the parameters a and b, we shall be able to compare the results of estimating techniques with these true values. First, consider the equation that results if least squares is inappropriately applied to $(4\text{--}1)a$. That equation is

$$C = 2.7 + .88Y$$

As expected from the earlier discussion, the value of b is greater than the true value, while the a value is smaller. Thus, the computed equation is tilted up in the manner of LS in Figure 4–3. The biased character of ordinary least-squares estimates will not lead to an improvement in these results even if the sample size is enlarged considerably. If we now fit the reduced form for Y, identified earlier as $(4\text{--}3)$, we obtain

$$Y_c = 268.4 + 4.77Ia$$

which is an unbiased estimate of

$$Y = 250 + 5Ia$$

Then, if we use the K_1 and K_2 results to solve back for the a and b values according to $(4\text{--}4)$ and $(4\text{--}5)$, we obtain:

$$b = 1 - \frac{1}{4.77} = .79$$

$$a = \frac{268.4}{4.77} = 56.4$$

giving as the consistent estimate of $(4-1)a$:

$$c = 56.4 + .79Y$$

which compares reasonably well with the true value and is substantially better than the least-squares results.

Many applications of interest in economics involve models that have at least some over-identified equations for which the reduced-form method is inappropriate, or which are overly complex for this method. We shall now discuss methods that uniquely contribute to structural coefficient estimation in this case, but which also apply in the case of exactly-identified models.

TWO-STAGE LEAST SQUARES

The most widely used technique in current econometric research is called two-stage least squares, and involves use of the familiar tools of least-squares in a somewhat different way. Because of its more frequent use, its simplicity in comparison with other alternative techniques, and its desirable properties as an estimator, this method shall be the focus of our discussion of simultaneous techniques. We shall only briefly survey other available techniques.

The thrust of two-stage least squares (TSLS for short) is to eliminate the condition of joint determinancy without also eliminating the structural equations. This is accomplished in two distinct stages. In the first stage, reduced-form equations as previously described are fit for each of the jointly determined (dependent) variables, with the independent variables consisting of all the exogenous and predetermined variables.

These regressions produce calculated values for each of the jointly determined variables, as functions of all the independent variables. The calculated values for the jointly determined variables have two valuable properties:

1. They are linear functions of only exogenous and predetermined variables, which means they can be unambiguously computed from the predetermined and exogenous values. Therefore, there is no way in which individual computed, jointly determined variables are influenced by other jointly determined variables.
2. The calculated values of the jointly determined variables are highly correlated with the actual values.

As these two properties suggest, the calculated values of the jointly determined variables are an attractive proxy for the actual values in equations where jointly determined variables appear on the right-hand side.

Employing this proxy is the crux of what is done in the second stage of the two-stage approach. The calculated values of jointly determined variables are used in place of actual values wherever the jointly determined variable appears on the right-hand side of an equation. Then, regressions are run on the structural equations so modified. The resulting estimates can be shown to eliminate the bias associated with simultaneity.

Consider, as an example, an over-identified system with Y_1, Y_2, and Y_3 jointly determined variables, X_1, X_2, X_3, and X_4 predetermined variables, and three specific behavioral (structural) equations as follows:

$$Y_1 = \beta_{11}Y_2 + \beta_{12}Y_3 + \beta_{13}X_1 + \mu_1$$
$$Y_2 = \beta_{21}Y_1 + \beta_{22}Y_3 + \beta_{23}X_2 + \mu_2$$
$$Y_3 = \beta_{31}Y_1 + \beta_{32}Y_2 + \beta_{33}X_3 + \beta_{34}X_4 + \mu_3$$

Successive algebraic substitution of Y_2, Y_3 into Y_1 and vice versa will result in reduced-form equations for the Y involving only predetermined variables. These reduced-form equations are:

$$Y_1 = K_{11}X_1 + \cdots + K_{14}X_4 + v_1$$
$$Y_2 = K_{21}X_1 + \cdots + K_{24}X_4 + v_2$$
$$Y_3 = K_{31}X_1 + \cdots + K_{34}X_4 + v_3$$

Performing regression on this reduced form produces three sets of calculated Y values, $\hat{Y}_1$, $\hat{Y}_2$, and $\hat{Y}_3$, each of which is a linear function of *all* the predetermined variables in the model (regardless of the structural equation in which the predetermined variable appears). This reflects the property of simultaneous models that variables influencing any of the Y influence all Y. As linear combinations of $X_1 \cdots X_3$, the $\hat{Y}$ from the first stage may be presumed to be free of the simultaneity present in Y. The $\hat{Y}$ are, to use a horrible phrase, quasi-predetermined in their use in the original structural equations. The structural coefficients may now be estimated directly by least squares in the second stage, as follows:

$$Y_1 = b_{11}\hat{Y}_2 + b_{12}\hat{Y}_3 + b_{13}X_1$$
$$Y_2 = b_{21}\hat{Y}_1 + b_{22}\hat{Y}_3 + b_{23}X_2$$
$$Y_3 = b_{31}\hat{Y}_1 + b_{32}\hat{Y}_2 + b_{33}X_3 + b_{34}X_4$$

where b_{11}, $b_{12} \cdots b_{34}$ are estimates of the true coefficients β_{11}, $\beta_{12} \cdots \beta_{34}$, which are negatively biased but consistent. In fact, it can be shown that the TSLS b coefficient estimates are identical mathematically to those resulting from solving algebraically the reduced-form estimates in the exactly-identified case, and therefore share the same properties of consistency and bias as reduced-form structural coefficients estimates.[8] However, the TSLS estimates have the advantage of being applicable in the case of over-identified models. Perhaps more important, TSLS

---

[8] Johnston, *Econometric Methods*, p. 237. See also pp. 258–60.

provides a comparatively easy way to estimate the coefficients in complex many-equation models, since equations are estimated one at a time rather than as parts of a complete system, as in the case of the algebraic solution of reduced-form equations.

In our previous numerical example, the first-stage equations expressing the jointly determined variables as functions of the predetermined variable would be:

$$Y = K_{11} + K_{12}Ia + v_1$$
$$C = K_{21} + K_{22}Ia + v_2$$

In our example, only Y appears on the right-hand side of a structural equation; therefore the computed C is not required in the second stage and need not be computed in the first stage. Discarding this expression and fitting the remaining equation (identically as was done in the reduced-form computation) gives:

$$Y = 268.4 + 4.77I_a$$

From this expression, inserting the known values of I_a gives the calculated $\hat{Y}$ values for use in the second stage. Then the second-stage regression:

$$C = a + b\hat{Y}$$

is computed. This result is:

$$C = 56.4 + .79Y$$

which indeed is the same as that obtained earlier by solving algebraically from the K values in the first stage.

MAXIMUM LIKELIHOOD ESTIMATES

Another technique for computing biased but consistent estimates of structural coefficients in simultaneous systems is the method of maximum likelihood, either *full-information* or *limited-information*. The full-information method is the most computationally complex of the consistent estimating techniques. We shall only discuss the general nature of this estimator here. The technique is based on manipulation of a stochastic function called the likelihood function L. To understand L, consider a single observation from a sample. Given the assumptions of Chapter 2 about the error term, a normal probability distribution characterizes μ such that, for an equation $Y = a + bX + \mu$, if we are given values of a, b, and X, we may compute the probability that a given value of Y would occur. For observation i, call this probability $P(Y_i/a,b,X_i)$, where the slash mark indicates the probability of Y_i occurring *given* a, b, and X_i did occur.

The likelihood function is the joint probability distribution of these P for all points in the sample:

$$L = P(Y_1/a,b,X_1)P(Y_2/a,b,X_2) \cdot \cdot \cdot P(Y_n/a,b,X_n)$$

The estimation of a, b is then obtained by maximizing L jointly on a, b, i.e., solving simultaneously

$$\frac{\partial L}{\partial a} = 0, \qquad \frac{\partial L}{\partial b} = 0$$

This procedure selects the values of the parameters a,b, which give the observed sample of Y, X values the highest probability of occurrence from among all possible choices of a, b, i.e., which maximize the joint probability of occurrence of the observed sample of Y and X.[9] In the full-information approach, the likelihood function is jointly maximized on all the parameters present in the model. For example, consider a small aggregate econometric model with six structural equations, 12 variables, and 18 total coefficients, including constants. Besides the problem in constructing L, its joint maximization in this case would involve the solution of the 18 equation system resulting from setting the respective partials equal to zero. These equations are nonlinear and quite complex. The complexities of the full-information method have given rise to the limited-information, maximum likelihood version of the approach, which constructs and maximizes the likelihood function based on subsections of the model, usually on a single equation at a time. This usually provides a greatly simplified likelihood function and a smaller resulting system of equations for solution. As will be seen, the results are quite comparable with the full-information approach, which means the limited-information approach receives greater use. Both full- and limited-information approaches provide consistent estimates for simultaneous systems.

CHOOSING ESTIMATING TECHNIQUES
FOR SIMULTANEOUS SYSTEMS

Ordinary least-squares estimators (OLS) were seen to be biased and inconsistent when used to estimate the coefficients in simultaneous systems. Reduced-form estimators, or the mathematically equivalent but more general two-stage, least-squares esitmators (TSLS), were found also to be biased but consistent. Full-information, maximum likelihood estimators (FIML) and limited-information, maximum likelihood estimators

---

[9] Where the statistical assumptions of Chapter 2 are met and where only predetermined variables are on the right-hand side, ordinary least squares can be mathematically demonstrated to be a maximum likelihood estimate.

(LIML) were found to be also generally biased but consistent. As earlier noted, the property of consistency possessed by the TSLS, FIML, and LIML techniques indicates that as sample sizes increase, these estimators will produce increasingly better estimates.

Since OLS does not share this property, when large samples (greater than 40, for example) are involved, the consistent techniques should deliver clearly superior parameter estimates for simultaneous systems. However, the large-sample performance of these estimators is not as practically important as the small-sample performance for n from, say, 15 to 40. Samples in this size range characterize most of the empirical research involving simultaneous economic systems. Therefore, the small-sample properties of these estimators are of specific interest to those interested in performing or evaluating empirical research on simultaneous systems.

Unfortunately, general descriptions of the comparative small-sample properties of TSLS, FIML, and LIML techniques are not available due to the mathematical difficulties involved in deriving general solutions. Reliance must be placed on the results of simulation studies that have been performed using known true parameter values and employing small samples. We shall confine our discussion to some of the results of a representative study by Summers in which OLS, TSLS, FIML, and LIML estimators were compared as to their small-sample performance under a number of circumstances.[10] Summers considered the relative performance of these four estimators when applied to samples of size 20 under conditions where no specification error occurred and where a specification error was present in the data (achieved by generating the data in the latter case with some fluctuation in the jointly determined variables due to a variable omitted in the curve fitting). He also considered jointly the case where multicollinearity was present and absent among the independent variables.

Although it is not possible or appropriate to state all his results here, his findings indicate:

1. When specification errors are not present in the model, FIML and LIML provide the least biased estimates of structural coefficients, followed by TSLS, and finally OLS.
2. Considering the overall accuracy of the estimates in approximating the true value of the coefficients, FIML was the best, followed by TSLS, then LIML, with OLS being generally the most inaccurate.
3. When specification errors are present (truly influential variable omitted) the TSLS, LIML, and OLS show equal bias, and the FIML greater bias in estimating the structural coefficients.

---

[10] R. Summers, "A Capital Intensive Approach to the Small-Sample Properties of Various Simultaneous Equation Estimators," *Econometrica* (Vol.. 33, No. 1), pp. 1–41.

4. With specification errors, the TSLS estimator shows the best accuracy, followed by LIML, OLS, and FIML.

5. When significant multicollinearity is present in the data and no specification errors exist, the bias ranking remains about the same, but the TSLS becomes as accurate as FIML, followed by OLS and then LIML.

6. When significant multicollinearity is present along with specification errors, the ranking both on bias and accuracy is TSLS, OLS, followed by LIML and FIML.

Summers also compared the relative predictive performance of the various estimators. Conditional forecasts of Y were made, given the true Xs, using each set of estimates. From the point of view of forecasting applications, this is the most interesting comparison of all. The results show that any of the TSLS, FIML, or LIML techniques were superior in conditional forecasts to OLS. However, it was not possible to designate a clearly superior technique among TSLS, FIML, and LIML. Summers' conclusion is, ". . . it appears that as far as conditional predictions are concerned, economy in computation can safely supplant statistical efficiency as a basis for choosing between FIML, LIML, TSLS, and LSNR."[11]

Other studies similar to that of Summers have both supported the results of his work and produced evidence contrary to it. Johnston has reviewed the evidence from a number of simulation studies including the Summers' study, and has reached the following general conclusion:[12]

On structural parameters the evidence would appear to be that FIML is the best method. Its disadvantages, however, are still very serious; the computational burden is very heavy, and the optimal properties of the estimator depend heavily upon the correctness of the *a priori* specification of the model. This latter fact alone, given our present ignorance and uncertainty about specification, is probably sufficient to rule out FIML as a practical tool. Concentrating then on single-equation estimators and leaving to one side the special case of indirect least-squares (reduced-form least-squares) for exactly identified relations, the best choice among the remaining methods would appear to be TSLS first, LIML second, and OLS third, but this is by no means a hard and fast ruling.[13] (parenthesis added)

The focus of attention has been on TSLS in this chapter, due to its (at least) comparable statistical properties with other consistent tech-

---

[11] LSNR stands for Least-Squares–No-Restrictions, which is the same as what we earlier called reduced-force least squares. Summers also computed conditional forecasts based on the reduced-form equations, and found them to compare favorably with the TSLS, LIML, FIML estimates based on the structural equations.

[12] J. Johnston, *Econometric Methods*, pp. 275–95.

[13] Ibid., pp. 293–94.

niques, and its relative computational ease, given the availability of easily accessable library computer programs for performing least squares and associated calculations. Summers' finding that the technique is superior in accuracy in the case of specification errors, if generally true, enhances the attractiveness of this estimator in those common cases where the analyst is not sure a priori of the accuracy of his model specification.

RECURSIVE SYSTEMS

Occasionally, econometric models may be specified in such a way that the variable determined by the first equation is used to help explain the value of the dependent variable in the second equation. This variable is then used to help explain the value of the dependent variable in the third equation, and so forth. Such a model is called *recursive*. The determination of endogenous variables within a recursive model occurs sequentially in what Professor Herman Wold, a pioneer in the area, calls a causal chain. The following system is an example of a recursive model:

$$Y_1 = C_{11}X_1 + C_{12}X_2 + \mu_1 \tag{R1}$$
$$Y_2 = C_{21}Y_1 + C_{22}X_3 + C_{23}X_4 + \mu_2 \tag{R2}$$
$$Y_3 = C_{31}Y_2 + C_{31}X_5 + \mu_3 \tag{R3}$$

where $X_1 \cdots X_5$ are exogenous and where μ_1, μ_2, μ_3 are normally distributed random variables that are independent of each other.

Notice in this system that the first of the three dependent variables, Y_1, is completely a product of exogenous variables. Therefore, from the standpoint of equation (R2), the value of Y_1 can be taken as having occurred in an exogenous fashion. Therefore, using this exogenous-like value along with X_3 and X_4 in (R2) produces a similarly exogenous-like estimate of Y_2 insofar as equation (R3) is concerned. This pattern continues throughout any truly recursive model.

Thus, in general, an m-equation recursive system involving n exogenous variables has the following appearance, where some C_{ij} are zero.

$$Y_1 = C_{11}X_1 + C_{12}X_2 + \cdots + C_{1n}X_n + \mu_1$$
$$Y_2 = C_{21}Y_1 + C_{22}X_1 + C_{23}X_2 + \cdots + C_{2,n+1}X_n + \mu_2$$
$$Y_3 = C_{31}Y_1 + C_{32}Y_2 + C_{33}X_1 + C_{34}X_2 \cdots + C_{3,n+2}X_n + \mu_3$$

.

.

.

$$Y_m = C_{m,1}Y_1 + \cdots + C_{m,m-1}Y_{m-1} + C_{m,m}X_1 + \cdots + C_{m,n+m}X_n + \mu_m$$

The exogenous-like character of the successive Y terms in such a recursive system enables good estimate of coefficients to be obtained by the single-equation methods discussed in Chapters 2 and 3. It may be shown that ordinary least squares applied to recursive systems produces consistent and unbiased estimates.

At this point, it may seem that recursive systems offer a way to skirt around the problems of simultaneity discussed in this chapter. That is, manipulating simultaneous systems algebraically will, in general, enable their assemblage into a system having a recursive appearance. Does this mean we may perform such manipulations on simultaneous systems and proceed to estimate them with ordinary least squares? Decidedly not. The problem is with the exogenous-like nature of succeeding endogenous variables. A large contributing factor to this exogenous-like property is that the error terms in each equation are independent of error terms in other equations. Such independence means that the Y variables used as successive explanatory variables will not contain elements of fluctuation resulting from the endogenous variable they seek to explain. If this does not hold, then succeeding Y terms will contain endogenous fluctuations resulting from the systematic correlated pattern in the error term. As a result, they will lose their exogenous-like character. If a truly simultaneous system were algebraically manipulated into a recursive appearance, the manipulation would produce a highly intertwined set of error terms that, as a result, would be intercorrelated. Thus, to correctly employ ordinary least squares, the recursiveness must occur naturally. Further, independence in the error terms of recursive equations is most probable under circumstances where the proposed model structure is recursive due to the assumed nature of the endogenous-exogenous relationships.

That is, if the recursiveness is a natural product of the model due to the economic character of the system modeled, then the assumption of independence among the error terms is most reasonable.

Recursive models have appeal in several forecasting applications. For example, consider a sales-profit forecasting model for a particular firm. Assume that profits follow closely the pattern of sales. Also assume that sales are a small but predictable portion of industry sales. Finally, assume that industry sales are a predictable share of GNP. The following recursive system is suggested:

$$\text{Industry Sales} = f(\text{GNP}, X_i)$$
$$\text{Firm Sales} = g(\text{Industry Sales}, X_j)$$
$$\text{Firm Profits} = h(\text{Firm Sales}, X_k)$$

where X_i, X_j, X_k are groups of exogenous variables.

Each equation in this system may be estimated by ordinary least squares. If the resulting three error terms are statistically independent, in addition to each being small in average size and free of autocorrelation and heteroscedasticity, the resulting model may be expected to lead to useful predictions of sales and profits.

In this chapter, we have considered the special problems of estimating coefficients in simultaneous system, and have reviewed the available techniques for dealing with the simultaneous estimation problem. Also, we have compared to the extent possible the relative properties of various estimators. Finally, we have discussed recursive systems. Two areas where these tools and those of Chapters 2–3 find fertile ground for application is in the quantitative analysis of demand and production relationships. We now turn to a consideration of these applications.

DISCUSSION QUESTIONS

1. Would an under-identified model prohibit the estimation of coefficients by two-stage least squares? Explain.
2. Distinguish between first-stage and second-stage equations as estimated by two-stage least squares. Can you define unique and common uses for each set of equations?
3. Is it correct to say a recursive model is simultaneous but a simultaneous model is not recursive? Explain.
4. How do obtained coefficient estimates of the structural equations in a simultaneous system contribute towards determining whether a model is identified?
5. What, if anything, is the difference between specification and identification?

CASE 3—MIDWEST EQUIPMENT COMPANY [B]

In September, 1969, Mr. Salnas was again faced with the annual task of determining next year's production capacity. (See Midwest Equipment Company [A].) Luckily, the investment in the new machines had not been made last year because of information that a new breakthrough in technology of aluminum casting had been achieved and a much more efficient machine would be available within a year. It had been decided to postpone the investment and wait for the release of the new machines. As it turned out, the forecasted sales had not developed and instead had taken a significant drop from the previous year, such that if the company had made the investment, a considerable drop in earnings would have occurred.

Mr. Lewander, the new marketing manager, was putting the finishing touches on his report to Salnas. In conjunction with the consulting firm of Ammer & Ammer a new forecasting model for the Power Division had been constructed. In this model, Sales (S) were hypothesized to be dependent on both the division's expenditures on advertising (A) and on regional family formations (FF). $(FF$ led to home purchases and lawn equipment demand.) In addition, experience with Midwest's management revealed that advertising budgets were approved at the top in light of the year's cash flows (CF). This was particularly interesting since cash flow directly depended on sales, thus completing a circular loop of dependence. In addition, cash flow was also affected by the productivity of the production process (PI). (Productivity in production was mainly a function of the state-of-art in the industry.) The company also had a policy that the advertising expenditures should always remain responsive to levels of competitive advertising expenditures (CA), regardless of cash flow. This seemed to be necessary to keep up with the industry advertising "noise level."

Considering the above factors, Lewander formulated and prepared to test the following hypothesized model.

$$S = a_0 + a_1A + a_2FF$$
$$A = b_0 + b_1CF + b_2CA$$
$$CF = c_0 + c_1S + c_2PI$$

The accompanying table gives the values for Sales, Advertising, and the other related variables over the past 20 years.

Questions

1. Is the model identified? Explain.
2. Construct the reduced-form equations. If only a sales forecast is of interest, would all three reduced-form equations be necessary?
3. What information can the structural form of the above model provide other than a forecast of sales?
4. Use regression analysis to find the coefficients of the reduced-form equations.
5. Are all the variables significant? Are your results reliable? Explain.
6. Given the following information, forecast Sales (S) for 1970 and 1971.

1970	1971
$FF = 130.4$	$FF = 132.7$
$CA = 405.6$	$CA = 414.9$
$PI = 120.1$	$PI = 127.0$

7. Use two-stage least squares to find the coefficients of the structural equations. Are all hypothesized variables significant?
8. What would sales be in 1970 and 1971 if advertising was increased by 20 percent?

MIDWEST EQUIPMENT COMPANY

Year	Sales (S)	Cash flow (CF) millions of (dollars)	Advertising (A)	Family formation (FF) (millions)	Competitive advertising (CA) (millions of dollars)	Productivity index (PI)
1950.........	472.4	26.52	18.40	80.2	352.1	82.7
1951.........	492.0	25.97	17.87	78.0	301.1	87.1
1952.........	367.1	27.34	16.52	85.4	334.2	86.4
1953.........	201.6	19.96	15.41	94.7	279.7	83.1
1954.........	368.5	23.27	17.34	95.1	357.2	82.0
1955.........	369.9	26.13	17.15	100.0	350.0	85.4
1956.........	490.6	24.02	19.23	95.1	381.4	83.3
1957.........	258.3	23.37	14.49	102.9	351.2	80.7
1958.........	179.0	17.91	11.15	105.2	300.4	83.9
1959.........	266.2	17.35	14.90	107.5	285.6	98.1
1960.........	128.0	14.26	13.43	110.7	312.1	84.0
1961.........	321.5	27.74	19.67	115.3	347.3	104.2
1962.........	389.3	28.72	18.41	108.0	353.1	102.5
1963.........	791.1	38.20	26.44	102.0	470.2	99.2
1964.........	753.4	41.51	28.70	101.1	451.0	100.0
1965.........	923.8	40.62	27.42	95.6	480.7	102.4
1966.........	825.7	44.49	27.92	100.4	432.4	124.1
1967.........	929.2	42.80	24.57	104.8	411.1	122.3
1968.........	741.0	40.37	23.73	112.7	401.3	125.6
1969.........	592.2	34.21	20.07	126.0	382.2	123.4

PART II

Analysis of Demand, Cost, and Market Prices

Analysis and forecasting demand for its products and services is an essential and inescapable task of corporate management. In addition, measurement and analysis of production and cost relationships can lead to lower costs by making better use of available labor and capital. Finally, a broad understanding of product market environments can be a valuable tool in mapping corporate pricing strategy. These are the major topics taken up in Part II.

DEMAND RELATIONSHIPS

A significant area of joint application of the tools of econometrics and the apparatus of microeconomic theory is in the measurement and prediction of demand relationships. Business decisions relating to pricing matters are conditioned by the sensitivity of product markets to alterations in price, by the relative weights to attach to competitors' advertising expenditures versus the firm's advertising expenditures in affecting market demand, by the effect of general business fluctuations upon industry and firm sales, and by an array of other similar questions relying upon quantitative relationships between pertinent variables. Whereas microeconomics has forged a forceful theoretical apparatus to help understand some of these relationships, econometrics has developed the means to recover relevant concepts from the theoretician's blackboard in specific numerical form. Still, the ability to unequivocally answer the key questions pertinent in the formulation of management policy regarding price leaves much room for improvement. It shall be our task in this chapter to explore the extent to which we may use these two areas of knowledge in analyzing and measuring demand relationships for firms and industries.

THE DEMAND FUNCTION

In a professional lecture on the theory of price, demand functions often seem to appear as readily as rabbits from a magician's hat. Although the logical argument for the general slope, and characteristics of this function seem impenetrable, at some point it is usually simply announced that the resulting function is of a given form, such as:

$$Q = a + bP$$

where, for example, $a = 10$, $b = -5$.

This approach, perfectly appropriate for those primarily concerned with the development or understanding of theory, is not sufficient for those concerned with using the apparatus to analyze problems. In the latter case, a more detailed understanding is necessary of the process that delivers the conclusion that $a = 10$ and $b = -5$. At its roots, that process is concerned with separating demand relationships from supply relationships, and estimating the quantitative magnitude of these relationships.

MEASURING DEMAND AND SUPPLY

A demand function is a schedule of intentions reflecting the behavior of buyers in a particular market. Specifically, a demand function is an attempt to quantify the relationship between influential variables such as price and the associated quantity buyers will want. Expression (5–1) is illustrative:

$$Q_D = a + bP + cY + dA + \mu, \tag{5–1}$$

where Q_D = quantity demanded, P = price, Y = consumer incomes, A = advertising expenditures, $a \cdot \cdot \cdot d$ are fixed coefficients, and μ, a random error term. This expression formalizes the factors that together explain the amount buyers will *want* to buy. Normally, actual market conditions do not create all possible combinations of P, Y, A such that a thoroughly exhaustive evaluation can be made of the relative impact of each on Q_D when the others take on various values. Necessarily, many of the actual computed values of Q_D that result from various sets of P, Y, and A are inferences established on the basis of other observations. In the measurement of demand, we must have a sufficient pattern of fluctuation in P, Y, A to enable these inferences to be reliable. In addition, simultaneity must be considered. When we specify price in a competitive market, the implication is that quantity demanded is known, as price is the product of quantity demanded and supplied. But we are using it to estimate Q_D. This problem thus must be handled by the special estimation methods of Chapter 4. Finally, it is normally the case that the quantity sellers will *want to* supply on the market, Q_S, can be represented by a supply function analogous to the demand function, for example:

$$Q_S = e + fP + gL + hT + \mu_2 \tag{5–2}$$

where L = labor productivity, T = index of production technology, $e \cdot \cdot \cdot h$ fixed coefficients, and μ_2 an error term. This means that other variables such as L and T affect the value of Q_S and therefore P and Q_D. Any estimation of the coefficients in (5–1) must take into account the variables in (5–2), and vice versa. Attempts to build quantitative models of one part of a market therefore must involve a model of the entire market when the parts are jointly determined.

As an example of these ideas, consider the data of Table 5–1. These data are of the type normally available to an analyst concerned with

TABLE 5-1

Time period	Price	Sales quantity	Index of labor productivity	Index of production technology	Income	Advertising expense
1........	33.60	993	89	91	72	500
2........	22.00	1018	92	94	71	510
3........	31.10	1033	95	96	73	520
4........	31.60	1063	98	98	76	540
5........	36.20	1123	100	100	80	550
6........	42.20	1151	102	104	86	560
7........	48.80	1228	104	108	93	570
8........	44.80	1218	108	110	96	610
9........	58.70	1314	112	115	105	640
10........	62.50	1360	116	119	112	700
11........	62.20	1381	117	123	110	680
12........	57.60	1363	118	120	109	660
13........	55.30	1374	119	120	109	650
14........	55.00	1373	121	121	112	660
15........	61.80	1415	124	124	115	700
16........	64.70	1462	127	126	118	720
17........	61.40	1486	129	129	121	710
18........	73.20	1566	134	130	129	750
19........	75.80	1593	140	132	137	800
20........	88.40	1655	145	137	142	850
21........	85.30	1702	148	141	144	850
22........	80.60	1708	150	144	147	860
23........	82.20	1733	153	147	149	860
24........	87.30	1786	155	148	154	840
25........	81.50	1743	158	147	149	850

the measurement of demand. They are a record of past actual market performance. The observed values of market price (P) and quantity traded (Q) have been jointly determined through the interaction of demand and supply influences. For illustrative purposes, the data of Table 5-1 have in fact been produced by simulation in a manner following the demand and supply expressions (5-1) and (5-2). Accordingly, the true underlying determinants of equilibrium price and quantity are income (Y), advertising (A), labor productivity, and production technology (T). The observed P and Q values are particular points where the quantities demanded and supplied are in balance—i.e., where the two curves intersect. Thus, while we would like to have many locations on the demand function of (5-1) to provide evidence for a statistical equation, the data restricts us to those locations where an equilibrium point has occurred. The same is true in establishing the quantitative influence of the other variables in the (5-1) demand function, Y and A.

As indicated in Chapter 4, one aspect of the data we cannot tolerate is excessive stability in the equilibrium P and Q values, as depicted in

Figure 5–1. In this figure, the dotted lines represent the band of stochastic variation associated with the supply and demand functions. With normal fluctuations in both these functions, equilibrium price-quantity combinations would occur generally within the rectangular area formed by the intersection of the two sets of dotted lines. In other words, observed

FIGURE 5–1

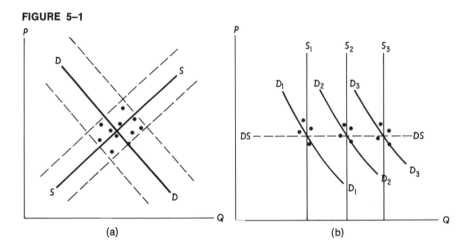

(a)   (b)

data would normally occur in the area defined by the dotted lines. Only a small range of the demand and supply functions are involved in the production of these data; therefore, they tell us little if anything about the overall shapes of the two curves. Any estimates we could produce of the coefficients of the demand or supply curves in this situation would be unreliable.

Similarly unreliable would be the situation depicted in panel (b) of Figure 5–1. This illustrates the situation where the demand for the product shifts over time from $D1$ to $D2$ to $D3$. But the supply also increases in approximately the amount to cover the demand increase. The result is a roughly stable price with increasing volume over time, and almost no relevant information as to the shape of the demand function. This depicts the situation as it often exists from the standpoint of the individual producer.

The reader has by now probably recognized that we are discussing an illustration of the identification problem introduced in Chapter 4. In terms of that earlier discussion, the situation of Figure 5–1 does not involve enough statistically significant and unique determinants of either the demand or supply curve to enable their reliable estimation. If independent influences were present and themselves fluctuating, they would cause shifts in the functions that would produce market evidence at other locations along the curves. If sufficient, shifts in these independent variables could generate the evidence for reliable estimates of the underlying functions. But in Figure 5-1, panel (a), we instead appear to have the situation where c and d in (5-1) and g and h in (5-2) are near zero, producing:

$$Q_D = a + bP$$
$$Q_S = e + fP$$
$$Q_D = Q_S$$

Applying the concepts of Chapter 4, both equations and the model are underidentified.

In the example, if c or d is nonzero but g and h are not, then we would have an identified supply function and an unidentified demand function, since the independent fluctuations in the Q_D function would produce evidence along the constant supply function as to its shape. If c and d are zero, but either g or h is not, then the same reasoning indicates the demand curve is estimatible but the supply curve is not. If *either* c or d and either g or h is nonzero, then the system is exactly identified with one unique independent determinant for each equation. Finally, if c, d, g, and h are nonzero, the equations are over-identified. So the a priori specification of our illustrative market model of (5-1), (5-2) indicates that each equation is over-identified. But this must stand the rigors of a statistical test of the significance of the structural coefficients before a final conclusion can be reached as to the identification status. A simple inspection of the data of Table 5-1 reveals that every variable employed in (5-1) or (5-2) has fluctuated substantially over the sample period. This offers some encouragement that the situation of Figure 5-1, panel (a), has not characterized the data. Additional approximate evidence on this point may be obtained by results of a t-test of the c, d, g, and h coefficients upon their statistical estimation.[1]

Returning to the position of an analyst with the data of Table 5-1 available, expressions (5-1) and (5-2) represent a beginning hypothesis about the nature of the economic process that produced the data. The true nature of this process would, of course, be unknown to the analyst. In fact, the best the analyst can hope to do is draw inferences from statistical results about the reasonableness of particular hypotheses similar to (5-1) and (5-2). In our case, we shall profit by departing from reality concerning this uncertainty and instead present the true underlying functions that produced the data of Table 5-1 by simulation. Those functions are:

$$Q_D = -7.0P + 10.0Y + 1.0A + \mu_1$$
$$Q_S = 3.0P + 5.0L + 5.0T + \mu_2$$

[1] A discussion of the t-test is found in Chapter 2.

and μ_1, μ_2 are normally distributed variables with mean $= 0$ and $\sigma_\mu = 20$. The data in Table 5–1 resulted from drawing randomly from a normal distribution with $E(\mu) = 0$ and $\sigma_\mu = 20$, and adding this to the sum of the Y, A, L, and T contributions.

The simultaneity apparent between P and Q in the market we are attempting to model indicates the applicability of one of the consistent simultaneous estimation techniques discussed in Chapter 4. Since our model is over-identified, the procedure of estimating the reduced-form coefficients, then solving backwards for a, $b \cdot \cdot \cdot h$ is not feasible. Among remaining estimators, we shall choose two-stage least squares to apply to the data of Table 4–1. Accordingly, regressions are computed for each of the jointly determined variables as functions of all the independent variables. This is equivalent to estimating the reduced form of the model. In our case, solving (5–1) and (5–2) simultaneously for the jointly determined variables P and Q gives:

$$P = \left(\frac{e-a}{b-f}\right) + \left(\frac{g}{b-f}\right)L + \left(\frac{h}{b-f}\right)T - \left(\frac{c}{b-f}\right)Y$$
$$- \left(\frac{d}{b-f}\right)A + \left(\frac{\mu_2 - \mu_1}{b-f}\right)$$

$$Q = \left(\frac{af-be}{f-b}\right) - \left(\frac{bg}{f-b}\right)L - \left(\frac{bh}{f-b}\right)T + \left(\frac{fc}{f-b}\right)Y$$
$$+ \left(\frac{fd}{f-b}\right)A + \left(\frac{f\mu_1 - b\mu_2}{f-b}\right)$$

Each expression involves all the independent variables. The expected value of P, Q—given L, T, Y, and A—occurs where $\mu_2 = \mu_1 = 0$ (expected value of the error term). In the two-stage approach, the computed values of the jointly determined variables (call them $\hat{P}$ and $\hat{Q}$) are the product of the first stage. These computed values then replace actual P and Q values wherever these occur on the right-hand side as independent variables in the structural equations. In our case, Q never appears on the right-hand side of a structural equation; therefore its computed value is not needed in the second stage. All that is necessary from the first stage is the $\hat{P}$ value. Computing a least-squares fit for this first stage gives:[2]

First Stage

$$P = 5.52 - 0.83L - 0.23T + 1.18Y + .07A$$
$$(.30) \quad (.35) \quad (.31) \quad (.04)$$

(5–3)

[2] The true value of this first-stage equation, when $\mu_1 = \mu_2 = 0$, is:

$$P = -0.5\,L - 0.5\,T + 1.0\,Y + 0.1\,A$$

Inserting the observed values of Y, A, L, and T into (5-3), the $\hat{P}$ values are computed for use in the second stage.

These $\hat{P}$ are used in the original expressions (5-1) and (5-2) in place of P to yield consistent estimates of the structural coefficients. Again applying least squares to fit these expressions yields:

Second Stage

$$Q_D = 234.76 - 4.79P + 12.30Y + 0.09A \qquad (5\text{-}1)\text{e}$$
$$ (1.39) \quad\; (1.10) \quad\;\; (0.18)$$

$$Q_S = -13.71 + 2.83P + 4.65L + 5.56T \qquad (5\text{-}2)\text{e}$$
$$ (0.82) \quad\; (1.07) \quad\;\; (1.40)$$

the final estimated equations. Numbers in parentheses are standard errors.

Table 5–2 shows these estimates, the true coefficient values, and the values that result when ordinary regression equations are directly computed for (5-1) and (5-2), ignoring the simultaneity problem. It is clear from Table 5–2 that ordinary least squares produces a rather poor estimate of the b and d coefficients. Two-stage least squares produces a better estimate in general, including a considerably improved estimate of b. Comparing the two-stage estimates with the true coefficient values, both supply and demand functions show a tolerable correspondence. The b and d estimates are the most errant. In fact, the d estimate is not significantly different from zero on the basis of a t-test, even though it actually is an integral part of the process that simulated our data. As noted in Chapter 4, t-tests cannot be strictly interpreted regarding the significance of coefficients in simultaneous-equation models. Assuming their approximate validity in this case, the explanation for this result is found in the intercorrelations among the independent variables—the situation described as multicollinearity in Chapter 3. In particular, the correlation coefficients between L and T, Y and A, and $\hat{P}$ with both Y and A, are all significantly greater than zero. The separate effects of P, Y, and A in the demand function are thus difficult to reliably discern. This common problem usually lessens our faith in the specific magnitude of regression coefficients, and in the interpretation of t-tests. As we have seen, our coefficient estimates made in the presence of multicollinearity are not all that could have been expected, and one t-test has produced a finding we know to be wrong. The data of the problem therefore illustrates the need to explore multicollinearity and other problems of reliability in the process of coefficient estimation in economic models.[3]

In our illustration, perfect knowledge of the makeup of the two structural equations eliminated the possibility that we would incorrectly either include or exclude variables from our equation. But in a world

---

[3] See Chapter 3 for a discussion of other problems of reliability.

TABLE 5-2
Coefficients

	Demand function, (5-1)				Supply function, (5-2)			
	a	b	c	d	e	f	g	h
True value..........	0.0	−7.0	10.0	1.0	0.0	3.0	5.0	5.0
Ordinary Least Squares.........	364.33	−0.26 (1.04)	9.78 (1.14)	−0.08 (0.22)	−30.69	2.58 (0.59)	4.72 (0.96)	5.75 (1.21)
Two-Stage Least Squares....	234.76	−4.79 (1.39)	12.30 (1.10)	0.04 (0.18)	−13.71	2.83 (0.82)	4.65 (1.07)	5.56 (1.40)
Two-Stage Least Squares with Specification Error (Y, L omitted)	322.64	6.16 (2.60)	omitted	1.03 (0.42)	−54.22	3.55 (1.09)	omitted	10.23 (1.22)
Two-Stage Least Squares with Specification Error (Y, L in wrong equation)...........	198.74	−15.21 (6.42)	23.42 (6.78)	0.95 (0.54)	128.87	−2.40 (2.42)	0.89 (1.92)	2.96 (1.71)

NOTE: Numbers in parentheses are standard errors.

where we have only the resulting data and not the true underlying functional relationships behind these data, the possibility always exists that we will incorrectly specify the correct variables to include in equations. This is called a specification error. In models of complex economic systems, at least some specification error seems a virtual certainty, because of the many variables exerting influence upon the dependent variable(s). In successful models of such system, the specification errors will be small, because all highly significant variables will have been included. But if some fundamentally related variables are incorrectly excluded, the coefficient estimates for the remaining variables may be affected. In such a case, the portion of the variation in Y that is related to the omitted variable attaches incorrectly to the remaining coefficients, causing them to deviate from their true value.

This effect is illustrated in the fourth row of Table 5–2, where the second-stage regressions have been recomputed with Y omitted from the demand function estimate and L omitted from the supply function estimate. The effect on the coefficients of the demand function of omitting Y is pronounced, particularly in the b coefficient estimate, which moves from -4.79 to $+6.16$. The specification error thus causes even the measured direction of the effect of price on quantity demanded to change. Moreover, the incorrectly positive b coefficient is significant on the basis of a t-test. Apparently, a large portion of the combined effect of the P and Y variables now is reflected in the b coefficient. P in effect becomes a proxy variable for the combined effect of P and Y. This will be misleading if we are interested in interpreting price elasticity or other price-quality relationships through use of the b measure.

In the supply function, the omitted effects of the L variable have mostly attached to the h coefficient on the T term. That coefficient nearly doubled from the previous estimate, and is over twice as large as the true value. Interestingly, the weight given to the h coefficient is approximately equal to the true combined weight of the g and h coefficient, which suggests the remaining T variable now measures the combined effect of both variables in the equation. As with the mis-specified b coefficient, it is statistically "significant" at this incorrect value. Again, interpretations about the role of T in price determination are likely to be misleading in this mis-specified case.

A similar distortion in the coefficient estimates is to be expected if extra variables are included in the equations. Superfluous variables will pull the regression plane away from the true position as long as the superfluous coefficients have a nonzero value, even though these coefficients may be insignificant in size. The last row of Table 5–2 contains computed second-stage equations with a variable added to each equation that is truly in the other equation. L has been added to the demand function, while Y has been added to the supply function. The effects on the original coefficient estimates are as pronounced as in the case of omitted variables. In the demand function, the *b* coefficient estimate is lowered below its earlier estimate and its true value, while the *c* estimate is doubled over its earlier value. Thus, this error of commission incorrectly shifts the relative weights assigned by the least-squares fit. An example is seen in the supply function where the price coefficient *f* is now measured as negative. The general lesson is clear: *Specification errors, either of omission or commission, can have a substantial distorting effect on other coefficient estimates in the model.*

The problems encountered in this confrontation of econometric techniques with messy but realistic data have been perhaps disturbingly complex. We have not totally solved them in all instances. So it is with quantitative research in economics. Let us now turn to a more pleasant topic.

USES OF DEMAND AND SUPPLY RELATIONSHIPS

Given reasonable estimates of the demand and supply functions from consistent estimation procedures, several uses are suggested by the apparatus of microeconomics. In exploring these uses, we will basically employ the model of (5–1) and (5–2) with the true coefficient values.

Elasticity

Elasticity refers to the sensitivity of movements in one variable to movements in a second variable. One important specific case is price elasticity, defined as the percentage change in quantity demanded divided by the corresponding percentage change in price. Values of this ratio greater than one indicate a greater-than-proportionate response of quantity demanded to price changes, while values less than one indicate a proportionately insensitive quantity-price relationship.[4]

If the demand function has been identified and estimated, an estimate of price elasticity can be prepared. Point elasticity of price is defined as:

$$e_p = \frac{\dfrac{dQ}{Q}}{\dfrac{dP}{P}} = \frac{dQ}{Q} \cdot \frac{P}{dP} = \frac{dQ}{dP} \cdot \frac{P}{Q}$$

Where the numerator and denominator are small percent changes in quantity and price respectively. In the demand curve of (5–1), the rela-

---

[4] For a more extensive discussion, see L. Reynolds, *Economics* (4th ed. Homewood, Ill.: R. D. Irwin, Inc., 1973) for a complete discussion of this and the following elasticities.

tionship between P and Q is linear. Therefore, since dQ/dP in our elasticity expression is the slope of Q with respect to P, it is just equal to the coefficient b. Therefore, for our demand function:

$$e_p = \frac{bP}{Q} = \frac{-7P}{Q}$$

At the mean sample values of P and Q, this is:

$$e_p = \frac{(7)(58.43)}{1379} \cong .30$$

where the minus sign has been dropped for convenience. So, at average price-quantity combinations, demand is relatively price inelastic in our data. At the most recent price-quantity combination in period 25, the value is $e_p = .33$, still inelastic. Applying our two-stage point estimate of b, rather than the true value, gives $e_p = .22$.

The techniques of Chapter 2 suggest we could also examine the uncertainty in our estimate of e_p by considering a confidence region constructed around our b estimate. For the data in the example, a 95 percent confidence interval for b is given by: $-4.79 \pm (2.08)(1.39) = -7.68 < b < -1.90$. Putting these boundaries into our elasticity expression yields a similar 95 percent confidence interval for the true value of the elasticity: $.08 < e_p < .32$. This interval in fact contains the true value of .30. It provides additional evidence as to the statistical uncertainty in our estimate. The finding that the obtained interval occurs entirely in the inelastic region heightens the confidence we have in drawing conclusions based on the premise that demand is inelastic.

A finding that demand in our market is relatively price-inelastic indicates that price changes do not elicit proportionate changes in quantity demanded. In fact, over the period of the sample, a 10 percent rise in price only produces approximately a 3 percent decline in quantity demanded.

The apparatus of price theory tells us that when $e_p < 1$, price and dollar sales move in the same direction, but when $e_p > 1$, they move in opposite directions. This follows directly from the definition, since if price changes bring disproportionately smaller quantity changes, then price increases will not decrease the number of units sold sufficiently to offset the greater revenue per unit on the remaining units. As a result, total sales will rise. The reverse is true for price decreases. When demand is inelastic, price decreases will not increase the quantity demanded sufficiently to offset the lower revenue per unit on the expanded volume. Accordingly, dollar sales will decline with a price decline.

The opposite is true in the case of $e_p > 1$. In these cases, quantity demanded responds by greater than proportionate amounts relative to a price change, causing price increases to produce declines in dollar sales and price reductions to increase dollar sales.

Price increases are usually rewarding when $e_p < 1$. The logic is as follows: The price increase *cuts* physical volume of sales and production but *raises* total dollar sales. The cut in physical volume reduces total variable costs (material, direct labor, etc.) and therefore, total costs. With total costs declining and total sales increasing, profits must be increasing, *ceteris paribus*. By the same reasoning, cutting prices when $e_p < 1$ will reduce profits, since revenues will fall while variable total costs rise. Therefore, a reliable finding that $e_p \cong .33$ at present prices, or that an entire estimated 95 percent confidence interval for e_p lies in the inelastic region, represents an opportunity for the producer to increase profits through increasing prices. At the same time, $e_p < 1$ warns the producer that price reductions may be expected to reduce profits. When $e_p > 1$, price increases produce a decline in both physical and dollar volume. But costs are reduced as a result of the cut in physical volume. The net impact on profits depends on the relative amounts of the revenue and cost decline. We may anticipate that for an initial elastic range, price rises may cut revenues by less than costs, but as the rises continue, the market response is likely to become more elastic, leading to greater revenue losses relative to cost decreases, and finally resulting in profit declines. For price cuts when $e_p > 1$, both revenues and costs will rise. Analogous to price increases, the comparison is between the revenue increase and the cost increase.

Estimation of the demand curve also enables computation of income elasticities. This measure is defined as the sensitivity of quantity demanded to income change. Specifically, we may express income elasticity of demand (e_Y) as follows:

$$e_Y = \frac{\dfrac{dQ}{Q}}{\dfrac{dY}{Y}} = \frac{dQ}{Q} \cdot \frac{Y}{dY} = \frac{dQ}{dY} \cdot \frac{Y}{Q}$$

In the linear demand function of (5–1), dQ/dY is the coefficient of the Y term (slope on Y whose true value is 10.0. Thus,

$$e_Y = \frac{10Y}{Q}$$

At the average Y and Q values, this is

$$e_Y = \frac{10(110.8)}{1379} \cong 0.80$$

and at the most recent Y, Q values in the data, $e_Y = 0.85$. If $e_Y > 1$, this means that increases (decreases) in income bring about proportionately greater increases (decreases) in quantity demanded. Goods whose demand shows $e_Y > 1$ are thus called *luxury* goods, as they are in porportionately greater demand with income increases. Goods for which $0 < e_Y < 1$ are often called *normal* goods. They show demand changes in the same direction as income changes, but by less than proportionate amounts relative to the income change. Finally, if $e_Y < 0$, then income increases (decreases) reduce (increase) the demand for the goods, as buyers shift their purchases to more attractive goods. In this sense, goods with $e_Y < 0$ may be called *inferior* goods.

In our example, the product involved is revealed to be a normal good; we should expect about an 8 percent rise in quantity demanded for a 10 percent rise in income. Thus, demand for this product should be expected to react in about these proportions to changes in general business conditions. On the other hand, producers of luxury goods can be expected to enjoy comparatively booming markets during business expansions and suffer quite weak markets during recessions. Inferior goods are recession goods, and provide producers with counter cyclical demand patterns.

The coefficient on the advertising variable in our example tells a somewhat different story than the price or income coefficients. Assuming Q is in thousands of units sold, and A is in thousands of dollars of advertising expenditure, the true value of 1.0 for the coefficient says that, over the range of the data, a dollar in new advertising yields a unit of additional demand. If the profit margin on that additional unit is greater than one dollar, then the advertising outlay has yielded more than it cost. Of course, after some point, a linear relationship between A and Q such as has characterized our example would surely break down, as further additions to a would fail to produce the same incremental result. Indeed, any attempt to extend interpretations of coefficient values beyond the range of observed data must consider this possibility.[5]

In many markets, the price of related products is an important determinant of demand. In such cases, these variables will be influential in demand functions, and will enable estimation of the cross-elasticity of demand, defined as follows:

$$e_{A,B} = \frac{\dfrac{dQ_A}{Q_A}}{\dfrac{dP_b}{P_b}} = \frac{dQ_A}{Q_A} \cdot \frac{P_b}{dP_b} = \frac{dQ_A}{dP_b} \cdot \frac{P_b}{Q_A}$$

where A is the subject market and B is a related product. If a linear demand function for A has been estimated that contains the price of related product B, then as before the coefficient on that term is equal

---

[5] Even over the range of observed observations, the linear assumption is always an approximation. In cases where it is a poor approximation of a systematically nonlinear relationship, autocorrelation will often develop. Thus, the test for autocorrelation discussed in Chapter 3 becomes a partial test for linearity.

to dQ_A/dP_b. This enables calculation of $e_{A,B}$ for given combinations of P_b and Q_A. Obtained $e_{A,B} > 0$ imply goods A and B are substitutes, since a price rise (fall) in B shifts demand towards (away from) A, thereby increasing (decreasing) Q_A. Obtained $e_{A,B} < 0$ imply goods A and B are complementary products, since a price rise (fall) in B, by reducing (increasing) its demand, similarly reduces (increases) demand for A, thus producing a negative $e_{A,B}$.

Cross-elasticity provides an analytical tool to classify goods as substitutes (competing goods) or complements (companion goods) purely on the basis of observed statistical data. In many instances, product managers in firms do not need such an analytical device to determine who their competitors are; in other instances the tool can be helpful in ascertaining the nature of competitive relations. A classical example of the latter is a court case involving the Dupont Corporation's cellophane. The antitrust division of the U.S. Justice Department contended that cellophane did not compete with other flexible packaging materials to any important degree, but rather had a near monopoly in their product area. The company argued that many flexible packaging materials competed with cellophane so that their product was in effect only a comparatively small part of the flexible packaging market. In this case, whether or not competition had been revealed between the two areas was an important consideration. Cross-elasticities are an analytical figure of merit relevant to such circumstances.

The expressions for price and income elasticity imply these measures are interrelated. The nature and implications of the interrelationships can be seen by referring to the original expressions:

$$e_P = \frac{-7P}{Q}; \; e_Y = \frac{10I}{Q}$$

Now substituting for Q the demand function gives:

$$e_P = \frac{-7P}{-7P + 10I + A}; \; e_Y = \frac{10I}{-7P + 10I + A}$$

which illustrates several interesting influences upon price and income elasticities for our illustrative demand function:

1. An increase in income will make demand more price inelastic, *ceteris paribus*, as the denominator of p will increase. In fact, for all products where income is an important demand determinant, an increase in income should cause the demand to become more price-inelastic. In effect, at higher income levels, demand is greater at given prices and the same absolute effect on demand of price changes is smaller, percentage-wise.

2. An increase in price reduces the denominator of y and therefore makes demand more income-elastic. At higher prices, the product now acts more like a luxury good.

3. An increase in advertising lowers both price and income elasticity. A central purpose of advertising is often considered to be to make demand more price-inelastic, which in turn gives producers a larger element of control over price. Greater income inelasticity thus affords the producer some insulation from income cycles, which may be advantageous.

The reader by now has probably recognized that the specific conclusions we may draw about interrelationships among elasticities depend upon the specific factors included in demand functions. In general this is true. We may compute an elasticity for any factor found to be a significant determinant of demand and from it derive impressions as to the sensitivity of demand to fluctuations in that variable.

We have now discussed the problem of estimating demand relations and forming various elasticity measures from these estimates. We have seen how the partial regression coefficients enter directly into the calculation of price, income, and cross-elasticities. Some useful interpretations of these elasticities have been outlined. It may by now be obvious that useful elasticity estimates depend entirely upon useful demand function estimates, so that we must solve the problems of estimating the latter as a prerequisite to obtaining the former. This further indicates that a given set of data will not yield reasonable elasticity measures if it will not yield a reasonable demand function estimate.

LIMITATIONS ON MEASURING DEMAND

In the discussion of demand estimation, several factors eminating from the empirical data were identified that implied an inability to produce an estimated demand function from data. To summarize these factors, demand function (and elasticity) estimates were seen to be prohibited by the nature of the data under the following circumstances:

1. The basic demand and supply functional relationships are too volatile to be significantly explained by analytical functions.
2. There are insufficient *statistically* viable relationships present among candidate variables to identify the demand function, i.e., models mathematically identified a priori may become under-identified when the statistical evidence is gathered.
3. There is too much multicollinearity inherent in the variables to allow their separate effects to be disentangled.
4. The data seriously violates one or more of the statistical assumptions about the error term.

Thus, the demand estimation procedures we have considered are not a pure path to reliable results, but instead are more of a navigational mapping of an ocean channel. If the tide is right, uncharted reefs not encountered, and stormy weather avoided, the map will guide the ship safely through. But as competent captains, we should not count on this. Rather, we should sail with the tide, continuously sound out the channel bottom, and, above all, keep our lookouts aloft. Finally, if our ship is scuttled by an unforeseen obstacle, we should take to the lifeboats with dignity.

We have now discussed the topic of estimating demand curves and formulating from them elasticity measures. A closely related but distinct topic is that of forecasting demand and evaluating the results of forecasting models. In the next chapter we turn our attention to these topics.

DISCUSSION QUESTIONS

1. Describe the principal steps involved in formulating an estimate of the price elasticity of demand for automobiles, starting from market data on automobile unit sales patterns and associated data.

2. Suppose consumer incomes importantly influence product demand in a certain market. What, if any, value would income elasticity be to the firm when it is recognized that the firm has no control over consumer incomes?

3. Point out three examples of pairs of goods that you expect would have a positive cross-elasticity, and three examples of pairs of goods you expect to have a negative cross-elasticity.

4. What seems to be the most important basic influence on the width of a confidence interval constructed for price elasticity? What, if anything, could be done to narrow the span of a confidence interval thought to be too large?

5. Considering potential interrelationships among price and income elasticities, does it follow that as the society moves steadily to higher income levels, it should also progress steadily towards more price-inelastic demand for most products and services?

CASE 4—TEXAS BELT, INC.

The Texas Belt Corporation manufactures a leading line of genuine cowhide belts for men sold widely through department stores and men's shops. Retail prices for the firm's belts have remained constant at $3.95, regardless of style or size, for the last two years. This is due primarily to an explicit policy by the firm's management that stipulates frequent fluctuations in prices or price differences due to style are bound to impugn the company's sought-after image of fair play, and are to be avoided.

In addition, the company's management felt that frequent price fluctuations were likely to lead to erratic short-run patterns in sales, as many shoppers would be likely to wait for anticipated markdowns at certain times of the year. However, cost factors now made serious consideration of a price increase imperative. Because prices had not been changed for two years, the company's management felt very uncertain as to how demand for their product would react. In particular, the most comfortable action on the part of the firm would be a move to $5.95, which would represent slightly greater than a 50 percent increase in price. Such an increase would produce generous profit margins and insure price stability for at least another two years, and perhaps longer. On the other hand, an increase of only about 8 percent, to $4.29, would be adequate to restore profit margins to acceptable levels. But in this case any further escalation of costs would begin to exert pressures on margins immediately, and a further price adjustment would then be required. The company's management had no clear picture as to how likely or how large further cost increases might be.

In choosing between these alternatives, the question of how the market would react to a 50 percent versus an 8 percent price increase was clearly the key. To add information, a study of price elasticity of demand was undertaken by the company's market research department. First, monthly data were collected for the past 3½ years (42 months' observations) on sales, prices, and other market inputs thought relevant by the company's sales personnel. These data included consumer incomes, overall clothing prices, general fashion movements, and so forth, encompassing 23 statistical series in all. Various combinations of these variables were regressed on sales along with price. The final resulting equation chosen had the highest R^2 value of any combinations considered, and was essentially selected on that basis. It was as follows:

$$S = 14.1 - 0.03P + 14.3DPI + 23.4CL$$
$$(0.11) \quad (0.80) \quad (1.91)$$
$$+ 3.48U - 4.2PD + 0.43AD$$
$$(0.91) \quad (1.17) \quad (2.11)$$
$$R^2 = .894$$
$$D.W. = 0.45$$

where:

S = dollar sales, net
P = retail price of belts
DPI = disposable personal income
CL = index of clothing sales
U = unemployment rate
PD = dummy variable to account for last previous shift in price, zero for first 18 months' data and one for last 24 months'.
AD = company advertising expenditures and where numbers in parentheses are computed t-values.

In reviewing these results with the company's management, the market research project leader who directed the work pointed out that seasonal patterns were evident in the data and were not adequately handled by the equation. However, these were seen as not having an important effect on the significance of price in affecting sales, as they would even out over the course of the sample period. The dummy variable was described as necessary due to the essentially stairstep nature of price fluctuations over the sample period.

In his presentation, the market research representative pointed to what he felt was the key conclusion of the work: the finding that the price had little if any impact on sales. "Even the dummy variable incorporated to smooth out the stairstep pattern is not statistically different from zero in its statistical effect," he declared. The conclusion and recommendation was as follows: "Therefore, it is clearcut on the basis of our work that sales of our product are not sensitive to the retail price, i.e., in the jargon of economics the demand is price-inelastic. We thereby feel that a 50 percent price increase will not importantly affect belt sales."

Questions

1. Based on the information in the case, review the conclusion of the market research group. Do you agree or disagree? Why?
2. What other information or data would you like to have? Would you do the analysis any differently? If so, how?

Chapter

6

FORECASTING DEMAND

In this chapter we shall focus upon the problems of forecasting economic variables with particular emphasis on perhaps the most common business forecasting problem—projecting the demand for individual products or services. Real-world firms may be more concerned about the value of projected sales revenues than about the shapes of underlying demand curves. In these cases the pitfalls of demand curve estimation discussed in the previous chapter need not be confronted. We may often obtain useful projections of equilibrium sales revenue projections in the presence of no information as to the shape of the basic product demand function. Of course, if the objective is pinpointing or analyzing the effects of specific demand determinants (i.e., arguments in the demand function or elasticities), or with exploring the impact of independent shifts in demand or supply relationships, the structural demand equation is indispensible. In practice, these objectives are often overshadowed by that of forecasting equilibrium values of key variables. In this, the concern of the forecaster is with biulding a model of the net effect of supply and demand variables upon price, quantity, total sales, or other relevant variables. In the case of a simple supply-demand model, the forecasting objective will be met if the supply-demand equilibrium position can be predicted reliably.

COMPOSITION OF DEMAND FORECASTING MODELS

A demand forecasting model in a particular market logically contains all variables significantly affecting both supply and demand. In the example presented in the preceding chapter, all the exogenous determinants of (5–1) and (5–2) appear in such a model, since each alters the equilibrium. The following forecasting model for price results:

$$P = C_0 + C_1L + C_2T + C_3Y + C_4A + e$$

where:

$$P = \text{equilibrium market price}$$
$$L = \text{labor productivity}$$
$$T = \text{technology index}$$
$$Y = \text{income}$$
$$A = \text{advertising expenditures}$$

This is identical to the reduced form of (5–1) and (5–2). Recall that the reduced-form equation contained the net relationship between the dependent variable and all the model's predetermined variables. That is precisely what we are concerned with in the forecasting model—reflecting the net impact of the independent variables upon a dependent. In fact, if our model is specified correctly, it will contain all the variables in either the demand or supply functions, and none that are not in these expressions.

Many forecasting models used by firms are constructed without formal hypotheses about the variables in the underlying structural equations. Some such models make no effort to deal with the structural nature of the model, preferring to let the data tell their own story on a purely empirical basis. Variables are included in such models on the basis of the statistical fit they produce, upon the results of t-tests, and upon a general logical conceptual connection between the independent and dependent variables. In some instances, such models may have impressive forecasting records. In these cases, the record is hard to discount by arguments that the forecaster is ignorant of the true underlying structure of his successful reduced-form model. The situation is similar to that of a medicine that cures a disease for reasons not understood by the physician. Unfortunately, statistically observed economic behavior is likely to be considerably more tricky to interpret than directly observed medical behavior.

The incidence of nonsense correlations is painfully high in economic data. More broadly, the pitfalls of regression applications discussed in chapters 3 and 4 lead many researchers to a wary position in assessing a variable as "significant" only on the basis of obtained statistical results. As examples, specification errors and multicollinearity are two often unrecognized influences upon the statistical significance of an individual forecasting variable. This same wariness produces a reluctance among researchers to accept the reduced form of a model in the absence of a careful consideration of the underlying structure. What is essentially involved is a question of reliability. A forecaster may reasonably assign greater confidence to a model whose structure is known than to one whose structure is unknown, even if all necessary forecasting outputs are derivable from the reduced form. This confidence factor probably subsides in importance after considerable application of a forecasting model over an extended period of time. But in choosing among fore-casting schemes for initial application, it is bound to be at least an important and perhaps a predominant consideration. Professor L. R. Klein, a pioneer and leading expert an econometric forecasting models, addressed this question in the following remark:

> For some time, I have maintained the position that there is no point in trying to construct models that are purely of use in prediction and deny that such models have an existence of their own apart from structural models. I would repeat earlier assertions that best predictions will be made from best structural models.[1]

Whether one explicitly holds Klein's view is largely a matter of one's philosophy of science, a consideration of which is far from our purpose here. But a summary word of caution on the subject is mandatory. Interpretation of forecasting results from unspecified and unknown structural systems should be undertaken in the same spirit as accepting the potion from a witch doctor when you are sick. Although many may have recovered after having taken the potion, it is hard to establish that recovery was *due* to the potion. A more bothersome question arises regarding those who took the potion and subsequently died. As medical science provides reasoned analysis and success probabilities with its cure, analysis of underlying structural systems supplies confidence and credibility in obtained forecasting models.

FORECASTING WITH SIMULTANEOUS MODELS

Forecasting with single-equation models presents no computational problem of solution, since insertion of values of the exogenous variables leads directly to a solution for the dependent variable. This is not the case for simultaneous models. For these models, direct substitution of the exogenous variables into the estimated structure of the model does not directly produce a solution for the exogenous variables, as illustrated by the following example:

$$Y_1 = C_{11}Y_2 + C_{12}X_1$$
$$Y_2 = C_{21}Y_1 + C_{22}X_2 + C_{23}X_3$$

and where Y_1 and Y_2 are endogenous, X_1, X_2, and X_3 are exogenous, and the C_{ij} are estimated coefficients.

The problem, of course, is that in addition to the Xs, Y_2 must be known in the first equation to calculate Y_1, and at the same time Y_1 must be known for the calculation of Y_2.

The usual solution to this problem in forecasting applications is to solve the estimated structural equations simultaneously to obtain expres-

---

[1] L. R. Klein, *Theory of Economic Prediction* (Markham, 1971), p. 99.

sions for the Y variables strictly in terms of the X variables. In our example, this can easily be accomplished by inserting the expression explaining Y_2 in the expression explaining Y_1 as follows:

$$Y_1 = C_{11}(C_{12}Y_1 + C_{22}X_2 + C_{23}X_3) + C_{12}X_1$$

or

$$Y_1 = \frac{1}{1 - C_{11}C_{21}} (C_{12}X_1 + C_{11}C_{22}X_2 + C_{11}C_{23}X_3)$$

Then this expression for Y_1 may be inserted into Y_2:

$$Y_2 = C_{21}\left[\frac{1}{1 - C_{11}C_{21}} (C_{11}C_{22}X_2 + C_{11}C_{23}X_3 + C_{12}X_1) \right] + C_{22}X_2 + C_{23}X_3$$

which gives

$$Y_2 = \left(\frac{C_{21}C_{22}}{1 - C_{11}C_{21}} \right) X_1 + \left(\frac{C_{21}C_{11}C_{22}}{1 - C_{11}C_{21}} + C_{22} \right) X_2$$
$$+ \left(\frac{C_{21}C_{11}C_{23}}{1 - C_{11}C_{21}} + C_{23} \right) X_3$$

which is often referred to as the solved structure of the model.

With the coefficients and the X values known, this solved structure yields direct estimates of the Y variables. This procedure applies readily to all simultaneous linear models. Solving the structure is only a matter of re-expressing the system such that each Y variable is a function of only exogenous variables. Moreover, for any linear model this may be accomplished through straightforward algebraic manipulation of the general type illustrated by our example.

For nonlinear models, such manipulation may not be expected to necessarily yield a unique solution for the endogenous variables in terms of the exogenous. For these systems, other methods of solution have been employed, based mainly on methods of successive approximation.[2] We shall not pursue those methods here except to note they are somewhat more complicated than linear methods.

LIMITATIONS ON FORECASTING DEMAND

In the previous chapter, four circumstances were listed in which retrieval of a demand function from raw data was impossible. We now review these as they apply to estimating a forecasting equation. The

---

[2] The interested reader may wish to consult M. K. Evans, "Computer Simulation of Nonlinear Econometric Models," in *The Design of Computer Simulation Experiments*, T. H. Naylor (ed.) (Durham, N.C.: Duke University Press, 1969), and the references cited there.

first condition that stipulated a stable and systematic pattern of covariance between dependent and independent variables must, of course, still hold. The second circumstance, regarding identification, is also not a problem with single-equation forecasting models, or with the reduced forms of multi-equation models. In either case, one independent variable techni-cally identifies the equation. However, concern remains in simultaneous models that the reduced form continues to characterize a known struc-tural system. In this context, identification of the underlying structure remains a consideration in interpreting the reduced form of a simul-taneous-equation forecasting model.

Multicollinearity remains a consideration in the estimation of forecast-ing models. From a strictly goodness-of-fit point of view, multicollinearity presents no problem in forecasting applications, as long as the pattern present in the data used to estimate the model coefficients persists into the forecast period. If explanatory variables only take on values highly correlated with other explanatory variables, errors in the estimation of individual coefficients will not damage the usefulness of the measured combined effect, as our discussion in Chapter 3 illustrated. Thus, multi-collinearity is a problem that often may be lived with in forecasting models.

However, as seen in Chapters 3 and 5 in connection with demand curves, when an a priori specification of the model exists and the analyst is interested in estimating and interpreting the structural coefficients, living with multicollinearity is not reasonable (as plainly indicated in Table 5–2). Only where the structural coefficients in the model are not of interest for simulation or for inferences about an a priori hypothesis is accepting multicollinearity a reasonable solution.

Alternatively, if a forecasting model contains six independent variables, three of which are highly intercorrelated, then two of these three could be eliminated, resulting in four independent variables. Although inter-pretation of the remaining coefficients is now altered (they now reflect the joint impact of the original six variables), the high intercorrelation should result in such surgery having a small effect on the goodness-of-fit statistics of the modified model, and the now less complicated model may be expected to predict as well as the original model. For forecasting applications, this is usually the primary concern of the analyst.

The fourth limiting circumstance involving the statistical assumptions must hold in the case of forecasting functions, since it relates to the statistical viability of the least-squares procedure. Therefore, the tests of reliability of Chapter 3 concerning these assumptions must be met.

In general, this discussion suggests the circumstances affecting our chances of producing a reasonable forecasting model are less restrictive than in the case of estimating the parameters of a structural model such as a demand function. This suggests that we may be able to generate usable forecasting results in circumstances where demand curve estimation is precluded by the data.

In the example developed earlier in the previous chapter, the reduced-form equation for P was estimated by least squares to be:

$$P = 5.52 - 0.83L - 0.23T + 1.18Y + .07A$$

Given values of L, T, Y, and A, this model can be used to forecast the expected equilibrium market price. If we apply the observed L, T, Y, and A values in the sample, we obtain a set of values that would have been forecast by the equation.

FIGURE 6–1

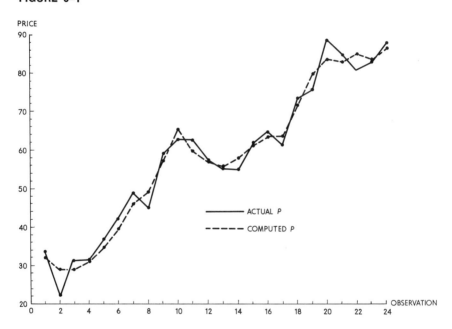

For the data of Table 5–1, these values are plotted in Figure 6–1 along with the actual values. The fit of these computed values to the data shown in Figure 6–1 is rather good. However, this provides only a weak indication of the worth of the model as a forecasting mechanism due to the use of the same data to establish the coefficients as we are plotting in Figure 6–1. Vagaries in the sample will be reflected in the coefficients, as the least-squares technique establishes coefficient values that maximize the fit of the curve to the data. Such results would be much more impressive if they were produced by applying the model to a sequence of observations not included in the data used to establish the coefficients, since the stability of relationships measured between the data period and the forecasting period would be demonstrated. This is called a conditional forecast, as it is a simple simulation of a forecasting circumstances with only the condition that the values of L, T, Y, and A are assumed known with certainty. In the construction of economic models, the number of observations is often not large enough to permit splitting the data into two parts, establishing the equation coefficients on the basis of one part, and then testing the predictive strength on the second part. However, if sample size permits, this is a recommended and often used procedure as it provides the most insight into the probable performance of the model over the actual forecasting period. For final forecasting, the coefficients are often re-estimated with the entire data, thus being based on all currently available data.

EVALUATING FORECASTING MODELS

Suppose sample size does permit the data to be split into two parts and tested. This process results in a number of conditional forecasts along with actual values. How might we proceed to evaluate these results? In answering this question, we shall consider two techniques, both due to Theil.[3] The first involves construction and interpretation of a graphical display of the results. The framework of this tool is shown in panel (a) of Figure 6–2. The horizontal axis contains actual percent changes in the forecast variable from period to period, which we will call (A). The vertical axis contains forecast percent changes (F) from the previous period's actual value. Thus, a 45° line passing through the origin contains the points where $F = A$, meaning the forecast was perfect. This is called the line of perfect forecast (PF). If the forecasting model is effective and undistorted, most of the points in both the upper and lower halves of the graph should lie close to the line PF, with a random scatter of deviant points throughout the rest of the graph. When the pattern of deviant points becomes noticeably nonrandom, the forecasting model produces distorted results. For example, in panel (b) the forecasts uniformly underestimate the magnitude of the movement in A, although they equally uniformly estimate the direction of movement correctly. The scatter of points lies in the lower half of the positive-positive quadrant and in the upper half of the negative-negative quadrant. This systematic underestimation should be the cause of further forecasting model development. In the opposite case, where forecasts consistently overestimated the magnitude of change but correctly forecast the direction, the scatter of points would fall in the area labeled TL.

In panel (c), the forecast produces close estimates as long as the direction of movement in the forecast variable does not change. The model

---

[3] For a complete treatise of both, see H. Theil, *Applied Economic Forecasting* (Amsterdam: North Holland, 1966).

FIGURE 6–2

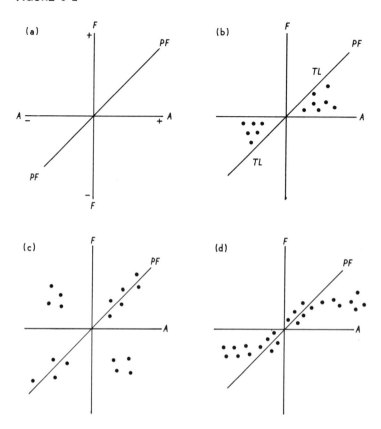

does poorly in forecasting directional changes or turning points, as all deviant points are in the positive-negative or negative-positive quadrants. Such a scatter is typical of a simple trend line fit through data over time. Over the long run, the trend line would capture the direction of movement and produce points along *PF*; however, being a linear line, it could not reflect short-term downswings and upswings in the forecast variable, and therefore would produce observations in the positive-negative or negative-positive quadrants whenever turning points occurs. Every downturn would produce a deviant point in the negative-positive quadrant.

Panel (*d*) illustrates a situation where small changes in the forecast variable are forecast well, but large actual changes are systematically underestimated. In this case the model cannot capture the magnitude of change when that change is large. These illustrations have perhaps sensitized the reader to the many possible forecasting distortions that can be reflected in the graph by significant nonrandom patterns.

Besides distortions, we are usually concerned with the general accuracy of our forecasting model. Theil has proposed a figure of merit for this purpose, called the Inequality Coefficient, I^2, which is given as follows:

$$I^2 = \frac{\sum_{i=1}^{n} (F_i - A_i)^2}{\sum_{i=1}^{n} A_i^2}$$

where F and A, as before, are the forecast and actual percent change in the forecast variable, and n is the size of the quasi-forecasting period. Obviously, the smaller is I, the more accurate the forecast, with $I = 0$ if it is perfect, i.e., if $F_i = A_i$ for all i. A second value of I is also subject to direct interpretation. If the forecast $F_i = 0$ was made for each period (the forecast of no change in the forecast variable), then $I = 1.0$. Thus, forecasts producing $I > 1$ are not as accurate on the whole as the naive forecast of $F =$ no change for every period. We must produce $I < 1$ to defend our forecasting procedure as being better than this naive strategy. Needless to say, the grudging objectivity of I as a figure of merit can be embarrassing to proponents of "non-naive" models with $I > 1$.

ON EXTRAPOLATIVE BASELINES

In addition to the special naive forecast that next period's values will be the same as this period's value ($F_i = 0$) a number of other simple extrapolations are often used by forecasters as a way to judge the effectiveness of a proposed forecasting model. Three of the most common are:

$$Y_t = a + bY_{t-1} \qquad \text{(autoregressive)}$$
$$Y_t = a + bt \qquad \text{(time series)}$$
$$Y_t - Y_{t-1} = Y_{t-1} - Y_{t-2} \qquad \text{(same change)}$$

where Y is the variable to be forecast and t is an index of time. The first of these relies exclusively on serial regularity in the dependent variable. For data with important trends over time, this approach may provide a demanding standard for comparison. The second model projects the forecast variable as a linear function of time. This approach seems to be incorporated into a considerable amount of subjective-type forecasting, and offers a basis for comparison of model results with those of time-trend extrapolations. The third approach projects the forecasted change as equal to last period's change. This is one step removed from the original naive model that projected the forecasted *level* of Y at the previous level of Y.

Wide variations on these extrapolative models are possible. For example, one variant on the autoregressive scheme is to consider a weighted average of past Y values rather than only Y_{t-1} as follows:

$$Y_t = a + b \sum_{i=1}^{n} w_i Y_{t-i}$$

where n is the length of the lag period and w_i are weights. If the w_i are defined as exponentially declining in magnitude, this would provide an exponentially smoothed series as the basis for a linear extrapolation. On the other hand, if the w_i are all defined as equal to $\dfrac{1}{n}$, the $\sum_{i=1}^{n} w_i Y_{t-i}$ term becomes a moving average $\left(\dfrac{1}{n} \sum_{i=1}^{n} Y_{t-i}\right)$ and the projection becomes based on a projected moving average.

One important facet common among extrapolative techniques such as we have outlined is their absolute failure to predict turning points in an economic time series. They share the property of forecasting by extending a facet of the time trend in the forecast variable forward. This complicates their use as a standard of comparison. For while such baselines may perform as well as more extensive models during periods of continued expansion or contraction in the economic series, in some circumstances good forecasts may be far more important at the turning points of the series. In these cases, the baselines clearly yield no standard for comparison. Moreover, in cases where turning points are critical, such measures as Theil's inequality coefficient or average absolute errors of forecast may be misleading since they will count mid-expansion and mid-contraction performance as having equal weight as turning point performance, a procedure that will cause these figures of merit to favor the extrapolative models. Some forecasters explicity recognize the crucial nature of turning point forecasts by computing the number of correct turning points predicted by a proposed model over an historical period, and using this as an additional criterion by which their model may be judged.

Up to this point in the chapter our discussion has been concerned with techniques of constructing and evaluating forecasting models. We have seen that formulation of forecasting models constitutes an important area for application of the tools of regression analysis. It is now of interest to consider some major findings produced by empirical research with respect to reasonable structures and specifications of predictive models for various kinds of goods.

FORECASTING DEMAND FOR DURABLE GOODS

Durable goods are often defined as having useful lives of greater than one year. Consumer durables normally include automobiles, major home appliances, TV and electronic equipment, furniture, and the like. Producer durables consist of such things as machine tools, manufacturing and office equipment, and (for some purposes) new plant and office facilities. Residential buildings are somewhere between a consumer and a producer durable due to their special treatment by the U.S. income accounting system, which treats a residential structure as an investment-like expenditure, implying it is a producer's durable good. Yet, a home represents the largest most durable good purchased by consumers. Fortunately for our discussion, a clear categorization of housing is not crucial as we find many more similarities in the nature of consumer and producer durables than we find differences between them.

A Stock Adjustment Principle

One such similarity deals with the basic structure of durables prediction models. Many such models have found important statistical support for a stock adjustment framework, in which emphasis is placed on the relationship between actual holdings (or stocks) of a good and the desired holdings of that good. The basic behavioral thesis contained in the stock adjustment framework is that the actual change in holdings of a good can be usefully represented as a function of the difference between desired and actual stocks of the good. One commonly used form of the stock adjustment framework assumes that the actual change in holdings of the good will be a constant proportion of the difference between actual and desired holdings, as illustrated by the following expression:

$$K_t - K_{t-1} = W(K_t{}^* - K_{t-1}) \qquad (6\text{-}1)$$

where K_t, $K_t{}^*$ are respectively actual and desired holdings of the good at the end of period t and W is the constant adjustment coefficient. The left-hand side of (6-1) is increased by new expenditures on the good and is decreased by depreciation or depletion in existing stocks. In stock adjustment models such depreciation is often a significant contributor to changes in holdings of goods over time. To deal with this factor, it is often assumed that the volume of depreciation can be approximated as a constant fraction of the value of the holdings of the good. Symbolically, incorporating this assumption gives the following expression for the left-hand side of (6-1):

$$K_t - K_{t-1} = E_t - bK_{t-1} \qquad (6\text{-}2)$$

where E is the level of new expenditure on the good, b is the assumed constant rate of depreciation, and K is the stock of goods as before. Combining (6-1) and (6-2) gives:

$$E_t - bK_{t-1} = W(K_t{}^* - K_{t-1})$$

or:

$$E_t = W(K_t^* - K_{t-1}) + bK_{t-1} \qquad (6\text{-}3)$$

Expression (6–3) provides a framework for the prediction of E that assigns key roles to current holdings of the good and to those factors influencing the desired holdings of the good. To construct a forecasting model from this stock adjustment framework, it is necessary for the forecaster to build an explanatory model for K^* in terms of useful forecasting variables. This model might be of the following form:

$$K_t^* = C_0 + C_1 X_{1t} + C_2 X_{2t} \qquad (6\text{-}4)$$

wherein X_1 and X_2 are exogenous variables assumed to importantly determine desired holdings of the good.

One dominant feature of (6–4) is that usually the dependent variable K^* is unobservable, i.e., we do not normally have an available statistical series on desired holdings of a good. This means it will usually be impossible to directly test the empirical significance of (6–4) by econometric methods. Instead, we are left with only an indirect test of the significance of X_1 and X_2 as explanatory variables obtained through substitution of (6–4) into (6–3) as follows:

$$\begin{aligned} E_t &= W(C_0 + C_1 X_{1t} + C_2 X_{2t} - K_{t-1}) + bK_{t-1} \\ E_t &= WC_0 + WC_1 X_{1t} + WC_2 X_{2t} + (b - W)K_{t-1} \end{aligned} \qquad (6\text{-}5)$$

Assuming E, X_1, X_2, and K are observable, we may draw conclusions about the significance of both the stock adjustment framework and the choice of X_1 and X_2 as exogenous variables through analysis of the empirical results obtained from statistically estimating and evaluating (6–5). However, in this case we will not be able to obtain measures of the basic structural parameters W, C_0, C_1, C_2, and b. The estimates of the coefficients of 6–5) will in all cases be combinations of the basic parameters, and in this case their recovery is prohibited due to the existence of only four expressions in five unknowns.[4]

Some Illustrations

Our discussion has by now probably suggested that the stock adjustment framework can accommodate a wide variety of specific forecasting models. We now consider some specific applications of the stock adjustment principle in the formulation of models of durable goods demand.

---

[4] Restating (6–5) as follows:

$$E_t = K_0 + K_1 X_{1t} + K_2 X_{2t} + K_3 K_{t-1}$$

the four expressions are $K_0 = WC_0$, $K_1 = WC_1$, $K_2 = WC_2$, and $K_3 = b - W$. However, if we know one parameter a priori (such as the depreciation rate), it is then possible to solve for the remaining unknown w, C_0, C_1, and C_2 via these expressions.

First, a study of the demand for nonfarm housing by Richard F. Muth is a direct illustration of a predictive-type model employing our stock adjustment framework.[5] Muth presents the following final stock adjustment model:

$$h_g' = d(h_d - h) + kh$$

where

h_g' = per capita gross rate of housing construction
h_d = desired stock of housing
h = actual stock of housing

and d, k are stock adjustment and depreciation constants respectively.

This is seen to be almost identical with our earlier presented expression (6–3), except for Muth's use of the current rather than lagged stock of houses.

The essential determinants of the desired stock of housing were proposed to be long-run equilibrium price (p), per capita income (y), and the long-run equilibrium interest rates on mortgages (r), as follows:

$$h_d = b_0 + b_1 p + b_2 y + b_3 r$$

which produces Muth's model as follows:

$$h_g' = db_0 + db_1 p + db_2 y + db_3 r - (d - k)h$$

The coefficients of this model were estimated with data from 1915 to 1941 (excluding war years) by ordinary least-squares methods, producing the following equation:

$$h_g' = -2.49_p + 0.438 y_p - 8.34 r - 0.282 h$$
$$ (0.589) \quad (0.0919) \quad (4.47) \quad (0.0695)$$
$$R^2 = .621$$

where numbers in parentheses are standard errors of regression coefficient estimates.

As seen, all the coefficients in the equation appear to be significant statistically, providing positive evidence for both the stock adjustment framework and Muth's choice of the determinants of the desired stock of housing. Using the results of this regression as a baseline, differing alternative choices of explanatory variables for the desired stock of housing were explored. In general, Muth concluded that his original selection of explanatory variables was surely of fundamental importance, but possibly not exclusively important, indicating additional explanatory variables may lead to improved results.

[5] See Richard F. Muth, "The Demand for Non-Farm Housing," in *The Demand for Durable Goods*, Arnold C. Harberger (ed.) (Chicago: University of Chicago Press, 1960), pp. 29–98.

A second illustration of the application of stock adjustment concepts is provided by a study done by Gregory C. Chow of demand functions for automobiles and their use in forecasting.[6] In commenting on the framework to be used in his study, Chow states:

A salient feature of the demand for consumer durables in general, and for automobiles in particular, is that annual purchase is only a part of the total stock available for the satisfaction of wants. Purchase is made primarily to fill the gap between the quantity of total stock desired and the quantity of old stock remaining from the preceding period. In order to explain the demand for purchase therefore, the demand for desired stock will be first explained. By "desired stock" is meant that level of ownership which actual ownership will approach in the course of time, given that the determining variables remain unchanged. (p. 149)

In his study, Chow initially deals with several difficult problems of measurement, such as obtaining a meaningful measure of the stock of cars on the road. On this subject, the student is invited to read Chow's study as an illustration of the handling of such problems in actual predictive research. Chow proceeds to define the desired stock of automobiles during a particular year as follows:

$$\dot{X}_t = a + bP_t + cI_t + e$$

where

$\dot{X}_t$ = desired stock of automobiles for t^{th} year
P_t = automobile prices for t^{th} year
I_t = consumer incomes for t^{th} year
e = error term summarizing the combined effect of omitted influences.

The desired stock is related to new expenditures through two stock adjustment models. The first is as follows:

$$E_t = (\dot{X}_t - X_{t-1}) + (1 - k)X_{t-1}$$

where

E_t = new automobile expenditures (per capita)
$\dot{X}_t$ = desired stock per capita at year end
X_t = actual stock at year end
$(1 - k)$ = rate of replacement of existing stock.

In this expression, Chow points out that explanation of E is divided into two parts. The first $(\dot{X}_t - X_{t-1})$ is the demand for desired change in stock during the year; the second $(1 - k)X_{t-1}$ is the demand for replacement of old stock. In this model, no adjustment coefficient appears in front of the first term. This reflects Chow's first assumption that the

---

[6] Gregory C. Chow, "Statistical Demand Functions for Automobiles and Their Use in Forecasting," in Harberger (ed.) *The Demand for Durable Goods*, pp. 149–78.

process of adjustment toward desired levels will be entirely completed during year t ($\partial = 1$).

As a second more general version of the stock adjustment model, Chow considers the more conventional version of the stock adjustment model in which $0 < \partial < 1$ as follows:

$$E_t = \partial(\dot{X}_t - X_{t-1}) + (1 - k)X_{t-1}$$

which allows for the possibility the amount purchased in a year may be insufficient to keep the stock in equilibrium at the end of the year. Inserting the earlier expression into this framework gives:

$$E_t = \partial a + \partial bP_t + \partial cI_t + (1 - k - \partial)X_{t-1} + v$$

where $v = \partial e$. This version was fit statistically for data from 1921–1953, giving:

$$E_t = 0.07791 - 0.020127P_t + 0.011699I_t - 0.23104X_{t-1}$$
$$R^2 = 0.858$$

In addition, the equation was estimated with an alternative measure of income.

From previous evidence, Chow reasons the value of k is likely to be close to .75. Then, the empirical result enables an estimate of the adjustment coefficient ∂ as follows:

$$-0.23104 = (1 - .75 - \partial)$$
$$\partial \cong .48$$

This suggests that adjustment to new desired levels is quite incomplete over the course of a year, even when starting from an equilibrium position.

In his study, Chow presents various forecasting results, using an updated version of the model. These results only encompass a few forecasting points, but do suggest the model produces very reasonable conditional forecasts of automobile demand.

Time Lags

One aspect of the demand for durable goods discussed only indirectly so far through our adjustment coefficient is the time lag that often occurs between the point when purchase desirabilities are altered by economic influences and the time when actual expenditure changes occur. This lag is probably most pronounced in the case of plant and equipment expenditures by business, but occurs to a degree in the purchase of every durable. For a new plant, an increased inclination to invest in a new plant leads to corporate staff work and management decision making, soliciting bids, negotiating contracts, and awaiting completion of production and delivery. Analysts of plant and equipment have measured this lag period to be up to two years in duration. In the case of these expenditures in particular, considerable attention has been devoted to explicit measurement of the way in which past values of economically significant variables influence current expenditures. In general, forecasts of any durable good can be expected to profit from careful and explicit consideration of the lag with which relevant explanatory variables work their effects.

FORECASTING DEMAND FOR NONDURABLES OR SERVICES

A nondurable good is often defined as one that is used up relatively soon after purchase, say within a year or so. Items such as food, drink, soap, some clothing, and gasoline are examples of nondurables along with hundreds of other similar goods found on the shelves of grocery and variety stores. Services are similarly defined as products used up upon or very nearly upon purchase. Things like entertainment expenditures, medical and dental care, legal and professional services, recreational outlays, rental payments, and governmental programs are examples of the large number of purchases that fall in the services category.

Generally speaking, nondurables and services constitute the types of continued week-to-week purchases that most people think of when discussing an individual's or the economy's "standard of living." Many of these expenditures are programmed by contractual-type arrangements (i.e., rents, tennis club dues, six-month dental checks), while others are based on habits. This characteristic is an important factor in nondurable and service demand, for it imparts a "the more you get, the more you want" effect upon new expenditures. Past levels of expenditure set standards for minimum levels of current expenditure. Standards of consumption, once attained, become minimum benchmarks for new levels. This means that current consumption of nondurables and services may be expected to be importantly influenced in a positive direction by past levels of attained expenditure.

This attribute of nondurables and services is in direct contrast to the durable goods category. For durables, past expenditures add to the available stock of goods and by doing so contribute to a lessening of demand. As the existing stock of goods withers through depreciation, a new positive demand influence is generated. The effect has often been referred to as a maximum ownership level. Markets are seen as only prepared to absorb new units of a durable good at a rate that will keep the existing stock in line with desired levels. Thus, the final impact on new durables demand of previous outlays on durable goods is negative, *ceteris paribus*, which is exactly the opposite of our expectation about the effect of past nondurables and services expenditures on new demand.

In our earlier discussion of durables, no attempt was made to list general determinants of the desired stock of durables, and therefore of demand. This is due to the highly diverse set of factors that may be meaningful for predicting demand for specific durable goods. Indeed, continued review of empirical studies of the demand for durable goods offers no persuasive common denominator for the determination of desired durable holdings. Frequently found determinants of desired holdings include income measures, liquid-asset measures, price credit-conditions measures, and proxies for general economic expectations.[7]

In contrast to the diversity found in the determinants of the demand for durable goods, nondurables and services expenditures have overwhelmingly been found to be responsive to household income measures and to past expenditure patterns. Differences in the way income best explains expenditures have been found, as have differences in the length of the relevant past period of expenditures. But the pattern of empirical findings is strong enough to suggest that predictive models for nondurable goods or services not involving income and past expenditure measures cannot be expected to be of much predictive value.

The relevance of income measures to nondurables and services expenditures undoubtedly derives from these expenditures nearly all being made by consumers who in turn have been repeatedly found to set their consumption standards based on income levels. Indeed, differences in the specific way income has been used in various models has usually derived from differing hypotheses as to the consumer's response to income change. These hypotheses range from the simple assumption of a proportional response of demand to income change, to complex assumptions of an assimilation period applicable to unusual periods of income change during which consumption habits adjust to the altered income flow or to the consumer's altered view of income flow.

Similarly, differences usually found in the role of past expenditure patterns in influencing current expenditures have involved such questions as whether the most recent past should be given more weight than the more distant past, or how many past periods contribute to the influence on current expenditures.

Finally, variables such as relative prices and consumer liquid assets have been found by some analysts to importantly contribute to the explanation of nondurables and services expenditures along with income and past expenditure measures. Thus, our focus on these latter two variables should not imply their use in forecasting models is exclusive of other variables.

---

[7] For a good discussion, see Michael K. Evans, *Macroeconomic Activity: Theory, Forecasting, and Control* (New York: Harper and Row, 1969), especially Chapters 4 and 6.

Some Illustrations

The ideas now discussed may be sharpened by reference to some examples of predictive models for nondurable and service type goods.

First, a simple illustration of a predictive model for total U.S. expenditures on nondurable goods is provided by an equation taken from a quarterly 36-equation simultaneous model of the national economy developed by a team of econometricians for use in the U.S. Department of Commerce's Office of Business Economics.[8] Based on post-World War II data, this equation was estimated as follows:

$$C_n = 31.1 + .252Y_r + .210 \frac{1}{8} \sum_{i=-1}^{-8} (C_n)_i \qquad R^2 = .995$$

where

C_n = constant dollar expenditures on nondurables
Y_r = disposable income, constant dollars

As seen, consumer income enters this model in a current linear fashion, assuming no assimilation period or no period of expectational adjustment to income change. The influence of past expenditures is assumed to be via a simple eight-quarter moving average of past expenditures. Thus, although quite simple, the Commerce Department equation produces a high R^2 and apparently satisfied the group of researchers who formulated the model as to its worthiness as a predictive tool.

Second, a contrast is provided by the more complex predictive equation for nondurables and services developed for use in the Wharton model by M. K. Evans and L. R. Klein.[9] The Wharton model is a quarterly 47-equation simultaneous model of the U.S. economy that has been in continuous widespread use for forecasting since the early 1960s. Due to a series of statistical problems, the authors decided to predict the ratio of nondurables and services expenditures to disposable income, rather than the level of expenditures directly. Estimated with data from 1948 to 1964, their equation is as follows:

$$\frac{C_{ns}}{Y} = 0.2273 - 0.4590 \left[\frac{\Delta Y}{Y} + 0.75 \left(\frac{\Delta Y}{Y} \right)_{-1} + 0.50 \left(\frac{\Delta Y}{Y} \right)_{-2} \right.$$
$$\left. + 0.25 \left(\frac{\Delta Y}{Y} \right)_{-3} \right] + 0.7232 \frac{1}{4} \sum_{i=1}^{4} \left(\frac{C_{ns}}{Y} \right)_{-i} \qquad R^2 = .825$$

---

[8] For a complete description of this model, see *The Survey of Current Business* (Washington, D.C.: U.S. Government Printing Office, May 1966), pp. 1–35.

[9] See Evans, "Computer Simulation," pp. 429–42.

where

C_{ns} = nondurable and services expenditures, constant dollars
Y = disposable personal income, constant dollars
ΔY = change in Y from previous quarter

As seen, the income term of the Wharton equation is considerably more complicated than our earlier illustration, involving the current rate of change in disposable income ($\Delta Y/Y$) and three past quarterly rates of income change, each assigned a reduced weight. This scheme reflects the assumption that recent income patterns rather than current levels are more pertinent to expenditures. Moreover, the specific thesis behind this formulation is that consumers must begin to view changes in income flow as permanent before they will adjust their consumption patterns accordingly.[10] Operationally, the effect of the specific income term employed is to make expenditures a function of a four-quarter smoothed income series rather than a raw income series, thus reducing the responsiveness of expenditure-income ratios on short-term income fluctuations. It is interesting to note the measured coefficient on the income term has a negative sign. This stipulates that increasing *rates* of change in disposable income associate with falling *ratios* of nondurables and service outlays to income, thus further emphasizing the author's assumed nonproportional response of expenditures to current and short-run income change.

The past expenditure term in the Wharton equation is similar to the Commerce Department illustration in proposing a moving average of past expenditure-income ratios as a measure of the effect of consumption standards. In this case, only four quarters are chosen for this average rather than the eight terms in the previous case.

A third illustration of predictive models of nondurables and services as well as consumer durables is provided by a study undertaken by H. S. Houthakker and L. D. Taylor of consumer demand in the United States.[11] In this study, the authors dissected total consumer goods into 83 separate durable and nondurable categories and fit a stock adjustment-type model to each category separately. In this model, desired holdings or purchases were proposed to be basically a function of consumer incomes. The stock adjustment mechanism also suggested an explanatory role for existing stocks of goods. The basic equation formulated was:

$$q_t = a + bS_t + cx_t \qquad (6\text{-}6)$$

---

[10] The idea has been discussed by T. M. Brown, "Habit Persistence and Lags in Consumer Behavior," *Econometrica*, vol. 20, no. 3, pp. 355–71 and more fully explored by M. Friedman, *A Theory of the Consumption Function* (New York: NBER, 1957).

[11] See H. S. Houthakker, and L. D. Taylor, *Consumer Demand in the United States, 1929–1970* (Cambridge, Mass.: Harvard University Press, 1966).

where

q_t = constant dollar expenditures
S_t = measure of consumption standard (nondurables, services) or existing stocks of goods (durables)
x_t = consumer incomes

The stock-of-goods variable (S_t) is of particular interest. For durables, this was proposed to measure the negative saturation effect of existing stocks on current demand. In contrast, for nondurables and services it was taken to reflect consumption standards, thus having a positive impact on current demand. Measurement of existing stocks in all 83 diverse consumption categories presented a substantial problem to the researchers. They began by formulating the identity

$$dS_t = q_t - w_t$$

where dS_t stands for a very small change in the physical or psychological stock over a very small time interval t, q_t is new purchases during t, and w_t stands for the average using up or depreciation of the stock over t. Next, the depreciation was assumed to be an approximately constant proportion of the stock of goods, f, giving:

$$dS_t = q_t - fS_t \qquad (6\text{--}7)$$

To eliminate the usually nonmeasurable S_t term from this expression, the original forecasting equation (6–6) may be solved for S_t as follows:

$$S_t = \frac{1}{b}[q_t - a - cx_t]$$

This expression may now be substituted in for the S_t term in (6–7), giving:

$$dS_t = q_t - \frac{f}{b}[q_t - a - cx_t] \qquad (6\text{--}8)$$

Next, Houthakker and Taylor formulate a "first-differences" version of (6–6). This can be derived by first lagging (6–6) by one of our very small time periods as follows:

$$q_{t-1} = a + bS_{t-1} + cx_{t-1}$$

and then subtracting this lagged expression from the original, which gives:

$$q_t - q_{t-1} = a - a + b(S_t - S_{t-1}) + c(x_t - x_{t-1})$$

or

$$dq_t = bdS_t + cdx_t$$

The earlier developed expression for dS_t, (6–8), may now be substituted into this differenced expression, giving:

$$dq_t = b\left[q_t - \frac{f}{b}(q_t - a - cx_t) \right] + cdx_t$$

or

$$dq_t = bq_t - fq_t + fa + fcx_t + cdx_t$$

or

$$dq_t = fa + (b - f)q_t + fcx_t + cdx_t \qquad (6–9)$$

Expression (6–9) expresses a very small change in quantity demanded over a very small period of time to be a function of the existing level of demand, the level of income, and the change in income over t. This formulation is an interesting dynamic expression for demand. However, its formulation over a very short time period does not coincide with the longer time periods (typically quarters) over which actual data occur on incomes and expenditures. Thus, estimates of the coefficients of (6–9) cannot be found. Therefore, the researchers were led to develop an approximation to (6–9), which is reasonable given the quarterly data available to them for estimation.

This approximation proceeds along the same lines as the original model with nearly identical expressions to (6–6) and (6–7) developed. Subsequent algebraic manipulations and a numerical approximation led to elimination of the instantaneous-change aspects of the original model and produced a model of the following form for statistical estimation:[12]

$$q_t = A_0 + A_1q_{t-1} + A_2x_t + A_3x_{t-1} \qquad (6–10)$$

which is a quarterly approximation and algebraic transformation of (6–9). Variable definitions are as before, but t subscripts now are understood to refer to quarterly periods rather than very short periods. In addition, x_t refers to the change in x from quarter to quarter.

Expression (6–10) is appropriately described as the reduced form of the original equation:

$$q_t = a + bS_t + cx_t \qquad (6–6a)$$

where, as above, t now is quarterly periods.

The researchers obtain estimates of a, b, and c by estimating the parameters A_0, A_1, A_2, and A_3 by regression methods and then solving the reduced-form expressions:[13]

---

[12] For details, see Houthakker and Taylor, *ibid.*, pp. 11–14.

$$a = \frac{2A_0(A - \frac{1}{2}A_3)}{A_3(A_1 + 1)}$$

$$b = \frac{2(A_1 - 1)}{A_1 + 1} + \frac{A_3}{A_2 - \frac{1}{2}A_3}$$

$$c = \frac{2(A_2 - \frac{1}{2}A_3)}{A_1 + 1}$$

Estimates of equation (6–10) were obtained for each of the 83 categories of consumption and from the estimated A coefficients, values of a, b, and c, were calculated from the above expressions.[14] Forecasts were also made from the estimated equation (6–10) for periods up to 1970 (four years beyond the data). Changes in some income accounting definitions since 1966 make these results somewhat difficult to interpret, as does the authors' assumption of specific baseline income figures (round numbers). However, one result of interest in light of our earlier discussion of the role of stocks of goods on expenditures is the estimated coefficient on the stock variable in the structural equation (6–6a).

Table 6–1 lists the 83 categories for which estimated equations were presented along with the sign of the b coefficient attached to the stock variable in the structural equation. The results correspond to our expectations of a negative b-value in clear-cut durables categories such as (49) New Cars and Net Purchase of Used Cars, (20) Furniture, and (23) Other Durable Home Furnishings as for all we would anticipate a saturation effect. Similarly, the positive sign measured for (15) Barbershops, Beauty Parlors, Baths, (1) Alcoholic Beverages, (33) Other Household Operations, and (38) Professional Services are clear-cut examples of a standard-of-living effect of past expenditures. The measured properties of other not-so-clear categories are also interesting. For example, (41) Funeral and Burial Expense is seen as a durable in that good years for the grim reaper beget bad years. This probably reflects the stable time pattern of deaths over the long run.

GENERALIZATIONS ON FORECASTING MODELS

In the final analysis, Professor Klein is probably right in his statement that the best forecasts will come from the best structural models. As

---

[13] See Chapter 4 for details of this procedure.

[14] In addition, the authors added prices as an explanatory variable on the grounds that it served to specify the *ceteris paribus* condition. Because its use was completely ad hoc to their basic model, we have not shown that variable. It would merely be added to (6–1a).

TABLE 6–1. Stock Effects for Consumer Goods

	(b) Effect of past spending		(b) Effect of past spending
1. Alcoholic Beverages	+	46. Legal Services	+
2. Carry-out Food	+	47. Interest on Personal Debt	+
3. Purchased Meals	+	48. Other Personal Business Expense	NC*
4. Food Furnished Government	−	49. New Cars and Net Purchase of Used Cars	−
5. Food Produced/Consumed on Farms	NC	50. Tires, Tubes, Accessories, and Parts	−
6. Tobacco Products	+	51. Automobile Repair, Servicing, etc.	+
7. Shoes and Other Footwear	NC	52. Gasoline and Oil	+
8. Shoe Cleaning and Repairs	+	53. Bridge, Tunnel, Ferry, and Road Tolls	+
9. Clothing, including Luggage	−	54. Auto Insurance Premiums	+
10. Uniforms for Military Personnel	+	55. Street and Electric Railway and Local Bus	NC*
11. Laundering in Establishments	+	56. Taxicabs	−
12. Jewelry and Watches	+	57. Railway	+
13. Other Clothing, Accessories, etc.	−	58. Intercity Railway	+
14. Toilet Articles and Preparations	+	59. Intercity Bus	+
15. Barbershops, Beauty Parlors, Baths	+	60. Airline Travel	+
16. Rental Value of Owner-Occupied Housing	+	61. Other Intercity Transportation	NC*
17. Rental Value of Tenant-Occupied Housing	+	62. Books and Maps	+
18. Rental Value of Farm Houses	+	63. Newspapers and Magazines	NC*
19. Other Housing	+	64. Nondurable Toys	+
20. Furniture	−	65. Wheel Goods, Durable Toys, Sports Goods	+
21. Kitchen and Other Appliances	NC	66. Radio and TV Receivers, Records, etc.	+
22. China, Glassware, Tableware	+	67. Radio and TV Repair	NC*
23. Other Durable House Furnishings	−	68. Flowers, Seeds, and Potted Plants	+
24. Semidurable House Furnishings	−	69. Motion Pictures	+
25. Cleaning, Polishing, and Household Supplies	+	70. Legitimate Theater and Opera	+
26. Stationery	+	71. Spectator Sports	NC*
27. Electricity	+	72. Clubs and Fraternal Orgs.	−
28. Gas (household)	+	73. Commercial Participant Amusements	+
29. Water	−	74. Parimutuel Receipts	+
30. Other Fuel and Ice	−	75. Other Recreation	+
31. Telephone, Telegraph	+	76. Higher Education	−
32. Domestic Services	−	77. Elementary & Secondary Education	+
33. Other Household Operation	+	78. Other Educational Expense	+
34. Drugs and Sundries	+	79. Religious and Welfare Expenditures	−
35. Ophthalmic Products	+	80. Foreign Travel by U.S. Residents	+
36. Physicians	−	81. Expenditures Abroad by U.S. Government Personnel	+
37. Dentists	+	82. Net Personal Cash Remittances Abroad	NC*
38. Other Professional Services	+	83. Expenditures in U.S. by Foreign Residents	NC*
39. Private Hospitals, Sanitariums	+		
40. Medical Care, Hospitalization	+		
41. Funeral and Burial Expense	−		
42. Brokerage Charges, etc.	NC*		
43. Bank Service Charges	+		
44. Services of Financial Intermediaries	+		
45. Expense of Handling Life Insurance	+		

* Not computed.

Source: Taken from Houthakker and Taylor, *Consumer Demand in the U.S., 1929–1970* (Cambridge, Mass.: Harvard University Press, 1966). The plus or minus refers to the sign of the coefficient on the "stock-of goods" variable in the structural equation.

forecasters, we should accept this principle. But we should not confuse best with complex. In our illustrations, we have moved from very simple to reasonably complex model structures, with the Houthakker-Taylor study an example of the latter. This complexity may aid in prediction if it moves us toward the true approximating model structure. But it may add nothing or even detract from our predictions if it moves in a different direction.

Since there is no way presently known to make a definitive test of whether an alteration in model structure leads in the direction of the true structure or not, enlightened forecasters live with the assumption that their structural problem is not completely solved.

Unfortunately, incorrectly specified models may predict for particular periods of time in which omitted structural components are inactive or unimportant or where inappropriately included variables work no havoc with results. Such periods cause some forecasters to lose interest in questions of underlying structure in favor of reduced forms of unknown systems that "work." When these periods pass, the unacceptable nature of forecasting results usually sparks renewed interest in structural questions. This pattern suggests the approach too often followed of picking a potful of variables having some intuitive association with the forecast variable and combining them in a reduced-form equation to maximize goodness-of-fit over the sample period can be recommended as a sure road to eventual forecasting disaster.

This chapter has discussed the subject of economic forecasting as one fertile area for joint application of the tools of econometrics and the ideas of economic theory. Another such area is the analysis of production relationships in the firm. In the next chapter our attention turns to this topic.

DISCUSSION QUESTIONS

1. Distinguish between a demand curve and a demand forecasting equation.

2. What is the difference between a conditional and an unconditional forecast?

3. You are assigned the job of developing a forecasting model for furniture. Use the framework developed in the discussion of durable goods and specific ideas drawn from the illustrative examples to formulate a reasonable model. Outline a procedure for testing and evaluating this model.

4. Explain in your own words the difference that patterns of past expenditures usually have upon current expenditures on durables as opposed to nondurables.

5. What is the solved structure of a demand forecasting model? How does it compare with the first-stage equations in a two-stage estimation procedure?

CASE 5—ENCORE BREWING COMPANY

The Encore Brewing Company produced a bottom-of-the-line variety of beer that sold at 10 to 20 percent less than most other brands. Over the years, the Encore company had clearly staked out this end of the product line and had successfully kept other competitors out through a combination of unconventional advertising, an insistence on lower shelf prices than other makes, and hard-nosed dealings with their merchandisers. Examples of recent Encore's advertising slogans are:

1. "We don't sell the best beer—but we're cheap."
2. "Encore beer—friend of the Proletariat."
3. "After the first one, only your wallet will know it's Encore."
4. "More belch for your buck with Encore."
5. "Buy Encore and support ecology. Plant a tree with the money you save."

The firm's approach had led to widespread acceptance among college students and younger citizens, resulting in a rapid rise in sales for the past decade. To some in the company, the rise was too fast. Company policy never seemed to be explicit, and lines of authority were ill-defined. Communication was often unacceptably poor. Fortunately, work was under way in several areas to solve, or at least reduce, critical management problems.

One such area was sales and profit forecasting. The firm maintained a monthly profit and loss statement upon which it based crucial operating decisions. Among the decisions regularly influenced by the monthly statement were: (a) product price, (b) marketing budgets, (c) production levels, and (d) inventory position.

The whipsaw pattern of these decisions over the recent past made clear a need for a near-term projected outlook to serve as a backdrop for current decision making in categories a to d. More specifically, if each month's figures were accompanied by a reasonably accurate six-month projection of the income statement, the decisions could be made in such a way to "smooth" the now existing peaks and valleys in the variables involved, and probably lead to increased efficiency in the use of the funds involved, particularly for advertising programs and in scheduling production.

Two of the company's analytical-type junior staffers were assigned the job of producing this six-month forecast. The first, Leo Lippe, was a recent MBA graduate who had only been with the firm a short time. The second, John Ammerman, had been employed somewhat longer as an economic analyst. His background included an MA in economics.

There was quick agreement among the two that some type of econometric model was probably appropriate to the situation, primarily due to the repetitive nature of the forecast. Management's idea was to have an updated six-month-ahead projection every month for the income statement.

One of the first questions the analysts considered was how their proposed forecasting model would be structured. Leo Lippe produced a list of accounts similar to Figure 6–3 and said, "Why not have an equation explaining each line in this statement?"

Ammerman replied, "Just hold it, OK? Before we get locked into anything like that, I want to take a closer look at the statement."

FIGURE 6–3
Income Statement Format

Line	Item	
1	Net Sales	XXX
2	Cost of Goods Sold	*XXX*
3	Gross Margin	XXX
	Other Expenses	
4	Sales Promotion Expense	XXX
5	Advertising Expense	XXX
6	Other Marketing Expense	*XXX*
7	Total Marketing Expense	XXX
8	General and Administrative Expense	XXX
9	Earnings from Operations	XXX

The two analysts agreed that a close look at the statement was likely to yield productive results. They proceeded to make a careful line-by-line analysis of the income statement, noting points they felt were pertinent to the model construction. The first point they agreed upon was that since net sales is a product of unit sales and price, and since price is one of the variables management wants to control, the prediction would have to be made on unit sales and converted to dollars. Secondly, they observed that the ratios of sales promotion expense and advertising expense to total marketing expense have remained largely stable over the past several years. In the analyst's opinion this was probably due to the highly simplistic budgetary policies of Harold Hunsaker, the director of marketing. He typically gave a constant piece of the budgetary "pie" to each of his departments.

Upon reflection on this point, Ammerman threw down his pencil and began pacing slowly in front of his desk. "Hunsaker's approach makes about as much sense as choosing secretaries on the basis of bustlines," grumbled Ammerman.

"He does that too, I hear," said Lippe. "But the point is, we are trying to forecast at this point, and policies like Hunsaker's have to be accounted for, whether we like them or not."

"Actually," said Ammerman, "the old fool has simplified our job. We can focus our prediction on total marketing expenditures and just employ his ratios to get back to advertising, sales promotion, and other expense."

"Just great," said Lippe. "And what happens when he changes his ratios?"

"Then we change ours," said Ammerman.

Lippe didn't like it; but, having nothing better to offer, he accepted this concept.

The two analysts now turned their attention to relationships between marketing expenditures and sales. One thing they completely agreed upon was that marketing expenditures were effective in generating sales. A plot of the data showed a perceptible (though not stable) changes in sales in the month following a change in marketing outlays. Occasionally, an effect was apparent for longer periods. The effect seemed generally to wear off rather rapidly, however. As Ammerman put it, "Our level of marketing expense must be an explanatory factor in predicting upcoming unit sales. If it isn't, our company is wasting one hellava lot of money on these programs."

On the other hand, the two noted what seemed to be an unwritten policy that marketing expenditures were not to exceed a certain percentage of gross margin. The main reason for this policy was apparently to buffer net profits from downward movements in gross margins by partially offsetting declines in marketing expense.

This connection between gross margins and marketing expense was particularly interesting to the analysts, since it suggested that sales and marketing expenses were jointly related. As marketing budgets were enlarged, sales normally rose, producing a larger gross margin and thus enabling further enlargements in marketing expenses.

The two analysts felt this simultaneous view of sales and marketing expense was intriguing. At the same time, they were concerned as to how well it fit with the intuition of the company's marketing personnel. At this point, Lippe volunteered to spend some time visiting with key marketing people on the subject.

Upon his return, Lippe reported complete agreement among marketing managers as to the importance of gross margin in setting marketing budgets, and upon the importance of marketing budgets in producing sales. However, they also pointed out that marketing budgets almost always responded to recent changes in market share. While it was reportedly difficult to sell top management on an increase in marketing budgets when market share was increasing, it was equally easy to obtain larger marketing budgets when market share declined. When questioned as to the specific meaning of "recent changes," the most frequent responses was that last month's market share counted the most in this month's decisions.

In the meetings with the marketing personnel, Lippe had come across two other ideas he felt were helpful. Both dealt with predictions of unit sales. When he inquired as to basic determinants of the demand for beer, population in the 21 to 35 age group and the index of industrial production were two statistical series commonly used by the department for forward planning. The latter was thought to have an inverse relationship by most salesmen, who had a rule of thumb that beer sales rose in recessions and fell in expansions, other things being equal. Some salesmen, noting their own behavior when commissions were low, called beer "the scotch drinker's retreat."

Prediction of cost of goods sold was the next problem faced by the analysts. Ammerman produced calculations showing that unit costs had shown almost no trend over the past few years, although they tended to rise above and fall below their average value with no particular pattern. On the basis of these data, the two analysts decided to represent cost of production as a simple linear function of sales.

Finally, the analysts considered the prediction of general and administrative expenses. These expenses consisted of general management salaries, interest, property taxes, utilities, and several other overhead-type charges. Lippe had just finished plotting these costs as a function of sales. In commenting on the results, Ammerman said, "Fixed costs, hell. These go up and down with sales."

"Well," said Lippe, "I imagine the reason is that management authorizes more of these kinds of fixed costs when sales are rising and orders them cut out when sales are falling."

"Right," said Ammerman. "So we should probably use sales to predict our fixed costs."

"I agree," said Lippe. "But I wish you'd stop calling them fixed. By definition, they are not."

"Aw, shuddup," said Ammerman. "You sound like my old econ professor."

While Ammerman rambled on about his former economics professor, Lippe quickly calculated the ratio of general and administrative expense to sales for the recent past.

He broke into Ammerman's discourse: "The ratio has steadily risen," he announced.

"What the hell are you talking about?" said Ammerman.

"The ratio of these expenses to sales is rising. See for yourself. We need another variable to account for the rise."

Ammerman lurched forward to see Lippe's worksheet. "How about a simple index of time?" he said.

"It's worth a try," said Lippe.

At this point, the two analysts began to collect data on all the pertinent variables that their deliberations had suggested might be relevant to the problem at hand, producing the battery of information shown in Appendix 6-A.

Questions

1. Formulate a forecasting model for the monthly profit and loss statement, using the ideas and findings of Lippe and Ammerman.
2. Outline a complete plan for estimating and testing this model.
3. Use the data of Appendix 6-A to estimate the model for the data period January, 1969 through June, 1971. Evaluate your results.
4. Prepare a forecast with your model of the income statement for the last six months of 1971. Is the forecast any good?

Appendix 6-A: Encore Brewing Company

TABLE 6–2
Population 21–35 Age Group (index 1968 = 100)

	1969	1970	1971
J.......	101.2	102.8	105.0
F......	101.3	103.0	105.1
M.....	101.3	103.3	105.3
A......	101.5	103.4	105.6
M......	101.7	103.6	105.9
J.......	101.8	103.8	106.2
J.......	102.0	104.1	106.1
A......	102.1	104.2	106.2
S......	102.2	104.3	106.3
O......	102.5	104.5	106.4
N......	102.6	104.7	106.4
D......	102.8	104.9	106.5–e

e = estimated

TABLE 6–3
Index of Industrial Production (1967 = 100)

	1969	1970	1971
J.......	108.4	107.4	105.3
F......	109.7	108.0	105.7
M.....	110.3	107.6	105.5
A......	110.2	107.5	106.2
M.....	110.2	107.5	107.0
J.......	110.8	107.6	107.2
J.......	111.5	107.5	106.1
A......	111.4	107.5	104.8
S......	111.9	106.5	105.3
O......	111.7	103.7	105.7–e
N......	110.3	102.6	106.2–e
D......	109.9	104.6	106.8–e

e = estimated

TABLE 6–4
Company Sales

	1969			1970			1971		
	Units (thousands)	Average price	Dollar sales (thousands)	Units (thousands)	Average price	Dollar sales (thousands)	Units (thousands)	Average price	Dollar sales (thousands)
J..........	30.1	15.10	454.8	29.2	15.00	437.4	32.6	15.40	502.3
F..........	29.6	15.10	447.1	31.8	15.00	476.7	31.3	15.40	481.6
M..........	26.6	15.20	404.2	32.2	15.05	484.9	30.9	15.45	478.1
A..........	27.5	15.30	421.2	30.2	15.05	455.2	32.8	15.50	508.6
M..........	29.9	15.10	451.3	29.6	15.10	447.0	33.4	15.40	514.3
J..........	28.1	15.10	423.8	31.7	15.10	479.2	32.1	15.40	494.1
J..........	29.5	15.00	442.1	31.9	15.10	482.2	32.0	15.45	494.5
A..........	31.0	15.00	464.8	30.2	15.15	457.5	33.5	15.50	519.1
S..........	28.2	15.00	423.3	32.8	15.15	497.6	34.7	15.50	537.6
O..........	27.6	14.95	413.0	32.9	15.30	503.0	32.9	15.55	511.5
N..........	30.7	14.95	458.4	30.6	15.30	467.7	35.4	15.60	551.6
D..........	30.9	14.90	460.3	29.4	15.35	450.6	33.8–e	15.60–e	526.9–e

e = estimated

TABLE 6–5
Industry Sales and Market Share

	1969		1970		1971	
	Industry (thousand units)	Encore's share	Industry (thousand units)	Encore's share	Industry (thousand units)	Encore's share
J..........	734.6	.041*	560.8	.052	572.3	.057
F..........	722.1	.041	623.1	.051	548.7	.057
M..........	618.4	.043	644.3	.050	533.6	.058
A..........	611.8	.045	617.3	.049	556.2	.059
M..........	649.7	.046	569.3	.052	521.8	.064
J..........	623.6	.045	622.2	.051	509.3	.063
J..........	669.8	.044	638.6	.050	533.5	.060
A..........	688.6	.045	603.9	.050	558.1	.060
S..........	575.9	.049	597.1	.055	542.0	.064
O..........	521.3	.053	566.8	.058	483.7	.068
N..........	601.2	.051	536.2	.057	520.0	.068
D..........	630.5	.049	542.2	.056	489.5–e	.069–e

* Calculated by dividing Encore's Unit Sales from Table 6–4 by Industry Unit Sales
e = estimated

TABLE 6–6
Cost of Goods Sold (thousands)

	1969	1970	1971
J.......	272.3	261.7	301.0
F.......	268.6	286.4	289.6
M.....	243.5	291.5	287.1
A......	251.9	273.2	304.9
M....	270.6	267.8	308.2
J.......	255.0	288.4	296.6
J.......	266.2	290.0	296.7
A......	278.6	274.7	311.5
S......	255.1	297.5	322.0
O......	248.4	302.4	306.7
N......	274.9	280.2	331.4
D.....	276.5	270.6	316.6–e

e = estimated

TABLE 6–7
Industry Advertising Levels (index 1967 = 100)

	1969	1970	1971
J..........	1.10	1.22	1.22
F..........	1.14	1.20	1.21
M........	1.16	1.18	1.21
A........	1.18	1.16	1.23
M........	1.20	1.15	1.25
J..........	1.25	1.14	1.27
J..........	1.30	1.15	1.29
A........	1.20	1.16	1.29
S........	1.20	1.17	1.30
O........	1.21	1.20	1.30
N........	1.20	1.21	1.29
D........	1.22	1.23	1.31–e

e = estimated

TABLE 6-8
Encore's Gross Margin (thousands)

	1969	1970	1971
J	182.5	175.7	201.3
F	178.4	190.3	192.1
M	160.7	193.3	191.1
A	169.3	182.0	203.7
M	180.7	179.2	206.1
J	168.8	190.8	197.6
J	175.9	192.1	197.8
A	186.2	182.8	207.5
S	168.2	200.0	215.7
O	164.6	200.6	204.8
N	183.5	187.5	220.2
D	183.8	180.1	210.3–e

e = estimated

TABLE 6-9
Encore's Marketing Expense (thousands)

	1969	1970	1971
J	36.1	37.4	41.1
F	34.4	39.3	40.4
M	32.1	39.1	40.8
A	34.4	37.9	41.2
M	36.6	37.4	42.5
J	34.6	38.7	42.7
J	35.1	38.8	42.0
A	36.9	37.5	43.7
S	33.5	40.4	44.2
O	34.4	41.4	43.7
N	38.3	39.5	47.0
D	37.7	38.7	44.9–e

e = estimated

TABLE 6-10
Encore's General and Administrative Expense (thousands)

	1969	1970	1971
J	69.8	91.9	126.1
F	71.3	99.6	124.1
M	66.3	102.6	125.7
A	71.6	99.8	132.6
M	77.9	101.5	134.7
J	75.1	107.7	134.0
J	80.5	110.4	136.0
A	85.3	107.3	142.6
S	81.2	116.5	146.9
O	82.5	119.9	144.6
N	91.2	116.3	152.9
D	92.8	115.6	151.3–e

e = estimated

TABLE 6–11
Encore's Net Profits*

TABLE 6–12
Industry Liquor Sales (index 1967 = 100)

	1969	1970	1971		1969	1970	1971
J.........	76.6	46.3	34.1	J.......	103.0	102.4	100.5
F.........	72.8	51.3	27.5	F......	104.1	103.0	100.7
M........	62.2	51.6	24.6	M.....	105.5	102.6	100.5
A.........	63.3	44.3	30.0	A......	105.4	102.5	101.4
M........	66.2	40.4	28.9	M.....	105.5	102.6	102.0
J.........	59.1	44.4	20.8	J.......	106.0	102.6	102.3
J.........	60.3	42.9	19.9	J.......	106.2	102.5	104.0
A.........	64.0	37.9	21.2	A......	106.4	102.5	106.2
S.........	53.5	43.1	24.5	S......	107.0	101.5	109.3
O.........	47.8	39.4	16.5	O......	106.7	98.7	111.0
N.........	54.0	31.6	20.3	N......	105.3	97.6	111.1
D.........	53.3	25.8	14.0–e	D......	104.9	99.8	111.7–e

* Equal to gross margin minus marketing expense minus general and administrative expense

e = estimated

e = estimated

CASE 6—THE MARIONETTE STATE MANAGEMENT GAME

Marionette State, a small Midwestern university, recently acquired a computerized packaged management game for use in connection with their MBA program. The game attempts to simulate real-world activity based on decisions about price, production, marketing, and finance policies and about overall corporation resource allocation. These decisions are made by competing teams of students. Each team functions as the executive head of a competing firm in a particular industry. The industry represented in the game is the packaged soap industry, with a number of firms engaged in the production and sale of detergent to wholesalers, who in turn sell to retailers. The industry exhibits a strong seasonal demand with peak sales occurring during the summer months. Upon initially using the game, the school found certain aspects to be highly unrealistic. Accordingly, various adaptions were made to enable the game to more closely mirror the real world. In one such modification, they utilized actual time-series data, such as population trends and income patterns to establish the prevailing economic and market conditions in the industry. On the other hand, the small enrollment in the MBA program limited the total industry to only two firms.

In the most recent six months of the game's operation, an interesting contrast developed between the two firms in the simulated industry. Firm 2 quickly routinized its decision process, kept its team meetings short and delegated decision-making responsibility entirely to the president's immediate staff. In contrast, Firm 1 developed a loosely-structured committee-type format for their executive actions, where the individual or individuals with the most factual or intellectual artillery determined the decision. Most notably this democratic process produced shifting strategies and often inconsistent decisions resulting in declining sales and loss of market share.

Bob Dude, president of Firm 1, called a team meeting to attempt to remedy the current situation. "Gentlemen," he began, "I've always felt that a democracy only works in a textbook, and now I'm convinced of it. From now on, all decisions will be channeled through me, and I will have the final vote on all decisions. The starting point obviously is an accurate sales forecast," Dude said. "The rest of our decisions will follow in a routine manner from that." Dude pointed to the simulated firm's chief financial officer, John Ammerman. "You do the forecast," he said. "Impossible" replied Ammerman. This exchange promoted a lengthy and far-ranging discussion of student responsibilities, school policy, and concepts of equity among team members. Finally, Ammerman agreed he would attempt to come up with a sales forecast since he could use the results in a seminar in econometrics he was taking, thereby killing two academic birds with one stone. He decided to start with the player's manual that came with the game.

"Hmmmm, here's something interesting," he thought as he began reading. "Actual historical time series have been incorporated into the game to enable analysis of past patterns. Maybe these could be incorporated into a predictive model using econometric methods." Reflecting upon the simulated industry involved, he decided to incorporate an index of dry cleaning into this analysis. He felt the more clothes that required dry cleaning, the less soap sales would be. In addition, he felt that some other series such as population, disposable income, or time should be included, although he wasn't sure which ones. Reading on further, he thought, "It appears that our sales and Firm 2's are dependent on each other, although our marketing expense also affects our share of the market. Our marketing expense, however, is partly determined by what our sales are and by the amount of funds available within the firm at the start of the month. In turn, the funds on hand at the start of the month correspond to the cash generated in the previous months." Similar statements, he noted, could be made from Firm 2's standpoint. This was something of a chilling thought, as it implied that in order to forecast his firm's sales, he may need his marketing expense and his available funds, as well as his competitor's sales. But, if his competitor's sales were similarily influenced, this meant he would need their available funds and marketing to forecast their sales. "This could get complicated fast," thought Ammerman, as he quickly dismissed the idea and went on to an easier aspect of the problem. A way was needed to represent available funds. Ammerman decided to use the following expression for the amount of funds readily available and uncommitted within the firm at any one time. Denoting this flow of Discretionary Cash as *IF*, it derives as follows:

$$IF = \text{Sales} - \text{Production Costs} - \text{Taxes} - \text{Dividends}$$

Ammerman proceeded to compile series of data that he felt might be relevant to his analysis. (See Appendix 6–B.) The source of most of his data came from two years of background data given to their firm at the start of the course. Having compiled the data, Ammerman was ready to formulate a model and "come up" with a forecast for the next six months.

Questions

1. Formulate the structure of Ammerman's model, explaining sales in such a way that interdependence between the two firms' strategies is explicitly recognized.
2. Is your model identified? Explain.
3. Estimate the coefficients of the structural equations in your model. Do your results support your hypothesized model?
4. How would you go about preparing a forecast for the next six months? Explain the details of how you get from your estimated structure to the forecast values.
5. Present forecasting results for the next six months. How do you feel about the reliability of your results?

Appendix 6–B: The Marionette State Management Game

TABLE 6–13
Unit Sales—Firm 1

	1969	1970	1971
January........	416	258	294
February......	375	289	377
March.........	352	338	300
April.........	450	423	430
May..........	440	395	550
June..........	523	359	556
July..........	398	489	
August........	457	432	
September.....	475	497	
October.......	327	429	
November.....	358	316	
December......	292	350	

TABLE 6–14
Unit Sales—Firm 2

	1969	1970	1971
January........	548	727	1102
February......	710	964	1340
March.........	770	926	1035
April.........	1142	1029	1235
May..........	1274	1199	1389
June..........	1221	1191	1365
July..........	1009	1672	
August........	1221	1470	
September.....	1342	1490	
October.......	1197	1150	
November.....	1053	1184	
December......	1049	1162	

TABLE 6–15
Marketing—Firm 1

	1969	1970	1971
January........	983	720	787
February......	763	647	639
March.........	757	663	782
April..........	845	909	811
May..........	876	1133	1112
June...........	1029	995	1237
July...........	1087	1280	
August........	972	1124	
September.....	979	900	
October........	917	1005	
November.....	711	892	
December......	717	734	

TABLE 6–16
Marketing—Firm 2

	1969	1970	1971
January........	1259	2504	2165
February......	1675	2405	2158
March.........	1803	2135	1905
April..........	2089	2492	2893
May..........	2429	2165	2674
June...........	2749	2913	3013
July...........	2563	2787	
August........	3009	3188	
September.....	2869	2992	
October........	2825	2820	
November.....	2343	2473	
December......	2713	2660	

TABLE 6–17
Discretionary Cash (*IF*) Firm 1

	1968	1969	1970	1971
January........	242	264	191	215
February......	271	235	197	220
March.........	260	213	202	222
April..........	255	287	289	308
May..........	260	309	320	343
June...........	280	310	325	351
July...........	297	305	325	
August........	310	305	326	
September.....	323	305	328	
October........	327	223	245	
November.....	310	199	218	
December......	302	191	213	

TABLE 6–18
Discretionary Cash (*IF*) Firm 2

	1968	1969	1970	1971
January........	263	498	822	880
February......	272	588	816	871
March.........	278	642	814	866
April..........	280	824	955	1007
May..........	285	928	1035	1093
June...........	300	988	1078	1138
July...........	308	1024	1104	
August........	327	1051	1122	
September.....	393	1070	1138	
October........	405	944	1006	
November.. .	410	880	936	
December......	352	842	900	

TABLE 6–19
Index of Dry Cleaning

	1969	1970	1971
January	135	112	90
February	137	108	88
March	143	105	93
April	129	102	91
May	125	98	85
June	128	106	84
July	132	104	88–e
August	123	101	89–e
September	119	96	83–e
October	115	94	80–e
November	110	97	78–e
December	114	93	76–e

e = estimated.

TABLE 6–20
Population Index

	1969	1970	1971
January	132	137	146
February	132	140	147
March	133	140	149
April	132	140	150
May	132	141	154
June	133	142	152
July	134	142	153–e
August	135	143	156–e
September	135	144	160–e
October	136	144	158–e
November	137	145	159–e
December	137	146	159–e

e = estimated.

TABLE 6–21
Disposable Income (billions)

	1969	1970	1971
January	345.3	377.2	412.2
February	347.4	380.5	413.0
March	349.5	383.3	414.5
April	351.3	387.1	416.0
May	354.7	389.9	416.5
June	356.1	393.9	420.6
July	359.0	392.7	423.7–e
August	361.5	400.5	427.1–e
September	364.7	401.8	428.8–e
October	369.3	405.1	429.7–e
November	372.6	407.4	435.6–e
December	375.2	409.6	444.3–e

e = estimated.

Chapter	PRODUCTION RELATIONSHIPS
7	IN THE FIRM

As defined by economists, production is a process of converting inputs into output. Inputs are such resources as labor hours, machinery, facilities, and materials. Output is the product produced. The process of production involves the mingling of these inputs in the right proportions at the right time to create the desired output.

Production technology is defined as the level of specific technical and engineering know-how with regard to the process of converting inputs into output. Our analysis of the economics of production will not attempt to encompass production technology. This technology is a product of specific industries, and even of specific firms within industries, and is concerned with chemical and physical processes of conversion and techniques of materials processing, preparation, and assembly. Our concern is more general, involving the fundamental efficiency trade-offs that characterize input choice, given an existing level of production technology. We shall also be concerned with the general nature of expansion and contraction of the scale of production processes.

CRUCIAL ASSUMPTIONS

In cases where a production process is characterized by two or more inputs, conclusions emerging from our analysis rest upon three assumptions about the nature of the production process. These assumptions are:

1. The relationship between inputs employed and output produced is sufficiently stable to be represented by a constant functional relationship, called a *production function*. In other words, when various sets of inputs are used, we can count on a systematic relationship to exist between these input combinations and the resulting output produced.

2. Inputs to a production process are at least to some extent substitutes for each other. That is, we normally require that several combinations

154

of the same inputs *could* be employed in producing a fixed output, such as more machinery and less labor or vice versa.

3. The incremental output resulting from additional employment of a unit of an input depends upon the level at which all other inputs are being utilized. That is, we cannot specify the output that can be produced by an additional man-hour of labor until we know the level of machinery being utilized in a production process involving these two inputs. In other words, the productivities of various inputs are interrelated. For example, we expect an additional unit of labor to be more productive when added to a large machinery input than when added to a small machinery input, and similarly for the addition of a unit of machinery.

Of course, if only one input characterizes the production process, the latter two assumptions would be meaningless.

A SPECIFIC FUNCTION FOR DISCUSSION

In our analysis, we are ultimately concerned with actually measuring crucial production relationships. Accordingly, we must avail ourselves of a mathematical structure that will enable production relationships to take on concrete and statistically viable forms. We also are interested in a structure consistent with the three assumptions given for two or more inputs. The following general function meets these requirements:

$$Q = b_0 I_1^{b_1} I_2^{b_2} \cdots I_n^{b_n} \qquad (7\text{--}1)$$

where Q is quantity produced, $I_1 \cdots I_n$ are inputs, and $b_0 \cdots b_n$ are coefficients. Functions of the general type of (7–1) are called Cobb-Douglas production functions after Professors C. W. Cobb and P. H. Douglas, who pioneered in their application. The Cobb-Douglas function offers a systematic functional rule (assumption 1) that accommodates substitute relationships between the I variables (assumption 2), and provides a structure to measure interrelationships among productivities (assumption 3), since the I terms bear a multiplicative rather than additive relationship.[1]

The Cobb-Douglas function has several useful properties for purposes of statistical analysis, the consideration of which we shall defer until the following chapter. The Cobb-Douglas function is also a convenient

---

[1] Consider the marginal product of input I_1 in 7–1):

$$\text{marginal product} = \frac{\partial Q}{\partial I_1} = b_1 b_0 I_1^{b_1 - 1} I_2^{b_2} \cdots I_n^{b_n}$$

which is clearly a function of all other input values. For example, assuming $b_2 \neq 0$, an increase in the level of I_2 input would increase the marginal productivity of a unit of I_1 input.

tool for evaluating key economic concepts regarding production functions, which is our immediate purpose in this chapter. Three such concepts are of interest in our present analysis: (a) the measurement of returns to a given input, (b) evaluating input elasticities, and (c) the analysis of returns to scale, to be considered in that order.

RETURNS TO A SINGLE INPUT

One important characteristic of a production process is how changes in a single input affect output when other inputs are held constant. The *marginal product* of an input is defined as the ratio between small changes in output ΔQ and input ΔI, with all else constant. Considering the mathematical limit of this ratio as $\Delta I \to 0$, we have

$$\text{Marginal Product of } I = \lim_{\Delta I \to 0} \frac{\Delta Q}{\Delta I} = \text{slope of } Q = \frac{\partial Q}{\partial I} = MP_I$$

For the input I_1 in (7–1) this would result in the expression:

$$MP_{I_1} = \frac{\partial Q}{\partial I_1} = b_1 b_0 I_1^{b_1-1} I_2^{b_2} \cdot \cdot \cdot I_n^{b_n} \qquad (7\text{–}2)$$

Notice in (7–2) that if $b_1 > 1$, the exponent on I_1 is positive and increased use of I_1 will increase the marginal product of I_1. This means greater and greater increases in output result as I_1 is uniformly increased. In other words, if the nth unit of I_1 produces 14 additional units of output, the $(n + 1)$st unit of I_1 produces more than 14 additional output units. The circumstance of $b_1 > 1$ in the Cobb-Douglas function is therefore called *increasing marginal productivity* of I_1.

Increasing marginal productivity is not the usual case in production analysis. More common is the situation where $0 < b < 1$. Notice in (7–2) if this is the case for I_1, then $(b_1 - 1)$ is negative, and increases in I_1 will reduce MP_{I_1}. Additional units of I_1 will increase output, (MP_{I_1} is still positive), but by diminishing amounts. If the nth unit of I_1 added 14 units of output, the $(n + 1)$st unit would add less than 14.

This case, called *diminishing marginal productivity*, is sufficiently common that some writers of economic tracts have declared it to be a law— the law of diminishing returns. In one sense, this tendency has the force of a physical law. For it is perfectly safe to assert that diminishing marginal productivity (or returns) will undoubtedly eventually characterize a production process, since with other input quantities fixed, continued increases in the variable input are bound to be of reduced usefulness past some level of utilization.[2] But the crucial and more practical question

---

[2] Consider, for instance, fixed inputs of a 10 ft.-square plant size with one machine. It is probably safe to say that the addition of the fiftieth worker's labor will add less to output than did the addition of the second worker's labor.

is whether that point occurs in the midst of the usual operating range of output for a particular production process. If it does, the concept is important for decision making, as we shall later see. In the final analysis, the empirical data produced by a production process is the final judge on the legitimacy of our law, as these data will establish the most probable numerical estimate of b.

Input Elasticities

We have seen that the b coefficients in a Cobb-Douglas production function directly indicate either increasing marginal productivity ($b > 1$) or decreasing marginal productivity ($0 < b < 1$). A second dimension can be added to this interpretation by considering the elasticities of output relative to various inputs. Elasticity of input I_1 is defined as follows:

$$e_{I_1} = \frac{\frac{\Delta Q}{Q}}{\frac{\Delta I_1}{I_1}} = \frac{\Delta Q}{Q} \frac{I_1}{\Delta I_1} = \frac{\Delta Q}{\Delta I_1} \cdot \frac{I_1}{Q}$$

where ΔQ stands for a small change in Q, and ΔI_1 a small change in input I_1. e_{I_1} measures proportional relationships between a specific input change and the resulting output change, *ceteris paribus*. If $e_{I_1} > 1$, then a given percentage change in input I_1 produces a proportionately greater increase in output, and vice versa when $e_{I_1} < 1$.

In the limit, the term $\Delta Q / \Delta I_1$ is readily seen as the marginal productivity of $I_1 (MP_{I_1})$ defined for the Cobb-Douglas function in (7–2). Thus, at a point:

$$e_{I_1} = MP_{I_1} \cdot \frac{I_1}{Q}$$

If we insert (7–2) in this expression for MP_{I_1} and (7–1) for Q, we may rewrite it as follows:

$$e_{I_1} = \frac{b_1 b_0 I_1^{b_1 - 1} I_2^{b_2} \cdots I_n^{b_n} (I_1)}{b_0 I_1^{b_1} I_2^{b_2} \cdots I_n^{b_n}}$$

Combining I_1 in the numerator gives:

$$e_{I_1} = \frac{b_1 b_0 I_1^{b_1} I_2^{b_2} \cdots I_n^{b_n}}{b_0 I_1^{b_1} I_2^{b_2} \cdots I_n^{b_n}} = b_1$$

This same result occurs for the elasticities of each input in a Cobb-Douglas function. The coefficient thus becomes a direct measure of input elasticity. Combining this with our earlier discussion of the measurement of marginal productivities in Cobb-Douglas functions, we may construct a correspondence between elasticities and marginal productivities for such functions as follows: When e_{I_1} is relatively elastic, increasing marginal productivity characterizes $I_1(b_1 > 1)$. When e_{I_1} is relatively inelastic, diminishing marginal productivity is present $(b_1 < 1)$. For example, if $b_1 = 0.8$, we can interpret this as indicating that a 10 percent increase in I_1 produces about an 8 percent increase in Q for the data. We may also interpret the 0.8 as indicating that diminishing marginal productivity characterizes the data.

RETURNS-TO-SCALE

The question of scale in production analysis refers to the input-output relationships that apply over the long run when all inputs can be varied. Economists usually separate the long and short run by reference to fixed commitments. In the short run, the producer has certain fixed commitments that produce fixed inputs to the short-run production process. Manufacturing and office facilities, specialized machinery, and lease agreements are examples of such fixed commitments. Over some period of time, these commitments can be changed or eliminated. That period of time separates the long run from the short run. The concepts of marginal productivity and input elasticities just discussed implicitly refer to short-run analysis, as both deal with input-output relationships in the situation where a single input varies while all others are held constant.

In this context, scale of production refers to the level at which all inputs are employed in the long run. If even one input remains fixed, the scale is constant. Therefore, the scale of a production process is altered only when all the inputs are altered. Since some inputs are fixed in the short run, it is tautological that scale changes can only occur in the long run. *Returns-to-scale* refers to the behavior of the production function when proportional changes are made in all inputs. The analysis of returns-to-scale is usually undertaken by considering an equal percentage change in all inputs compared with the resulting output change. For example in the production function of (7–1) each of the inputs I_1, $I_2 \cdots I_n$ would be changed by an equal percentage in analyzing returns. Three possible results are possible from such a scale change:

1. The resulting increase in output is of a greater percentage than the percentage increase in the inputs. There are *increasing returns-to-scale*. Larger-scale input use yields greater than proportional output increases. The production process thus yields economies of scale, becoming more efficient as it becomes larger.

2. The increase in output is of the same percentage as the input increase. There are *constant returns-to-scale*. Larger-scale input levels produce proportional output increases. The general efficiency remains the same as the process grows larger.

3. The increase in output is of a lesser percentage than the input increase. There are *decreasing returns-to-scale,* as larger-scale input levels produce less than proportional output increases. The production process becomes less efficient as it becomes larger.

The scale category to which a particular production function belongs is affected both by the mathematical characteristic of the function and by the specific coefficient values in the function. We can usually interrogate a production function directly to determine its scale relationship by algebraically exploring the effect on output of proportional input changes. For example, consider the Cobb-Douglas function of (7–1). Assume a specific set of inputs I_1^*, $I_2^* \cdots I_n^*$ that produces Q^* output when inserted in (7–1):

$$Q^* = b_0(I_1^*)^{b_1}(I_2^*)^{b_2} \cdots (I_n^*)^{b_n}$$

If the I are doubled in magnitude, to $2I_1^*$, $2I_2^* \ldots 2I_n^*$, and these doubled values are reinserted, the following results:

$$Q^{**} = b_0(2I_1^*)^{b_1}(2I_2^*)^{b_2} \cdots (2I_n^*)^{b_n}$$

where Q^{**} is the new quantity produced by these enlarged inputs. This can be rewritten:

$$Q^{**} = [2^{b_1}2^{b_2} \cdots 2^{b_n}] \cdot [b_0(I_1^*)^{b_1}(I_2^*)^{b_2} \cdots (I_n^*)^{b_n}]$$

Since the second bracket in this expression contains the original expression for Q^*, we can further write:

$$Q^{**} = 2^{(b_1+b_2 \cdots +b_n)}Q^* \qquad (7-3)$$

For the immediate problem, (7–3) shows that the output that will result from doubling all inputs will be $2^{(b_1+b_2\cdots+b_n)}$ times as large as the original output. The specific scale category depends on the magnitude of the b_i. If the sum of the b_i is greater than 1, then the function shows increasing returns to scale, as the resulting output will be more than doubled. If the sum of the $b_i < 1$, then decreasing returns to scale characterize the production process. Finally, with constant returns the b_i sum to 1.

The result shown in (7–3) is in fact general for all Cobb-Douglas functions, if we replace the 2 by any constant multiple k. In general, if all inputs are increased by k, output will increase by $k^{(b_1+b_2+\cdots b_n)}$, so that the returns-to-scale in the production process will depend upon the sum of the b_i. Thus, in Cobb-Douglas functions we may determine the returns-to-scale by arithmetic inspection of the function. With other functions, it may be necessary to derive expressions similar to (7–3) for this purpose.

We have now discussed three properties of production functions, the returns to a single input, input elasticities, and return-to-scale. These concepts aid in the development of production models that, when operationalized, provide reasonable answers to some pertinent questions in production. We now consider these models, beginning with the simplest case of a single-variable input production process.

A SINGLE-VARIABLE INPUT MODEL

In the short run, some plant and equipment inputs to production processes are usually fixed. This means the choice of the best overall combination of labor, physical capital, and other inputs by the firm's production management is largely irrelevant. The firm must accept the fixed capital input as essentially given and make its production decisions regarding use of the variable inputs. To see the economic considerations in such a restricted decision-making case, we now consider the simplest version of this circumstance—where the firm's production process is characterized by only one input that is variable in the short run. All other inputs can be varied only over a long-run period.

In this circumstance, the major concern is with the problem of efficiency in the use of the fixed and variable inputs. To specifically explore this problem, consider a two-input production process involving a fixed input of capital (K) and a variable input of labor (L). We define efficiency of an input as the ratio of output to units of the input employed.

$$\text{Efficiency of } L = \frac{Q}{L} = \text{Average Product of Labor} = AP_L$$

$$\text{Efficiency of } K = \frac{Q}{K_F} = \text{Average Product of Capital} = AP_K$$

Thus, more units of output per unit of labor input means more efficient use of labor in our definition. Similarly, more units of output per unit of capital means more efficient use of capital. In other words, the higher the Average Product, the greater the efficiency. We envision a production function in which:

$$Q = f(L,K)$$

Therefore, it is clear that increasing Q by using more capital makes labor more efficient, i.e., (AP_L) would rise, and increasing Q by employing more labor makes capital more efficient.

Under our circumstances where K is fixed at a specific value K_F, the crucial consideration is how far to push the use of L in terms of the resulting efficiencies of L and K. To explore this question, we turn to a graphical model.

If we plot the output of the production process Q against units of the variable input employed, the result can be called the total product curve. We may expect this curve to have the general shape shown in Figure 7–1, panel (a). Now the AP_L will have the general shape shown

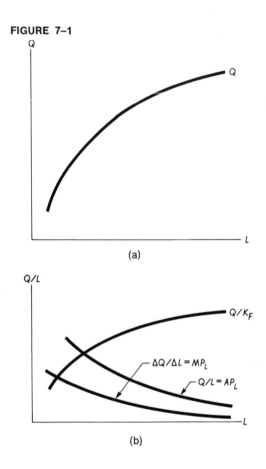

FIGURE 7–1

(a)

(b)

in panel (b) of the figure, which derives directly from the shape of the total product function. This correspondence is best seen by reference to the marginal product of labor (MP_L) curve which plots the change in Q relative to changes in L, i.e., it is a plot of the slope of the total product curve. The MP_L curve is shown in panel (b) of Figure 7–1. If MP_L is above AP_L, increments of Q and L are being added which are greater than the average value of Q and L. Thus, the average value (AP_L) must rise. When the MP_L falls below AP_L, increments of Q/L are being added which are less than the average Q/L and the average will fall. The maximum value of the AP_L thus occurs where $MP_L = AP_L$. In our

Figure, $MP_L < AP_L$ immediately so that AP_L is continuously falling. With K fixed, AP_K will just be the value of Q divided by the constant value of the input K_F. Thus, the AP_K in this case is merely a direct reflection of the total product curve of panel (a).

The correspondence between efficiency in the use of the K input (AP_K) and the level of output illustrates an interesting property of this single-variable input case; as long as we can increase output produced by the fixed capital input (however inefficiently we do so regarding labor's use), we will increase the efficiency with which the fixed K is used. At the same time, the MP_L reveals that the efficiency of L declines all the while that of K rises, thus proposing a basic efficiency trade-off in the case of these two inputs. If the total-product curve also had a region where MP_L increased, then this trade-off would cease to exist over this range, increasing MP_L range, since increased use of the variable L input would result in it being *more efficiently* used as well as providing more efficient use of K. A firm would be expected to move entirely through this rising MP_L region into the region of the efficiency trade-off we have discussed. However, within the region of trade-offs, the decision as to how inefficiently to employ labor hinges on the relative costs of L and K. If K is very expensive relative to L, we would expect to see the trade-off favor heavier use of K at the expense of L efficiency, and vice versa if L is expensive relative to K.[3]

A TWO-VARIABLE INPUT MODEL

Many real-world production processes are characterized by more than a single input being variable in the short run. In these circumstances, the firm has a choice as to the proportions in which it employs each input. If labor and machinery are the two primary inputs, then a given output may in most cases be produced by highly labor-intensive (hand) methods, by highly capital-intensive (automated) methods, or by some combination of resources in between. In such a situation, the question of efficiency now outlined is broadened to encompass a consideration of the appropriate combination of inputs for production of a given output. When we adopt a long-run perspective, this same input trade-off consideration is relevant for all production processes having more than one total input. We now consider the economics of this input trade-off. For convenience in discussion, we shall consider a two-variable input process. Later we shall generalize the results to the case of more-than-two-variable inputs.

---

[3] For the reader interested in an extensive treatment of one-variable input production models, including a more detailed discussion of the stages of production, see the appropriate chapters of a price theory text such as D. S. Watson, *Price Theory and Its Uses* (New York: Houghton Mifflin, 1968).

Consider the following general production function:

$$Q = F(L,K) \qquad\qquad (7\text{--}4)$$

where L is labor input and K machinery and facility input. Assume this function follows the three production function assumptions considered earlier. The basic question we now wish to answer with this model is: What are the most efficient combinations of L and K to employ to produce given levels of output?

Isoquants

Consider a series of fixed output levels, $Q_0 < Q_1 < Q_2 < Q_3$. Since L and K are at least partial substitutes, if we fix Q at, say Q_0, we may envision many combinations of L and K that could be employed in its production. The same is true of Q_1, Q_2, and Q_3. For normal production processes (that could be characterized reliably by, say, a Cobb-Douglas function) we would expect these L, K combinations to bear a systematic relationship to each other, generally similar to that shown in Figure 7–2. These L, K trade-off curves for given Q are called *isoquants*. It is logical to assume they are (a) nonintersecting—i.e., that the same L, K combination would not correspond to two different Q levels, (b) concave from above—i.e., at very high levels of utilization of one, and low levels of utilization of the other (such as point A on isoquant Q_0), more of the abundant resource could be exchanged for a given amount of the scarce resource (and still retain Q) than at any other location on the curve. In other words, our abundant input can be traded off for our scarce input in proportionately larger quantities in the extreme regions of the isoquant. For example, notice that in moving down the curve from point A in Figure 7–2, less and less L would be given up as K was added in equal increments: i.e., $(K_1 - K_0) = (K_2 - K_1) = (K_3 - K_2)$, while $(L_1 -$

FIGURE 7-2

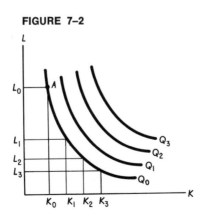

$L_0) > (L_2 - L_1) > L_3 - L_2)$. This property is usually called *diminish-ing marginal rate of substitution*. This diminishing marginal rate of substi-tution results entirely from the assumption of concavity.

Let us consider this rate of substitution further by examining the slope of an isoquant. Refer to Figure 7–3. Beginning with combination

FIGURE 7–3

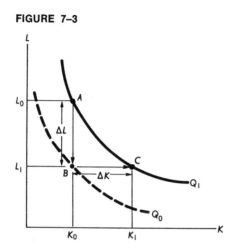

L_0K_0 at point A, withdraw $L_1 - L_0 = \Delta L$ units of labor, which now leaves L_1 units of L and K_0 units of K and enables the production of a smaller output Q_0. Now the decline in output $Q_0 - Q_1$ can be expressed as follows:

$$Q_0 - Q_1 = -\Delta L \times MP_L \qquad (7-5)$$

where MP_L = the marginal product of labor. Since MP_L measures the change in output associated with a small change in L, multiplying MP_L by ΔL (as long as ΔL is small) results in the change in total output $Q_0 - Q_1$. Consider now substituting for the withdrawn L input a sufficient addi-tional amount of K to return to the original isoquant. This involves adding $(K_1 - K_0) = \Delta K$ units of capital. Reasoning as before, the addi-tional output resulting from increasing K by ΔK units is:

$$Q_1 - Q_0 = \Delta K \times MP_K \qquad (7-6)$$

In adding ΔK we return to the same curve from which we departed, (Q_1), thus the absolute magnitude of the output change is identical for (7–5) and (7–6). Therefore,

$$MP_k \times \Delta K = -MP_L \times \Delta L$$

and

$$\frac{\Delta L}{\Delta K} = -\frac{MP_k}{MP_L} \qquad (7-7)$$

Expression (7–7), a logical product of our definitions, reveals the slope of an isoquant (the limit of $\Delta L/\Delta K$ as $\Delta K \to 0$) is equal to the ratio of the two marginal productivities.[4] At point A in Figure 7–3, a large amount of L is being employed relative to K. Thus, the MP_L can be expected to be low relative to the MP_K, thus producing a large absolute value for the ratio of MP_k/MP_L. On the other hand, at point C in the figure, more k employed, lowering MP_k, and less L is employed, raising MP_L. The absolute value of MP_k/MP_L would thereby fall—in fact would fall all down the isoquant. This pattern is only a reflection of the assumption that more extensive use of an input relative to another input will lower its marginal productivity relative to the other input, i.e., the assumption of a diminishing marginal rate of substitution.

Budget Constraints

The slope of an isoquant tells us how the marginal productivities of two inputs compare. This is important information in formulating a rational choice of inputs, but it is not all we need to know. In addition, we need to know how the costs of the inputs compare. For a unit of input I, we may have twice the marginal productivity of a second input I_2, but if I_1 costs four times as much as I_2, it will not be rational to use more I_1, and less I_2—indeed just the opposite. To see these ideas more clearly, consider the following expression for total outlay B:

$$B = P_L \times L + P_k \times K \qquad (7\text{–}8)$$

where P_L, P_k are the prices per unit of labor and machinery respectively.

Plotting this expression on the same graph as an isoquant will most clearly reveal the essential relationships between costs and productivities. To do this, we must re-express (7–8) with L on the left-hand side and K on the right-hand side, as follows:

$$P_L \times L = B - P_k \times K$$

and

$$L = B/P_L - \frac{P_k}{P_L} K \qquad (7\text{–}9)$$

---

[4] This result can also be seen by reference to partial derivatives, as follows:

$$\frac{\partial L}{\partial K} = \frac{\partial Q}{\partial K} \cdot \frac{\partial L}{\partial Q} = \frac{\partial Q}{\partial K} \cdot \frac{1}{\partial Q/\partial L} = \frac{\partial Q/\partial K}{\partial Q/\partial L}$$

Since $\partial Q/\partial L = MP_L$ and $\partial Q/\partial K = MP_K$, this means

$$\frac{\partial L}{\partial K} = \frac{MP_K}{MP_L}$$

which would plot as shown in Figure 7–4, given $B = B_1$. For $B_2 > B_1$, the intercept of (7–9) would be enlarged, repositioning the budget line to the right in parallel fashion as shown in Figure 7–4. In general, as long

FIGURE 7–4

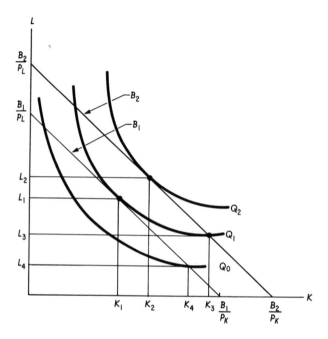

as P_k and P_L remain fixed, changes in B will shift the budget curve accordingly. Changes in either P_K or P_L, on the other hand, will rotate the curve by changing its slope.

LEAST-COST INPUT COMBINATIONS

The information on costs contained in the budget line enables derivation of a minimum cost combinations of inputs for the production of a stipulated output level. This point of least-cost occurs at input combination L_1K_1 for output Q_1 and L_2K_2 for output Q_2, which are called *least-cost* input combinations. To see this property, pick any combination of L and K that lies on isoquant Q_1 other than L_1K_1, for example L_3K_3. Any such combination would enable Q_1 output to be produced. As long as the input prices remain fixed, the cost of producing Q_1 with another combination would be given by passing the budget line through that point. Thus, since budget line B_2 passes through point L_3K_3, the cost of producing Q_1 with this combination is B_2, which is greater than the B_1 cost of Q_1 at L_1K_1.

This same result occurs for all other combinations of L and K on Q_1—they necessarily correspond to rightward-positioned budget lines and therefore greater costs than the budget line that is just tangent to the isoquant. At the fixed input prices, there is no way to shift the budget line to the left any further than the point of tangency and still be on isoquant Q_1. That output is being produced at least-cost. Similarly, there is no input combination that will enable production of as great an output as Q_1 for the budget allocation B_1 than L_1K_1. Any other combination of L and K that lies on budget line B_1, for example L_4K_4, corresponds with positions on an isoquant that lies to the left of Q_1, meaning a smaller output level, as Q_0 for L_4K_4.

The least-cost points in Figure 7–4 are points of tangency between isoquants and budget lines. At a point of tangency between two curves, the slopes of the curves are equal. Since the budget line given in (7–9) is a linear equation of the form $L = a + bK$, its slope is simply the coefficient of the K term, $-P_K/P_L$. We earlier saw in (7–7) that the slope of an isoquant is equal to $-MP_K/MP_L$. Thus, at least-cost:

$$\frac{-P_K}{P_L} = \frac{-MP_K}{MP_L}$$

This may be reexpressed as follows:

$$\frac{MP_L}{P_L} = \frac{MP_K}{P_K} \qquad (7\text{–}10)$$

Expression (7–10) shows a fundamental property of a two-input, least-cost point. At this point, the marginal product of labor inputs per dollar of cost is brought into equality with the marginal product of machinery inputs per dollar of their costs. In other words, the last (marginal) dollar allocated to the purchase of labor produces the same increase in output as the last (marginal) dollar allocated to machinery use. Assuming the marginal products of both inputs decline, we can do no better than we do at L, K combinations that satisfy (7–10). For if $MP_L/P_L > MP_K/P_K$, i.e., where the output-return from a dollar committed to labor is greater than for capital, we could increase output with no increase in costs by withdrawing a dollar from the low-return capital category and reallocating it to the high-return labor category. The above inequality provides that the incremental gain in output due to the additional L will be larger than the incremental loss due to K. The result will be higher total output for unchanged total costs. A suboptimum cost-output relationship will characterize all combinations of L and K for which (7–10) does not hold.

The least-cost position in (7–10) has involved two inputs. However, the same least-cost result applies to as many inputs as are present in the production function:

$$\frac{MP_{I_1}}{P_{I_1}} = \frac{MP_{I_2}}{P_{I_2}} = \cdots = \frac{MP_{I_n}}{P_{I_n}} \qquad (7\text{–}11)$$

Expression (7–11) indicates that changes in input prices will change the least-cost point. If P_{I_1} is lowered, then I_1 is more productive at the margin per dollar spent. More of I_1 should be employed and less of the other inputs until (7–11) is again restored. Such a change has enabled more total output to result from the given outlay. Alternatively, the same output could now result with a lower outlay. For two inputs, this situation is shown graphically in Figure 7–5. Beginning at least-cost

FIGURE 7–5
Least-Cost Relationships

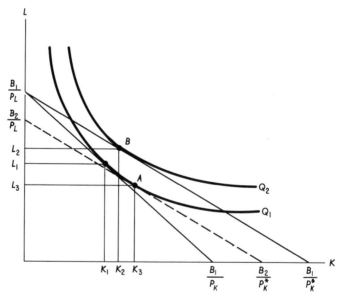

combination $L_1 K_1$ involving budget B_1, for output Q_1, the price of K is lowered from P_K to $P_K{}^*$. The budget line pivots out, since the absolute value of its slope $-P_K/P_L$ has been reduced, but its L intercept, B_1/P_L is unaltered. For the same outlay B_1, a larger output Q_2 can now be produced by redeploying the additional money freed by the price decrease $(P_K{}^* - P_K) \times K_1$ to purchase more labor $(L_2 > L_1)$, and more capital $(K_2 > K_1)$. Or, the total budget can now be reduced to retain the initial output level Q_1.

This is shown in Figure 7–5 by the dotted line, whose slope reflects the new input prices, and which involves a smaller budget outlay B_2, more utilization of K than before the price change $(K_3 > K_1)$, and less usage of L $(L_3 < L_1)$. This option shows the substitution of the now cheaper K for L in the least-cost input combination. We may call this the pure *input substitution effect* of the price change, since it shows the different L, K combinations involved in the production of the *same* output levels, before and after the change. Notice also in Figure 7–5 that the increased usage of both L and K that accompanies the production of Q_2 appears to involve a greater quantity of L than K (assuming the L and K scales are comparable), even though K is the cheaper resource.

In fact, the final least-cost quantity of K, K_2 is *less* than K_3, the amount resulting from the pure substitution effect. The reason for this is related to the basic scale characteristics of the underlying production function. Specifically, the relative shape of the two isoquants Q_1 and Q_2 in Figure 7–5 indicates that for this case L becomes more productive relative to K as the scale of production is expanded from Q_1 to Q_2. Therefore, the least-cost combination tends toward proportionately greater L usage and smaller K usage as Q is increased. It is this effect, which we will call the *scale* effect, that accounts for $K_2 < K_3$, and that causes the K price decrease to increase L proportionately more. We could, in fact, call the movement from least-cost combination L_3K_3 to combination L_2K_2 the *pure scale effect*, since it is equivalent to an expansion of the budget at given prices from B_2 to B_1. Comparing the least-cost points A and B resulting from this scale expansion, we find that for this particular isoquant mapping, *less* K would be employed in least-cost location B $(K_2 < K_3)$. In this case, the increasing productivity of L relative to K has thus produced a negative scale effect for K.

Scale effects can be more thoroughly evaluated by inspecting the pattern produced by the least-cost combinations associated with several successively larger levels of outlay. Such a pattern is shown in Figure 7–6, where the outlay is increased in least-cost fashion, from B_1 to B_4, resulting in increases in output from Q_1 to Q_4. The trace of least-cost points that results, characterized by the connecting line EP, can be interpreted as the efficient expansion path of the firm. It shows the general pattern of L,K usage if least-cost input combinations are used to produce successively higher output levels. Thus, for given input prices, output Q_1 is being produced most efficiently at L_1K_1 while output Q_4 is produced efficiently at L_2K_2 input combination. If the shape of the production surface indicated extensive automation was efficient at higher output levels, then the expansion path would begin to flatten parallel to the K axis as higher levels of output were reached. Such a circumstance implies expansion would thereafter occur with much greater emphasis on the K input than on the L input, i.e., the most efficient ratio of

FIGURE 7–6
Scale Effects

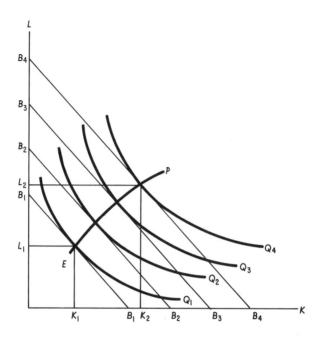

K to L would rise. If the expansion path were a straight line, then the most efficient input proportions would be unaffected by level of production. Scale effects would have no impact on efficient input usage.

INPUT CHOICE FOR MANY INPUTS

In the case of two-variable inputs, it was possible to obtain a specific solution for least-cost quantities of the two inputs for a given output by equating the ratio of the two marginal productivities (slope of a given isoquant) with the ratio of input prices (slope of the budget line), identically as was done in the graphical case. This resulted in expression (7–10). When more-than-two-variable inputs are present, the same least-cost condition was stated on intuitive grounds to extend over all inputs, as illustrated by expression (7–11), repeated here for convenience:

$$\frac{MP_{I_1}}{P_{I_1}} = \frac{MP_{I_2}}{P_{I_2}} = \cdots = \frac{MP_{I_n}}{P_{I_n}} \qquad (7\text{--}11)$$

A more explicit but equivalent procedure can be employed to arrive at (7–11), which also yields the results obtained earlier for two-inputs as a special case. It involves the construction and solution of a Lagrangian expression employing the unknown multiplier λ.[5]

In considering this computational approach, the general Cobb-Douglas function will be used with n inputs $(I_1, I_2 \cdots I_n)$ having prices P_1, $P_2 \cdots P_n$. Although the approach is completely general, this specific choice allows direct comparisons with earlier illustrations. The general Cobb-Douglas function is given as follows:

$$Q = b_0 I_1^{b_1} I_2^{b_2} \cdots I_n^{b_n}$$

The associated budget equation is:

$$B = P_{I_1} I_1 + P_{I_2} I_2 + \cdots + P_{I_n} I_n$$

where B is the total budget outlay. In the Lagrangian expression L, the objective of the analysis is to minimize the budget outlay under the constraint of producing a given level of output (call that level Q_0). The Lagrangian expression is as follows:

$$L = P_{I_1} I_1 + P_{I_2} I_2 + \cdots + P_{I_n} I_n + \lambda(b_0 I_1^{b_1} I_2^{b_2} \cdots I_n^{b_n} - Q_0)$$

which includes the budget expression to be minimized as well as the constraint that Q_0 units must be produced. The constrained minimum of L may be obtained by taking partial derivatives of L on I_1, $I_2 \cdots I_n$, λ, setting each of these expressions equal to zero, and simultaneously solving this system of $n + 1$ equations in $n + 1$ variables. This gives:

$$\frac{\partial L}{\partial I_1} = P_1 + \lambda b_1 b_0 I_1^{b_1 - 1} I_2^{b_2} \cdots I_n^{b_n} = 0$$

$$\frac{\partial L}{\partial I_2} = P_2 + \lambda b_2 b_0 I_1^{b_1} I_2^{b_2 - 1} \cdots I_n^{b_n} = 0$$

$$\frac{\partial L}{\partial I_n} = P_n + \lambda b_n b_0 I_1^{b_1} I_2^{b_2} \cdots I_n^{b_n - 1} = 0$$

$$\frac{\partial L}{\partial \lambda} = b_0 I_1^{b_1} I_2^{b_2} \cdots I_n^{b_n} - Q_0 = 0$$

The last equation introduces the output constraint into the solution. This system of equations, set equal to zero, now can be solved for least-cost values of the I for the production of Q_0 units of output.

To conveniently see the equivalence of this approach with the earlier direct method of solution, we may apply the Lagrangian technique to

---

[5] The reader unfamiliar with Lagrangian multipliers should consult an elementary applied calculus text, such as J. E. Howell and D. Teichroew, *Mathematical Analysis for Business Decisions* (Homewood, Ill.: Richard D. Irwin, 1971), p. 161.

the specific two-variable input case discussed throughout this chapter, where:

$$Q = b_0 L^{b_1} K^{b_2}$$

and

$$B = P_L L + P_K K$$

The Lagrangian expression is given as follows:

$$LE = P_L L + P_K K + \lambda(b_0 L^{b_1} K^{b_2} - Q_0)$$

and:

$$\frac{\partial LE}{\partial L} = P_L + \lambda b_1 b_0 L^{*b_1-1} K^{*b_2} = 0$$

$$\frac{\partial LE}{\partial K} = P_K + \lambda b_2 b_0 L^{*b_1} K^{*b_2-1} = 0$$

$$\frac{\partial LE}{\partial \lambda} = b_0 L^{*b_1} K^{*b_2} - Q_0 = 0$$

where the * indicates the least-cost quantities of L and K.

In solving simultaneously, we may divide the second expression by the first, and subtract P_L and P_K from both sides of the equations in which they appear:

$$\frac{\lambda b_2 b_0 L^{*b_1} K^{*b_2-1}}{\lambda b_1 b_0 L^{*b_1-1} K^{*b_2}} = \frac{-P_K}{-P_L}$$

which gives:

$$\frac{b_2}{b_1} [L^{*b_1} L^{*1-b_1} K^{*b_2-1} K^{*-b_2}] = \frac{P_K}{P_L}$$

and

$$\frac{b_2 L^*}{b_1 K^*} = \frac{P_K}{P_L} \qquad (7\text{--}12)$$

It was earlier shown that conceptually least-cost points occur where the slope of an isoquant equals the slope of an isocost. Expression (7–7) earlier established that the slope of an isoquant could be expressed as a ratio of the marginal productivities of the inputs:

$$- \frac{MP_K}{MP_L} \qquad (7\text{--}7)$$

Since:

$$MP_K = \frac{\partial Q}{\partial K}; \quad MP_L = \frac{\partial Q}{\partial L}$$

(7–7) is equivalent to:

$$-\frac{\dfrac{\partial Q}{\partial K}}{\dfrac{\partial Q}{\partial L}} \qquad (7\text{–}7\text{a})$$

For our two-variable Cobb-Douglas function:

$$\frac{\partial Q}{\partial K} = b_2 b_0 L^{b_1} K^{b_2 - 1}$$

$$\frac{\partial Q}{\partial L} = b_1 b_0 L^{b_1 - 1} K^{b_2}$$

Inserting in (7–7) a gives:

$$-\frac{b_2 b_0 L^{b_1} K^{b_2 - 1}}{b_1 b_0 L^{b_1 - 1} K^{b_2}} = -\frac{b_0 L^{b_1 - 1} K^{b_2 - 1} b_2 L}{b_0 L^{b_1 - 1} K^{b_2 - 1} b_1 K} = -\frac{b_2 L}{b_1 K}$$

as an equivalent expression for the slope of the Cobb-Douglas isoquant. From expression (7–9) it is recalled that the slope of our assumed linear budget constraint is given by the coefficient on the K term, $-P_K/P_L$. Thus, setting the isoquant and budget constraint slopes equal gives least-cost where:

$$\frac{b_2}{b_1} \frac{L^*}{K^*} = \frac{P_K}{P_L} \qquad (7\text{–}13)$$

and where multiplying both sides by (-1) removes the minus sign. Expression (7–13) is identical to expression (7–12), thus illustrating the equivalence of the Lagrangian approach and the direct conceptual approach for two-input models. For many-input models, the same general correspondence is present. However, Lagrangian methods are considered more tractable computationally, as they boil down to the solution of a system of simultaneous equations. Solving such systems (particularly large systems) has been greatly facilitated by the widespread availability of standardized computer programs.

The models of input choice now considered can be applied at a qualitative level to explore the probable direction of effect of various influences on the production process. For example, we considered a change in input prices and saw the effect to be (a) a lowering of costs for a given output level, and (b) a shift in input mix towards the now cheaper input. We could as well trace through the general effect of a technological improvement, which would begin by shifting the production function to the right. There are in fact several such questions for which our model would produce interesting qualitative answers. In order to move beyond this qualitative level into situations where specific quantitative results can be given, we need to (a) make specific our assumptions about the structure of the production function, and (b) formulate reliable empirical estimates of their coefficients. We turn in the next chapter to these two topics.

DISCUSSION QUESTIONS

1. Distinguish between returns to a single input and returns-to-scale.
2. Under what circumstances might you expect to see increasing returns to labor in a single firm's production process?
3. Consider a production function fit to aggregate production data of an underdeveloped nation, along with total labor hours expended and total units of capital employed. Would you expect this production function to yield a least-cost labor-capital combination involving a high or low ratio of labor to capital? Why?
4. What does it mean to production decision making to find that the efficiency of all inputs are rising as use of variable inputs is increased?
5. How would a sudden technological advance affect the isoquant mapping for a particular production process?

Chapter 8

MEASURING PRODUCTION RELATIONSHIPS

In the previous chapter the major concern was with exploring the major economic questions of production and with identifying principles useful in a prescriptive way in production management. Applying principles such as those leading to least-cost input combinations depends upon statistical estimation of the underlying production function. Under circumstances where a statistically estimated production function is free of autocorrelation and other problems of reliability, we may indeed obtain explicit answers to some important questions of a prescriptive nature. Our purpose in this chapter is to explore the question of measurement as applied to Cobb-Douglas production functions.

APPLYING THE COBB-DOUGLAS FUNCTION

In the previous chapter, our discussion led to the identification of some interesting and potentially useful properties of the Cobb-Douglas production function. We saw that this function provided direct estimates of increasing or decreasing marginal productivity for each input, as well as direct measurements of input elasticities. It also enabled returns to scale to be easily determined. The multiplicative way in which inputs relate in a Cobb-Douglas function enables measurement of levels of interrelationship in input marginal products. To this summary list, we can now add a computational convenience: The Cobb-Douglas function is linear in logarithms. If we take natural logs of both sides of the general Cobb-Douglas function

$$Q = b_0 I_1{}^{b_1} I_2{}^{b_2} \cdots I_n{}^{b_n}$$

we obtain:

$$\ln Q = \ln b_0 + b_1 \ln I_1 + b_2 \ln I_2 + \cdots + b_n \ln I_n$$

which is a linear function of the natural logs of the data, and is therefore susceptible to the coefficient estimation and evaluation methods of multiple regression analysis. The factors mentioned here constitute the principal case for employment of the Cobb-Douglas structure in efforts to quantify production models.

Weighing against its use are three principal objections: (1) that mathematically the Cobb-Douglas function cannot measure a pattern of returns characterized by both an increasing and decreasing marginal productivity region, (2) that the function implies a linear expansion path where least-cost input combinations are assumed constant, and (3) that the function stipulates, a priori, a unitary elasticity of input substitution. We shall discuss these in order.

Regarding (1), since the Cobb-Douglas function is a power function, the direction of change in the slope is fixed, which gives the *MP* curve a monotonic shape. Such a pattern is illustrated in panel (b) of Figure 8–1. More generally, this monotonic slope means that the function could reflect only one of the two possible regions of the curve in panel (a) of Figure 8–1. If the Cobb-Douglas coefficient *b* was greater than one,

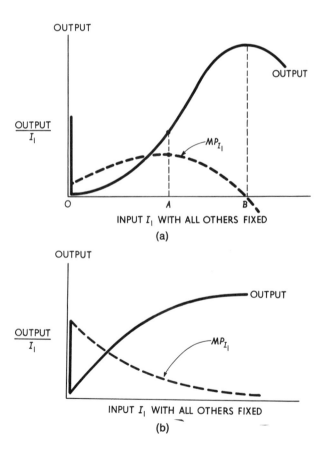

the Cobb-Douglas curve would have the shape of the region from 0 to A in panel (a). If $0 \leq b \leq 1$, the Cobb-Douglas curve would have the shape characterizing the portion of the curve in panel (a) from A to B. This latter possibility is the most common expectation and corresponds to the curve illustrated in panel (b). Also, no value can be assigned that would produce a shape similar to the portion of the curve in panel (a) to the right of B.

If a particular production process has both a significant region of increasing and decreasing marginal productivity, and if the observed data from the process spans this region, then estimated Cobb-Douglas coefficients will be distorted, as the data from the former region will confuse estimates of the latter region coefficients, resulting in a kind of average of the values over the two ranges. An indication of this condition in empirical regression results may appear in two places. First, the t-values associated with input regression coefficients may be measured to be small, since a monotonic function will not fit the true quadratic pattern closely. Therefore, the input will be found to be quantitatively insignificant. Secondly, autocorrelation is likely, as the nonlinear pattern in the partial slope of the production function can be expected to carry over to the error term, producing a pattern in that term. If a region of increasing returns exists, but is confined to quite low levels of production not included in observed data, then Cobb-Douglas estimates will be unaffected by this limitation, as we will be fitting an essentially correct structure to the diminishing marginal productivity region. However, if t-tests and the presence of autocorrelation suggest that specific data contains both increasing and decreasing productivity regions, then the Cobb-Douglas function is probably not a useful model of the production process.

The second objection to the Cobb-Douglas function is revealed by a slight modification of expression (7–12) derived in the previous chapter. In (7–12) it was shown that in least-cost, the following property held for a two-variable Cobb-Douglas function:

$$\frac{b_2 L^*}{b_1 K^*} = \frac{P_k}{P_L} \tag{8-1}$$

where b_1, b_2 are exponents on labor and capital inputs respectively, L^* and K^* are least-cost quantities of labor and capital for a given output level, and P_k, P_L are prices of capital and labor respectively. Multiplying both sides of (8–1) by (b_1/b_2) gives:

$$\frac{L^*}{K^*} = \frac{b_1 P_k}{b_2 P_L} \tag{8-2}$$

This shows that the least-cost ratio of labor to capital is invariant with respect to output level in the Cobb-Douglas case. As output increases, the best input ratio is constrained to remain constant. This structural constraint produces an expansion path that is linear.

But what if the production process is such that higher ratios of capital to labor are efficient at higher output levels? With no structural apparatus for reflecting such a pattern, a statistically estimated Cobb-Douglas function will produce the best constant ratio over the data. If such departures from a linear expansion path are serious, then in effect the Cobb-Douglas is not an appropriate production function to represent the data. As with our earlier single range limitation, this may be expected to show up as autocorrelation in the case of serious departures of the data from the assumed structure. Thus, we have a crude check on the severity of the effect of our first two limiting features of the Cobb-Douglas in the form of the Durbin-Watson statistic.

The third limitation of the Cobb-Douglas function for real-world applications is its constraint of unitary elasticity of input substitution. Elasticity of input substitution between any two inputs, say labor (L) and capital K, may be defined as follows:

$$e_{L \cdot K} = \frac{\% \text{ change in } (L/K)}{\% \text{ change in } (\Delta L/\Delta K)}$$

The numerator of this expression shows the porportionate change in comparative input use resulting from a movement along the $L - K$ isoquant. If $e_{L \cdot K} > 1$, then the isoquant is shaped such that a one-percent change in $\Delta L/\Delta K$, the slope of the isoquant (resulting from moving along it), produces greater than a one-percent change in the associated ratio of L to K. Thus, the constraint that $e_{L \cdot K} = 1$ implied by the Cobb-Douglas function, represents a constraint on the curvature of the family of isoquants resulting from the estimated production function.

The best way to see the $e_{L \cdot K} = 1$ constraint is to formulate the above expression in specific terms. In expression (7–7) in the previous chapter it was shown that the slope of an isoquant for labor and capital $(\Delta L/\Delta K)$ was equal to a ratio of their marginal productivities:

$$\frac{\Delta L}{\Delta K} = \frac{MP_K}{MP_L}$$

Substituting this into the denominator of the present elasticity expression, and formulating a point measure gives:

$$e_{L \cdot K} = \frac{\dfrac{\partial (L/K)}{L/K}}{\dfrac{\partial (MP_K/MP_L)}{MP_K/MP_L}} = \frac{\partial (L/K)}{\partial (MP_K/MP_L)} \cdot \frac{MP_K}{MP_L} \cdot \frac{K}{L}$$

The first term on the right-hand side of this expression can be conveniently written by formulation of an expression for L/K that can be partially differentiated on (MP_K/MP_L). For the two-variable illustrative Cobb-Douglas function $Q = b_0 L^{b_1} K^{b_2}$, this proceeds from expressions for MP_K and MP_L as follows:

$$MP_K = \frac{\partial Q}{\partial K} = b_2 b_0 L^{b_1} K^{b_2-1}$$

$$MP_L = \frac{\partial Q}{\partial L} = b_1 b_0 L^{b_1-1} K^{b_2}$$

and

$$\frac{MP_K}{MP_L} = \frac{b_2}{b_1} \cdot \frac{L}{K}$$

Reexpressing in terms of L/K gives:

$$L/K = \frac{b_1}{b_2} \cdot \frac{MP_K}{MP_L}$$

which leads to the needed derivative:

$$\frac{\partial(L/K)}{\partial(MP_K/MP_L)} = \frac{b_1}{b_2}$$

Combining these results in the expression for $e_{L \cdot K}$ yields:

$$e_{L \cdot K} = \frac{b_1}{b_2} \cdot \frac{b_2 L}{b_1 K} \cdot \frac{K}{L} = 1$$

which shows that the Cobb-Douglas function produces $e_{L \cdot K} = 1$, regardless of the measured values of any coefficients.

The $e_{L \cdot K} = 1$ result shows that a constraint is imposed on the overall shape of the isoquant map by selection of the Cobb-Douglas structure. As with our first two limitations, to the extent that an actual production process does not at least approximately correspond to this assumption, the Cobb-Douglas structure will be inappropriate as a tool for measuring production characteristics.

In this chapter, we will recognize these limitations of the Cobb-Douglas structure, and proceed to use it to further consider the problem of estimation of actual production relationships.[1] We now turn our attention to methods of estimating the coefficients of Cobb-Douglas functions from raw data.

---

[1] An increasingly discussed alternative to the Cobb-Douglas function for empirical research is the constant elasticity of substitution (CES) production function. For a discussion, see K. J. Arrow, H. B. Chenery, B. S. Minhas, and R. M. Solow, "Capital–Labor Substitution and Economic Efficiency," *Review of Economics and Statistics* (August 1961), pp. 225–50.

COEFFICIENT ESTIMATION IN COBB-DOUGLAS FUNCTION

We earlier saw the Cobb-Douglas function to be logarithmically linear, as follows:

$$\ln Q = \ln b_0 + b_1 \ln I_1 + b_2 \ln I_2 + \cdots + b_n \ln I_n$$

If data are obtained for quantity Q produced and associated quantities of inputs employed for a production process, logs may be taken of the raw data Q, $I_1 \cdots I_n$. This transformation enables direct estimates of b_1, $b_2 \cdots b_n$ (the coefficients of a linear function fit through the log data). An estimate of b_0 can be obtained by then taking the antilog of the resulting regression intercept. Moreover, least-squares and the single-equation methods of equation evaluation discussed in Chapters 2–3 are appropriate tools for this purpose. For production functions, our fundamental prerequisite of single-equations estimation methods—that the independent variables are truly predetermined—is met. For short time periods such as monthly, over which much production data on inputs and outputs accrue in practice (and for which production decisions often have practical relevance), the inputs do indeed determine the output and not vice versa, in most production processes. Over much longer time periods, say yearly, this not so clearly the case.[2]

As with other empirical models, correct specification is an important consideration with Cobb-Douglas production functions. We must include all significant inputs to the production process, and none that is superfluous if we expect to obtain reasonable coefficient estimates. The effect of specification errors on our parameter estimates will be similar to those discussed in Chapter 3. However, obtaining a correct specification of inputs will usually be less difficult than in the case of many other classes of models, since the operation of a production process is normally highly visible, with major inputs usually being quite evident. (Labor, machinery, and so forth must be organized and paid for.)

A notable and common exception is the influence of technology and technological change. An increase in technology enables a set of inputs to produce more output, in effect shifting the production function to the right. In this sense, technological change can be considered as an input. In some cases, it may be possible to enter a technology variable directly into the specification of inputs. In others, where the technological change has been erratic, this may not be possible.

It is often possible in cases of periodic technological change to construct a dummy variable that coincides with the pattern of technological

---

[2] For a discussion of the theoretical position of inputs as endogenous or exogenous relative to neoclassical microeconomic theory, see M. Nerlove, *Estimation and Identification of Cobb-Douglas Production Functions* (Skokie, Ill.: Rand McNally, 1965), pp. 30–58.

change in the data. For example, consider a sample of 30 observations over time characterized by two major technological changes, one at period 8 and the other at period 22. The separate effects of two such technological changes on the position of the production function may be measured by using two dummy shift variables. The first corresponds to the period 8 change and has a value of 1.0 (arbitrarily chosen) for periods 1 through 7 and a different value, say 2.0, for periods 8 through 30. The second dummy variable corresponds to the period 22 change and has a value of, say, 1.0 for periods 1 through 21 and a value of 2.0 for periods 22 through 30. Then, the regression analysis would assign an empirically meaningful weighting to each of the two changes, in the form of the coefficients of the two dummy variables. In some cases, the technological pattern may be so erratic as to frustrate attempts to represent it quantitatively. In these cases, useful coefficients cannot be obtained due to the inability to specify technology's effects.

In some instances, technology can realistically be assumed constant over the sample. In these cases, it may safely be omitted from the production function. In other cases, changing technology will have to be brought into the equation and its effects accounted for statistically. Although we have no uniform procedure for separating these two cases, the effects of unaccounted-for changes in technology will show up as specification errors and often produce autocorrelation. In this way, a partial test can be made on this account.

Any specification of inputs for a particular production process is bound to omit the effects of small unsystematic influences on output. For example, if the foreman shows up somewhat ill on a given morning, he may not be as efficient in his duties as normal, and the result will be that a given set of specified inputs will not produce as much output as otherwise. One could envision a large number of such possible minor disturbances to the "normal" functioning of the production process. In fitting an equation to production data, we want to abstract from these disturbances to focus on the inherent underlying process. This can be accomplished through addition of an error term μ to our model representing the unsystematically determined portion of output:

$$\ln Q = \ln b_0 + b_1 \ln I_1 + b_2 \ln I_2 + \cdots + b_n I_n + \mu \qquad (8\text{--}3)$$

When we apply the single-equation estimation and evaluation procedures of Chapters 2 and 3 to (8–3), the four statistical assumptions about μ must hold if the estimates are to be reliable.[3] Thus, μ must be a stochastic variable, approximately normally distributed with zero mean and constant variance, non-autocorrelated, and not correlated with $I_1, I_2 \cdots I_n$. In addition, the discussion of multicollinearity in Chapter 3 applies here;

---

[3] See Chapter 2 for a discussion of these error term assumptions.

the I must not be seriously intercorrelated. If they are, our b estimates will have greatly reduced meaning. If these conditions are met, ordinary regression procedures will produce reasonable estimates of the b values.

AN ILLUSTRATIVE EXAMPLE

We now focus the ideas of this chapter on a numerical example, beginning with raw data of the variety normally available on the operation of production processes. As in earlier examples, we shall impose the unreality of knowing for certain the structure, specification, and coefficient values of the underlying function that produced our raw data. That "true" production function is:

$$Q = 50.0L^{0.3}K^{0.8}e^{\mu} \tag{8-4}$$

where Q is quantity produced per week, L is the total man-hours of labor per week applied, and K is the number of production lines brought into operation during the week ($K = 1$, 2, or 3 only). μ is a normally distributed variable with mean $= 0$ and standard deviation $= 15.0$. For statistical use, μ will be taken at its assumed value of 0, thus causing the last term to dissappear. With this function, data have been simulated for 25 weeks of operation. These data are shown in the first three columns of Table 8–1.

Our earlier discussion of marginal productivity and Cobb-Douglas functions showed that the equation coefficient provided a direct measure of this pattern. For example, knowledge that the L coefficient is 0.3 tells us our process is characterized by diminishing marginal productivity of labor. If this is true, it should be apparent in the data of Table 8–1, if only we could hold the K input constant. (Recall the concept of marginal productivity was premised upon other inputs being held constant.) Indeed, since only three values of K characterize the data, we can group the data into constant-K groupings of $K = 1$, 2, and 3, and observe the output-labor input pattern that results.

This is done in Table 8–2, where the nine observations for $k = 1$, eight observations for $k = 2$, and eight observations for $k = 3$ are grouped according to the L input. Average output for a given L are computed and shown. Then, a crude estimate of the marginal productivity of labor is computed, $\Delta Q / \Delta L$. All three groupings generally show the true diminishing pattern on the basis of this crude procedure, although the unsystematic factor in the data, μ, produces two exceptions: (a) for $k = 1$, chance variation has produced what appears to be a rising, then falling pattern of marginal productivity (we have earlier seen that such a systematic pattern cannot characterize the Cobb-Douglas function); and (b) a large disturbance value in the $k = 3$ grouping has produced

TABLE 8–1

Period (1)	Quantity produced (2)	Labor man-hours (3)	Production lines (4)	Quantity produced— shift in technology period 13 (5)	Quantity produced— constant increase in technology (6)
1..........	503	280	2	503	503
2..........	218	160	1	218	232
3..........	679	360	3	679	763
4..........	729	400	3	729	859
5..........	493	320	2	493	611
6..........	467	280	2	467	609
7..........	440	240	2	440	602
8..........	246	160	1	246	342
9..........	199	120	1	199	300
10..........	266	160	1	266	390
11..........	390	200	2	390	646
12..........	462	240	2	462	759
13..........	651	280	3	1304	1121
14..........	688	320	3	1367	1218
15..........	741	400	3	1467	1351
16..........	480	320	2	972	922
17..........	240	200	1	485	475
18..........	209	160	1	438	443
19..........	194	80	1	380	395
20..........	215	140	1	435	466
21..........	242	180	1	480	527
22..........	449	240	2	899	1017
23..........	672	300	3	1338	1551
24..........	678	320	3	1357	1615
25..........	726	380	3	1442	1757

a quirk in the MP_L pattern between 360 and 380 man-hours of L, which smooths out somewhat if 320 through 380 is computed instead.

We should be able to produce a similar pattern if we could fix L at some value and consider the use of 1, 2, and 3 units of K. There are, however, no instances in the data where this occurs. Where possible, such visual methods as shown in Table 8–2 are helpful preliminary steps in sizing up the data for irregularities and unexpected patterns. However, all the major conclusions derivable from empirical data flow from the estimated equation coefficients themselves.

Assuming we choose the true specification of inputs, the equation to be estimated is of the form:

$$Q = b_0 L^{b_1} K^{b_2}$$

taking logs gives:

$$\ln Q = \ln b_0 + b_1 \ln L + b_2 \ln K$$

TABLE 8–2

One Production Line ($k = 1$)

Average output	Man-hours (L)	$\dfrac{\Delta\ Output}{\Delta\ Man\text{-}hours}$
194............	80 (1)*	....
199............	120 (1)	0.13
215............	140 (1)	0.80
235............	160 (4)	1.00
242............	180 (1)	0.35
240............	200 (1)	−0.10

Two Production Lines ($k = 2$)

Average output	Man-hours (L)	$\dfrac{\Delta\ Output}{\Delta\ Man\text{-}hours}$
390............	200 (1)	....
450............	240 (3)	1.50
485............	280 (2)	0.88
487............	320 (2)	0.05

Three Production Lines ($k = 3$)

Average output	Man-hours (L)	$\dfrac{\Delta\ Output}{\Delta\ Man\text{-}hours}$
651............	280 (1)	....
672............	300 (1)	1.05
683............	320 (2)	0.55
679............	360 (1)	−0.10 ⎫
726............	380 (1)	2.35 ⎬ (0.72)
735............	400 (2)	0.45 ⎭

* Denotes the number of times man-hours were observed.

Taking the natural logs of columns (2) through (4) of Table 8–1 and fitting a regression line with ordinary least-squares gives:

$$\ln Q = 3.83 + .32 \ln L + .78 \ln k$$
$$\qquad\qquad (.06) \qquad\quad (.05)$$

$$R^2 = .990 \quad \text{Durbin-Watson} = 2.99$$

Taking the antilog of the estimated intercept 3.83 gives:

$$Q = 46.1L^{.32}K^{.78} \tag{8–5}$$

a reasonable estimate of the true value. The t-test outlined in Chapter 2 can be applied in this case to judge the significance of individual inputs; in our case the obtained t-values of 5.76 for L and 16.76 for k correctly reflect the fundamental importance of these inputs. The Durbin-Watson statistic does not indicate significant autocorrelation, nor do there appear to be other problems with the statistical assumptions.

In our example, the true production function underlying the data exhibited constant technology, as the only systematic influences upon

Q were L and K. Therefore, our estimate (8–5) correctly ignored technological change. But what if technology (or some other input) is not constant. Specifically, we shall consider two cases: (a) a shift in technology, and (b) a constant change in technology.

An outward shift in technology enables the same inputs to produce more output. Such a shift is present in the output data in column (5) of Table 8–1. These data were produced by enlarging the b_0 coefficient from 50 to 100 at the start of observation 13. As a result, the production function shifts to the right in the last half of the data. Given this shift, we should not expect our model

$$Q = b_0 L^{b_1} K^{b_2} e^{\mu}$$

to enable good estimates of b as it ignores this shift; indeed, our expectation is correct. The equation that results when the model is estimated with the column (4) data is:

$$Q = 150.0 L^{.14} K^{.98} \qquad (8\text{–}6)$$

With an active technological variable, the original, now mis-specified, model greatly understates b_1 and overstates b_2. As earlier suggested, one way to deal with such a shift is to employ a dummy variable D, representing a technological input having, for example, a value of 0.5 for observations 1 through 12 and a value of 1.0 for observations 13 through 25, giving:

$$Q = b_0 L^{b_1} K^{b_2} D^{b_3} e^{\mu}$$

When this model is estimated using the column (4) data, the result is:

$$Q = 83.5 L^{.34} K^{.76} D^{.99}$$

which is a considerable improvement over (8–6) and produces reasonable estimates of b_1 and b_2 in (8–4). The corrected estimates of b_0 allowing for the effect of the dummy variable would be $b_0 = 83.5(0.5)^{.99} = 42.1 =$ for $t = 1$, $2 \cdots 12$, and $b_0 = 83.5(1.0)^{.99} = 83.5$ for $t = 13$, $14 \cdots 25$, which are reasonably close to the true value of 50 and 100.

In some production processes, a common effect of technology is to cause a continual outward shifting in the production function over time. In such cases, constant improvements in techniques and quality of inputs are largely responsible. In Table 8–1, such a pattern has influenced the output data in column (6). The value of b_0 has been successively increased by 3.0 over the sample, beginning with $b_0 = 50$ for $t = 1$ and ending with $b_0 = 125$ for $t = 25$. Ignoring this technological pattern and fitting the original, now mis-specified, model gives:

$$Q = 350.0 L^{.01} K^{1.02}$$

an even poorer estimate than in the case of the technology shift. In fact, this estimate produces the conclusion of increasing marginal productivity of capital. (Additional production lines add output at an increasing rate.) This could be a rather serious consequence of a specification error if several more production lines were constructed on the strength of the finding.

Extending the dummy variable approach to this case of continuous technological change, a trend variable taking on values 1, 2 · · · 25 for the 25 observations can be used to capture the trend effect of the technological change. Fitting a regression with such a trend dummy (TD) included gives:

$$Q = 36.2L^{.32}K^{.79}TD^{.31}$$

which again is a reasonable estimate of the true coefficient values.[4]

The general conclusion suggested by these examples is that specification of all relevant inputs in production functions, particularly the effect of technological shifts and changes, is crucial in obtaining good regression estimates of the relevant coefficients. In turn, the goodness of these estimates will affect the principal conclusions flowing from our estimated equation. We now turn to some of these conclusions.

Conclusions

For convenience, we shall use the true coefficients in our original production function to draw conclusions about the nature of the production process characterized by expression (8–4), repeated here for convenience:

$$Q = 50.0L^{0.30}K^{0.80}e^{\mu} \tag{8-4}$$

By inspection of the L and K coefficients, our earlier discussion enables the following conclusions:

1. Labor exhibits diminishing marginal productivity over the period of the data ($0.30 < 1$) and is inelastic relative to output.
2. Addition of production lines exhibits diminishing marginal productivity for the data ($0.80 < 1$) is also inelastic relative to output.
3. Labor is more inelastic relative to output than production lines are ($0.30 < 0.80$).
4. The process is characterized by increasing returns-to-scale ($0.30 + 0.80 = 1.1 > 1$) over the period of the data.

---

[4] The "corrected" b_0 value would be $36.2TD^{.31}$, which would be 36.2 for $TD = 1$ and 98.2 for $TD = 25$.

LEAST-COST IN COBB-DOUGLAS FUNCTIONS

Returning to the ideas contained in our production model, it is now possible to stipulate least-cost combinations of L and K for specific output levels if we are given unit prices for both L and K. Earlier, we defined expression (8–2) as holding for all least-cost points on the firm's expansion path. It is repeated here for convenience:

$$\frac{L^*}{K^*} = \frac{b_1 P_k}{b_2 P_L} \qquad (8-2)$$

We earlier noted that the least-cost ratio L^*/K^* remained constant for production processes approximated by Cobb-Douglas functions. We now find the value of that constant ratio for our problem, for the case where $P_k = \$600$ per production line and $P_L = \$4$ per manhour.

$$\frac{L^*}{K^*} = \frac{(0.3)(600)}{(0.8)(4)} = 56.2$$

This result shows that the least-cost solution involves 56.2 labor manhours to each production line. A quick inspection of the data of Table 8–1 reveals that the actual observed ratios of L to K were regularly several times this amount and averaged $L/K = 133.5$. This means that the actual combination of inputs were rather seriously nonleast-cost, and that consequently total costs of L and K were more than necessary to produce the output produced. We shall come back to this point in Chapter 9.

Expression (8–2) defines a least-cost ratio of L/K, but it does not enable L^* and K^* to be selected given an output level. To obtain an expression appropriate to this task, define the least-cost L^*/K^* ratio as R:

$$R = \frac{b_1 P_K}{b_2 P_L}$$

Then

$$L^* = RK^*$$

and

$$K^* = \frac{L^*}{R}$$

This may now be inserted in the original production function in place of K, along with L^*:

$$Q = b_0 L^{*b_1} \left[\frac{L^*}{R} \right]^{b_2} = \frac{b_0 L^{*b_1} L^{*b_2}}{R^{b_2}}$$

$$Q = \frac{b_0 L^{*(b_1+b_2)}}{R^{b_2}}$$

Solving for L^* gives:

$$L^* = \left[\frac{R^{b_2}}{b_0}\right]^{\frac{1}{b_1+b_2}} \cdot Q^{\frac{1}{b_1+b_2}} \tag{8-7}$$

For our data, this gives:

$$L^* = .534Q^{.908} \tag{8-8}$$

which enables the corresponding least-cost value of K:

$$K^* = \frac{L^*}{56.2} \tag{8-9}$$

These expressions are used in Table 8–3 to compute least-cost combinations for output levels of 200, 400, and 600. These calculations are shown in the rectangular boxes.

TABLE 8–3

Q	L	K	L/K	*Cost*
	46	1.345	34.2	991
200	66	1.175	56.2	969
	86	1.065	80.7	983
	104	2.36	44.1	1832
400	124	2.21	56.2	1822
	144	2.09	68.9	1830
	158	3.34	47.3	2636
600	178	3.17	56.2	2614
	198	3.06	64.8	2628

Note: Numbers have been rounded.

In addition, for each output level the table shows two other input combinations involving a lower and higher K/L ratio than the least-cost value of 56.2. This allows a comparison of optimal with non-optimal input combinations. Costs are computed for each input combination, illustrating the least-cost property of the values of L and K that satisfy (8–8) and (8–9). Also notice the costs that result from the least-cost solutions. In the 100 percent increase in output from 200 to 400 units, costs rise by only 88 percent. In the 50 percent increase from 400 to 600 units, they rise by 43.5 percent. This arises from economics of scale in the production process which we earlier saw reflected by the condition that $b_1 + b_2 > 1$.

The function we have considered treats K as a continuous variable. Thus, our least-cost combinations in Table 8–3 have involved fractional units of K. In some cases, a variable such as K will have to take on an integer value. i.e., we will have to decide to use one, two or three production lines. In such cases we can only approximate the least-cost point by selecting the integer value that comes the closest to the least-cost value. In the example, this amounts to the selection of the integer value for K that will produce the lowest cost for a given output. A comparison of the unrestricted least-cost points and the integer values is contained in Table 8–4, where the first three columns contain the exact least-cost

TABLE 8–4

Q	Least cost unrestricted solutions			Least-cost approximations K = integer value			Cost— K fixed at 3	
	L^*	K^*	Cost	L'	K'	Cost	L''	Cost
100........	35	0.623	513.8	10	1	640	1	1804
150........	50	0.890	734.0	39	1	756	2	1808
200........	66	1.175	969.0	101	1	1004	5	1820
250........	80	1.424	1,174.0	34	2	1336	11	1844
300........	94	1.672	1,379.2	61	2	1444	21	1884
350........	109	1.938	1,598.8	103	2	1612	35	1940
400........	124	2.21	1,822.0	160	2	1840	54	2016
450........	137	2.44	2,012.6	80	3	2120	80	2120
500........	150	2.670	2,202.0	111	3	2244	111	2244
550........	164	2.92	2,408.0	157	3	2428	157	2428
600........	178	3.17	2,614.0	207	3	2628	207	2628
650........	191	3.40	2,804.0	269	3	2876	269	2876
700........	205	3.65	3,010.0	346	3	3184	346	3184
750........	218	3.89	3,206.0	442	3	3568	442	3568
800........	229	4.08	3.364.0	553	3	4012	553	4012

value of L^* and K^* along with the resulting costs, while the next three columns contain the minimum cost input combinations given the integer restrictions on K. As seen, the path of L' is rather bumpy with increasing output. This is due to the unrestricted least-cost K values becoming greater than an integer value (i.e., 1.175 for $Q = 200$), resulting in the use of more L than the unrestricted values but the smaller integer value of K. Then, at some point, such as $Q = 250$, it becomes economical to step to the next integer value (2) of K, i.e., it becomes economical to begin to use the second production line which is *greater* than the unrestricted value, and involves *less* labor. In the lower part of the table (beyond $Q = 650$ or so), the unrestricted least-cost combination involves a K approaching 4. However, our assumption was that only three lines were available. This means the K restricted input combinations would be able to generate the additional output only by additional labor applied to the now fixed input. As indicated by the earlier finding of diminishing returns to labor, this results in decreasing efficiency in the additional use of labor, and the costs are seen to rise sharply compared to their pattern in the unrestricted case, where scale changes in K can be made continuously as indicated by the K^* values.[5]

The final two columns in Table 8–4 show the pattern of costs associated with the strategy of operating all three production lines for the production of any output levels. As seen, the costs in low output ranges are substantially higher than for the use of less K, illustrating the cost consequences of substantial departures from least-cost L, K combination in this case. We shall return to this point in the next chapter.

ON NONEXPERIMENTAL DATA

One final problem that may be encountered in efforts aimed at production function estimation concerns the nonexperimental nature of production data in many real-world situations. Ideally, we would like to accumulate production function data on a wide variety of input combinations for various output combinations. This would span the input-output data space with well-dispersed observations. In terms of an isoquant mapping such as was discussed in Chapter 7, we would accumulate data from many regions of many isoquants. These data would support reliable production function coefficient estimates.

In particular applications, these ideal conditions may not be even approximately met. A firm that diligently monitors its input combinations may succeed in keeping these combinations at approximately the least-cost point. If so, input-output combinations will be observed only along the firm's expansion path. Consequently, only a small dimension of the production surface will be the basis for all the observable data. The result of this situation will be estimated coefficients that are quite unreliable as a representative measure of the overall production function. A similar problem would exist if the firm's production levels had been very stable over the data period. Data would essentially accrue on only one isoquant region of the curve. Accordingly, reliable measurements of coefficients would not be well supported.

Unfortunately, the analyst of production relationships may have little recourse when faced with data problems of nonexperimental data. The only fundamental attack on this problem is to seek more data in other regions of the production surface. But this implies the ability to make experimental production decisions involving unusual input combinations or unusual output levels. Often, this is a luxury that real-world·firms cannot afford. In such cases, there may be no way to circumvent potential data deficiencies of nonexperimental samples.

---

[5] In fact, the marginal product of labor measured incrementally when $K' = 3$ continuously declines from 1.6, 1.1, 1.0, 0.8, 0.6, 0.5, to 0.4 and the costs would similarly rise.

We have seen in this and the previous chapter that the costs of production are integrally related through input selection to the production function. In fact, if we know the production function characterizing a production process, we can derive relevant cost curves for analysis. A discussion of the specifics of this and other related concepts is the concern of the next chapter.

DISCUSSION QUESTIONS

1. In measuring production relationships, the discussion of this chapter has pointed out that the Cobb-Douglas function enables discovery of some important aspects of a production function, if we are prepared to assume other things. Distinguish between what we may discover and what we must assume.
2. In forming an estimated Cobb-Douglas function, how would you handle the occurrence of four successive technological changes in the form of machine improvements occurring over the sample period?
3. What are the practical implications of accepting the Cobb-Douglas assumption of a constant least-cost ratio?
4. If you could acquire historical data on input use and output produced for a production process, under what circumstances could you not obtain reliable empirical estimates of production function coefficients?
5. A statistically estimated production function yields the following results:

$$ln\ Q = 3.85 + 0.63\ ln\ L + 0.40\ ln\ K$$
$$(3.8) \quad (5.43) \quad (0.84)$$
$$R^2 = .86$$
$$D.W. = 1.87$$

where numbers in parentheses are computed t-values, where Q is output in units, and where L and K are labor hours and units of physical capacity respectively. From both a statistical and an economic viewpoint, how do you interpret these results? Do you need any more information?

CASE 7—A. O. JONES FURNITURE (A)

The A. O. Jones Corporation manufactures furniture. Its major product lines are sofas, easy chairs, coffee and end tables, and dining room sets. Specific products are put into production upon receipt of orders by furniture retailers or by large-volume buyers for apartment buildings. No conventional production line is employed. Rather, certain premanufactured pieces are combined with special parts on an item-by-item basis by furniture craftsmen. In the manufacture of both the premanufactured parts (table legs, chair spindles, frame parts), and the special parts, considerable latitude exists in the use of wood or other materials as opposed to the use of labor. Considerable labor can be saved by certain lathe and saw set-ups and techniques, at the expense of the efficient use of materials. Alternatively, production methods directed towards the most efficient use of materials generally absorb more labor. For example, squeezing the maximum usage from a bolt of sofa fabric means extra seams and considerable time-consuming calculations. Thus, a serious continued problem confronts the firm as to where to strike a balance in efficiency between labor use and materials use.

Since this appeared to be one type of problem to which the economics of production was addressed, the firm's analytical staff decided it might be appropriate to attempt to estimate a production function for the firm's output.

The first problem was that the firm produced a large variety of products that, while sharing many things in common, were far different in size and expense. For example, the least expensive end table sold by the company carried a manufacturer's price of $30.00, while the highest priced item, a decorative oak-trimmed sofa, sold for $440.00. So the firm's unit-production figures seemed to be a batch of oranges and apples. However, on further analysis, the staff members noted that the relative composition of items produced was largely constant over time, as shown in Table 8–5.

TABLE 8–5
Percentage of Total Production—1969 ($ value of units shipped)

Product category	January	March	May	July	September	November
End tables........	14	15	14	14	13	14
Coffee tables......	12	12	14	13	12	13
Sofas.............	23	25	23	24	24	25
Easy chairs.......	25	23	22	24	25	24
Dining sets.......	11	10	11	12	11	10
Decorative furniture........	10	12	13	10	12	10
Other.............	5	3	3	3	3	4

The pattern of Table 8–5 was typical of other recent years and encouraged the staff members' use of the total unit production data. The reasoning was that if the composition of total production remained approximately constant, then using data on total inputs employed and total units produced to establish key production relationships would be a reasonable procedure to follow.

Turning to a description of inputs to the production process, the staff established that the same plant size had been used since 1967, and that the machinery used had been largely the same from early 1966 to July 1969, at which time seven major new items of woodworking equipment were purchased, partially to replace older items and partially to expand and extend the woodworking capability. After this change, the items of machinery had remained the same up to the present time.

The major items of direct expense with which the company was concerned were skilled labor hours, quantity of wood, and quantity of upholstery fabric. To explore the statistical production relationships between these inputs and the total units produced, a Cobb-Douglas production function was chosen, as follows:

$$Q = aL^bW^cM^de^\mu$$

where

Q = total units of furniture produced per month
L = man hours of skilled labor employed per month
W = total board feet of wood used per month
M = bolts of upholstery fabric used per month
μ = a random disturbance term satisfying regression assumptions

Data were available on Q, L, W, and M stretching back to the early 1960s. However, since the nature of the factory and other conditions only approached stability since 1967, the period 1967 to 1970 was chosen for the study, involving 48 months of data. The data were next transformed into logarithms so that estimation of the coefficients a, b, c, and d could be accomplished by linear least squares according to:

$$\ln Q = \ln a + b \ln L + c \ln W + d \ln M + \mu$$

Upon performing regression on this transformed model, the following equation was obtained:

$$\ln Q = 1.792 + 0.61 \ln L + 0.30 \ln W + 0.23 \ln M$$
$$\qquad\qquad (2.95) \qquad (4.27) \qquad (3.35)$$

$R^2 = .92$ (coefficient of determination)
$S_\mu = 0.69$ (standard error)
$D.W. = 0.84$ (Durbin-Watson)
$\overline{\ln Q} = 5.01$ (average value of log of output)

In addition, correlations among the variables involved are:

	$\ln Q$	$\ln L$	$\ln W$	$\ln M$
$\ln Q$	1.00			
$\ln L$	.42	1.00		
$\ln W$	.51	.09	1.00	
$\ln M$	.73	.19	.20	1.00

Questions

1. What conclusions may be drawn about:
   a) returns to a single input
   b) returns-to-scale
   c) input elasticities
   d) appropriateness of the Cobb-Douglas function in representing the firm's production data?
2. Do you agree with the "lumping together" of the firm's products into a single production function?
3. How does this production function apply to the production of sofas, if at all?

CASE 8—A. O. JONES FURNITURE (B)

Having organized data on their production process and having fitted a Cobb-Douglass function to these data, the firm's analysts detected a substantial level of autocorrelation in the residuals, having obtained a Durbin-Watson statistic of 0.84. (See Part A for details.) They felt this result was probably due to either: (a) failure to specify correctly an important input to the production process; or (b) failure of the data to conform to the assumed Cobb-Douglas structure. Analysts Charles Tinder and Alfred Jones, Jr. were assigned to track down this problem. Upon further analysis of the error term, they found that 23 of the first 30 values of $(Y - Y_c)$ were negative, while 14 of the last 18 values were positive. Moreover, the "break-point" in this pattern occurred in July, 1969.

"Aha!" said analyst Tinder, "That is exactly the point where seven major items of equipment were introduced into service. That equipment must have had the effect of shifting our production function up."

"Yes" said Jones, "I'm sure that's right. When Dad bought that new equipment, productivity went up just like the equipment salesman said it would." (Jones' dad was the founder, chairman of the board, and president of the company. This usually caused young Jones' ideas to be popularly received.)

Jones went to a nearby blackboard and drew a sketch similar to Figure 8–2. He continued, "In fact, that explains all of the negative residuals followed by the positive. See, it's like this picture—our equation consistently misses on the high side for the data before July 1969, and consistently misses on the low side after that point."

Tinder replied, "You've hit it right on the head, Jones!" and grinned slightly at being able to say that truthfully for a change. The question the two analysts now pondered was what to do to account for the impact of this problem on their results.

After some discussion, they decided to introduce a dummy variable

FIGURE 8–2

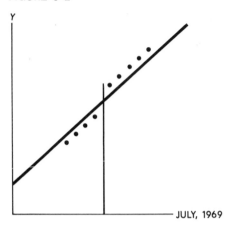

into their analysis, having a value of 1.0 for the period before the change and 2.0 for the period after the change. This made their modified Cobb-Douglas function:

$$Q = aL^bW^cM^dD^fe^\mu$$

where:

Q = output of furniture (units)
L = labor use (man-hours)
W = wood use (board feet)
M = upholstery fabric use (bolts)
D = dummy to account for machine purchase
μ = random error term

This function was re-estimated using the original data along with the new dummy series. The following regression equation resulted:

$$\ln Q = 1.609 + 0.61 \ln L + 0.02 \ln W + 0.25 \ln M + 0.28D$$
$$(4.01) \qquad (0.09) \qquad (4.22) \qquad (6.14)$$

where numbers in parentheses are computed t-values.
Also,

$R^2 = .98$ (coefficient of determination)
$S_\mu = 1.70$ (standard error)
$D.W. = 1.89$ (Durbin-Watson statistic)

Jones and Tinder were encouraged at the elimination of the autocorrelation by the dummy variable. However, a new concern was now present. "Look at the t-value associated with the W (wood use) term," said

Tinder. "It now suggests almost no significance in output attached to wood use."

"Come on now," said Jones. "Wood is obviously involved in our production process. Who's kidding who that it doesn't belong in our model?"

Tinder rubbed his ear. "Well, it certainly does nothing statistically for our production function."

At this point, the two analysts decided to consult a friend in the company who was currently taking a course in quantitative economic analysis at the university.

Question

You are the friend. What general ideas can you provide, apart from this specific problem, that may be helpful to the analysts?

After some soul searching, Jones and Tinder decided to re-estimate their equation, dropping out the wood use variable. The results obtained were:

$$\ln Q = 1.946 + 0.62 \ln L + 0.26 \ln M + 0.27 \ln D$$
$$(4.88) \qquad (5.01) \qquad (4.23)$$

where numbers in parentheses are computed t-values and:

$$R^2 = .98$$
$$S_\mu = 1.60$$
$$D.W. = 1.91$$

Upon seeing these results, Jones said, "Well, the R^2 is undamaged by the change, and the standard error of the equation has actually gone down. Since the Durbin-Watson is still o.k., I say this equation is a better representation of our production process than the first one."

With a rare display of gut reaction, Tinder replied, "I think you are wrong, Jones. We can't prove W doesn't belong in this equation just because of its low t-value and these results. Don't forget, we have only a sample of data containing only a sample of the fluctuations in the variables. Also, maybe multicollinearity is operating in a way we cannot detect to affect the value of the W coefficient. If either of these is true, the lower standard error in our second run may be due just to chance."

In order to interpret their results, they now needed to gather data on the costs of the inputs. First, there was the cost of labor. The average wage rate per manhour of labor was $4.10. However, fringe benefits, including hospitalization, vacation, an employer-paid life insurance policy, and contributions to a retirement plan, came to $1,760 per year per man. Figuring 2,000 hours in a standard company man-year, this came to an additional $0.88 per hour. Thus, the total labor cost for labor plus fringes was $4.98 per hour, which the company often rounded to $5 for purposes of quick analyses. The two analysts now struggled with the question of whether $4.10 or $5.00 was the more appropriate rate to use in their evaluations.

Upholstery costs were more straightforward. Although many different types and grades were used, the average cost was $17.10 per bolt.

Questions

1. Considering the specifics of this case, do you agree with their decision to drop the variable?
2. Given Jones' and Tinder's final form of the production function and the data on costs, present all the information it is possible to derive from these data about the nature of the production process.

Chapter 9

COST-OUTPUT
RELATIONSHIPS

A cost curve in economics is a relationship between costs of production and output levels. Relationships between monetary costs and output are direct products of relationships between physical inputs and output. Therefore, Chapters 7 and 8 have provided all the basic conceptual apparatus necessary for our analysis of costs. We shall build upon those ideas in developing the primary cost curves of interest in our analysis of firm behavior. We shall then consider conclusions that can be drawn from cost curves. As we have several differing costs of production, our analysis begins with a consideration of the definitional question, which costs? We shall discuss three primary definitions and one secondary definition relating to our specific problem.

THEORETICAL LONG-RUN COSTS

The first concept can be called theoretical long-run costs, defined as the costs associated with production of all output levels with unrestricted least-cost input combinations. Such a situation involves output levels being produced as cheaply as possible, using the most efficient scale of production. This accounts for the term *long-run* in the definition, since the premise is that all inputs are variable. This curve shows the cost of producing along the theoretical expansion path of the firm. Figure 9–1 shows the derivation of the firm's theoretical long-run cost curve from its isoquant mapping for the two-input case (L = labor, K = machinery, equipment and facilities). In panel (a), the total cost outlay B, at fixed prices P_L, P_K is increased sufficiently to produce at least-cost the outputs Q_1, Q_2, and Q_3 with total outlay B_1, B_2, and B_3. Values of these two variables, illustrating the net effect of the process of input choice, are then plotted in panel (b), which is the firm's theoretical long-run cost curve. This cost curve is a direct result of the production function from which the isoquant mapping of panel (a) was obtained. If the production function shifts (because of a shift in technology for

FIGURE 9–1

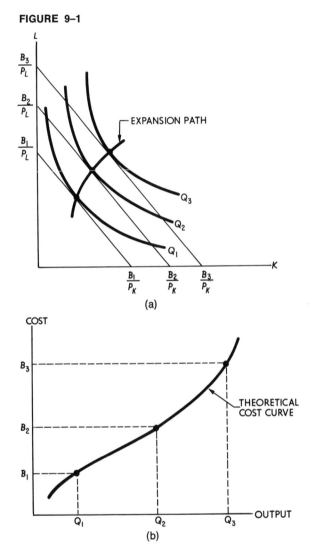

(a)

(b)

example), the cost curve will similarly shift. Or if input prices change, the cost curve will directly reflect this change by a shift in position.[1]

Since all inputs are free to vary in the theoretical long-run cost function, the general shape of this function will relate to the returns-to-scale characterizing the production function. If the process exhibits increasing returns-to-scale, then proportionate input increases produce greater-than-proportionate output changes. At fixed input prices, this means that cost-per-unit (C/Q where C is total costs and Q is output) will fall at larger

---

[1] Can you trace this through the graphical model of Figure 9–1?

scales of production, since the input costs will not rise proportionately with output. The reverse is true if decreasing returns-to-scale characterize the production process. Proportionately greater input quantities (and costs) are necessary to produce continued output increases, so that unit costs will rise. Accordingly, for constant returns-to-scale, unit costs would remain constant for increased output levels. From the total cost curve illustrated in Figure 9-1 panel (b), we could derive a second curve plotting unit costs (or average costs as they are often called) against output. The slope of this long-run unit cost curve directly indicates returns-to-scale. Figure 9-2 contains illustrative long-run unit cost curves reflect-

FIGURE 9-2

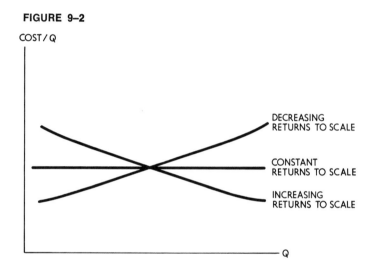

ing the three logical possibilities now outlined: (1) a positively sloped long-run unit cost curve indicating decreasing returns, (2) a negatively sloped curve indicating increasing returns, and (3) a horizontal curve showing constant returns.

For the numerical example of Chapter 8, unrestricted least-cost combinations were computed for the two-variable production function:

$$Q = b_0 L^{b_1} K^{b_2} \qquad (9-1)$$

where L is labor, K the number of production lines (L and K are the only inputs), and $b_0 = 50$, $b_1 = 0.3$, $b_2 = 0.8$. These computations were presented in Table 8-4. The resulting minimum total costs (for $P_K = 600$, $P_L = 4$) and associated output levels comprise the theoretical long-run cost function for the problem. It is plotted from the data of Table 8-4 and shown as the solid line in Figure 9-3. The associated long-run-unit cost curve for the same data is shown in Figure 9-4. As seen in Figure 9-4, long-run unit costs decline. With no other changes

FIGURE 9–3

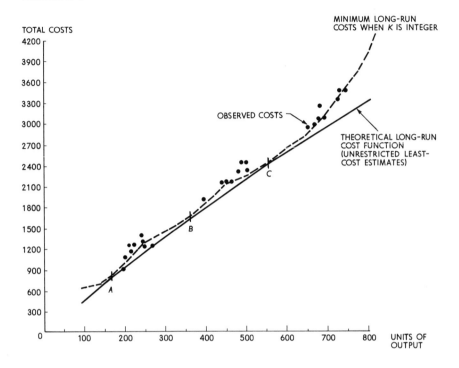

FIGURE 9–4

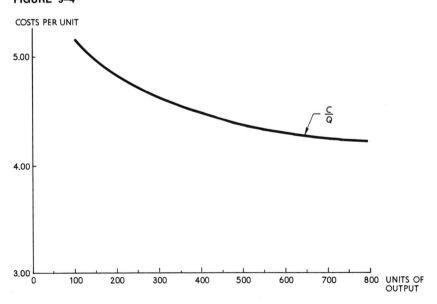

in prices, technology, and so forth, declining long-run costs occur because increasing return-to-scale characterize the production process generating those costs. Thus, Figure 9–4 indicates increasing returns-to-scale. This corresponds to the conclusion reached in Chapter 8 through algebraic analysis of the production function in the example.

$$(b_1 + b_2 = .3 + .8 = 1.1 > 1)$$

Restricted Long-Run Costs

The specific definition of K in the illustrative problem of this and the previous chapter indicated that certain productive inputs may not be alterable continuously in the least-cost direction. K could be changed only in integer values of 1, 2, or 3 production lines, with the latter being a maximum value for K. The result of this restriction is to cause the now minimum cost combination of L and K to involve more K than optimal when the least-cost K is somewhat less than an integer value, and less K than optimal the remainder of the time. The result will be higher cost than in the unrestricted case at all levels of output except those three points where the unrestricted least-cost combination involves exactly 1, 2, and 3 units of K, in wihch case the two costs would be the same. Minimum-cost combinations of L and K with this integer restriction were computed and given in Table 8–4 in Chapter 8. These values are plotted graphically in Figure 9–3 (dotted line) along with the unrestricted curve (solid line). As seen, at points A, B, and C the three curves are tangent, since at those points the unrestricted least-cost points involve exactly 1, 2, and 3 units of K. To the right of point A, costs rise above the solid line due to using the one line beyond its most efficient level. Then beyond 250 units, two lines are employed at less than optimal efficiency, thus causing the dotted line to remain above the solid. However, as output increases, the inefficiency is reduced and eliminated at point B, where the cycle begins again. However, beyond about $Q = 700$, the maximum and now fixed value of K produces increasing inefficiency in the use of labor, driving costs up considerably.

The long-run unit cost curve accompanying this restricted input case (obtained from the data of Table 8–4) is shown in Figure 9–5. The pattern is necessarily similar to that of Figure 9–3 since the C/Q curves are only the C curves of Figure 9–3 divided by a constant. The points of tangency in Figure 9–5 at A, B, and C between the restricted and unrestricted curves also similarly corresponds to the same output points.[2]

---

[2] We have taken two curves and divided them both by a constant. Thus, points of tangency on the original curves will remain points of tangency on the modified curves.

FIGURE 9–5

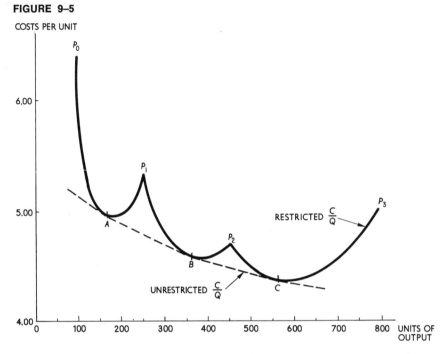

Figure 9–5 highlights the bumpy path of input costs under the kind of input restrictions assumed in the illustrative problem. Moreover, it suggests a heretofore undiscussed property of the unrestricted unit-cost curve of Figure 9–4.

THEORETICAL SHORT-RUN COSTS

To understand this property, we need to introduce the second major cost curve, the theoretical short-run cost curve. It is defined as the relationship between costs and output under conditions where some inputs are fixed. Fixing an input means the input combinations employed along the short-run cost curve will generally not be least-cost. Figure 9–6 illustrates the derivation of a short-run cost function from an isoquant mapping for the case where K is fixed at K_1. As seen in panel (a), the fixed commitment of K at K_1 in the two-input case means that selection of L merely determines the level of output that will result. As seen, this will not be a least-cost combination of L and K in the graph unless output Q_1 is produced, at which level the fixed K_1 is the least cost value along with L_1 for the given budget line BB. This circumstance is identical to the points of tangency A, B, and C in Figure 9–5. At output Q_0,K_1 is greater than the least-cost value (visually pass BB back

FIGURE 9–6

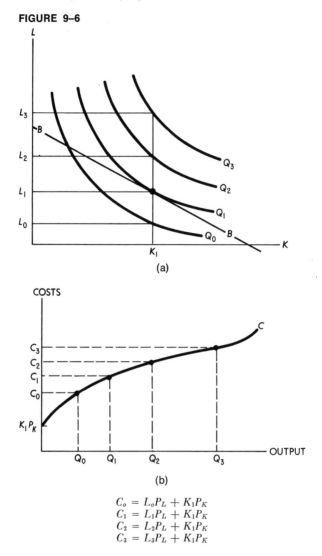

$$C_o = L_oP_L + K_1P_K$$
$$C_1 = L_1P_L + K_1P_K$$
$$C_2 = L_2P_L + K_1P_K$$
$$C_3 = L_3P_L + K_1P_K$$

parallel until it intersects Q_0), while at Q_2 and Q_3, K_1 is smaller than the least-cost value (do the reverse). Now the fixed cost of K_1 (P_KK_1), plus the varying cost of L (LP_L), gives the total cost C for each output. These C values are plotted against the associated output levels in panel (b), which gives the short-run cost curve. This curve shows the way costs and output relate when K is fixed. A similar short-run average cost curve can also be computed from these data.

Returning to Figure 9–5, the integer restriction underlying the solid curve in this figure now means this curve is actually composed of segments from three short-run average cost curves, P_0 to P_1 for $K = 1$, P to P for $K = 2$, and P_2 to P_3 for $K = 3$. When we increase the fixed K value, we simply shift to another short-run curve. In Figure 9–7, other portions of the three short-run curves have been filled in for

FIGURE 9–7

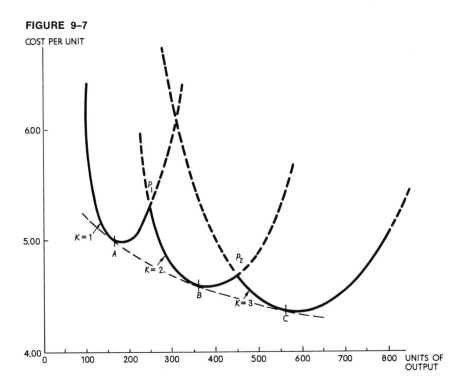

ranges beyond that of the data from which the graph was drawn.[3] This makes the general scale trade-off clearer. As output is expanded beyond the minimum point of the $K = 1$ curve, unit costs rise. At P_1 where the $K = 1$ and $K = 2$ curves cross, it is equally costly to (a) inefficiently overutilize the single production line; or (b) inefficiently underutilize two production lines. To the right of P_1', the underutilization of the two lines is less costly than continued overutilization of the single line until P_2, when a point of indifference is reached between 2 and 3 lines.

Returning now to the unrestricted long-run unit cost curve, recall it was defined as a plot of the unit costs associated with producing at least-cost along the expansion path. This implies a continuous change in scale occurs in order to retain the least-cost property at all points

---

[3] Complete data for the $K = 3$ curve were presented in Table 8–4 in Chapter 8.

along the curve. Given our definition of short-run costs, this also implies that each point on the long-run unit cost curve, representing a different scale, associates with a different short-run unit cost curve. Points *A*, *B*, and *C* on the unrestricted long-run unit cost curve in Figure 9–7 (which correspond to the $K = 1, 2$, and 3 short-run curves) are illustrative of this point, but we could fill in a short-run curve corresponding to each point on the long-run curve.

Thus, in addition to showing the unit costs of producing along the expansion path, the unrestricted long-run unit cost curve can be viewed as an envelope curve of the family of short-run cost curves produced by continuous scale changes.

OBSERVED COSTS

We have considered long-run cost curves, both restricted and unrestricted versions, and short-run curves. The third major type of cost curve suggested in Chapter 8 is observed costs. Returning to Figure 9–3, observed costs for the associated output levels of the Chapter 8 data are shown (the points) along with the unrestricted and restricted long-run costs. As seen, the observed costs are in most cases higher than the theoretical curves. In our illustration, this results from the actual use of more labor per production line than the 56.2 L/K ratio indicated in Chapter 8 as optimal. In the observed data, an average of slightly more than 133 L per unit of K was employed. The scatter of points in the vertical direction (including one below the theoretical unrestricted curve) reflects the true stochastic nature of the relationships we have heretofore assumed to be exact in our calculations. Notice the points are bunched in the horizontal direction into three general groupings. These groupings relate to the use of one, two, and three units of K.

Apparently, when a change in K was made, a corresponding change in L was also typically made. For example, when K was increased from one to two, the utilization of L was also increased, say from 130 to 260. As a result of this practice of maintaining a reasonably constant (although excessive) ratio of L to K, output would similarly be increased in stairstep fashion.

Fitting a curve through these observed data would result in an empirical version of the restricted long-run cost curve. The empirical curve would exhibit the actual behavior of the firm in contrast with minimum-cost behavior. The observed curve shows what costs *have been*, while the two theoretical curves derived from the production function tell us what costs *could have been*. Both kinds of curves have their uses as we shall consider. But first, we shall formalize the relationships between costs and production functions that were informally contained in our analysis so far.

RELATIONSHIPS BETWEEN COST AND PRODUCTION MODELS

In our earlier consideration of production models, three related curves were presented for the case of some variable and some fixed inputs:

$$Q = f(I_1, I_2, \ldots I_n) = \text{production function}$$
$$API_1 = Q/I_1 = \text{average product of } I_1.$$
$$MPI_1 = \Delta Q/\Delta I_1 = \text{marginal product of } I_1$$

We now formally define a family of analogous short-run cost curves:[4]

$$C = VC + FC; \text{ total costs} = \text{variable costs} + \text{fixed costs}$$
$$AVC = VC/Q; \text{ average short-run variable costs}$$
$$AFC = FC/Q; \text{ average fixed costs}$$
$$AC = C/Q; \text{ average short-run costs}$$
$$MC = \frac{\Delta VC}{\Delta Q}; \text{ marginal costs}$$

The characteristic shapes of both these sets of functions for data with first increasing then diminishing marginal productivity (the most general case) is shown in Figure 9–8. In panel (a), the MPI_1 function directly shows the increasing then decreasing marginal productivity characterizing the production process. It reaches a maximum at DR, an inflection point in the production function. In the region where MP lies above AP, it causes AP to rise, as the marginal additions to Q/I are above the average Q/I. This continues until MP crosses and falls below AP, after which point the lower MP causes AP to fall. AP thus reaches its maximum where MP crosses from above. In panel (b) the AFC curve continues to fall with greater output, since the numerator remains constant while the denominator continues to increase. The MC curve is shown to fall over an initial range, then rise. In the region where MC is below AC and AVC, unit costs are being added at a smaller rate than average unit costs, so that both AVC and AC will fall. When MC rises above AVC and AC, then the higher MC raises AVC and AC. Thus, both AVC and AC reach their minimums where they are crossed from below by MC.

We now consider two direct connections between the sets of curves in panels (a) and (b) of Figure 9–8. The first is between the AVC and AP curves, while the second is between the MC and MP curves. For convenience, assume that I_1 is the only variable input and that its price is fixed at P_{I_1}. In this case, variable costs are incurred solely for the purchase of input I_1, which means:

$$VC = (P_{I_1})(I_1)$$

---

[4] The short run is due to the existence of some fixed inputs in the production process.

FIGURE 9–8

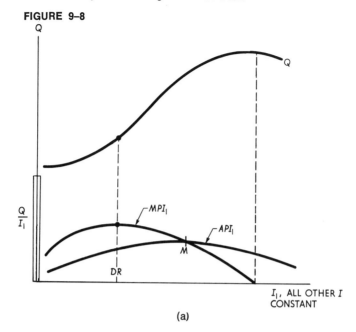

(a)

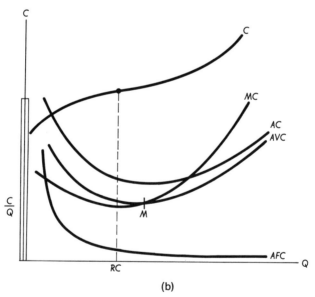

(b)

Then AVC can be reexpressed as follows:

$$AVC = \frac{VC}{Q} = \frac{(P_{I_1})(I_1)}{Q} = P_{I_1}\left(\frac{I_1}{Q}\right) = P_{I_1}\left(\frac{1}{API_1}\right)$$

$$AVC = \frac{P_{I_1}}{API_1}$$

This demonstrates the basic connection between AVC and AP in the single-variable input case: AP is the reciprocal of AVC multiplied by the constant input price. As such, when AP is rising, AVC must be falling and vice versa—when AP is falling, AVC must be rising. Moreover, the maximum of the AP curve corresponds to the minimum of the AVC curve (see points M on the two panels)—the AVC is the monetized mirror image of the AP curve.

In a similar analysis, MC may be reexpressed as follows:

$$MC = \frac{\Delta C}{\Delta Q} = \frac{(P_{I_1})\Delta(I_1)}{\Delta Q} = P_{I_1}\cdot\left(\frac{\Delta I_1}{\Delta Q}\right) = P_{I_1}\cdot\left(\frac{1}{MPI_1}\right)$$

$$MC = \frac{P_{I_1}}{MPI_1}$$

Thus, a monetized reciprocal relationship exists between the two marginal curves similar to that between the average curves: When MP is rising, MC is falling and vice versa. Also, the MP reaches its maximum value at the same output at which MC reaches its minimum. Thus, the rising marginal costs evident in Figure 9–8, panel (b), directly reflects the property of falling marginal productivity characterizing the production function.

USES OF COST CURVES

We now turn to some of the conclusions we may draw from analysis of cost relationships, focusing our attention for illustrative purposes upon the example of this and Chapter 8. First, the excess of observed costs over those derivable from the production function, assuming minimum cost input use (Figure 9–3), indicates that cost savings can be obtained (productivity can be increased) by shifting input combinations towards more use of K and less of L. Second, we know that employment of an additional production line over the existing three lines is likely to be proportionately more profitable than the third line, because the long-run trend of least-cost unit costs is down due to increasing returns-to-scale. Third, as long as the integer restriction of $K = 1, 2,$ and 3 characterizes the production process, production scheduling should try to produce output levels in the vicinity of points A (165 units), B (360 units), or C (560 units) in Figure 9–5 where labor and capital usage equates with least-cost values. By the same token, production levels in the vicinity of P_0, P_1, P_2, and P_3 should be avoided if possible, since they involve the most costly switchover points between production lines. Production levels much beyond point C in Figure 9–5 involve significant marginal cost increases due to inefficient use of additional labor on the fixed three production lines, and should be avoided.

In addition to conclusions of the type we have just reviewed, the family of cost curves provides insights into decisions about best levels of output under certain conditions.

COST CURVES AND PROFIT-MAXIMIZING PRODUCTION DECISIONS

Choice of an appropriate production level in a firm depends upon its objectives, the nature and position of its cost curves (and therefore its production function), and upon the position of its demand function, which establishes a feasible selling price or price range and gives an indication of the quantity that can be sold at that price or within that price range. At this juncture, we shall concentrate on the cost factors in this selection process, saying the market considerations until the next chapter. As a temporary bridge over demand-price considerations, we shall for now assume selling price is wholly determined by the market forces of supply and demand, and is given as fixed to the firm, remaining unaffected by the firm's decision on output level. We also assume output levels are selected in order to attempt to maximize profits.

Under these two sets of circumstances, we may stipulate an appropriate output level by reference to the firm's AC, AVC, and MC curves. Illustrations of these curves are shown in Figure 9–9. Given an objective

FIGURE 9–9

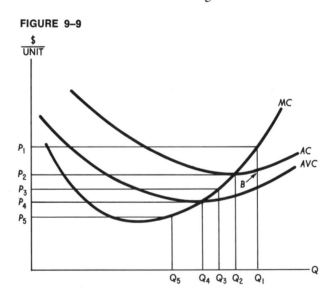

of profit maximization, the basic question involved in the decision to *change* output levels is what the impact of the change will be upon revenues (marginal revenues or *MR*) and upon costs (marginal costs or *MC*). With conditions of given prices, the evaluation of *MR* is quite straightforward. Since the price is unaffected by output changes, producing and selling one more unit of output adds to revenues by an amount equal to the price. The same is true for producing one less unit of output; the decrease in total revenues is simply the price of the lost unit. While *MR* is constant with respect to output, *MC* varies with output as indicated by the shape of the *MC* function in Figure 9–9. Specifically *MC* falls over an initial range, then rises continuously.

Under the circumstances that have now been described, we may unequivocally stipulate that the profit-maximizing output level occurs where $MC = MR$ and *MC* is rising. To see this, consider the given price P_1 in Figure 9–9, for which $P_1 = MR_1$. Now consider output levels to the left of Q_1. At all $Q < Q_1$, MR_1 is greater than *MC*. This means that output increases will produce more revenues than costs. Consequently, such output increases add to profits. This opportunity for additional profits through output increases exists as long as $MR_1 > MC$. However, as *MC* begins to rise, the addition to profits ($MR_1 - MC$) associated with production and sale of an additional unit declines. However, total profits continue to rise (although at at even slower rate) until $MR_1 = MC$. At output levels greater than $MR_1 = MC$, to the right of Q_1 in Figure 9–9, costs are being added at a greater rate than revenues, so that the production of additional units of output generates more costs than it produces revenues. $MR_1 = MC$ is the output level where all available profits have been realized.

Production where $MC = MR$ assures the best possible relationship between revenues and costs, but it does not mean that this "best" position will be profitable. Indeed, it may involve extraordinary, ordinary, or less than ordinary profits or it may involve losses. $MC = MR$ only corresponds to the point where, if losses are inevitable, they are minimized; or if profits are possible, they are maximized. This is shown in Figure 9–9, where the final level of profits is a function of the given price when cost curves are constant in position. For example, for $P = P_1$, production of output Q_1 maximizes profits. These maximum profits can be seen in Figure 9–9 as the difference between P_1 and *AC* for Q_1 (identified in the figure as point B), multiplied by Q_1, or:

$$\text{Total profits} = \text{profits per unit} \times \text{units} = \text{total revenues} - \text{total costs} = (P - AC)Q = PQ - QAC$$

If $P = P_2$, then the profit-maximizing output Q_2 occurs at the point where $P = AC$. This point, which appears to be a zero profit point, is usually understood to be a normal profit point, where opportunity costs consisting of normal profits are incorporated as a fixed cost of production. We shall have more to say on this point in the next chapter. If $P = P_3$, P_4, or P_5, then the loss-minimizing outputs Q_3, Q_4, and Q_5 correspond to increasingly larger losses as indicated in Figure 9–9 by the areas formed by the loss rectangles formed by the respective $AC–P$ and Q values. The notion of selecting output levels that will produce a loss raises the more general question of when a decision should be made to shut down the production process. We now turn to that question.

Referring to Figure 9–9, when $P = P_3$, a loss is incurred. However, P is above AVC at the associated loss-minimizing output Q_3. This means that the market price is high enough to pay the variable production costs and contribute the difference $(P − AVC)$ towards meeting fixed costs, and thereby towards reducing losses. In this circumstance, total losses are lessened by producing rather than shutting down the process over the short run. In the long run, when fixed costs can be eliminated, if the market price is not raised, the firm would be well-advised to pursue more profitable alternative productive opportunities for the use of its resources. At price P_4 and loss minimizing output Q_4, the AVC is just covered by the market price, so that the revenues from producing just cover variable costs. In this position, the firm's total losses are the same whether it produces or shuts down. The loss incurred is exactly the total fixed cost in either case.

Therefore, from the standpoint of total losses, P_4Q_4 is a point of indifference regarding short-run production or disbandment. It is often called the *shut-down point*. Finally, at P_5, even the minimum-loss output Q_5 corresponds to the situation where the revenues from production do not cover the variable costs incurred by production. Therefore, losses are greater if production takes place than if it does not. In this circumstance, the firm is better off shutting down over the short-run than remaining in production.

COST CURVES AND SUPPLY CURVES

This discussion of output selection, given various prices, has indicated the firm's optimal choice of a Q level for the short run is that which equates the price with a short-run marginal costs as long as that price lies above AVC. A supply curve is generally described as the relationship between market price and quantity supplied, *ceteris paribus*. For the profit maximizing firm, the portion of its marginal cost curve that lies above AVC therefore constitutes the firm's short-run supply curve, since it relates the amount supplied with the prevailing price, assuming profit-maximizing behavior. Below the shut-down price, the Q supplied would jump to zero for the profit-maximizing firm.

The interpretation of this portion of the *MC* curve as the firm's supply curve enables the considerations inherent in our production analysis and cost analysis to be brought directly into focus as they affect individual production decisions as to levels of output. For example, a decrease in the price of an input would shift the least-cost input combination towards that input, lower the total cost for a given Q, and lower the *AC* and *MC*. As the *MC* shifted down for a given price, a larger Q would correspond to profit maximization, since the new level of *MC* would not yet equal P. The firm's supply curve would shift out. Output would be increased and total profits enlarged.

TABLE 9–1

Q	C	VC	FC	AVC	AFC	AC	ΔC	$\dfrac{\Delta C}{\Delta Q}$
100.....	1804	4*	1800	.04	18.00	18.04	—	—
150.....	1808	8	1800	.05	12.00	12.05	4	.08
200.....	1820	20	1800	.10	9.00	9.10	12	.24
250.....	1844	44	1800	.18	7.20	7.38	24	.48
300.....	1884	84	1800	.28	6.00	6.28	40	.80
350.....	1940	140	1800	.40	5.14	5.54	56	1.12
400.....	2016	216	1800	.54	4.50	5.04	76	1.52
450.....	2120	320	1800	.71	4.00	4.71	104	2.08
500.....	2244	444	1800	.89	3.60	4.49	124	2.48
550.....	2428	628	1800	1.14	3.27	4.41	184	3.68
600.....	2628	828	1800	1.38	3.00	4.38	200	4.00
650.....	2876	1076	1800	1.65	2.77	4.42	248	4.96
700.....	3184	1384	1800	1.98	2.57	4.55	308	6.16
750.....	3568	1768	1800	2.36	2.40	4.76	384	7.58
800.....	4012	2212	1800	2.76	2.25	5.01	444	8.88

* The man-hours of labor resulting in these costs have been rounded to the nearest whole man-hour.

Table 9–1 contains cost and output data for the numerical example of this and the previous chapter for the case where K is fixed at $K = 3$, i.e., where the cost of $3 \times \$600 = \$1,800$ is fixed over the short run, being incurred regardless of whether production takes place. From the basic data on Q, variable costs (VC), fixed costs (FC), average variable costs (AVC), average fixed costs (AFC), average costs (AC), and incremental costs $\dfrac{\Delta C}{\Delta Q}$, are computed. Notice that the very inefficient use of all three production lines over low-production volumes results in a very efficient use of the labor input, so that AVC are quite low at low-production volumes. These data, characterized by a Cobb-Douglas production function, do not contain a region where MC or AVC falls. Therefore, the inefficiency in the use of K continuously declines with larger Q, while the inefficiency in the use of L continuously increases. As a result, the AVC overtakes the AFC at $Q = 800$. The AC data, reflecting the trade-off between these efficiencies, falls during the range $100 < Q \leq 600$. In this range, the increased efficiency in the use of K, as illustrated by the sizable declines in AFC, more than compensates for the more inefficient use of L, and therefore rising AVC. Beyond $Q = 600$, the situation is reversed.

The data of Table 9–1 are plotted graphically in Figure 9–10. The curves in Figure 9–10 have the general appearance of the portion of the curves of Figure 9–8, panel (b), where MC are rising (to the right of point M). That, in fact, is exactly the case in Figure 9–10, since MC starts out and continues to rise above AVC, as if it had already crossed through AVC at the minimum of AVC. Also, AC continues to drop until intersected by MC.

The short-run supply curve for our data for the assumptions earlier described thus is the entire plotted MC curve from $Q = 100$ to $Q = 800$, since nowhere in the graph is MC below AVC. In our data, AVC for $Q = 100$ is \$0.04, meaning the shut-down price per unit would have to be something less than this amount to shut down. With $AC = \$18.04$ at $Q = 100$, this means the units would have practically no market value relative to their cost before it would pay to leave the production lines idle. This is a direct result of the large fixed costs and low variable costs associated with our particular production process.

Recognition that the MC curve of Figure 9–10 is the short-run supply curve of the production process under conditions of fixed prices and profit maximization, enables the following additional conclusions to be drawn from the data of this and the previous chapter:

1. A market price of approximately \$4.35 to \$4.40 per unit (where MC crosses through and defines the low point of AC) will result in zero profits, if opportunity costs are zero as assumed in our calculation that $FC = 3 \times 600 = 1800$. At higher prices a profit is possible and at lower prices a loss will be incurred.[5]

2. Given a price where profits are possible, profit maximizing output levels range from about 620 units upwards. Thus, starting from the basic data of Chapter 8 on input employment and output produced, we have found it is possible to reproduce the curves of our production and cost model, and draw from these curves conclusions about the nature of the underlying production process, and about profitable levels of output and market prices. In the next chapter, we turn

---

[5] The term "is possible" is used to indicate that our evaluation is based on theoretical short-run costs as contrasted with observed costs. If observed costs are higher due to employment of nonleast-cost combinations, then a higher price would be required.

FIGURE 9–10

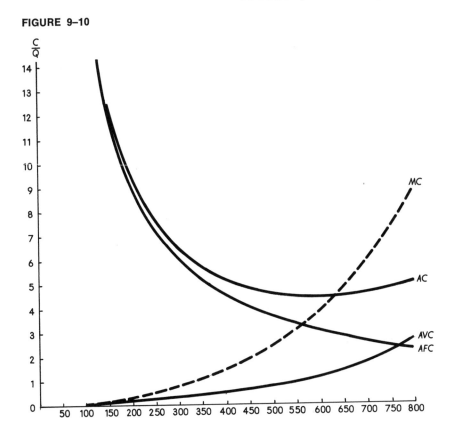

our attention to a consideration of the role the firm's short-run supply curve and other cost curves play in determining price in circumstances of pure competition.

DISCUSSION QUESTIONS

1. Distinguish between (a) theoretical long-run costs and restricted long-run costs, (b) theoretical long-run costs and theoretical short-run costs, (c) theoretical short-run costs and observed costs.

2. Provide an intuitive reason for the relationship described between average variable costs and average product. That is, why are AVC rising when AP is falling and vice versa?

3. A firm has developed two sets of cost curves. First, it has derived a cost curve from its statistically estimated production function in the manner shown in the chapter. Secondly, it has gathered data on costs and output and directly estimated a cost curve by econometric methods. It finds these two estimates are not the same. Why not?

4. Which of the two estimated cost curves in question 3 is more useful? Can you suggest unique uses for each?

5. For a profit-maximizing firm facing fixed market prices, cost curves were described as having an important bearing on the selection of output levels. In this framework, describe the final impact on company output of a technology-inspired shift in the firm's production function.

CASE 9—STA-BUILT COMPANY

The Sta-Built Company produces a leading brand of wood glue used mostly by industrial users. The firm's biggest customers are three furniture manufacturers, followed by a leading producer of children's toys. Retail sales to consumers comprise only about 15 percent of the total.

In the past the company has experienced steady growth in demand for its glue. This has led to 5 plant expansions over the past 16 years. Each expansion has produced an impact on costs that has been difficult to measure. This difficulty arises from a situation in which output levels move back into a more efficient range at the same time that additional capacity comes on stream. Separating these two effects on costs is a difficult problem for corporate management.

At the current time the company is interested in attempting to measure the impact of scale on their costs. In considering this project, the company finds the biggest problem to be measurement of the scale changes and their incorporation into an explanatory equation for costs. Originally, a regression equation was tried in which an output variable was used to explain unit costs, along with a dummy variable taking on values from one to five corresponding to each of the expansions. This was not a successful approach, as the statistical properties of the dummy variable suggested scale did not matter in explaining costs, a result the company knew to be incorrect. As a second approach, five dummy variables were added, corresponding to each of the plant expansions in the historical data. Each of these dummies was given a value of zero before the particular expansion and one after the expansion. When these dummies were regressed on unit costs along with output measures, the resulting regression coefficients show the separate impact of each of the plant expansions. The specific equation was as follows:

$$(C/Q) = 320.4 + 3.3(Q/CAP) - 4.2D_1 - 2.3D_2 - 0.8D_3 - 2.8D_4 - 1.3D_5$$

where

(C/Q) = costs per unit (100 gallons) of glue produced
(Q/CAP) = ratio of production levels to total production capacity
$D_1, \ldots, D_5$ = dummies corresponding to five previous expansions

The five expansions involved adding 3700, 2100, 1700, 4700, and 3800 square feet respectively to the company's original base of 35,000 square feet of plant space. These additions resulted in a proportional increase in unit production capacity in each case. According to the separate impact on costs in each case as measured by the coefficients on the dummy variables, the unit-cost effect of each of these changes is given as follows:

1. $-4.2/3700 = -.00113$
2. $-2.3/2100 = -.00109$
3. $-0.8/1700 = -.00047$
4. $-2.8/4700 = -.00060$
5. $-1.3/3800 = -.00034$

Questions

1. How do you interpret these unit cost ratios, i.e., what do they show? Do they tell the company something useful for future plant expansions?
2. Can you think of an alternative way to attack the problem in which the company is interested? Explain.

Chapter 10

PRICING MODELS IN PURELY
COMPETITIVE MARKETS

Previous chapters have discussed ways in which demand, production, and cost functions can be extracted from raw data. These functions enabled several important and useful inferences to emerge concerning the nature of the processes underlying these functions. In this chapter and the one which follows, we consider additional implications flowing from the general apparatus of those earlier chapters through their use in models of pricing behavior. These models principally are concerned with the explanation and price and output movements in various types of markets.

As such, they can be an aid in understanding pressures on and movements of prices in various market circumstances. Our discussion will range over a spectrum of market types, beginning in this chapter with pure competition as one end of this spectrum, and moving in the following chapter to imperfect competition, to monopoly on the other end of the spectrum, and finally to oligopoly (which may be positioned somewhere between imperfect competition and monopoly). The discussion will by no means encompass all the possible topics and issues relevant to pricing—e.g., we shall not consider such topics as f.o.b. pricing, loss-leader pricing, or antitrust legislation. Instead, we shall confine our discussion to a review of economic models concerned with pricing and output determination.

An important common denominator in the family of pricing models we shall consider is the reliance upon equilibrium analysis to formulate conclusions about pricing behavior. This makes a slight digression into the nature of equilibrium analysis per se, of value in our later discussion. We now undertake that digression.

EQUILIBRIUM ANALYSIS

In equilibrium analysis, attention is focused upon the prevailing value of variables if all external determinants of a model's performance were held constant, and all the behavioral relationships in the model remained constant. Under such conditions, the only forces generating changes in the model's variables would be those inherent in the logic of the model. With these *ceteris paribus* conditions, equilibrium is the state where no net forces are working internally to bring about a change in the model's variables. Take, for example, a simple supply-demand model of market price and volume. If the demand and supply determinants (e.g., income, price of other goods, technology) underlying both the demand curve and the supply curve are held constant except the price, and the demand and supply (behavioral) functions remain constant in their position and shape, then the price where the amount supplied is equated with the amount demanded is an equilibrium price per the "no net forces working for change" definition. At this price, both suppliers and demanders are happy to supply and purchase the same amount at the prevailing price. Neither is motivated to change his level of supply and demand.

Of equilibrium analysis, one may reasonably ask, "Why study models where all factors are held constant except one or two where all relationships are constant, when this is virtually never the case in the real markets and other systems represented by the model?" We may answer this important question by first recognizing a critical assumption in drawing conclusions from equilibrium analysis.[1] We assume that when we manipulate a model variable and observe the impact on equilibrium, the effect observed will be generally the same in our isolated *ceteris paribus* environment as that which would occur if the change were to be observed as part of an array of changes.

That statement may be illustrated by returning to our supply-demand example. Suppose the demand for a particular product is given by the following unstructured function:

$$Q_d = f(P,I,PR)$$

where Q_d is the quantity demanded, P is the price, I is income, and PR is the price of related goods. Suppose the supply function is given by:

$$Q_s = g(P,T)$$

where Q_s is the quantity supplied, P is as before, and T is the level of technology. If Q_d is a negative function of P and Q_s is a positive function of P (i.e., the demand curve slopes down to the right while the supply curve slopes up), then if the values of I, PR, and T are held constant, we

---

[1] It is not implied here that this is the only substantive assumption. Also assumed is that functional relationships will remain reasonably constant, that no quantitatively significant variables have been omitted from the model specification, and in most cases, that the patterns of rational action ascribed to human behavior will approximately persist. We are focusing on the single assumption in the discussion because it seems less apparent than these more conventional model assumptions.

can determine a value of P that will equate Q_d with Q_s and thereby generate an equilibrium position.

Now assume we are interested in estimating the effect on this equilibrium of a change in T, during a time period when I was rising and in which PR was falling. Equilibrium analysis would involve holding constant the effect of I and PR, and observing the impact of a change in T on equilibrium price. Since observation of real markets almost never provides direct evidence on relationships such as between T and P *in isolation*, we are generally required to assume that such relationships would be the same in isolation as they appear to be in the entangled clusters in which they exist empirically. If this assumption is realistically met, then we may answer our "why study" questions by asserting that equilibrium analysis gives us a useful tool to consider the unique impact of each specific variable in our model. In the example, we would have the ability to look at the individual effect of T, I, or PR on equilibrium P, as well as the combined effect.

Comparative Static Analysis

In focusing the model building of this and the following chapter upon equilibrium positions, we are employing what is often called static analysis. We proceed from a set of system variables to an equilibrium position with no concern as to the past or future performance of the system. Each set of variables is sufficient to determine an equilibrium. The reader can refer to Chapter 1 for a further discussion of static models.

The method of comparative statics involves analysis of the effect on equilibrium of changes in static model variables. Consider the supply-demand example given a change in T. We may trace the effect on equilibrium P. In comparing the equilibrium before the change in T with that after the change, we are using the method of comparative statics. Comparative static analysis goes no further than this comparison. It does not yield information as to the path followed in moving from equilibrium to equilibrium. For example, in saying that the effect of an increase in T is to lower the equilibrium market price in our supply-demand model, we are not dealing with the nature of the movement of price to that new equilibrium. We do not know if we would expect the price to fall below the new equilibrium, then recover to above the new equilibrium, then below, and so forth, or whether we would expect the price to move directly to the equilibrium. These further statements about the nature of changing equilibria would involve the use of dynamic models. In our discussion of market price models in this chapter, we shall build static equilibrium models and employ the methods of comparative statics to arrive at our conclusions. By choosing this approach, we are not implying that more sophisticated dynamic techniques are not useful, but merely that the simpler static models serve our purposes adequately at a lower level of analytical entanglement. We now move to the consideration of pricing models, starting with the simplest case of pure competition.

PURELY COMPETITIVE MARKETS

Markets are described by economists as purely competitive if they approximately correspond to the following conditions:

1. They involve the production and sale of a single uniform product that cannot be identified as to its producer. It is homogeneous. There are no brand names attached to the product.
2. There are many producers in the market, and each produces a very small fraction of the total industry output. The share of the market sold by each producer is so small that any conceivable pricing or production decision by an individual producer will have an unnoticeable influence on the total market.
3. Price is established on the basis of the interplay of the forces of supply and demand in the general market. Producers cannot sidestep or segment this general market arena. Price is a freely fluctuating regulator equating the two sides of the general market.
4. Resources are free to flow into and out of production of the product. In other words, there are no highly specialized productive inputs that cannot be used in the production of other products. Likewise, there are no institutional barriers to the entry of new producers, or the departure of existing producers.

These conditions obviously describe a rather specialized type of market. Indeed that is the case. Agricultural markets perhaps correspond most closely to the conditions we have described.[2] For example, corn delivered to the market is indistinguishable as to producer. Corn is produced by a large number of small producers, all of whom simply accept the going price, and given this price, decide how much they will bring to the market in a particular time period. Prices in the market are established impersonally on the basis of the forces of supply and demand. Finally, producers of corn can normally use most of their equipment, land, and labor in alternative agricultural productions; therefore productive resources are free to move into and out of corn production.

Besides agricultural markets, a few other markets in the economy demonstrate a reasonable although not perfect correspondence to the conditions of pure competition. Examples are the market for widely held securities (as the illustration of Chapter 1), the market for loanable funds,

---

[2] However, some agricultural product areas are increasingly violating the first assumption regarding unbranded products; e.g., brand name oranges and bananas as opposed to "off brands."

certain low-volume hardware items such as chain, nails, screws, plumbing pipe, and angle irons, and certain building products such as brick and various types of lumber.

In some countries where agricultural markets dominate the economy, purely competitive market mechanisms provide an important vehicle for understanding price movements in individual markets. In economically advanced nations such as the United States, agricultural and other approximately purely competitive markets do not account for a large fraction of total output. Therefore, the analysis of pure competition does not offer an important general explanation of product prices and output in the United States. Nonetheless, the ideas contained in models of purely competitive market systems provide a benchmark for comparison with other more applicable market models. Also, several of the conclusions that emerge clearly from the simplest purely competitive case apply as well in other market structures. We now explore the main conclusions emerging from analysis of purely competitive market structures, and the logic leading to those conclusions.

PRICES AND OUTPUT IN PURE COMPETITION

To begin, consider a general market arena where the price is free to fluctuate according to assumption three above, and is purely a product of the shape and position of the market demand and supply functions. Figure 10–1 illustrates the situation, where P_0 and Q_0 are values consistent with positions on both the demand function DD and the supply function SS. P_0 is a market equilibrium price, since at higher prices more Q would be supplied according to SS than would be demanded according to DD, and at lower prices than P_0 more would be demanded than supplied. We now consider the supply function further.

FIGURE 10–1

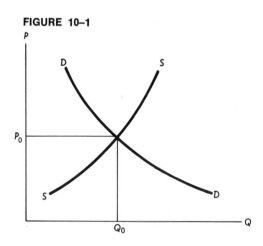

We assume that the production process involved with supplying a good on a purely competitive market is characterized by diminishing returns to the variable input(s) beyond an initial point, so that the family of cost curves has the general appearance shown in Figure 10–2 for a

FIGURE 10–2
Producer A

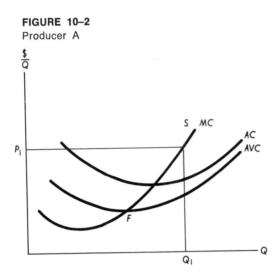

particular producer. Chapter 9 established that with such a family of curves, and assuming producers aim to maximize profits and are given fixed prices, the segment *FS* of the *MC* curve can be interpreted as the firm's supply curve. Now our logic about the impersonal establishment of price, coupled with assumption four regarding the insignificant size of individual producers, will indeed cause price to be beyond the control of specific producers, essentially being given to them as fixed. This means *FS* can be taken as a short-run individual firm supply curve in pure competition. It is then a simple matter to move to a market supply curve such as *SS*. The latter is only a horizontal arithmetic summation of individual producer's supply curves. Thus, if P_1 in Figure 10–2 will draw forth profit maximizing output Q_1 from producer A, we would add this quantity to that of producers B, C . . . , resulting in the total output drawn forth at price P_1—the industry supply curve.

The demand curve for an industry, illustrated by *DD* in Figure 10–1, can also be considered to be a horizontal summation of the individual demand patterns of participants on the demand side of the market. Its general properties are discussed in Chapter 5.

Consider now the situation illustrated in Figure 10–3. In this figure, the market demand and supply curves produce equilibrium price P_0 and quantity MQ_0. From the standpoint of the typical individual producer

FIGURE 10–3

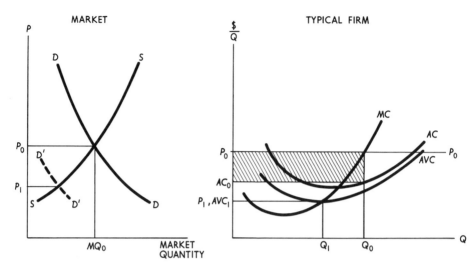

whose cost curves are illustrated in the figure, P_0 is the going price. The producer's only concern is with selecting an output level that will be in his best interests at that price. As we saw in Chapter 9, profits are maximized under such circumstances by selecting Q_0 production volume, where $MR = P = MC$. In this case, this selection produces a pure profit net of opportunity and explicit costs of $(P_0 - AC_0) \times Q_0$—the area of the shaded rectangle in Figure 10–3.[3] So, in this illustration, the market supply and demand relationships produce a price that yields a pure profit to individual producers in the short run. If the situation of Figure 10–3 were the production of corn, individual growers would find the market price higher than usual, and those who had planted corn would reap abnormally large profits on this acreage.

Still considering Figure 10–3 as corn, suppose research was made public that showed that feeding rats 100 ears of corn per day for five years caused a heart condition. Assume this created a scare among consumers and shifted DD to $D'D'$, lowering the equilibrium price to P_1. Now, at P_1, individual growers are indifferent in terms of profits as to whether corn should be (a) picked and taken to market, thereby incurring variable cost $(AVC_1 \times Q_1)$ exactly equal to total revenues $(P_1 \times Q_1)$, or (b) left to rot in the field. In other words, the typical grower would be at a short-run shutdown point if price were P_1.

Over the short run, the fixed resource commitment protects pure profits of the type produced by market price P_0 from the ravages of competition, since insufficient time elapses for other producers to enter the market. Also, the fixed resource commitment makes it rational for

---

[3] Opportunity costs are discussed in Chapter 1.

producers to supply the market at a loss, if by doing so they recover at least a part of their fixed cost. When we consider the long-run implications of our analysis, the situation is different.

COMPETITIVE ADJUSTMENT AND LONG-RUN EQUILIBRIUM

The abnormally large profits associated with P_0 in Figure 10–3 are as much a signal as they are a reward in purely competitive market systems. They are a signal that market demand is outpacing market supply—that the product's consumers are demonstrating an increased willingness to buy compared with the quantity available for purchase. In pure competition, such a signal is not likely to go unheeded. In the long run, the abnormally high profits will attract additional producers into the industry away from normal-profit and low-profit productions. This will bring an end to the abornmally high profits. The entry of new firms will add to the market supply, which will begin to bring the price down by reducing the excess demand. Profits will fall. The situation is illustrated graphically in Figure 10–4 for the corn market. P_0 results in pure profits for existing corn growers. These profits can be expected to influence the plans of farmers in closely related areas. The number of corn producers can be expected to rise as a result, along with the total supply of corn. The supply curve SS in Figure 10–4 will begin to shift to the

FIGURE 10–4

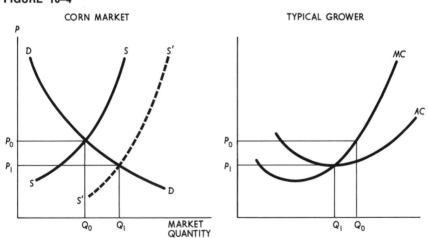

CORN MARKET   TYPICAL GROWER

right, which in turn will begin to lower the market price of corn. For a while, profits in corn production, while falling, will remain abnormally high, continuing to attract additional producers and lowering the price. This process can be expected to continue until the market supply curve has shifted to $S'S'$, resulting in P_1 and completely eliminating the abnormal profits for the typical grower, leaving $P_1 = MR = MC = AC$ at output Q_1. At this point, motivation would cease for further entry of producers, and the supply curve would stabilize as would the market price. Long-run equilibrium would be attained.

If the market price was pushed below P_1, profits would be abnormally low (or negative). This too would be a signal, which would discourage new producers from entering the industry, and at the same time encourage existing producers to leave the industry to pursue alternative opportunities. SS would shift back to the left as producers exited the industry. Market price would increase, which would begin to reduce the loss incurred by typical producers. Equilibrium would finally be restored at P_1 and Q_1. Thus, P_1Q_1 is the only price-quantity combination sustainable over the long run. Any other P would not persist as it would set up forces tending to move P towards P_1. Therefore, the minimum point on the firm's AC curve is the long-run profit-maximizing equilibrium output for the purely competitive firm.

This long-run equilibrium position produces the lowest unit cost possible, for the cost curves involved, i.e., the most efficient output level. Therefore, purely competitive markets have built-in pressures tending towards maximum efficiency equilibria. Ironically, these pressures do not originate from a concern with efficiency but instead from a pervasive attempt on the part of all producers to capture more than the average amount of profits. This causes productive resources to flow among markets in a manner corresponding to shifting patterns of market demand. For example, consider a shift in tastes by consuming groups away from corn and towards oats. The leftward shift in the market demand curve for corn is approximately offset by the rightward shift in the demand for oats. The price of corn falls while that of oats rises, producing similar changes in the profitability of the two. At the same time new producers are attracted into the production of oats, they are attracted away from corn. Over time, the profit-motivated output adjustments of producers will balance out the supply of both products with the altered quantities demanded, and the prices in both markets will yield suppliers only normal profits. If we consider an entire family of related purely competitive markets, a similar pattern can be expected, where prices and profits, as reflections of consumer demand, ultimately direct the flow of productive resources among alternative productions.

Consider the situation depicted in Figure 10–5, which again illustrates the corn market, beginning at P_0 market price and MQ_0 total output. This price just covers all costs and normal profits for the typical producer, leaving $P_0 = MC = AC$, and producing both short-run and long-run equilibrium. Now assume demand for corn increases sharply, shifting DD to $D'D'$ and causing the market price to be bid up to P_1 at a greater level of output Q_1. P_1 sets up short-run pure profits for the typical pro-

FIGURE 10–5

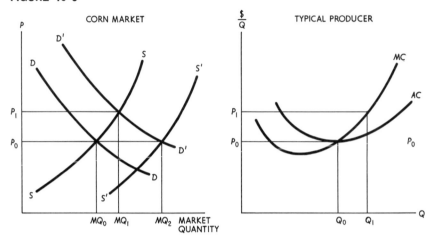

ducer, which attracts additional producers for the next growing season. As their supply begins to come onto the market, SS starts to shift towards $S'S'$, the price begins to fall, and output continues to expand. Finally, when all pure profits have been squeezed out, price will have been reduced back to the original value P_0 at the still larger output MQ_2. The typical producer will be at the initial output level Q_0, and the market will again be in both long-run and short-run equilibrium. In this circumstance, the increase in industry output, $MQ_2 - MQ_0$, would represent the output produced by the newly entering producers.

Figure 10–5 indicates that existing producers would not permanently share in supplying the increased demand, which may seem a strange result. Although the typical producer's output would rise in the short run (from Q_0 to Q_1) as new producers entered, their output would weaken price, and it would no longer be profitable to produce Q_1, forcing a retreat to more efficient output levels as the market price fell.

In some circumstances, an expansion of industry output similar to that illustrated in Figure 10–5 will affect the cost curves of individual producers. Production of a larger output generates a corresponding demand for larger quantities of productive inputs. (The demand curve for these inputs shifts out.) If the supply of inputs follows an upward-sloping curve, this increased demand will result in an increase in the price of the input. This, in turn, will cause the typical producer's unit costs to rise systematically as industry output is increased. The effect is illustrated in Figure 10–6. In this figure, an initial equilibrium position P_0Q_0 is disrupted by a shift in market demand from DD to $D'D'$. This causes P to increase to P_1 and produces pure profits. Industry volume is increased from MQ_0 to MQ_1, due to increased supply by existing

FIGURE 10–6

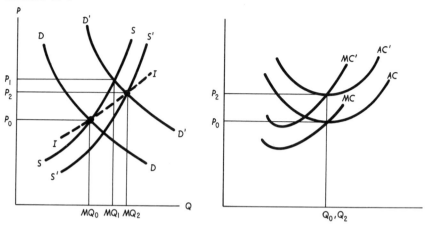

producers. Under conditions of rising supply curves of inputs, this increased volume begins to cause the cost curves to rise towards *MC'*
and *AC'*. At the same time, the pure profits attract additional producers
into the industry. As these producers add to supply in the long run,
a scissors effect is applied to the pure profits. Prices weaken as the industry supply curve moves towards *S'S'*, while costs continue to rise
as total volume increases towards MQ_2. The pure profits are squeezed
out at the new equilibrium P_2, which is higher than P. The situation
of P_2P_0 means that long-run increases in industry output associate with
rising equilibrium prices in this case.

The locus of equilibrium points II in Figure 10–6 can be interpreted
as the *long-run supply curve* for this industry. It slopes up due to the
increased price of inputs associated with greater demand. If input prices
were not affected by increased industry demand, as earlier assumed in
Figure 10–5, then the locus of equilibria would be horizontal, giving
the industry a horizontal long-run supply curve. In other words, if demand were permanently doubled for the situation of Figure 10–5, the
equilibrium price would eventually return to its original level, *ceteris
paribus*. By contrast, in the situation of Figure 10–6, equilibrium price
would remain permanently higher.

In certain cases, such as infant industries, increased industry volume
might produce decreased costs to individual producers. In such cases,
the final equilibrium prices would trend downward at greater volumes,
thereby producing a downward-sloping long-run industry supply curve.

SCALE RELATIONSHIPS

In the analysis of Figure 10–5, the scale of the production process
for the typical producer has not been changed. We now consider the

situation where the increase in P to P_1 increases the typical producer's profit maximizing Q to the point where the existing scale is now being very inefficiently utilized relative to larger scales. It pays producers to expand their scale of production. Figure 10–7 illustrates two possible

FIGURE 10–7

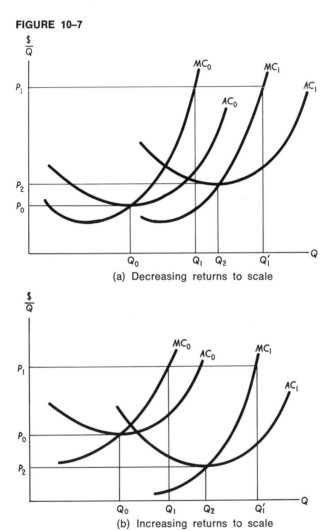

(a) Decreasing returns to scale

(b) Increasing returns to scale

situations. In panel (a), increases in scale are accompanied by decreasing returns, while in panel (b), increasing returns-to-scale characterize the production process. In both panels, we begin from an equilibrium position at $P_0 Q_0$ with normal profits. Now, as before, assume price rises to P_1. In both cases, Q is expanded to Q_1 where $P_1 = MC_0$. In both cases, it is now profitable for the firm to employ a larger scale of production, represented by AC_1, to produce the new output Q_1 since unit costs with the larger scale are lower for both increasing and decreasing returns. (Q_1 crosses AC_1 at a lower point than AC_0 in both cases.) However, once the scale change has been made, the firm in both cases finds it is even more profitable to expand output beyond Q_1 to Q_1' where $MC_1 = P_1$. The larger scale enables profitable production of an increased level of output. But Q_1' associates in both cases with a pure short-run profit, which we can expect to attract competitors and weaken the price. Here is where panels (a) and (b) become divergent in their conclusions. In the case of (a) all normal profits will have been squeezed out by the time the price falls to P_2, which is above the initial P_0. In (b), the P_2 normal profit price will lie below the initial price. Both correspond to higher output levels Q_2 in equilibrium.

So if the production process is characterized by increasing returns-to-scale, we have seen that increases in scale by individual producers will reduce AC for larger volumes of output. But under such conditions, the drive for greater profits could be expected to induce virtually all producers to enlarge their scale of production to realize the economies of scale.[4] In fact, producers who did *not* expand their scale of production would soon discover their profits were not as great as their competitors' profits. Finally, increased supply associated with expansion of existing firms and entry of new firms would drive prices to the normal profit level for larger-scale producers. At this lower P, the nonexpanding producers would be incurring low or negative profits, which would induce them either to expand and realize the scale economies, or leave the industry. The surviving firms in pure competition can thus be assumed to have taken advantage of all prevailing economies of scale.

Similarly, if continued enlargement of the production process resulted in decreasing returns to scale as in panel (a) of Figure 10–7, producers who continued to expand would find a continually increasing normal profit price as scale was enlarged. To expand scale under such circumstances would mean producing a higher normal profit price than a producer not expanding. This would give smaller-scale producers a profit advantage for a given price. As price was driven to the lower normal profit level, the expanding producers would incur low or negative profits, and would either contract their scale or exit the industry. Thus, the competitive forces inherent in the purely competitive situation would tend to force individual producers, for their survival, to realize all scale economies produced by increasing returns and avoid scale diseconomies associated with decreasing returns.

If we assume that a given production process is characterized by an

---

[4] This analysis assumes that no financial or other restrictions stand in the way of such expansion—that if a producer wanted to expand, he could expand.

initial region of increasing returns, a region of constant returns, and finally a region of decreasing returns, the path of the AC curve through time will take on the general appearance shown in Figure 10–8. In this figure, three representative production scales, AC_0, AC_1, and AC_2, reflect the region OQ_A of increasing returns. Continued expansion to scales such as AC_3 and AC_4 yields constant returns ($Q_A Q_B$), while expansion beyond AC_4 produces decreasing returns.

FIGURE 10–8

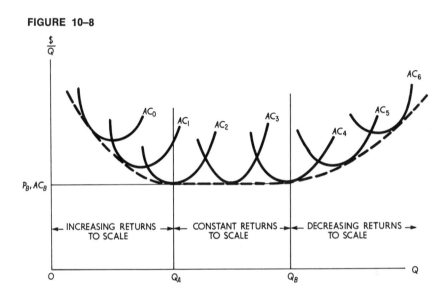

Our discussion has indicated that we expect to find the scale of production prevailing over the long run in pure competition to be in the region $Q_A Q_B$ where economies have been realized. In fact, since an individual producer could move entirely through this region without incurring diseconomies, we would expect the scale to move towards Q_B, the maximum economical size. Q_B is often referred to as the *optimal scale of production* since it delivers the lowest unit cost technologically possible. We have just seen that producers are pushed towards this optimal scale over the long run in pure competition by their profit-seeking motives in conjunction with competitive pressures inherent in the market environment. They are thereby led to the achievement of an ultimate efficiency objective— lowest technologically possible unit cost—in which paradoxically we ascribed to them no particular interest per se. Finally, if it is possible to produce a product at AC_B unit cost in Figure 10–8 and there are no obstructions to this attainment, then we may safely assume that as producers move to this position for the additional profits available, price will be driven to $P_B = AC_B$. The long-run result is as low a price as is technologically possible, which will yield normal profits only for producers who have realized all possible efficiencies.

PRODUCERS IN PURE COMPETITION—TWO VIEWS

Purely competitive markets are socially advantageous from the standpoint of efficiency. As we have seen, in long-run equilibrium they result in:

1. production at the low point of the producer's average cost curve for a fixed scale of production.
2. production at the optimal scale of production.
3. payment of profits to producers just sufficient to retain those producers in the industry (producers are paid their opportunity costs).
4. continuing commitments of productive resources to those productions in current demand, with built-in mechanisms for adjusting resource commitments to changing demands.

These are powerful advantages from the standpoint of efficient use of the productive resources of an economy. However, viewed from the position of an individual producer, pure competition leaves something to be desired. For example, the producer does not know what price he will receive for his output during its production. His efforts at achieving efficiencies and cost reductions, while profitable for a while, are ultimately all wiped out by reductions in price. When market prices move below his costs, his only alternatives are to (a) take his productive resources out of the industry; or (b) supply the market at a loss, hoping enough of his competitors will leave to reduce supply sufficiently to restore a profitable price. His efforts at expanding his scale of production are inevitably halted at the point where decreasing returns-to-scale occur. In short, the producer in perfect competition is not in a position to feel particularly secure in his enterprise, nor can we expect him to be overjoyed with the situation he is locked into by his market environment.

Indeed, given the rational behavior we have ascribed to producers in pure competition, one would almost expect these producers to behave in a way to attempt to reduce the insecurity of their market position. The roots of their problem are contained in the behavior of market prices over which individual producers have no control. Therefore, we might further expect that efforts aimed at reducing the misery of producing in perfect competition would be focused on gaining some control over the market price. If we review the history of older, approximately purely competitive markets in the United States, these expectations are fully borne out. Producers have in most cases gained some control over prices by introducing distinctive features in their product, affixing a brand label to it, and advertising its advantages. For example, consider older retail markets in the United States for such products as salt, sugar, soap, beans, crackers, and pickles, to name a few. These markets were once characterized by a high degree of product homogeneity, with brand indentification weak or nonexistent. Producers suffered the vagaries while being forced into the efficiencies of approximately pure competition. The emergence of sharp and effectively advertised brand distinctions transformed these markets into somewhat more secure arenas for producers by enabling these producers to develop a brand-conscious following for their product, with whom each producer could deal directly in the market place.

This type of modified market is often referred to as imperfectly competitive. Most once purely competitive markets in the United States have been transformed into imperfectly competitive markets with the passage of time. In fact, markets (such as some in the agricultural sector) that still remain approximately purely competitive probably do so because producers have not discovered a way to effectively differentiate their product. We turn in the next chapter to a consideration of imperfectly competitive and other markets.

DISCUSSION QUESTIONS

1. What market segments in the United States approximately correspond to conditions of perfect competition?
2. Is it correct to say that market prices in perfectly competitive markets are not really set by producers?
3. Where on the perfect competitors' cost curve is the most efficient point of production in the short run? What is the most efficient long-run position?
4. "What is good for the society is good for its business firms." Given that perfectly competitive markets are more efficient than other alternatives, comment on this statement.
5. Do you think it is reasonable to call the marginal cost-price model of this chapter the economic theory of the firm? Why or why not?

Chapter 11

PRICING MODELS IN NONPURELY COMPETITIVE MARKETS

Our discussion in Chapter 10 has suggested that purely competitive markets contain at least some of the motivational seeds of their own demise. In the United States many once purely competitive markets have evolved into structures that economists often call imperfectly competitive. Other markets have developed into oligopolistic structures, often from imperfectly competitive beginnings. Indeed, in the history of U.S. business, an often repeated scenario is a market characterized by approximately purely competitive conditions that is converted through product differentiation into a group of imperfectly competitive firms producing highly substitutable but brand-labeled products. Later, a competitive shake-out causes consolidations and failures of less profitable producers with less distinct products, resulting in an oligopolistic structure involving a small number of economically potent competitors.

In addition, various legal and other conditions combine to produce markets in the United States served by a single monopoly producer. In the discussion that follows we consider models of market prices applicable for imperfectly competitive, monopoly, and oligopolistic market structures. Since these models derive from the purely competitive model framework, Chapter 10 has already provided much of the needed conceptual apparatus for our discussion.

IMPERFECT COMPETITION

Of the four assumpitons of pure competition given at the start of the previous chapter, the second, defining a large number of producers, and the fourth, regarding freedom of resources to move in and out of the industry, continue to apply in imperfect competition. However, the first pure competitive assumption of product homogeneity does not characterize imperfect competition. Producers in imperfect competition have succeeded in distinguishing their product from that of their competitors. We no longer just have pickles from the pickle barrel. We have Jones' green wonders, Smith's pickles cured by a secret process, and so forth. What once was a single market demand curve for pickles has now been fragmented into many small but distinct and highly interrelated markets for individual brands of pickles. For his own brand, each producer sells to the entire market, dealing directly with his customers. When the producer decides how much to supply his market, he sets the price that will just take this supply off the market. So, unlike the producer in pure competition, the imperfectly competitive producer is a price setter who can decide upon and implement different pricing strategies. For example, the producer can decide to be a high-price, low-volume producer, or vice

FIGURE 11–1

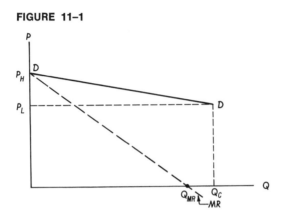

versa, and within limits imposed by the market, achieve this result. The producer as a price setter in imperfect competition violates the third pure competitive assumption, which stated that price was established impersonally by the forces of supply and demand and given as fixed to the producer. Quite the contrary, price is very personally a product of the strategies of individual producers.

While the market fragmentation of imperfect competition creates as many individual demand curves as producers, the smallness of the actual differences among brands can be expected to make these curves individually price-elastic and highly interrelated. A typical demand curve of this type for a particular brand of pickles is illustrated by DD in Figure 11–1. Over the short-run, with at least one fixed input, an absolute capacity level of production Q_C exists for the individual producer. The portion of the demand curve DD to the right of Q_C is irrelevant for short-run analysis, since the producer would never select a price below P_L, which would correspond to larger volumes of production than could be produced. On the other end of the spectrum, P_H corresponds to a price so high that volume shrinks to zero. Thus, P_H and P_L constitute the applicable price range over which the producer has discretion in setting his price. This price range is a function of the shape and position of the demand curve and the value of Q_C.[1]

In pure competition with prices given to the firm, the marginal revenue resulting from the sale of an additional unit of output was simply the price of the additional unit. With the downward-sloping demand curve of Figure 11–1, the sale of an additional unit of output can only be accomplished by a lower price, all other things equal. Thus, the increase in revenue associated with the price of the additional unit sold is reduced by the loss of revenue on existing sales volume, due to the sale of the existing volume at a now-lower price. This trade-off is illustrated by the following expression:

$$\Delta TR = P_2 - (P_1 - P_2)Q_0$$

where ΔTR is the change in total revenue associated with lowering price enough to sell one more unit of output, P_1 is the initial price, P_2 the final price, and Q_0 the initial volume. As Q grows, a fixed price change $(P_2 - P_1)$ produces greater and greater retardation in the ΔTR. With P falling as Q grows, the positive addition to ΔTR (P_2) is reduced while the negative component grows. In these two ways, a scissors effect upon ΔTR causes it to decline with further price reductions/output expansions, and eventually become negative when $(P_1 - P_2)\ Q_0 > P_2$. Marginal revenue (MR) is defined as $\Delta TR/\Delta Q$ for small ΔQ. Therefore MR would show the same pattern as ΔTR when Q was enlarged, shown as the dotted line MR in Figure 11–1. MR shows that increases in Q produce increases in revenues at a declining rate until Q_{MR}, at which point revenues are maximized, marginal revenues are zero, and beyond which negative MR causes total revenues to fall with further price decreases/output expansion.

Since the major difference between pure and imperfect competition is found in the nature of the demand curves, the typical family of cost curves characterizing the producer in pure competition can also be expected to characterize imperfect competition. Illustrative MC and AC curves along with demand and MR curves are shown in Figure 11–2. The producer in this circumstance is faced with selecting jointly the price and output level at which he will serve his market within the applicable price range. Assuming profit maximization, the same general decision rule discussed under pure competition applies in this case for profit maximizing levels of P and Q. Output should be increased and price reduced as long as the revenue added are greater than the additional costs incurred. Since MR is falling and MC rising, a point will be reached where MR has fallen to the rising level of MC, where output increases

---

[1] Since the demand curve attains its position because of the behavior of the product's consumers, we may assign to them the ultimate cause of the value of P_H and P_L.

add to revenues at the same rate they add to costs. At this point, further increases in Q reduce profits since $MC > MR$. As before, $MR = MC$ is the maximum profit. This corresponds to price P_0 and output Q_0 in Figure 11–2, which for the curves shown produces a pure profit equal to $(P_0 - AC_0)Q_0$ in the short run. Generally, we may define short-run equilibrium in imperfect competition as the price and quantity where $MR = MC$, which may correspond to either a profit or a loss (assuming we are above the shut-down point).

FIGURE 11–2

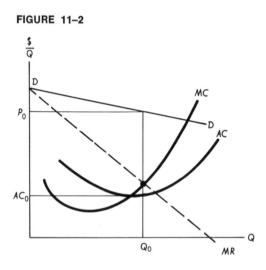

But what of the long run in imperfect competition? Realization of pure profits cannot lead to the entry of new producers of an existing brand name product, since that is legally protected. However, since imperfect competition is characterized by free entry and exit of firms into the general product group, we may expect the competitive reaction to pure profits to take the form of imitations, or perhaps improvements, which will be close substitutes in the market for the original product. For example, consider Green-Wonder Pickles produced by the Mudgett Pickle Company. Let us say that vigorous research and development by its producer has perfected and patented a smooth-skinned pickle. The product is marketed as the new improved Mudgett's Wart-Free Green-Wonder Pickle. We assume it is an immediate success, attracts a following of customers, and produces pure profits for the producer similar to those of Figure 11–2.

Other pickle producers see the advantages of this technological break-through and begin related research of their own. Shortly, two new break-throughs occur. In one, a new and different process is discovered by the Ahill Pickle Company that eliminates the warts while at the same time changes the color of the pickle to red. This product is marketed as the new smooth Ahill's Red Devil Pickle. In the other development, the Erdman Pickle Company has found a way to produce vitamin enriched pickles, which provide 100 percent of all daily vitamin requirements. It is marketed as Erdman's Eat-Your-Way-to-Health Pickles. These two new products, Ahill's and Erdman's, can be expected to attract some of the customers away from the original Mudgett's Wart-Free Green-Wonders. The effect will be to shift the Green-Wonder demand curve down to the left as the size of the total Green-Wonder market has now been reduced. After these adjustments brought on by the entry of the

FIGURE 11–3

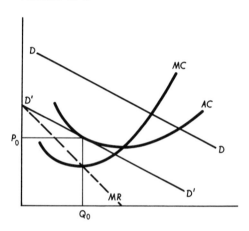

two new pickle concepts, if pure profits still remain, we may expect additional breakthroughs to be sought. Finally, the array of different but competing pickle innovations can be expected to reach a point where only normal profits are available in the field, at which point further innovation will be discouraged. This situation is illustrated in Figure 11–3. The encroachment of new substitutes reduces the market demand for Green-Wonders from its original level represented by DD involving pure profits, toward position $D'D'$ where only sufficient numbers of customers remain to provide normal profits at P_0Q_0 where $P = AC$ and $MR = MC$, where the innovation process for speciality pickles would cease to be motivated by pure profits. Therefore, we could describe the situation of $P = AC$ and $MR = MC$ as a long-run equilibrium in imperfect competition.

Such equilibria can be expected to be interrupted frequently in imperfectly competitive markets by new innovations. Our analysis of the effects of innovation has suggested that they may be quite profitable for the innovator during the period before competition can respond with close substitutes. Thus, wihle temporary, these initial pure profits represent a potential stimulus to the use of product innovation as a competitive tool. In most U.S. markets where imperfect competition prevails, the pace of product innovation is rapid and continuous. This indicates the stimulus of profits during the catch-up period may indeed be quite important.

The long-run equilibrium now described is similar to that of pure competition in its implications for overall resource allocation. Recall that in pure competition, price and profits were a signal to producers directing productive resources towards the products and services in heavy demand. The ultimate result was more output and a reduction in price. In imperfect competition, the same signal would produce an expansion of the list of substitute products (rather than more of the same product) to the maximum the market could support. In both cases, the market directed the resource adjustment towards the areas of heavy demand.

Over the long run, we would expect producers in imperfect competition to take advantage of scale economies the same way and for the same reasons as in pure competition. Unit costs could therefore be expected to be reduced through expansion to the extent possible. However, a glance at Figure 11–3 suggests that the process of expansion will not carry on as far as it would in pure competition due to the downward-sloping demand curve. This would cause the equilibrium point to occur at less than optimal output, with unit costs remaining higher than is technologically feasible. In this sense, imperfect competition is not as efficient as pure competition, and results in higher product prices than technologically feasible.

ADVERTISING AND IMPERFECT COMPETITION

In pure competition, producers have no need for advertising or marketing programs as their product is homogeneous, and producers can sell all they want at the going price. However, with the differentiated products in imperfect competition, producers have a clear need to undertake advertising programs. In fact, these programs are often an important way in which the distinctive characteristic of a particular product is heightened and sold for its advantages. In the final analysis, it is the consumer's perception of distinctions among products that establishes the fragmented individual demand curves of imperfect competition, and not the true extent of these differences.

The effect of advertising expenditures on the producer in imperfect competition is twofold. First, the expenditures can be considered a fixed cost that add to unit costs at all levels of output. Second, the effects of the program are expected to shift the demand curve outward. These effects are illustrated graphically in Figure 11–4. From the original long-run equilibrium position of P_0Q_0 involving normal profits with MC_0 and

FIGURE 11–4

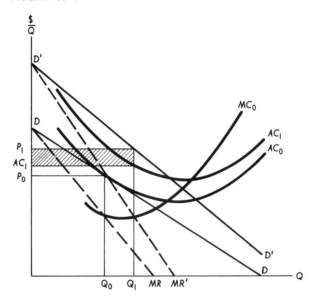

AC_0 cost curves, introduction of an advertising expenditure shifts the AC to AC_1 but does not alter the MC. It affects the demand curve in two ways: (a) shifting it outward, and (b) pivoting it towards a more inelastic position (more brand loyalty). In the hypothetical case illustrated, the expenditure has been worthwhile, since pure profits of $(P_1 - AC_1)Q_1$ now are being realized on Q_1 volume as compared with only normal profits on Q_0 volume before. Thus, the advertising outlay under these circumstances is more than fully recovered by the producer through the higher resulting selling price and the larger resulting quantity.

In view of the increase in profits associated with the introduction of advertising in our illustration, marginal analysis suggests that a further increase should be undertaken until the point is reached where the shift in the demand curve resulting from advertising no longer produces changes in revenues that offset the cost of advertising. At that point, all profits from advertising would have been taken, resulting in an optimal advertising outlay.

In our illustration, further increases in advertising outlay promise to increase profits. This may not always be the motivation for producers in imperfect competition. They may instead be concerned with trying to protect their market positions from erosion due to the "wearing off" of the distinctive character of their product. That is, producers may be able to forecast that their demand curves will shift backwards *unless* advertising expenditures are increased. Even so, the earlier analysis still applies—we are concerned with whether the advertising outlay produces additional revenues beyond its costs (the additional revenues would be those associated with the unshifted demand curve).

The principal distinctive feature of the model of imperfect competition is that each producer has his own segmented market of brand-loyal customers, however fragile this segmentation may be. As the only seller to these customers, the producer has a monopoly on the sale of his brand. As we have seen, this mini-monopoly position is only of limited advantage to the producer due to the close proximity of good substitutes for the producer's brand. If these close substitutes were not present, the monopoly position would be of greater consequence to the producer. Let us now consider this case.

MONOPOLY MARKETS

Economists define a monopoly as a situation involving a single seller of a product with no close substitutes. A monopolist serves the entire market, deciding upon the price he will charge and the quantity he will offer. His customers either buy from him at this price, or they do without the product. Unlike imperfect competition, the monopolist's customers cannot simply switch to another brand, for there is none.[2] This usually gives the monopolist increased security and often yields increased profitability. However, this is not always the case. The monopolist still must deal with a market that can be expected to buy more at lower prices and less at higher prices. In this sense, his plight is similar to that of the imperfect competitor with a feasible price range and a downward-sloping MR function. However, we may expect one important difference. Whereas the close substitutes in imperfect competition usually will cause the demand curve to be highly elastic over a good part of its range, the lack of these substitutes in the case of monopoly should produce somewhat less elastic demand curves. This in turn should widen the price range over which the monopolist has latitude in setting the selling price. We have no reason to expect the monopolist's production function or cost curves to be shaped differently from those of producers in imperfect competition; therefore we continue to assume the same family of cost curves. Pricing in monopoly markets can therefore be characterized by the model of Figure 11–5, in which the market demand is shown as DD, along with familiar MC, AC, and MR functions. In Figure 11–5, the profit-maximizing output level and price are Q_0 and P_0, which yields the pure profit $(P_0 - AC_0)Q_0$ and where $MR = MC$. This result and the logic behind it is exactly the same as that of imperfect competition. Thus, the profit-maximizing monopolist is not relieved from the

---

[2] This definition has led some economists to proclaim that a true monopolist has never existed because no physical product exists that has no close substitutes from the standpoint of basic want satisfaction.

problem of selecting the best *PQ* combination merely because he serves the entire market.

In Figure 11–5, at the optimal output level the monopolist is realizing a pure profit equal to the shaded area. This profit is the joint product of the relationship between market demand and the firm's production and cost curves. Monopolists are often characterized as being able to procure such pure profits at will as they bleed their markets. This is a myth. Clearly, there is no necessary reason why the demand and cost curves must relate in such a way as to produce a pure profit as in Figure 11–5. Figure 11–6 helps illustrate this point. In this case, the market demand for the monopolist's product does not come up to his costs. At the optimal output Q_0, a loss is still incurred as given by the shaded

FIGURE 11–5

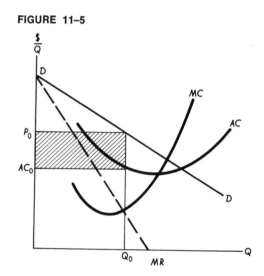

FIGURE 11–6

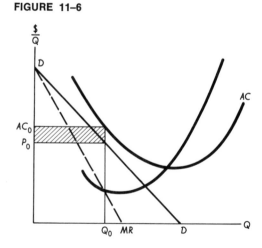

area in the figure. The monopolist's unit production cost is simply greater than the price for any related quantity of production. The monopolist of Figure 11–6 cannot profitably produce for his market given the current demand.

Over the long run, the pure profits of Figure 11–5 could be maintained as long as close substitutes did not emerge. Of course, for monopolies in which the product distinctiveness is simply the result of a technological innovation, substantial pure profits would motivate intensive efforts aimed at discovering parallel technological innovations that would eliminate the monopoly position and yield the innovator a share of the profitable market. This kind of reaction has in fact eliminated most of the technological monopolies in the private sector of the U.S. economy. Conversely, over the long run, the loss situation of Figure 11–6 can be expected to cause either: (a) dissolution of the market by the producer, by simply refusing to serve it and taking his resources elsewhere, or (b) introduction of marketing and advertising efforts aimed at moving the demand curve into a profitable region.

Monopoly markets usually can be expected to be more inefficient than imperfectly competitive or purely competitive markets. There are no market forces leading to the normal profit price, so that the price could remain above this level indefinitely. If the monopolist were a dogged profit maximizer, he still would be motivated to take advantage of scale economies and avoid diseconomies, as doing so would add to long-run profits. But the higher-than-normal profit price, if present, would restrict output levels below those occurring in pure competition, and mean higher unit costs than technologically possible. Finally, the monopolist would receive a greater reward than necessary to keep him supplying the market, and from the standpoint of the entire economy we may question the economic usefulness of such a surplus bounty.

Monopoly markets may be inefficient from the standpoint of market prices and resource allocation. Nonetheless, these markets are advantageous from the standpoint of the individual producer. The situation is almost exactly the opposite of pure competition. Given a profitable price, the producer can earn these profits indefinitely. Increased profits from cost-cutting or product development programs can be retained. There are no pressures beyond the monopolist's own profit motives stimulating him to attain scale economies. He can therefore expand and modernize at his own pace. If the price falls below a profitable level, he can usually exit and produce elsewhere. Compared to a producer in pure or imperfect competition, the monopolist is indeed in a plump and secure position. However, in the United States antitrust legislation has eliminated many monopolists in the private sector of the economy, while technological innovation, through substitute products, has taken care of most of the remaining private monopoly positions.

Most continuing monopolies in the United States gain their positions by legal restrictions upon competition by substitutes. Common examples are the power and light and other utilities affected by the public interest in the services they provide. Although legal restrictions provide the necessary barriers to entry for monopolists in these cases, restrictions are usually also placed on the monopoly profits earned serving these markets, typically in the form of price restrictions tied to a maximum return on investment. This return on investment is generally set at an amount necessary to enable the utilities to continue to compete in acquiring new capital. We can easily characterize the impact of such price restrictions on the price and output behavior of a regulated monopolist. Figure 11–7

FIGURE 11–7

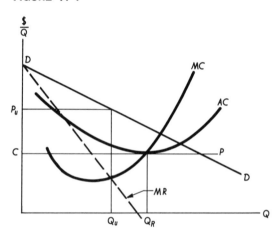

illustrates the situation. The unregulated price and quantity P_u and Q_u yield a pure profit to the monopolist. If the normal return on investment is included in the monopolist's cost curves, then the objective of regulation would be to set $P = AC$. This could be accomplished by the price ceiling CP. Imposing this ceiling, the portion of the demand curve DP now becomes inapplicable, and the $MR = P$ for the horizontal portion of the regulated demand curve, as in pure competition. The result of this ceiling in Figure 11–7 is to lower price and increase output produced. Looking more generally at the figure, a lower price will obviously occur whenever the ceiling is effective. But the increase in output occurred because the unregulated MR curve happened to lie to the left of the low point on AC (to which point the regulated Q will move for $P = AC$). If the unregulated MR had crossed MC to the right of the minimum point on AC (which is perfectly plausible), then the regulated output would decline.

Perhaps the possibility of earning pure profits over the long run in unregulated monopolies and the security of the market position is what causes this structure to be sought by producers in other market forms. For example, how many advertising programs hammer at the message, "Accept No Substitutes—There Is Nothing Like . . . ." However, few producers in a free economy succeed in this endeavor over the long term, even though they may achieve regular and significant technological breakthroughs. The reason for this (besides antitrust laws) apparently relates to widespread acceptance of the adage that to the innovator in a market economy goes at least a temporary monopoly position, and with this position go greater than average profits and increased market options. When many producers hold this view, the innovative competition makes it uncommon for a single producer to break away from his rivals over the long run in product design and distinctiveness. Quantitatively speaking, the most important market structure in the composition of U.S. output is that of oligopoly. We now consider this market structure.

OLIGOPOLY MARKETS

Oligopoly markets are served by only a few sellers. Each seller has captured a significant share of the market, and is importantly concerned with maintaining or increasing his market share. The prices of each producer are carefully watched by the other producers, who can be expected to react via their own prices to any change in the prevailing price relationships in the industry. The product in oligopoly can be either homogeneous or differentiated. The crucial feature of oligopolies is each producer's recognition in his pricing strategy of pricing interdependence with other producers. Examples of approximately oligopoly markets in the United States involving near homogeneous products are the primary steel and aluminum industries, copper production, and various materials and components bought according to specifications. Examples of approximately differentiated oligopolies are automobile production, television production, and major home appliances.

In pure competition, imperfect competition, and monopoly markets, the profit-maximizing selection of output and price was based upon variables found within the firm in conjunction with variables representing the firm's markets. In oligopoly markets, the reaction of rivals to price changes enters and interrupts this picture. The oligopolist who sets his price based on the position of a downward sloping demand curve is likely to discover that the setting of that price has caused a price change by his competitors, which in turn has shifted his demand curve and caused his established price to now be nonoptimal. If he readjusts his price to $MR = MC$, he again invites a reaction.

This process of play and counterplay has not been found logically to lead to any particular equilibrium position as in the case of other market models. The establishment of an individual producer's price appears to be largely a result of a kind of calculated guess by each producer as to what the other will be likely to do if such-and-such a price is announced by each. In cases where producers are familiar with and can predict the patterns of behavior of their rivals, a remarkable degree of price stability and relative uniformity can characterize oligopoly price patterns.

For example, let us say that in a three-producer oligopoly, each producer knows his unit cost curve to be approximately equally positioned as that of his competitors. Now assume an increase in labor costs associated with an industry-wide labor settlement has reduced profits below normal levels. Each producer knows not only that he would like to raise his prices sufficiently to restore profits, but that his rivals are in approximately the same cost-price situation as he is, and therefore they will be likely to follow such an increase. Moreover, if they do all follow an increase, *relative* prices in the industry will not have changed although the industry's product will now be higher in the general spectrum of prices. If, as we will assume in this case, the demand for the *industry's* product is relatively inelastic, such a general industry price increase would have a small effect on the volume of total demand. These conditions can be expected to produce a price increase by one producer, obediently followed by the other two competitors, with little fuss or resistance.

Each producer knew an increase in his price would be clearly advantageous if it were followed by his competitors, and each also knew the others were in the same pinch as he regarding profits. The risk of not having the increase followed is thus low. If the initiating producer's price increase was not followed by even one significant producer, the effects upon the market share of the price-increasing producers could be serious, as customers could be drawn away to the competitor's brand, possibly never to return. Moreover, to announce a "necessary" price increase due to pressing cost increases, and then rescind it when it became clear it would not be generally followed, would not likely be viewed kindly by the producer's customers who, as a result, might see the producer as a greedy merchant attempting to gouge them for every cent possible. So a clear degree of risk is associated with a price rise in the circumstance we have illustrated and in oligopoly generally. The extent of this risk is determined by how well each producer can predict the reactions of his rivals.[3]

The only circumstances for which formal models of pricing in

---

[3] The reader familiar with game theory may see in this illustration an inviting application. This has been explored by economists interested in forging a game-theoretic theory of oligopoly. In extremely simple cases, the logic is forceful and the model applicable. However, the actual empirical applications are virtually nonexistent.

oligopoly have been developed involve extremely specialized and mechanistic assumptions about the reaction of rivals. Therefore, such formal oligopoly models as have been developed are not of general interest in analysis of prices. For example, if we assume that any price cut by a particular producer will inevitably be followed by all producers, but that any price increase will not be followed, we can develop a model that offers an explanation within the *MR, MC* context, not of the level of price per se, but of why price is often "sticky" in oligopolies, moving in stairstep fashion. We shall not go into this model here, since the highly mechanical nature of the assumed reaction pattern of rivals greatly reduces application of the model, and also since the model does not offer an explanation of the actual level of price.[4] In fact, some of the most important price-related questions involved in the analysis of oligopoly concerns the nature of the reaction pattern expected as a result of changes in price relationships.

In many actual oligopoly markets in the United States, price does not appear to be used as an important competitive weapon. Producers in these oligopolies typically have learned that: (a) attempts to increase market share through price cutting usually lead to unfavorable outcomes for both the firm and the industry through price wars; (b) frequent manipulation of price breeds uncertainty on the part of customers, and promotes delayed purchases of postponable durables when price is increased, and (c) price increases if not followed promote shopping around by a firm's customers, produce general ill will, and can lead to serious erosion of market conditions.

Rather than rely on price to attain growth goals, many oligopolists have instead typically found that product research and development and effective marketing programs are less risky ways to achieve expansion of output. As a result, the product development and marketing programs in most U.S. oligopolies are generally extensive. With respect to pricing, customary pricing relationships among producers are often accepted by all, and changed only upon general realization of abnormally low profits, or as a result of downward pressures produced by abnormally high profits. In the latter case, we may often depend upon the ambitions of at least some producers to put downward pressure on oligopoly prices in cases where profits are in general abnormally high.

MARKET PRICES—AN EPILOGUE

The discussion of this and the previous chapter has not produced the kind of quantitative conclusions that characterized chapters 5 through

---

[4] A discussion of this model is contained in most intermediate-level price theory texts. For example, see D. S. Watson, *Price Theory and Its Uses*, Chapter 19, pp. 361–76.

9. The models discussed have been qualitative in nature. As such, they yield insights only into the direction of the effect upon markets resulting from manipulating market variables, and as to overall patterns that might be expected for certain sets of "givens." In some instances, these models provide no particular insights beyond those that result from our own common sense. For example, if market demand increases in pure competition, our model predicts the initial impact will be higher prices. That result is possible from much more elementary analysis. However, in other instances (such as the less than optimal long-run scale of production in imperfect competition), the model may lead to conclusions not emerging from other simpler techniques. In such instances, these models do uniquely contribute to understanding by providing a consistent framework for logical reasoning. As a framework for reasoning, the models of this chapter can be an aid to understanding and analysis of market price fluctuations.

A Concluding Note on "Being Competitive"

The analysis of pure competition has indicated that price is likely to be a key influence upon producers in these markets. With a homogeneous product and many small producers, being competitive is essentially a matter of taking advantage of all possible efficiencies and cost savings. If the perfect competitor is successful at this task, he will survive over the long run. In imperfect competition, the market abounds with prices, each reflecting the level of brand loyalty fostered by its product. The producer's price in this market structure measures the extent of the distinctiveness of his innovation and the effectiveness of his marketing programs. Being competitive for the imperfectly competitive producer is a matter of attaining efficiencies, as in pure competition. However, it is also a matter of maintaining the product's demand curve in a favorable position through effective marketing and product improvement programs.

In oligopoly markets, competing effectively is often a matter of producing a continuing stream of effectively marketed product innovations. Unlike imperfect competition, price is often a generally ineffective means to reap rewards from product innovation and marketing programs. Instead, the producer generally can be expected to rely upon increasing his share of the market as a means of realizing the fruits of his nonprice efforts.

The focus of attention in our analysis has been upon the pricing patterns in various markets. Our discussion of oligopoly has indicated that other areas such as marketing, research and development, new product decisions, and plant and equipment purchases constitute important areas of economic concern to producers in these markets. Indeed this is the case. Attempts to study other relationships among important economic variables in the firm have taken several directions, including behavioral and information-processing approaches, and simultaneous-equation econometric models. In the next section, we consider a representative sampling of other techniques for the analysis of economic behavior in the firm.

DISCUSSION QUESTIONS

1. What do you see as the short-run and long-run effect on price and other market data of a law that makes brand labeling of consumer products illegal?
2. Contrast the response of an imperfectly competitive market versus a perfectly competitive market to a shift in general demand for product goups.
3. Are monopolistic markets more or less efficient than imperfectly competitive markets, or can you generalize at all on the basis of the threoretical arguments in the chapter?
4. Would you characterize the distinction drawn between imperfect competition and monopoly markets as small and subtle, or large and fundamental? Explain.
5. What major factors preclude the application of the pricing model appropriate for perfectly competitive, imperfectly competitive, and monopoly markets to the analysis of pricing in oligopoly?

PART III

Analyzing Economic Behavior
of Firms

In recent times, a number of tools from quantitative and behavioral disciplines have been directed towards analyzing economic behavior of firms. Still more recently, econometrics has been employed to measure important financial relationships in firms. Application of these tools has led to development of a positive framework for a prescriptive theory of resource allocation in firms. In Part III we consider these topics.

Chapter 12

NONECONOMETRIC ANALYSIS OF CORPORATE ECONOMIC ACTIVITY

In this chapter, we shall survey analytical models and approaches directed towards understanding and predicting major economic and financial processes at work in the firm. In this endeavor, our concern is with explanatory schemes for overall performance as contrasted with models dealing with specific operational problems in the firm. Thus, we are interested in analyzing variables such as sales and production levels, budget levels, profits and cash flow as opposed to operational problems such as inventory levels, production scheduling, or selection of product mix. These latter topics are the usual concern of operations research, to which the interested reader is referred.[1]

In this chapter, we shall consider four approaches to the study of economic processes in the firm: (1) behavioral analysis, (2) industrial dynamics, (3) corporate simulations, and (4) programming models. These four approaches are not completely separable nor are they mutually exclusive. Our discussion of them separately should be understood to be only a matter of clarity and convenience. In practice, one increasingly finds two or more of these approaches intertwined.

One aspect common among the approaches of interest in this chapter is their reliance on measurement tools other than econometrics. In the following chapter we shall consider econometric analyses of corporate behavior.

A second common property of these four approaches is that they are primarily tools of measurement. Finally, with the exception of programming models, they are all descriptive analytical tools that do not yield optimal solutions to resource-related questions. Nor do they in general contain statements about the functioning of the firm that cannot later be evaluated and accepted or rejected on the basis of the available empirical evidence. Thus, the first three approaches we shall consider are largely instruments of description, while the fourth approach is a

---

[1] For example, see Hiller and Lieberman, *Introduction to Operations Research* (San Francisco, Calif.: Holden-Day, 1967).

source of prescriptive solutions. All may lead to quantitative insights into the often subtle economic relationships in the firm. In turn, these insights in the hands of management can often lead to redirection of resources towards more desirable deployments in terms of the firm's family of objectives. We now turn to the first of these approaches.

BEHAVIORAL ANALYSES

Analyzing economic relationships in the firm from a behavioral viewpoint begins by identifying the firm as a coalition of people, according to Cyert and March, who pioneered this area.[2] As such, all the distinctly human factors in the firm occupy the central role in analysis. Whereas other approaches such as the "strawman" firm, typically used in economics as a means to study market prices, dispensed with human facilities with the sweeping assumptions of rational behavior, perfect information, and profit maximization, nearly the whole of behavioral analysis is concerned with evaluating and measuring the effects of departures from such rigid sets of assumptions.

The behavioral analysis of Cyert and March was initially concerned with obtaining an analytical representation of the goals of a firm. This task is undertaken within a general theoretical framework that sees the firm's goals as largely resulting from a bargaining process between members of the organization, and relating to performance levels seen as attainable by members of the organization. In addition, the goals are viewed as fluid and sensitive to actual achievement. Cyert and March laid down the following guidelines:

1. In the steady state, aspiration level exceeds achievement by a small amount.
2. Where achievement increases at an increasing rate, aspiration level will exhibit short-run lags behind achievement.
3. Where achievement decreases, aspiration level will be above achievement.[3]

In addition to the general notion of a coalition of people who affect and are affected by the process of goal formulation, and the framework for measuring goals, five basic mechanisms are assumed:

1. A mechanism that provides for change in the demands of the organization.
2. A mechanism that focuses attention upon potential or latent problems at appropriate times, and away from problems no longer important.
3. A mechanism for sorting among the demands of members.

---

[2] R. M. Cyert and J. G. March, *A Behavioral Theory of the Firm* (Englewood Cliffs, N.J.: Prentice-Hall, Inc., 1963).

[3] Ibid., p. 34.

4. A mechanism for evaluating the significance of demands made on the resources of the organization.
5. A mechanism for choosing among potential viable organizational configurations.

Within this broad framework, Cyert and March considered the specific problem of establishing a model of the process by which a duopolist (two-firm oligopolist) arrives at the selection of output level. The container industry in the United States was used to develop the specific structure of this model. The skeleton of this model is summarized as follows: [4]

1. Forecast competitor's reactions
2. Forecast demand
3. Estimate average unit costs
4. Specify profit goal and other objectives
5. Examine and evaluate alternatives
6. Reexamine cost estimate
7. Reexamine demand estimates
8. Reexamine profit goal
9. Decide upon output

This skeleton represents the author's description of the process mechanism by which decisions about output level are assumed to take place in the sample firms. The framework is based on direct observation of these firms' historical decision-process for output selection. Each step was then spelled out in much more detail leading to construction of a computer simulation. This computer model enabled the assumed process to be operated to make simulated decisions. These simulated results were then compared with actual results for the American and Continental Can Companies. A reasonable correspondence was observed between actual and simulated results. Of the fit between the model and the data, Cyert and March observed:

It should be clear that the validity of the approach presented in this chapter is not conclusively demonstrated by the goodness of fit to the can industry data. We have demonstrated that under the appropriate assumptions, models of firm decision processes can be specified that yield predictions approximating some observed results. However, the situation is one in which there are ample degrees of freedom in the specification of parameters to enable a number of time series to be approximated. Although in this case we have reduced the number of free parameters substantially by specifying

---

[4] This is only an outline of what Cyert and March refer to as a skeleton and therefore is a greatly simplified version of their final model. See pp. 86–87 of their work for more details.

most of them *a priori*, the problems of identification faced by any complex model are faced by this one and will have to be solved. The general methodology for testing models that take the form of computer programs remains to be developed.[5]

This fundamental limitation recognized, Cyert and March proceeded with observations about the general category of process models with which they are concerned, as compared with classical economic equilibrium models:[6]

1. The models are descriptions of processes.
2. The models recognize the importance of the search process, as well as the final decision value.
3. The models allow for change in the profit objective over time as a result of experience.
4. The models postulate an important role for forecasts, and provide for the adjustment of these forecasts in accordance with experience.
5. The models deal with organizational biases in making cost, demand estimates.
6. The models all allow for organizational slack or, in other words, for the maintenance of nonoptimal positions over time. These nonoptimal positions are seen as a reservoir of potential economies available in time of need.

Besides describing the duopoly output selection process in the can industry, Cyert and March presented a description of pricing for a specific department store. In this they began with a highly aggregated model of the pricing decision based on four a priori notions about the fundamental ingredients in the process:

1. process-component to resolve conflicts
2. means to avoid uncertainty
3. process-component for problemistic search
4. process-component to provide organizational adaption

Figure 12–1 contains this aggregated model. In this process, initial estimates of prices and markups are made and checked against a markup goal (basic concept 1). If the goal is achieved, formal rules are applied to determine the actual item markups (basic concept 2). If not, a search is undertaken (basic concept 3), leading to possible changes in product mix and markup rules. An iterative reappraisal of markup goals is made in conjunction with each specific markup decision (basic concept 4).

---

[5] Ibid., p. 97, footnote.

[6] Ibid., p. 98.

FIGURE 12–1

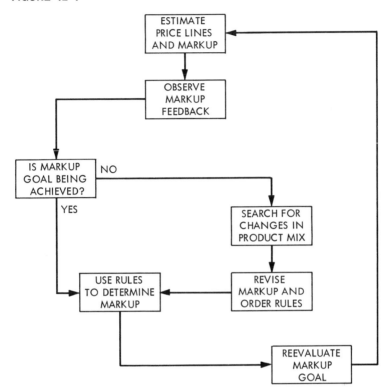

The process of Figure 12–1 is then successively disaggregated according to the specific characteristics of the subject department store. Finally, a flow diagram is developed that is sufficiently specific to enable preparation of computer programs for its simulated operation.

Simulations computed this way show a good correspondence between model and actual results, which lead Cyert and March to the conclusion,

> The tests that have been made of the model tend to support it. Clearly some of the tests are inadequate because of the paucity of the data. Also, we have not attempted to build alternative models and compare predictive ability. Undoubtedly, alternative models can be built and can be made to predict well. However, we have been interested in building a model that embodies the actual decision-making process. Our reasons for this position have been amplified elsewhere in the book. We do not believe a radically different model can be built that captures the actual decision process and predicts as well. Because our objective is to understand the actual process, we have not attempted to minimize the number of assumptions, the number of variables, or the number of inputs to the model.[7]

---

[7] Ibid., pp. 147–48.

We have considered enough of the specifics of the Cyert and March project to indicate its approach in dealing with an economic variable such as output or price. Their work has demonstrated that many behavioral patterns in the firm can be quantitatively expressed in computer-programmable form so that the behavior can be analyzed and predicted. Such inquiry is of course limited to behavior that exhibits a regular pattern. This limits applicability of behavioral analysis to areas of regular repetitive-type decisions in which distinct behavioral patterns exist.

Another behavioral project concerning the firm was developed by Bonini.[8] His project attempts to specify through a series of difference equations the behavior of individuals and groups in the firm as a function of the behavior of other individuals and of past and present information flows, the interlinking of which comprised the model. These relationships were specified for a hypothetical firm, which of course limits conclusions to being only illustrative. Bonini's "strawman" firm consisted of decision and information locuses, information channels, management policies, and behavioral systems displaying the operation of these structures. He introduced eight specific changes in his model and used a factoral experimental design to study the effects of the eight changes upon prices, inventory levels, costs, sales, profits, and organizational pressure, as well as the interactions among the changes. The changes considered were:[9]

1. large versus small changes in the external conditions surrounding the firm

2. small steady growth in demand versus large irregular growth in demand

3. a rapid versus slow adjustment of production standards in response to change

4. a stressful versus stress-free organization when under pressure

5. a situation where individuals in the organization are affected by pressure versus one where they are not

6. an average cost method of inventory valuation versus a LIFO method

7. a situation where company salesmen know the firm's inventory position versus one where they do not

8. primary use of present information for control versus past information

Bonini's analysis produced conclusions about the effect of each of the two possible states of these eight conditions plus all interactions. The specific conclusions are not of general interest due to the firm-peculiar and hypothetical nature of the data they reflect. However, they would be of obvious interest to the management of a real-world firm were

---

[8] C. P. Bonini, *Simulation of Information and Decision Systems in the Firm* (Englewood Cliffs, N.J.: Prentice-Hall, 1963).

[9] Ibid., pp. 86–87.

they based on that firm's data. In fact, possibly the most interesting aspect of the Bonini study is that it illustrates the use of behavioral analysis and simulation to explore the quantitative impact of such phenomena as organizational pressure and uneven economic growth. Thus, Bonini's study invites adaptation to real-world firms.

Behavioral models in general offer a vehicle for description, understanding, and analysis of repetitive decision-making processes in the firm. Applied to the circumstances of particular firms, we may gain insights through behavioral models into the actual factors brought to bear upon repetitive economic decisions. This data in turn can provide indications as to the direction of desirable changes in decision-making processes. In many applications proposed process alterations could be simulated in such a model prior to their application in the firm, thus providing a "laboratory test" of alterations of policies and information flows.

INDUSTRIAL DYNAMICS

Industrial dynamics is an approach to the analysis of economic relationships in the firm that emphasizes the study of patterns of instability inherent in business variables. In the words of the originator of the approach, Forrester:

> Industrial dynamics is the study of the information-feedback characteristics of industrial activity to show how organizational structure, amplification (in policies), and time delays (in decisions and actions) interact to influence the success of the enterprise. It treats the interactions between the flows of information, money orders, materials, personnel and capital equipment in a company, an industry, or a national economy.[10]

Forrester identifies four cornerstones in the industrial dynamics approach. These are: (a) the theory of information feedback systems, (b) a knowledge of decision-making processes, (c) experimental model approach to complex systems, and (d) digital computer for simulation.[11]

Information feedback systems exist in circumstances where the environment surrounding a system affects that system, which causes the system to produce outputs reacting back upon the environment. We have seen such a system in the analysis of pure competition, where pure profits in the industry produce a flow of new producers whose output affects the pure profits and therefore the continued flow. A second example at the level of the firm is found in inventories. Orders and inventory levels lead to manufacturing decisions that fill orders, correct inventories, and yield new manufacturing decisions. The study of feedback

---

[10] J. W. Forrester, *Industrial Dynamics* (Cambridge, Mass.: The M.I.T. Press, 1962), p. 13.

[11] Ibid., p. 14.

systems deals with the way information is used for the purpose of control. It helps understand how the extent of corrective action and the time delays in information processing can lead to unstable fluctuation.

The second cornerstone, knowledge of the decision making process, implies a substantial degree of regularity and stability in the process of decision making. Industrial dynamics is concerned with building information feedback type models of decision processes; therefore the processes themselves must possess sufficient stability and be sufficiently visible to enable such models. Forrester points to the experience obtained in military systems research as evidence that such regularity likely underlies individual business processes as well.

The third cornerstone of industrial dynamics, the experimental approach, consists of the construction of simulation models that interrelate various mathematical functions and which, upon operation, produce solutions approximating those obtainable from exact analytical solutions of the mathematical functions. Use of the experimental approach enables models to be developed and employed whose analytical solution is complex almost beyond solution. In fact, Forrester's evaluation indicates that the simulation approach is a necessity:

> Mathematical analysis is not powerful enough to yield general analytical solutions to situations as complex as are encountered in business. The alternative is the experimental approach.[12]

In some specific models presented by Forrester most mathematicians would grudgingly agree, although in others the use of simulation seems more a convenience than a necessity.

The final cornerstone, use of digital computers, is set down by Forrester as a factor in greatly reducing the costs of the large number of arithmetic computations required in simulation.

These four cornerstones comprise the primary apparatus of the techniques of analysis proposed by industrial dynamics. To better understand the flavor of their combined application, we consider a simple example presented by Forrester of a production-distribution system. It is illustrated in Figure 12–2, which contains a model of the interrelated flows of information, orders and goods in the production-distribution process. Omitted from consideration are three other flows with which Forrester is concerned in a complete simulation—flows of capital equipment, money, and personnel.

As Figure 12–2 implies, such a model requires information about the physical structure and organization of the production-distribution process, and also information about the processing locations and time requirements. As seen, goods flow from the factory to the factory inventory

---

[12] Ibid, p. 17.

FIGURE 12–2

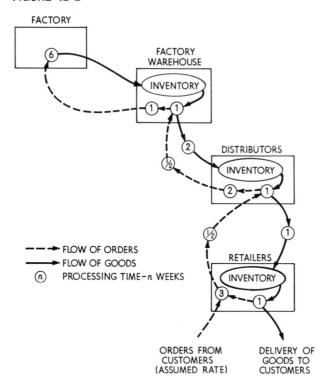

on receipt of an order after a six-week delay. A one-week processing delay and two-week shipping delay characterize the flow of goods from the factory inventory to distributor's inventory, assuming an in-stock condition. Two more weeks are required to process and ship goods to retail inventories, also assuming in-stock conditions. Finally, a one-week processing time is required for retailers to distribute the goods to customers. The flow of orders from customers to retailers, from retailers to distributors, from distributors to the factory warehouse, and from the factory warehouse to the factory follows a similar pattern, where the processing consists of a sales analysis and a purchasing delay at each distribution level, and a transmission time of one-half week each between retail, distributor, and factory levels.

The illustration of Figure 12–2 is reduced to a series of mathematical functions that quantitatively express the various information linkages, flows, and feedback loops (such as between factory and factory inventory) in the model.[13] This mathematical version can now be directly

---

[13] Forrester has presented the equations for this model. See *Industrial Dynamics*, Chap. 15.

translated into a computer program, enabling a variety of analyses to be undertaken. The simplest type of analysis is where only one variable is altered with all else fixed, enabling the pure effects of each to be seen. In the illustration under discussion, this type of analysis brings out the major contribution of information feedback-type simulation since it demonstrates the extent and magnitude of the instability associated with an innocent appearing step change in one activity among several interrelated and time-spaced activities of the Figure 12–2 type. For example, starting from an equilibrium, the model of Figure 12–2 was subjected to a 10-percent step increase in sales, then maintained at this higher constant level. The effects of this change upon other major variables

FIGURE 12–3

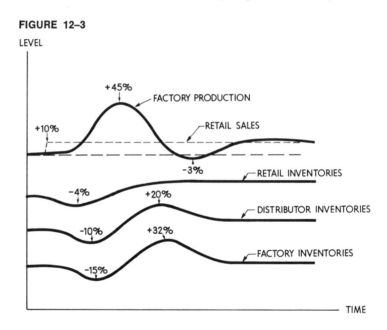

are generally as shown in Figure 12–3. Notice that a damped cyclical pattern in sales is produced by the change. Sales rise substantially above, then fall below the new level of demand, finally returning to the original level. This is a function of the buildup of orders to replenish buffer inventories at various levels. Finally, when the orders related to the 10 percent increase begin to affect factory production levels, several weeks have passed and the positions of all inventories have deteriorated further, to a maximum of 15 percent at the factory level. To replenish these stocks and produce for the additional demand, factory production rises to a peak increase of 45 percent as the inventories begin to build.

Then as the catch-up process overshoots, inventories at distributor and factory levels rise above intended levels and production is cut back to as much as 3 percent below *initial* levels. The flow of orders undergoes a similar process of instability. Eventually (after about 70 weeks have passed in the example of Figure 12–2) production, orders, and inventories return to their long-run values. But the length and magnitude of the intervening instability, all in response to a simple 10 percent increase, has been rather remarkable. Forrester presents a similar analysis for a regular cyclical pattern of fluctuation in demand and for an erratic pattern of demand. He considers the case of a capacity constraint and the impact this has upon patterns of instability. Finally, he analyzes the results if the processing times of Figure 12–2 were reduced by various amounts, or if certain new information linkages were created. These results demonstrated that certain changes in the information flows and processing times could sharply reduce the magnitude and length of cyclical patterns inherent in the original process. Through simulation, proposed changes of this nature could be evaluated as to their dynamic effect prior to implementation.

Forrester's techniques are particularly well suited for understanding and analysis of cyclical instability in interrelated systems with specific processing points and time delays of the type illustrated in the example. In this regard, they contribute uniquely to the available techniques for analysis of economic variables in the firm. However, as in the case of behavioral analysis, Forrester's techniques require the process under investigation be fully visible, systematic, and repetitive. This limits the analysis to routine-type processes that sometimes are not a primary source of trouble in firms. Nonetheless, the techniques of industrial dynamics offer an often powerful tool for the analysis of cyclical instability in regular economic processes in the firm.

CORPORATE SIMULATIONS

In this section we are concerned with exploring the nature of simulation-type models developed to explain overall aspects of corporate financial performance. Perhaps the most striking thing about developments in this area during the latter part of the 1960s is the diversity of model types and structures that have been called corporate simulations. This makes it particularly difficult to pinpoint a definition or clear-cut description of corporate simulations, since they have evolved along different lines for different corporations.

However, observation of a number of specific corporate projects brings to mind some statements as to attributes of corporate simulations that appear to be common denominators. Among these are:

1. Most models are primarily tools for formal financial planning at the level of the overall corporation.

2. Most models find primary application in answering "what-if" questions about financial relationships.

3. Virtually all models consist of sets of equations comprising analytical structures that relate sets of inputs to performance-type outputs.

4. Most models are of the descriptive variety that do not attempt to prescribe optimal solutions.

5. Most models are deterministic in character, as opposed to stochastic models (see Chapter 1 for a discussion of this property).

Both behavioral analysis and industrial dynamics approaches have been largely developed in academic institutions. By contrast, the initiation and continued development of corporate simulation projects by firms for their own use has been rather widespread. By 1970, a study undertaken by George Gershefski indicates more than 100 such models were in development or in use by U.S. corporations.[14] The primary uses for these models were found to be: (1) as tools in the preparation of one- and five-year financial plans, and (2) as an aid in long-run planning. It is difficult to explore the specifics of these uses without reference to specific model structures. Thus, we now turn to some illustrations of corporate models that together should help illustrate the nature of this tool.[15]

The Xerox Project

According to those involved, the Xerox Corporation's efforts at constructing a corporate model were aimed at providing essentially a computational aid in their financial planning. In essence, their initial model was a computer-programmed version of the company's basic financial planning process. A simplified hypothetical example of such a planning structure is shown in Figure 12–4. As seen, the structure of this type model is in accordance with conventional income statement lines, with each line essentially being a variable to be explained. The method of explanation is by defining simple ratios relating the income statement lines, and by accepting as "given" the necessary starting point variables. In the structure shown, sales, depreciation, and values for all the ratios (values of all underlined variables in Figure 12–4) are assumed to have been predicted separately and made available for use in the model structure.

The model then estimates the income statement significance of the predictions. This function should be distinguished from predicting the

[14] See Gershefski's article in *Corporate Simulation Models*, A. N. Schreiber (ed.), (Seattle, Wash.: University of Washington, 1970), pp. 26–42.

[15] These examples are derived from reports presented at a Symposium on Corporate Models held at the University of Washington. The reader should consult *Corporate Simulation Models* for more details and examples.

income statement from top to bottom. Indeed, a look at the required input predictions in Figure 12–4 suggests that the tough prediction job for many firms is completed upon assembling the inputs for this planning structure.

In addition to providing a computational framework to relate together the variables and ratios in the model in a consistent way, the planning-structure model of Figure 12–4 enables a number of basic "what-if" types of questions to be answered. For example, the question, "What if sales were 150 rather than 100?" could be answered relative to the income statement implications.

FIGURE 12–4
Hypothetical Planning—Structure Model

Variable		*Explained by*
1.	Sales	100 or 150 or 190 or 200 or ?
2.	Manufacturing costs	.35 × sales
3.	Selling expense	.04 × sales
4.	R&D expense	.02 × sales
5.	Other expense	1.5 + .07 × sales
6.	Total expense	Sum of lines 2–5
7.	Depreciation	3 or 3 or 3 or 3 or ?
8.	Profit before tax	Line 1 − (line 6 + line 7)
9.	Income tax	.50 × line 8
10.	Profit after tax	Line 8 − line 9

Note: Underlined variables are required inputs.

In a backward look on their original project, Xerox model builders pointed to a number of criticisms of their original approach. Among these were:

1. The required inputs were often combinations of firm-controllable and uncontrollable variables. For example, the proportion of sales represented by manufacturing costs (.35) in Figure 12–4 is influenced by company strategies and input choices, as well as by market labor and material costs. This character of the input made it difficult to explicitly evaluate "what-if" questions relating to firm-controllable variables, as it was not possible to reliably unbundle the separate types of effects.
2. Many of the inputs were too simply done to enable representation of many interesting "what-if" planning questions.
3. The model did not contribute to the basic need for financial forecasts, as most inputs assumed these data.

Follow-up efforts at Xerox probed specific ways to overcome these weaknesses, and produced more highly disaggregated model structures with separations between controllable and uncontrollable factors. Efforts to transform the planning model into a forecasting model were reportedly frustrated by difficulties in assembling reliable data for use in statistical analyses. To enhance the attractiveness of their model as a planning tool, the later Xerox developments also were designed to involve more people in the model and embed it more deeply in the firm's planning process.

Dow Chemical

A sharp contrast in model structure is provided by a project undertaken at the Dow Chemical Company. As in the previous example, a major objective of the Dow model was to answer "what-if" questions

FIGURE 12–5
The Dow Chemical Company—First Generation Financial Model

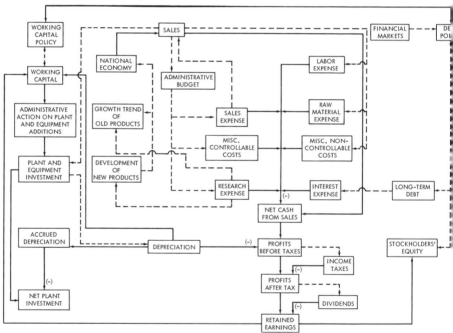

Note: Broken lines indicate lines of influence, while solid lines represent fund flows.

for financial planning purposes. However, to accomplish this, Dow investigators became directly concerned with the firm's processes for decision making, from which they derived conventional income statement data. The general structure of the initial Dow model is shown in Figure 12–5. Notice in the figure that two specific influences upon overall company sales are proposed—national economic conditions and the firm's own sales expense. Sales are presumed to influence the firm's administrative budget, which is described as influencing the level of sales expense, research expense, and miscellaneous controllable costs. In addition, sales are shown to be the driving variable behind labor expense, raw material expense, and miscellaneous noncontrollable costs. These various expense categories combine with sales levels to produce the net cash from sales, which leads to profits before taxes, profits after tax, and retained earnings. Similarly, the left-hand side of Figure 12–5 shows the firm's procedure for establishing levels of plant and equipment expenditure.

The structure of the Dow model attempts to describe the channels through which decisions and market activities exert an impact upon income statement variables. Although it is not clear how Dow quantified the various relationships illustrated by the lines in Figure 12–5, the best indication is that a combination of assumed values and rule-of-thumb magnitudes and ratios was employed.[16] These assumptions reduce the predictive content of the Dow model since they must involve the results of prior forecasts. For example, the extent to which Dow's sales depend on the GNP is a complex question involving several exogenous factors, and this result is an input to the model of Figure 12–5. Indeed, the company did not describe prediction as one of the objectives of the model. These objectives were constrained to be the pursuit of "what-if" planning questions and to provide a tool to assist overall corporate planning.

In further work with the model structure of Figure 12–5, Dow investigators have attempted to draw more model inputs from the firm's planning staff by dis-aggregating the input requirements into those in which existing planning channels in the firm could provide useful data.

Further Thoughts on Corporate Models

Discussions with corporate managers involved with model projects often lead to the conclusion that models of the general variety of our two illustrations have found a niche in their company's planning structure as a result of a process of change in the structure of the model, the objectives of the model, and the company's planning structure itself. Usually, the uses of the model considered most productive by the firm's management were not the uses envisioned for the model upon its initiation. For example, financial forecasting is a continuing important component in corporate planning—yet our illustrations are reflective of a pattern of development of models that do not have great primary value in predicting. This result has undoubtedly come about due to a shortage

---

[16] See *Corporate Simulation Models*, pp. 374–95, for a more complete account of the Dow project.

of historical data considered relevant by the firm upon which the reliability of statistically oriented forecasts rests. Thus, the model structure that typically has developed has taken the form of a structure involving rules of thumb, ratios, and so forth, but not demanding extensive historical data concerning company operations. This is a pattern of development we may expect to see continue. As firms feel more confident of their data base, they will likely tackle the prediction objective in greater numbers. The result will be a more explicit development of the kind of relationships depicted in Figures 12–4 and 12–5 along statistical lines. In turn, this will lead to a new class of uses of such models. In Chapter 13 we return to this general topic by considering econometric models applied to the data of firms. For now, we turn our attention to a class of noneconometric models of the firm having the unusual property of being prescriptive in nature. Our discussion to this point has dealt exclusively with descriptive models, which comprise the dominant proportion of all recent applications (95 percent according to a 1969 survey). The less-frequent development of prescriptive or optimizing-type models has almost unanimously been of one form—programming models of the firm. We now consider these models.

PROGRAMMING MODELS

Programming models of the firm have a very simple superstructure, a less-simple specific structure, and a complex solution procedure that fortunately is readily programmable on most computers. Basically, the superstructure consists of an economic objective function for the firm and a set of constraints on the unlimited achievement of that objective. The objective function quantifies the answer to the question, "What is the economic goal towards which the firm is directing its activities?" The constraints quantify the answer to the question, "Why can't the firm infinitely achieve its objective?"

The specific structure of a programming model typically consists of an objective function that expresses some measure of performance as a function of the various production outputs of the firm, such as:

$$P_t = f(0_{1,t}, 0_{2,t}, + \cdots + 0_{n,t}) \qquad (12\text{–}1)$$

where P_t is a performance measure for time t such as profits, and $0_{1,t}$, $0_{2,t} \ldots 0_{n,t}$ are alternative outputs of the firm in t that typically compete for the firm's resource inputs. The extent of such input trade-offs as well as overall company limits on available inputs are typically defined by a series of constraints, written to take into account limits on performance maximization imposed by such factors as market absorption rates, labor availability, plant space, machine time, warehouse space, and working capital needs. For example, the following constraints may be applicable:

$$0_{1,t} \leq g_1(M_{1,t}, 0_{1,t-1})$$
$$\cdot$$
$$\cdot \qquad \cdot$$
$$\cdot \qquad \cdot \qquad \qquad \qquad (12\text{--}2)$$
$$\cdot$$
$$0_{n,t} \leq g_n(M_{n,t}, 0_{n,t-1})$$

$$M_{1,t} + M_{2,t} + \cdots + M_{n,t} \leq CF_t \qquad\qquad (12\text{--}3)$$
$$CF_t = h[(0_1 + 0_2 + \cdots + 0_n)_t, LC_t] \qquad\qquad (12\text{--}4)$$
$$c_1 0_{1,t} + c_2 0_{2,t} + \cdots + c_n 0_{n,t} \leq LM_t \qquad\qquad (12\text{--}5)$$
$$d_1 0_{1,t} + d_2 0_{2,t} + \cdots + d_n 0_{n,t} \leq CE_t \qquad\qquad (12\text{--}6)$$
$$\cdot \qquad\qquad\qquad\qquad \cdot$$
$$\cdot \qquad\qquad\qquad\qquad \cdot$$
$$\cdot \qquad\qquad\qquad\qquad \cdot$$

etc.   etc.

where new variables are:

$M_{i,t}$ = marketing expenditures on product i in time t
CF_t = total available cash flow
LC_t = unit labor costs in t
LM_t = maximum available labor hours in t
CE_t = maximum available machine time in t
h, g_i = denotes some function
c_i, d_i = denotes unit labor and machine requirements respectively.

This partial listing of typical constraints should suggest the flavor of the specific constraint structure of programming models. For instance, the reason $0_{i,t}$ cannot be made infinitely large for all products is partly due to marketshare limitations. The first set of constraints (12–2) formalizes these limitations by stipulating that current maximum output levels are a function of marketing outlays and past output levels. Constraint (12–3) formulates a budgetary constraint on the total size of the marketing budget, relating this sum to a measure of available cash. Expression (12–4) in turn shows available cash to be a product of output levels in all product areas plus labor costs. Expression (12–5) and (12–6) formulate constraints on the available labor and capital resources of the firm as functions of the quantity of various outputs produced.

In real-world applications, our listing of constraints would be drawn up to encompass all important limitations on the firm's attainment of performance objectives. Specific functional relations and coefficients would be chosen by reference to historical data. Then solution of this system for time t would involve selecting those values of $0_{1,t} \ldots 0_{n,t}$ that maximize P_t subject to meeting all the constraints. A new solution would result for $t + 1$ and so forth. Thus, the model yields prescriptions as to optimal output mixes over time given the real-world constraints involved. A second major output of such models is analysis of the particular constraints that are most sensitive in attaining better performance. Once an optimal solution is attained, the impact of relaxing any constraints via specific management efforts can be easily found. For example, the working capital constraint (12–3) in our illustration could be relaxed by acquiring additional funds externally. The effect of such funds on sales and performance measures can be ascertained in the context of the programming solution. In addition, it is the normal case that not all constraints are actually met in optimal solutions. Some are not operative due to the prior effects of others. These circumstances reveal "slack" in some resources and show the critical constraining nature of others. In our example, if slack existed in the cash flow constraint, more cash would not contribute to the performance objective. However, more resources of another more critical type may importantly impact on the objective. Programming models can discover answers to such questions.

Solution algorithms for constrained optimization systems have been developed rapidly in recent years by operations researchers and can by now accommodate a wide variety of differing objective-function constraint systems. For examples, the reader should consult the growing operations research literature. We may obtain a better feeling for the way in which programming models have been applied and the uses to which they may be put by considering an actual application of a programming model by a large lumber company.

Boise Cascade

According to a spokesman for the firm, "Boise Cascade is a firm with a very clearly stated objective—to increase the value of the company for its shareholders."[17] In applying a programming model to their firm, Boise operations research personnel thus outlined the nature of the objective function in a programming formulation of Boise's resource allocation problem. The resource constraints and allocative options operative in the case of a large lumber company such as Boise are numerous and sometimes complicated. The nature of the problem is depicted in Figure 12–6.

Notice in Figure 12–6 that the firm's three major products—plywood, lumber, and paper—emanate from a single raw material, timber and logs. This presents a major allocational problem for the company—how to

---

[17] See the article by J. H. Dickens, "Linear Programming in Corporate Simulation," in *Corporate Simulation Models*, p. 292.

divide the available material supply among these outputs in such a way to increase the value of the company to its shareholders by the maximum amount. In moving from company timber supplies to marketable plywood, lumber, and paper products, the firm has a number of options available to increase or decrease its resource input, as shown in Figure 12–6. Initially, the company can muster more timber than its own supplies will yield by buying timber in the open market. Secondly, after conversion of the timber into logs, the firm has the option of selling part of

FIGURE 12–6
Boise Cascade Resource Flow

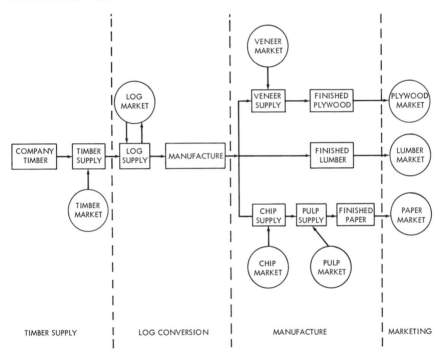

this output in log markets, retaining it entirely for its own use, or buying more logs in the market. Its level of participation in both the timber and log markets will depend on prices in these markets and on demand for the company's final products.[18]

The figure next shows that additional inputs may be purchased in veneer, chip, and pulp markets for the purpose of supplementing internally

---

[18] Indeed, the figure shows a secondary potential activity of the firm as a log wholesaler. If timber prices are low and log prices high, it may be profitable to buy timber for direct resale as logs as long as slack capacity exists in log-producing facilities.

produced inputs. The purchase of inputs at this level is clearly a substitute for purchasing either timber or logs, and depends on relative prices in all areas as well as availability of processing facilities in the log conversion and manufacturing stage. Finally, the result of these various purchase and make-or-buy decisions are outputs in the firm's three product areas.

The major interrelated questions to which the programming model was addressed are thus:

1. How much timber to buy versus cut
2. What quantity of logs should be bought or sold
3. What amount of veneer, chips, and pulp should be bought[19]
4. What quantities of plywood, lumber, and paper should be produced in order to maximize the shareholder value of the company.

One complicating factor in Boise's programming formulation is that the firm's timber supplies, lumber manufacturing, plywood manufacturing, and pulp and paper manufacturing facilities are geographically spread out over nine management regions. These regions encompass eight timber producing areas, fourteen sawmills, eight plywood plants, and four pulp and paper mills. Thus, part of the problem to which the programming model is addressed is which timber areas should be used to obtain timber, which sawmills should be used to cut which timber, and which plywood and pulp and paper manufacturing facilities should receive cut timber from which sawmills.

These various considerations and constraints resulted in a giant 5800-equation linear programming model involving some 25,000 variables. Given (a) prices for timber, logs, green veneer, pulp, and chips, (b) log conversion costs, (c) key manufacturing costs, (d) product prices for lumber, plywood, and paper, and (e) market share data by products, the model produced a constrained optimal solution stipulating which timber should be cut, where and in what form it should be sold or manufactured, and what proportion of output each product should occupy.

In obtaining quick and visible answers to these kinds of questions, Boise saw several advantages. Among these were the capability to make highly reasoned decisions about new plant or sawmill additions. Since the sawmill and plant capacities entered the model as constraints, the potential construction of a new facility in a certain geographic area had the effect of relaxing the constraint by the amount of the new capacity. Quick and consistent answers are possible to the question of the total impact upon company operations and ultimately upon shareholder value

---

[19] Although not shown in Figure 12–6, one additional conceivable option is for the company to sell in veneer, chip, or pulp markets.

of such proposed plant additions. Furthermore, analysis of an optimal solution of the model can identify the operative constraints and the non-operative or slack constraints. By focusing on the operative constraints, the firm might learn the best possible location for additions to facilities. Thus, the highest-return size and location of new sawmills and other productive resources can be identified. In addition, by focusing on possible alternative uses of slack resources, the firm may be able to cut costs. Finally, the rapid response to inquiry provided by their programming formulation led to quick and defensible suggestions as to the company's best response to changes in market prices for timber, logs, green veneer, chips, pulp, and finished goods—responses that are best considering all other related materials and product prices.

With all the advantages of programming models, the fact that programming applications to overall firm input-output processes are rare may seem surprising. Perhaps the largest practical limitation contributing to this situation is the immense data requirements of such projects (consider data for 25,000 variables). Secondly, many firms, perhaps most, may not find their allocational problem as well structured as Boise, particularly multi-industry firms. For them the errors and costs involved in formulating such models are probably seen to exceed the value. Rapidly changing product lines and market structures greatly complicate the picture for many new-product-oriented firms. For others, the assumption of fixed input-output coefficients (c_i, d_i in our example) has been found to be unreasonable, as has the assumption of fixed resource constraints.

Even in circumstances where programming models reasonably fit the circumstances, it is important to note that primary prediction of performance and operational variables is a function not performed by these models. The inputs to programming models include market share or other forecasted data used to establish output constraints, and predicted market and input prices in order to produce a priori allocations of resources to products. By contrast, prediction requires the construction of analytical bridges from market and industry environments to firm operating decisions, resource flows, and performance measures. At the present time, the tools of econometrics have been the unique source of such predictive analytical bridges. In the next chapter, our attention turns to a consideration of econometric models applied to firms.

DISCUSSION QUESTIONS

1. Which two of the approaches surveyed do you think are the most similar? Which approach is the most uniquely different from all the others? Why?
2. Describe a corporate management problem for which behavioral analysis would provide potentially valuable insights.

3. What do you think is the major advantage of industrial dynamics in analyzing particular company problems? What is the major disadvantage?

4. Distinguish between a corporate simulation model and a behavioral model of the firm's cash-flow allocation process. What are the biggest similarities in the two approaches?

5. "The biggest limitation in applying programming models to resource allocation in the modern corporation is that it is impossible to quantitatively approximate the true objective function of the firm." Comment.

Chapter 13

ECONOMETRIC ANALYSIS OF CORPORATE ECONOMIC ACTIVITY

This chapter is concerned with exploring the extent to which the tools of econometrics can contribute to the analysis of corporate economic activity. Since many interesting questions regarding the economic dimension of modern corporations hinge upon the nature of relationships among variables within the firm, and upon relationships of such internal variables with external variables, the use of econometric models in this regard seems a natural extention of their application to the analysis of total economic systems. Perhaps so, yet applications to individual corporations have occurred only rather recently and in relatively small numbers. In considering the nature of such actual and potential applications, it is useful to begin by considering the special types of endogenous and exogenous variables that are bound to be involved in such model developments.

VARIABLES AND MODEL STRUCTURES

Econometric models of economic processes in the firm are concerned with measuring and analyzing relationships among variables within and around the firm using the statistical and mathematical tools of econometrics. In published econometric models and studies of the firm, three general classes of endogenous and exogenous variables have been of interest, as follows:

1. *Environmental variables* influencing the firm's decisions from outside the firm, generally exogenous in nature
2. *Control variables* that are within the control of the firm's management, and are either endogenous or exogenous
3. *Performance variables* that measure the firm's economic and financial performance, and which are usually endogenous

We now consider these classifications in more detail.

Environmental Variables

Generally speaking, the firm is embedded in an industry environment. This industry environment, in turn, is influenced by overall general business conditions. General business conditions exert influences upon particular industries in several ways. Total volume of demand, product prices, labor costs, material costs, money rates, and general expectations are among the industry variables affected by the general business environment. Thus, through its impact on the industry, variables such as the GNP affect economic relationships within individual firms. Variables such as total industry output, purchasing power of the industry's customer group, and average industry prices are specific examples of measures that bind the firm to its industrial and competitive environment through the influence they exert on the economic variables in the firm. In oligopolistic market structures in particular, such influences operating upon the firm are likely to work back upon the industry in a feedback loop similar to that discussed in Chapter 12 under industrial dynamics.

Control Variables

The firm has a number of influential economic variables over which its management exerts some control. Among these we may list: (1) the firm's price structure and production level; (2) the size and character of its sales and advertising programs; (3) the size and direction of its product research and development programs; (4) the rate and direction of its capital investment programs; (5) outlays upon and management of its industrial engineering program; (6) the size and nature of its management and organizational structure; (7) the extent of its equity and external debt financing and the financial leverage represented thereby; (8) the size of its cash balances and liquid asset position; (9) the size of its management and employee development programs; and (10) the overall market and product areas in which the firm competes, including its new product and acquisition policies. These variables influence the economic performance of the firm. Moreover, at least some of these variables jointly influence each other, in working their effects upon the performance variables of the firm. Since management's selection of values for these control variables is likely to be vital to the progress of the firm, efforts aimed at understanding relationships between environmental, control, and performance measures through econometric models are potentially of high value.

Performance Variables

Finally, the firm is typically responsive to a number of different parties in its performance. Stockholders are likely to be concerned with: (1)

the firm's level of earnings; (2) growth in earnings; (3) projected earnings; (4) growth in sales; and (5) overall market outlook and management reputation to the extent these measures influence the market capitalization rate. Lendors of the firm's long- and short-term debt are likely to be directly concerned with (6) cash flow, (7) debt-to-equity ratio, and (8) overall liquidity position as indicated by current ratios, quick ratios, and times-interest earned, as well as less directly concerned about (1) through (4). The firm's top managers are likely to be evaluated on the basis of (1), (2), (4), and (5) as well as upon the smoothness of the path these variables take over time. Bonus and incentive systems are typically biased towards steady patterns of growth in sales and profits, as opposed to erratic patterns. The interests of managers and stockholders are in this respect largely similar. However, the firm's top management inherits the responsibility of arbitrating between the demands of several groups, such as labor unions, whose demands tend to be inversely related to (1) through (3); civic groups, whose requests are similarly inversely related; and social welfare projects, which also generally substitute for profits. While high and growing earnings and sales are directly in the interests of top management, they must successfully arbitrate between various conflicting demands in order to maintain an orderly climate for the firm's main economic task of production. To achieve this, management may well be prepared to accept levels of profits and growth in profits that are less than a strict short-term stockholder's viewpoint would council. Therefore, the weights we should attach to various of the performance variables outlined in arriving at an overall measure of the firm's progress is likely to be a very complex problem. Fortunately, such a single figure of merit is of little specific use in management decision making.

Model Structure

The structure of published econometric models of the firm has tended to follow a general framework. If we define $E_1, E_2, \ldots E_n$ as n environmental variables, $C_1, C_2 \ldots C_m$ as m control variables, and $P_1, P_2 \ldots P_y$ as y performance variables, that structure is given as follows:

$$P_1 = f_1(P_2, P_3 \ldots P_y, C_1, C_2 \ldots C_m, E_1, E_2 \ldots E_n) + \mu_1$$

$$\cdot$$
$$\cdot$$
$$\cdot$$

$$P_y = f_y(P_1, P_2 \ldots P_{y-1}, C_1, C_2 \ldots C_m, E_1, E_2 \ldots E_n) + \mu_y$$
$$C_1 = f_{y+1}(P_1, P_2 \ldots P_y, C_2, C_3 \ldots C_m, E_1, E_2 \ldots E_n) + \mu_{y+1}$$

$$\cdot$$
$$\cdot$$
$$\cdot$$

$$C_m = f_{y+m}(P_1, P_2 \ldots P_y, C_1, C_2 \ldots C_{m-1}, E_1, E_2 \ldots E_n) + \mu_{y+m}$$

where f_i is a general functional notation, μ_i is an error term as discussed in Chapter 2, where some variables do not appear in each equation, i.e., the coefficients of a subset of variables in each equation are zero, and where specific equations are omitted for specific models. In this structure, the general objective is assumed to be prediction of the P variables; therefore they appear as the endogenous variables. However, if we are interested in studying the behavior of the control variables, some of the C_i may be cast as endogenous, resulting in a combination of P_i and C_i variables appearing on the left-hand side of the equations. The general structure indicates that the performance variables are interrelated such that P_1 is in effect a product of the value of P_2, P_3 . . . P_y, which means the P variables are jointly determined as part of a simultaneous system. In the construction of specific models, the C variables may also be jointly determined and significantly interrelated with the P variables. The general structure enables the measurement of these effects when some of the C_i are designated as endogenous. Recognizing the potential simultaneous nature of performance and control variables in the firm is an essential feature of econometric models of the firm. In effect, these models presume that the entire set of endogenous variables may be uniquely evaluated by reference to the previously determined set of exogenous variables. Estimating the coefficients in a simultaneous system can be accomplished by one of the simultaneous estimation techniques discussed in Chapter 4.

Given favorable empirical data, these techniques will yield rational estimates of the *existing* relationships among variables. The tools of econometrics will not tell us the optimal values for our control variables, although data may be provided by application of these tools which bear upon that question. The specific examples of this chapter suggest that the choice between the many different kinds of econometric models possible at the level of the firm and the particular specification of these models largely depends upon the objectives of the model builder. For example, if we are concerned with jointly selecting the best levels of marketing, research and development, and capital programs, these variables would be structured as endogenous in the model. The various coefficients attached to their explanatory variables might yield data pertinent to the selection of optimal levels of these variables.

To better explore the specific results obtainable from econometric models of firms as well as survey differing examples of econometric models, we have selected four specific studies for discussion. While these do not exhaust all the relevant work in the area, the number of projects aimed at measuring relationships at the level of the firm with the objective of explaining performance are surprisingly small as yet, which greatly simplified the choice.

A SPECIFIC STUDY OF FOUR INTERRELATED DECISIONS

A study by Mueller focused upon four decisions in the firm: capital investments, research and development, advertising, and dividend payments.[1] A basic assumption of this study is that the firm's decision concerning levels of any one of these variables is made while considering the other three, i.e., that these four strategic-type expenditures are important substitutes in the firm. A second assumption was given by Mueller as follows:

> In what follows we assume the firm acts implicitly so as to maximize the present net worth of its stockholders. It may use its funds to pay out dividends, or employ them in some combination of the three competitive strategies included in the model. The trade-off between dividend payments and the strategy variables will depend upon: (1) the time-preference schedule of the firm's stockholders; (2) the extent to which the market reflects increases in expenditure on the strategies in increases in the value of equity shares; and (3) the expected returns from the three strategies.[2]

The variables employed in Mueller's analysis are given as follows, using our classification:[3]

Environmental

IRD = Ratio of industry R&D to industry sales (X)
IAS = Ratio of industry assets to industry sales (X)
IA = Ratio of industry advertising to industry sales (X)

Control

RD = Firm R&D outlays (Y)
I = Gross capital investment (Y)
A = Advertising (Y)
D = Cash dividend payments (Y)
DP = Depreciation plus depletion (X)
TRD = Total R&D undertaken during a previous one-year period (X)

Performance

S = Sales (X)
P = Profits (X)
G = Ten-year change in sales (X)
ds = One-year change in sales (X)

---

[1] Dennis C. Mueller, "The Firm Decision Process: An Econometric Investigation," Quarterly Journal of Economics (Vol. 81, February 1967) pp. 58–87.

[2] Ibid., p. 61.

[3] All variables not already ratios were divided by sales to produce ratios of these variables to sales. This was done to reduce the suspected heteroscedasticity associated with the cross-sectional sample used. For a discussion of heteroscedasticity and the use of ratios, see Chapter 3.

where X = predetermined or exogenous variable
     Y = endogenous variable

Since Mueller's objective was the analysis of the decisions made as to four key control variables, he formulated his model with these variables, RD, I, A, and D, on the left-hand side, as functions of other control. performance, and environmental variables. So, rather than studying the influence of control variables on performance, his analysis results in the evaluation of the effect of performance variables upon control variables. With this objective, Mueller assumed all performance variables including sales and profits to be exogenous. In addition, rather than study the resulting patterns for individual firms using time series data for each firm, he employed a cross-sectional sample involving observations from 67 firms for each of the four years 1957 to 1960. With this type of sample, the conclusions of the study can be interpreted as represented general patterns common across different kinds of firms.

In specifying the particular variables to be included in each equation in his model, Mueller selected the environmental and performance variables to be included in each equation, as well as DP and TRD on an a priori basis. The four endogenous variables I, RD, A, D were admitted as independent variables in other equations on a statistical basis, primarily on the basis of t-tests. This resulted in a model with the following structure:

$$I = f_1(RD,A,TRD,IAS,dS,P_{t-1},DP_{t-1})$$
$$RD = f_2(I,A,D,IRD,G,P_{t-1},DP_{t-1},S)$$
$$A = f_3(I,D,G,IA,S)$$
$$D = f_4(RD,P,D_{t-1})$$

Estimates of the coefficients for the terms in these four equations were computed for each of the four years in the sample, using two-stage, least-squares techniques. A study of these coefficients and their t-values produced a number of implications about general economic patterns among sample firms. Without developing the reasoning (which occupies the bulk of Mueller's paper), some of the more interesting conclusions are:

1. Based on analysis of the measured effect of lagged depreciation (DP_{t-1}) upon investment (I):

The extent to which a firm chooses to use the available flow-of-funds from depreciation to restore the previous period's capital stock depends upon the comparative advantage this alternative has over others at the firm's disposal. The results for the I and RD equations viewed together stress the flexibility the firm has in allocating the funds at its disposal among their many potential uses.[4]

---

[4] Mueller, "The Firm Decision Process," p. 69.

2. In terms of its influence on the model, sales change (dS) acts primarily as a surrogate for profit expectations with respect to new capital investment.

3. R&D can be highly influential in inducing future capital investment, apparently by producing technological obsolescence and creating a need for capital investment related to new products.

4. Dividends apparently have little effect on capital investment.

5. Evidence is found that "a shifting of resources from investment to R&D occurs in years when the returns on the former activity are low."[5]

6. The industry index of R&D intensity was the most important variable in the R&D equation, and the analogous variable in the advertising equation was similarly important, both indicating these environmental variables are quite significant influences upon both types of expenditures.

7. Neither profits nor depreciation importantly influenced advertising outlays. Mueller interpreted this as suggesting "that firms regard advertising more as a necessary business expense than as an investment."[6]

8. Comparing the four equations, advertising expenditures proved the most difficult to explain, judging by the multiple correlation coefficients for this equation, which were uniformly lower for all sample years than for other equations.

Mueller then considered the effect of a cut in the personal income tax rate upon the variables in his estimated model. He observed that all four budget outlays, I, RD, A, D, would initially be increased, with dividends receiving proportionately the largest increase and R&D the smallest. However, the role of lagged profits in the model implies that later adjustments by the firm would result in substantial increases in R&D and capital investment, an actual reduction in advertising investment, and another secondary rise in dividends. Further analysis of the model along these lines leads to the conclusion that an increase in R&D by a firm's competitors results in an increase in its own R&D and a reduction in its advertising. Likewise, when industry advertising rises, the firm increases its advertising and reduces its R&D. Of these results, Mueller comments, "They indicate that while long-run competitive pressures result in a high allocation of funds to R&D and advertising, the short-run response of a firm to an intensification of a specific form of competition—say advertising—is a withdrawal of funds from the competing-strategy—R&D."

The results of Mueller's study are only implications based on statistical

---

[5] Ibid., p. 71.

[6] Ibid., p. 74.

findings. They cannot be laid down as laws, principles, or even proven hypotheses. But they do yield illustrative evidence bearing upon some rather subtle and seemingly unapproachable issues, and they provide an illustration of a potential use of econometric models applied to cross-sectional data in search of general conclusions. We now turn to a second example of the application of econometric models to time-series data in the firm.

A MODEL TO ANALYZE AND PREDICT
FINANCIAL PERFORMANCE

A study undertaken by the author was concerned with exploring (among other things) the extent to which econometric models of the firm may be useful in forecasting sales and other elements of performance in the firm's income statement.[7] The model developed to pursue this objective was structured with 11 equations designed to simultaneously explain each major line in a typical corporate income statement, as follows:

Sales (*S*)		(equation 1)
Less:	Production Costs (*PC*)	(equation 2)
	Marketing Expense (*MK*)	(equation 3)
	Research and Development (*RD*)	(equation 4)
	General and Administrative Expense (*GAE*)	(equation 6)
	Depreciation Expense (*DPP*)	(equation 7)
	Fixed Financial Charges (*FFC*)	(equation 8)
Equals:	Before-Tax Profits	
Less:	Taxes	
Equals:	Profits (*PRFT*)	(equation 9)

Other related items:

Capital Investment (*CP*)	(equation 5)
New Long-Term Debt (Δ*DBT*)	(equation 10)
Inventory Investment (*INVS*)	(equation 11)

The simultaneous aspect of the model structure was constructed around the theoretical premise that flows of discretionary or uncommitted cash play an important role in corporate financial performance by motivating expenditures on sales-generating and cost-reducing programs, which result in sales and increased flows of discretionary cash, thus motivating greater flows of discretionary cash, and so forth. This concept

---

[7] J. W. Elliott, "Forecasting and Analysis of Corporate Financial Performance with an Econometric Model of the Firm," *Journal of Financial and Quantitative Analysis* (Vol. 7, March 1972), pp. 1499–1526.

FIGURE 13–1

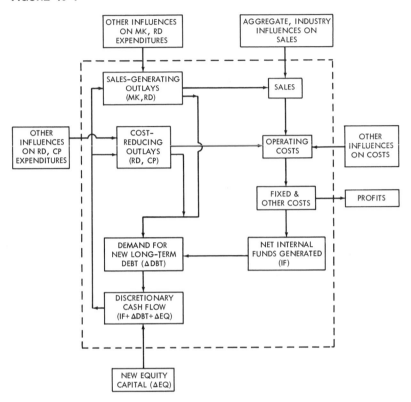

is illustrated in Figure 13–1. The portion within the dotted box represents the major elements envisioned in the simultaneous process, which are as follows:

1. Sales-generating outlays such as marketing respond positively to movements in discretionary cash flow.
2. Sales are substantially affected by sales-generating outlays.
3. Net internal funds and discretionary cash flow generated are an immediate product of sales.
4. These discretionary cash flows lead to further sales-generating expenditures.
5. A similar simultaneous linkage operates through the impact of cost-reducing outlays upon operating costs and upon net internal funds generated, and so forth.

The major implication of this simultaneity is that we must jointly determine all income statement items in order to reasonably determine each. As the figure also illustrates, this set of endogenous forces is assumed to be influenced by exogenous forces (outside dotted lines) influencing sales, sales-generating and cost-reducing outlays, and production costs.

Classification of the specific variables employed in the model is as follows:

Environmental Variables

PRA = industry prices relative to general prices (X)
IPA = industry output relative to aggregate output (X)
MS = money supply (X)
G = government expenditures (X)
i_e = yield on bonds (X)
t = index of time (X)

Control variables

$STKMK$ = stock of marketing assets (Y), measured by current and past marketing spending
$STKRD$ = stock of R&D assets (Y), measured by current and past R&D spending
GAE = general, administrative expense (Y)
$STKCP$ = stock of capital assets (Y)
PR = price of firm's industry output (X)
MK = marketing expenditure (Y)
RD = research and development expense (Y)
CP = capital expenditures (Y)
DPP = depreciation expense (Y)
FFC = fixed financial charges (Y)
DBT = long-term debt (Y)
DFD = demand for debt (Y), measured by the difference between total investmentlike expenditures $(MK + RD + CP)$ and internal funds
DE = debt-equity ratio (Y)
INV = inventory investment (Y)
ΔEQ = new equity capital (X)
DVD = dividend payments (X)

Performance Variables

S = sales (Y)
CU = unit production costs (Y)
PC = production costs (Y)
CF = discretionary cash flow (Y), defined as internal cash flow plus new debt capital and new equity capital
BTP = profits before taxes (Y)
$PRFT$ = after-tax profits (Y)
where X = exogenous variables
Y = endogenous variables

The equations of the model outlined above were structured approximately as follows:[8]

$$S = f(PRA,IPA,STKMK,STKRD,MS,G) \tag{1}$$

In (1), money supply (MS) and government expenditures (G) are measures of general economic activity, PRA and IPA are measures of price and demand shifts among industries, while $STKMK$ and $STKRD$ measure the influence on sales of the firm's marketing and product development efforts.

$$CU = f(GAE,STKCP,STKRD,S) \tag{2}$$
$$PC = (CU)(S) \tag{2a}$$

In (2) note that unit production costs are the subject of the structural equation, while total production costs are obtained by the identity (2a). This simplified the treatment of inventories, by assuming unit costs of sales are equal to unit costs of production.

General and administrative expenses are considered to be partially a substitute for production costs, mainly due to the staff expense portion of GAE. The same is true for additions to capital and technological stocks ($STKCP$, $STKRD$) which presumably lower production costs *ceteris paribus*. The inclusion of sales in (2) measures whether unit costs increased or decreased with sales.

$$MK = f(STKMK_{-1},CF,CU/PR) \tag{3}$$

Inclusion of the lagged stock measure in the marketing equation responds to the view of marketing expenditures as investmentlike in character, in which past stocks of assets play an important role. Specifically, the stock of assets term in (3), (4), and (5) responds to a flexible accelerator hypothesis such as discussed in Chapter 6. CU/PR measures profitability of new sales, while cash flow (CF) measures uncommitted funds and represents a key part of the earlier discussed simultaneous linkage.

$$RD = f(STKRD_{-1},CF,PRFT_{-1}) \tag{4}$$

Like marketing, R&D is seen as investment-like and thus responsive to past stocks ($STKRD_{-1}$). Also, R&D is assumed sensitive to the simultaneous variable cash flow and to profits, based on results of earlier specific empirical studies in this area.

$$CP = f(i_e,CF,MS,STKCP_{-1}) \tag{5}$$

In (5) capital investment is assumed to respond to past capital stocks; to current money market conditions and expectations, approximated by

---

[8] See the author's paper for elaboration on these definitions.

interest rates and the money supply; and to the firm's discretionary cash flow similar to marketing and R&D investments.

$$GAE = f(t, PRFT_{-1}) \tag{6}$$

In (6) general and administrative expense is taken to be affected by profits, which are seen to an extent to be substitutes for GAE, and by a range of other undescribed influences approximated by an index of time.

$$DPP = f(STKCP, t) \tag{7}$$

Depreciation expense is assumed to be determined by the size of the capital stock and by an array of miscellaneous factors summarized by t.

$$FFC = f(i_e, DBT) \tag{8}$$

Fixed financial charges, mainly interest payments, are represented as a function of interest rates and the level of long-term debt.

$$PRFT = f(BTP) \tag{9}$$

Equation (9) translates between before-tax and after-tax profits. As the income statement illustrates, before-tax profits were derived from a number of equations. Expression (9) uses this derived value to compute $PRFT$.

$$DBT = f(DFD, DE_{-1}, i_e, MS) \tag{10}$$

In this expression, the level of new debt is taken as a function of the firm's demand for debt, measured by the difference between investment-like expenditures and internal funds available, a function of market costs and availability of funds, measured by interest rates (i_e) and money supply (MS), and a function of the firm's debt-equity position, which is assumed to measure the firm's status as a borrower.

$$INV = f(S, t) \tag{11}$$

In the final equation, inventory investment is explained as a function of sales (implying a systematic inventory-sales ratio) and of time to reflect unspecified influences on inventory investment over time.

This model was tested statistically on the data of nine large corporations over the period 1948 to 1968. On the basis of goodness-of-fit statistics, the indications were that the model fit the data of the firms reasonably well, particularly with respect to the simultaneous linkages outlined earlier. This constituted statistical support for the general ideas reflected in the model, as well as support for the specific relationships of equations (1) through (11). As a test of predictability, the ability of the model to forecast the income statement beyond the data used to establish the equations was undertaken, assuming values of the exogenous variables (X) known for the forecast period.

Forecasts were prohibited in two of the nine cases due to major mergers during the forecast period that made the data used to establish the coefficients uncompatible with the prediction data. For the remaining seven firms, 15 predictions were obtained for various combinations of 1968, 1969, and 1970.[9] Since 1970 was a recessionary year, forecasts of individual corporate income statements for this year were particularly challenging.

In having been estimated by two-stage, least-squares, the model actually yielded two separate forecasts of the income statement variables of equations (1) through (11). The first, called P_1, is obtained from the first-stage equations. It will be recalled from Chapter 4 that these equations are regressions containing all endogenous variables on the left-hand side and exogenous model variables on the right-hand side. The second forecast P_2 is obtained from the second-stage structural equations by solving the structure algebraically for the endogenous variables as functions of the exogenous variables using the final structural coefficients. The basic difference between P_1 and P_2 is that the former measures the net effect of all the model's exogenous variables upon each endogenous variable directly while P_2 derives this net effect by working through the structural restrictions and measured coefficients of equations (1) through (11).

In order to shed some light on the question, "How good is a good forecast?," two basic forecasts were computed for comparison with the results of the model. These two baseline forecasting schemes were defined as follows:

$$NI: \quad Y_t = Y_{t-1}$$
$$NII: \quad \Delta Y_t = \Delta Y_{t-1}$$

In *NI*, this year's value is simply assumed equal to last year's value, while in *NII* the forecast *change* year-to-year is assumed equal to the previous period change. As a minimum, the model should compare well with *NI* and *NII* if it is to be considered as having forecasting potential.

Table 13–1 shows the comparative results of sales and profits forecasts for all four forecasting schemes now mentioned.[10] Entries in the table show the number of times the model forecast listed down the side of the table was closer to the actual value than the model forecast listed across the top. For example, P_2 was closer to the actual value than P_1 in 10 of 15 cases, and also closer than both *NI* and *NII* in 10 of 15

---

[9] Various individual-year forecasts were also missing due to unavailable exogenous variables.

[10] Results were obtained for the entire income statement. The two shown are representative.

cases. This comparison suggests that the model made a marked improvement over both *NI* and *NII* in the prediction of sales, and that the structural sales prediction was more effective in two thirds of the cases than the first-stage prediction.

TABLE 13–1
Predictive Comparisons

Sales (15 predictions)

	P_2	P_1	*NI*	*NII*
P_2	✕	10	10	10
P_1	5	✕	11	13
NI	5	4	✕	8
NII	5	2	7	✕

Profits (13 predictions)

	P_1	*NI*	*NII*	P_2
P_1	✕	8	9	7
NI	5	✕	8	8
NII	4	5	✕	8
P_2	5	5	5	✕

Results of one firm omitted due to explosive nature.

TABLE 13–2
Inequality Coefficients

Sales		Profits	
P_1	0.14	P_1	0.97
P_2	0.32	*NI*	1.00
NI	1.00	*NII*	.2.76
NII	1.44	P_2	7.99

Note: P_1 = first-stage forecast
P_2 = second-stage forecast
NI = "this year same as last"
NII = "change same as last year's change"

In forecasting profits, a contrasting result occurred. Here the P_2 forecast was inferior to the first-stage results in eight of thirteen instances, and inferior to *NI* and *NII* in an equal number of cases. However, P_1 provided a closer prediction than *NI* or *NII* in eight and nine of thirteen cases, respectively, indicating its comparative merit over simple autoregressive models.

Table 13–2 provides an index of forecasting merit of the four models in the form of Theil's inequality coefficient.[11] It will be recalled from Chapter 6 that the inequality coefficient has a value of zero in the case of

---

[11] For a discussion of the inequality coefficient, see Chapter 6.

the perfect forecast and of 1.00 for the "no change" forecast (*NI*). With these two bench marks, Table 13–2 shows that the model makes a substantial quantitative improvement over *NI* and *NII* in predicting sales. However, the order of importance of P_1 and P_2 is now reversed over that of Table 13–1, due mainly to a few instances where the P_2 forecast was extremely poor, thus weighing heavily upon the computed inequality coefficient.

For profits, Table 13–2 shows that the improvement of P_1 over *NI* is only slight in quantitative terms, even though P_1 is superior to *NI* in eight of thirteen cases. Also, the inferiority of P_2 to the other methods is quite substantial, as the 7.99 value plainly shows.

Overall, the forecasting results obtained in the study provide positive if not overwhelming evidence suggesting simultaneous-equation models structured along the lines of equations (1) through (11) can be useful predictive mechanisms for major income statement variables.

Besides income statement predictions, the estimated coefficients in the model enable inferences to be made relative to the impact of fluctuations in individual exogenous (*X*) variables upon the set of endogenous variables (*Y*). By establishing a baseline solution for the *Y* variables, the differential impact of a given departure of an *X* from its baseline enables its individual effect to be computed. For example, if high-employment government expenditures are increased, the impact on sales and profits of sample firms was found to be generally inconsequential. By contrast, fluctuations in the nation's money supply were seen to generally exert a complicated but eventually powerful impact on corporate sales and other performance variables. Such simulation analysis represents an additional use of econometric models beyond that of confirming a priori hypotheses or predicting income statement variables. The interested reader is invited to read the author's earlier cited paper for more details.

A THREE-SECTOR CORPORATE MODEL

A study by Saltzman provides a third illustration of the construction of an econometric model of a specific firm.[12] Saltzman's model involved 10 structural equations and several identities. The objective of the study was not to explore any particular hypothesis, as with Mueller, or to embrace any particular theoretical construct as with the author's cash-flow orientation, but rather to "develop a relatively comprehensive simultaneous-equations model of a firm."[13]

The variables used in the study, classified as before into environmental, control, and performance categories, are given as follows:

[12] S. Saltzman, "An Econometric Model of a Firm," *Review of Economics and Statistics* (August 1967, Vol. 49) pp. 332–42.

[13] Ibid., p. 332.

Environmental Variables

NRM = total potential market (X)
PDI = personal disposable income (X)
INR = current interest rates (X)
$SV1, SV2, SV3$ = seasonal shift variables (X)
MPI = machinery and allied products index (X)
APM = average price of materials (X)
AWR = average wage rate (X)
APW = average industry price for the product (X)
SVP = shift variables accounting for periods of zero expenditures (X)
UCF = fixed expense (X)

Control Variables

SE = selling expense (Y)
PE = product engineering expense (Y)
AP = average price (Y)
ID = dollar value of inventories (Y)
CE = capital expenditures (Y)
ME = manufacturing engineering expense (Y)
AE = administrative expense (Y)
MEF = miscellaneous expense term (Y)

Performance Variables

SD = dollar sales (Y)
SU = unit sales (Y)
AC = average costs (Y)
CS = standard costs of sales (Y)
OD = dollar value of output (Y)
OP = operating profit (Y)
PTS = firm's share of market (Y)
MC = manufacturing costs (Y)
where X = exogenous variables
Y = endogenous variables

The model is conceptually broken into three sectors: (1) sales, prices, inventory, and output; (2) investment and expenses; and (3) cost and profit relationships.

The first equation in the first sector gives total sales as a product of environmental and control variables:

$$SD_t = a_0 + a_1 SD_{t-1} + a_2(SE_t/AWR_t) + a_3(PE_t/AWR_t)_v + a_4 AP_t$$
$$- a_5 INR_t + a_6 NRM_t + a_7 SV1_t + a_8 SV2_t + a_9 SV3_t$$
$$+ a_{10}(PDI_t/APW_t) + \mu_{1,t}$$

where the subscript v refers to the average value over several periods. In this expression, selling expense, product engineering expense, and average prices are control variables assumed to exert influence upon sales. In addition, personal disposable income, interest rates and market potential are assumed to be major external influences upon sales. $SV1$, $SV2$, and $SV3$ are dummy variables that measure the seasonal effect present in the data.

The hypotheses contained in this and the following equations were tested through use of data from one sample firm, a producer of home laundry equipment. Thirty-six successive quarters of data provided the data for the tests. The coefficients of each equation were estimated both by two-stage least-squares and ordinary least-squares methods. Only minor differences were found between the two methods, which resulted in the author reporting only the ordinary least-squares results in his paper.

For the sales equation, these results indicated a significant role for all the control variables. Of the environmental variables, the influence of interest rates INR was not significantly different from zero on the basis of a t-test. The same was true of the first two seasonal shift variables, $SV1$ and $SV2$. The measured effect of income PDI on sales was negative contrary to expectations. The author thereby deleted this variable from his final equation. The final equation explained a significant 83 percent of the variation in dollar sales.

The second equation identified determinants of the average price set by the firm:

$$AP_t = b_0 + b_1 AP_{t-1} + b_2 AC_t + b_3(CS_t - ID_{t-1}) + \mu_{2,t}$$

This expression considers price a function of unit costs according to the hypothesis that keeping an acceptable markup over unit costs is an important consideration in price setting. Also, demand and supply factors and inventory position are assumed to affect price. These are represented by the expression $(CS - ID)$, which subtracts inventory investment from standard costs of sales, the latter used to represent demand. Thus, either increases in demand or decreases in inventory position are assumed to produce price increases. Finally, serial correlation in prices over time is measured by the lagged value of the dependent variable. The statistical tests indicated that both the unit costs and demand variables were significant in their effects on price, thereby upholding these hypotheses. The lagged AP value had an insignificant influence upon price, indicating the impact of lagged effects was weak. The overall equation produced an R^2 value of .765, indicating significant explanatory properties.

The dollar value of output was formulated as follows:

$$OD_t = c_0 + c_1 OD_{t-1} + c_2(CS_t - ID_t) + \mu_{3,t}$$

as a function of past output as well as the same demand-inventory proxy variable used in the AP expression. In this case, both explanatory variables were clearly significant statistically, and the equation accounted for 93.7 percent of the observed output variation, thus yielding an excellent fit to the data.

The standard cost of sales was given as follows:

$$CS_t = d_0 + d_1 SD_t + \mu_{4,t}$$

as a simple function of dollar sales. As one would expect due to the partial accounting dependence of CS upon SD, the d_1 coefficient was highly significant in the statistical test, as was the R^2 value of .954.

Selling expense, earlier seen as an important factor in determining sales, was given as:

$$SE_t = e_0 + e_1 SE_{t-1} + e_2 SD_t + e_3 OP_t + e_4(CS_t - ID_{t-1}) + \mu_{5,t}$$

As seen, the level of this expenditure was assumed to be influenced by the firm's sales (thus completing a circular interdependence between the two), by operating profits, and by the same demand-inventory proxy considered earlier. In the statistical tests, all the variables in the equation were statistically significant except the demand-inventory variable. We may infer from the e_2 result that the circular relationship between selling expense and sales is significant for the firm studied, thus producing evidence on the operation of a significant $SE - SD$ multiplier. The overall equation accounts for 89.7 percent of the variation in SE.

Capital expenditures in the firm are given by the following expression:

$$CE_t = f_0 + f_1 CE_{t-1} + f_2 SD_t + f_3 OP_t + f_4 SVC_t + \mu_{6,t}$$

which proposes these expenditures are a function of dollar sales, operating profits, and a shift variable SVC that accounts for periods where CE was equal to zero. This equation proposes that capital expenditures are basically influenced by the same variables that influence selling expense (since the demand-inventory variable was insignificant in that earlier equation). As with the previous equation, all four variables were significant. The level of explanation was 73.8 percent.

Expenditures on product engineering were given by the following:

$$PE_t = g_0 + g_1 PE_{t-1} + g_2 SD_t + g_3 PTS_t + g_4 SVP_t + g_5 OP_t + \mu_{7,t}$$

In addition to the sales and profits variables of the previous equations, the firm's market share is presumed to influence product engineering expenditures. In the statistical tests, the unexpected sign of the g_5 coefficient caused that variable to be deleted from the equation. The lagged PE and SD variables were significant, while the PTS and the SVP shift variables were not significantly different from zero. The overall equation explained 91.6% of the variation in PE.

Manufacturing engineering expense, directed towards improvements in productivity, are given as follows:

$$ME_t = h_0 + h_1 ME_{t-1} + h_2 SD_t + h_3 OP_t + \mu_{8,t}$$

which contains the same basic ingredients as the other expense equations. The statistical test showed all three variables statistically significant, thus bearing out the parallel results of the earlier expense equations. The resulting R^2 value was .850.

Administrative expenses are considered to be given as:

$$AE_t = i_0 + i_1 AE_{t-1} + i_2 SD_t + \mu_{9,t}$$

which proposes these expenses to be a product of the trend in past values and of the level of dollar sales. In this expression, the lagged AE value was highly significant but the SD coefficient was not clearly different from zero. The overall level of explanation, largely attributable to the lagged AE value, was .889.

The final expression for manufacturing costs was as follows:

$$MC_t = j_0 + j_1 MC_{t-1} + j_2 SD_t + j_3 APM_t + j_4 AWR_t - j_5(PE_t/AWR_t) \\ - j_6(CE_t/MPI_t)_v - j_7(AE_t/AWR_t)_v$$

which gives these costs as a function of materials, prices, and labor costs in addition to dollar sales. Product engineering, capital equipment, and administrative expense categories are hypothesized to be substitutes for manufacturing expense, and thereby inversely influence MC expense. Empirically, the measured direction of the relationships in the case of APM, (PE/AWR), and $(AE/AWR)_v$ were not in accord with the hypothesis; therefore these variables were omitted in the final form of this equation. Of the remaining variables, only dollar sales had a regression coefficient significantly different from zero. Nonetheless the level of explanation was 92.5 percent, largely due to SD.

The various expense categories explained by the previous equations are combined as follows:

$$TC_t = MC_t + SE_t + PE_t + ME_t + AE_t + MEF_t$$
$$\text{(total costs as the sum of its parts)}$$
$$AC_t = TC_t/SU_t \quad \text{(average costs as total costs divided by units)}$$
$$OP_t = SD_t - TC_t - UEF_t$$
$$\text{(operating profits as sales minus total costs minus other costs)}$$

Also:

$$SU_t = SD_t/AP_t \quad \text{(units sold as dollar sales divided by average price)}$$
$$ID_t = ID_{t-1} + OD_t - CS_t \quad \text{(dollars of inventory as equal to} \\ \text{previous value adjusted by additions and deletions)}$$

These identities provide the necessary additional variables to "close" the system, enabling solution of the 10 basic equations as parts in a simultaneous system—for example, total costs and average costs include selling expenses. In turn, average costs influence the price charged, which influences dollar sales. Finally dollar sales influence selling expense, which influences unit costs, the original point of departure.

A similar simultaneity is present with regard to the factors in and role of operating profits, as the reader can verify by tracing the relevant effects through the model.

The numerical coefficient estimates obtained for the sample firm provide indications of the magnitude of the interdependencies present in the model. While Saltzman does not report on the specific multiplier effects of these interdependencies, he provides data on some partial and long-run elasticities. Included among these are the following:

	Short-run[14]	*Long-run*[15]
$E_{SE,SD}$	.977[16]	2.13
$E_{CE,SD}$	1.26	3.32
$E_{PE,SD}$	.411	.517
$E_{ME,SD}$	1.58	2.92
$E_{AE,SD}$	.197	.213

which shows the elasticity of key controllable expense categories with regard to sales. As seen, only PE and AE appear to be clearly inelastic with respect to sales. All other categories demonstrate elastic or nearly elastic short-run responses and clearly elastic long-run values. Similar elasticities regarding profits revealed:

	Short-run	*Long-run*
$E_{SE,OP}$	$-.152$	$-.280$
$E_{CE,OP}$	$-.295$	$-.474$
$E_{ME,OP}$	$-.432$	$-.944$

The negative long-run and short-run values indicate an inverse relationship between changes in profits and changes in the three expense categories, which suggests these expenses are increased as a response to eroding profits over the long run, and vice versa for decreases.

---

[14] This is the value obtained by considering only the directly related equations without considering the interactions.

[15] This is the value that results when the multiplier effects and time-lagged effects have run their course.

[16] The numbers mean that the elasticity of selling expense, given a change in dollar sales, was .977, or that a 1 percent increase in dollar sales produced a 0.977 percent change in selling expense in the same quarter.

The Saltzman study could enable financial forecasts as well as a simulation of the overall operation of the model, as in the case of the previous model discussed. Saltzman does not report on the results of such forecasts or simulations. However, if available, we could expect these results to deepen our understanding of the dynamics of this model.

AN APPROACH TO PREDICTING SALES AND PROFITS

In the econometric models considered so far, an important concern of the investigator has been to evaluate the reasonableness of the structural hypotheses contained in the equations of the model. Such evaluation has led to inferences about the extent to which the structure of the model is a plausible abstraction of the underlying corporate system. In the second example, the predictive relevance of the model was also examined, along with structural hypotheses testing. Some analysts have argued that in cases where prediction is the only objective of the model, one need not be concerned with drawing inferences as to the reasonableness of structural hypotheses. Instead, a reduced-form system may be drawn up on an essentially ad hoc basis to be judged primarily on the basis of how well it predicts. One project employing this approach is under development at Data Resources, Inc. by G. Fromm and E. Hyman.[17]

At the time of their project, Data Resources had already developed an econometric model of the U.S. economy that produced considerable detail on expenditures by various sectors of the economy. This macroeconomic model was in regular use by the firm to produce overall economic forecasts and component forecasts of various economic sectors.[18] The basic idea of the company model project was to use the appropriate sector predictions from the macroeconomic model as key explanatory variables in the prediction of company sales and profits. Through this means, the company sales and profit predictions could be linked up with the macroeconomic predictions. This provides a way by which the impact of federal economic policy changes, monetary changes, and a variety of other exogenous influences on the economy can be translated quickly and consistently into their impact on the performance of individual firms.

At the time of their paper (cited earlier), Fromm and Hyman had developed forecasting equations for approximately 30 companies. Their general procedure in this development was to predict sales through a single-equation regression model and then derive profits principally through sales relationships. Dividends were also predicted by relating them to profits and past dividends.

---

[17] For details, see G. Fromm, and E. Hyman, "Econometric Models of Company Performance," paper presented at the 1971 meetings of the Econometric Society (December 1971).

[18] These data are supplied to subscribers of Data Resources, along with other types of analytical material.

To specify the variables in the key sales equation, the analysts began with an examination of the firm's principal lines of business. The next step was to find the most closely related macroeconomic series of the type predicted by the aggregate model. For example, the sales of a large retail chain was related to national consumption expenditures on non-durables except foods and beverages and durables except automobiles. The sales of primary materials-producing companies such as Dupont were related to variables such as industry sales or shipments of the same type of goods. In addition to national economic variables, other explanatory data particularly applicable to the specific firm involved was used. To see illustrative results of this process, we now consider some specific sales forecasting models developed in the Data Resources project.[19]

Sears

The approach taken to explain Sears' sales is to relate them to national consumption expenditures for nondurables clothing and shoes plus non-durables—other and durables except automobiles. The equation is:

$$S = -680.2 + 111.5(CDEA) + 29.6(CNCS + CNO)$$
$$(153.2) \quad (20.6) \qquad\quad (12.8)$$
$$R^2 = .998$$
$$DW = 1.59$$

where numbers in parentheses are standard errors, and:

$$\begin{aligned}
S &= \text{dollar sales} \\
CDEA &= CD - CDA \\
CD &= \text{personal consumption expenditures—durables} \\
CDA &= \text{personal consumption expenditures—new and net used autos} \\
CNCS &= \text{personal consumption expenditures—clothing and shoes} \\
CNO &= \text{personal consumption expenditures—other nondurables}
\end{aligned}$$

As seen, the fit of the equation is high along with some evidence of autocorrelation ($DW = 1.59$). Two types of predictive evidence were presented. The first is ex-post predictions that assume the true values of the exogenous variables. The second is ex-ante predictions for 1970 as of August, 1970, using predicted values for 1970 for the exogenous variables. These results are:

		Predictions	
	Actual	*Ex-Post*	*Ex-Ante—August 1970*
1968	8198		
1969	8863	8860	
1970	E 9226	9388	9571

---

[19] Other equations were not presented in the author's paper.

These predictive results, although meager in frequency do seem to offer encouragement for the macroeconomic-microeconomic structure of Fromm and Hyman. Since the company models are all designed explicitly for predicting short-term performance, the results on this criterion constitute the major test of the approach taken in the project.

DuPont

The explanation of DuPont's sales is as follows:

$$S = 725.8 + 709.2(JFRB28) + 37.47(CDA) + 8.04(\Delta INVEAF)$$
$$(42.9)\quad (93.2)\qquad\qquad (8.3)\qquad\qquad (3.3)$$

where

$$S = \text{dollar sales}$$
$$JFRB28 = \text{Federal Reserve Board Index—Chemicals and Products}$$
$$CDA = \text{personal consumption expenditures—new and net used autos}$$
$$\Delta INVEAF = \text{change in nonfarm business inventories}$$

As seen, this equation relies on the related component of the Federal Reserve Board Index of industrial production, on a consumption expenditure component, and on the change in business inventories. The latter variable is intended to measure the cyclical behavior of prices, since according to the authors, inventories are a kind of pressure gauge reflecting cyclical demand and price patterns in the economy. Ex-post and ex-ante forecasting results for the DuPont equation are as follows:

	Actual	Ex-Post	Predictions Ex-Ante—August, 1970
1968	3481		
1969	3632	3670	
1970	3618	3494	3556

Again, the results are encouraging to the approach taken by the authors. Unfortunately, in their report the authors present such forecasting data on only four of the thirty or so firms they reportedly have studied. Our ability to judge the worth of their approach for prediction models would be greatly enhanced by a more complete account of these findings.

In forecasting profits, no results are available from the Data Resources project. However, the authors stated that errors in forecasting profits were approximately twice those in forecasting sales. Even with these limitations in reported results, the project of Fromm and Hyman provides an interesting contrast to the econometric models reviewed earlier in this chapter.

CONCLUSION

In this and the preceding chapter, we have seen a number of different approaches to the analysis of economic activity in firms. Behavioral analysis has provided a way to evaluate repetitive decision processes in firms by making these processes visible and by quantifying applicable decision rules. Industrial dynamics has offered techniques for measuring and evaluating processes of cumulative instability in the interaction of flows of orders, materials, money, and other resources in firms, and has suggested ways to evaluate process modifications leading to greater stability in resource flows. Corporate simulation models have developed as tools in tops-down financial and long-range planning by translating basic predictive data and operating rules of thumb into income statement projections, thus enabling quick and consistent "what-if" analyses. Although rare, successful applications of programming models can provide optimal answers to important resource-allocation questions in a manner that takes into account all relevant prices, costs, and constraints on resource availability.

Econometric models of the firm can be used to study behavior of firms or as a laboratory in which quick answers to questions dealing with the financial performance implications of changes in the firm's environment can be evaluated. These models can also be relevant for predictions of financial performance. Econometric models have also been used to measure linkages between national economic fluctuations and fluctuations in individual firm sales, then have used these linkages to prepare company sales and profits forecasts.

One striking aspect of the various tools we have considered is the variety of problems to which they are addressed. If any property is shared by these tools, it is that of being tailored to the particular problem at issue. It is thus rather meaningless to compare the merits of the various problem-approaches considered in our discussion as if they were competitors for the favor of corporate users. They clearly are not. However, this is not to say that a misguided behavioralist will always refrain from seeing all corporate problems-situations as behavioral in nature, or that a programming specialist will not see all corporate problems as programming problems. Such misuses of reasonable analytical tools have and will continue to occur, and will probably lead to inappropriate conclusions by management as to the usefulness and reliability of the ravaged tool. Ultimately, the case for all the analytical tools of this and the previous chapter rests with their judicious use in circumstances where they are appropriate.

In the next chapter, our attention turns away from tools and towards a theoretical structure designed to provide a framework for dealing with overall resource allocation in corporations. This structure leads to prescriptive guidelines for the level of resource use and the allocation of available resources to alternative strategic uses.

DISCUSSION QUESTIONS

1. Under what circumstances does it seem reasonable to predict the values of a control-type variable such as the firm's marketing expenditure?
2. Distinguish between applications of firm-level econometric models that depend upon the structural coefficients of the model vs. those that can be based on the reduced-form.
3. Do you see any applications for firm-level econometric models besides prediction?
4. The illustrations have contained examples of firm-level models estimated with cross-sectional data as well as time-series data. For what purposes would one approach be superior to the other?
5. Contrast an econometric model of a firm with a simulation model of a firm. Where are the similarities and the differences?

Chapter	A FRAMEWORK FOR
14	RESOURCE ALLOCATION
	IN THE FIRM

In nearly all firms, responsibility for major financial commitment resides at the top of the managerial hierarchy. This indicates the high priority typically assigned by chief executives to determining the allocation of corporate resources. The general strength of this pattern, regardless of industry, firm structure, or market is sufficient to warrant the conclusion that the primary economic decision issues of top management are likely to be found in the allocation of the corporation's scarce financial resources. In this chapter, we shall be concerned with defining a general structure for analysis of these financial flows. In Chapter 15, this structure will lead to formulation of prescriptive guidelines pertinent to major financial commitment decisions in firms.

A FUNDS-FLOW IDENTITY

Our analysis begins with a consideration of accounting relationships in the firm. Consider the hypothetical income statement given in Figure 14–1. The components in this statement are denoted by the corresponding symbols next to them in the table. The logic of such conventional income statement definitions enables construction of an identity for changes in financial position that is of interest in our analysis. This identity accounts for the sources and uses of the firm's uncommitted or discretionary cash flow. It is given in symbolic form in (14–1) and numerically in (14–1a) for the income-statement data.

Origins   *Allocations*

$$S - P - AD - INT - TX - PFD = IF = MK + RD + CP + DIV + \Delta CA$$
$$\text{(14–1)}$$
$$1000 - 600 - 100 - 10 - 95 - 20 = 175 = 45 + 35 + 40 + 35 + 20 \qquad \text{(14–1a)}$$

where IF is the firm's internal discretionary cash flow and all other symbols are as defined in Figure 14–1 and Figure 14–2. For Identity

FIGURE 14–1

Income Statement—XYZ Company

Sales (S)		1000
Less: Production Costs (P)		600
Gross Margin......................		400
Less: General and Administrative Expense		
Administrative Expense (AD)	100	
Marketing Expense (MK)	45	
Reserach and Development (RD)	35	
Total		180
Net Margin........................		220
Less: Total Depreciation Expense (DP)		20
Less: Interest Payments (INT)		10
Profit before Taxes...................		190
Less: Taxes (TX)		95
Profit after Taxes....................		95
Less: Preferred Dividends (PFD)		20
Available for Common................		75
Less: Common Dividend (DIV)		35
Balance to Retained Earnings...........		40

(14–1) to strictly hold, three assumptions are necessary, which we now make:

1. all strategic investmentlike programs can be included in one of the three categories shown (MK, RD, CP)
2. the entire difference between flows of IF and the sum of the allocation to DIV, MK, RD and CP programs will appear as a change in current assets accounts (ΔCA). That is, we assume no change in any other noncapital long-term asset accounts, and ignore the possibility of extraordinary or other write-offs in the capital account.
3. no change occurs in the firm's short-term or long-term debt position, or in its total equity position.

The meaning of these assumptions can be seen by reference to Figure 14–2, which contains a balance sheet corresponding to the income statement in Figure 14–1. The first assumption defines the firm's strategic programs and projects. The second assumption excludes the possibility that residual discretionary cash flows (i.e., not allocated to DIV, MK, RD, or CP) are applied towards other nonplant fixed assets or to an increase in good will. In Figure 14–2 no other asset categories exist, so that the residual is forced into the current asset category. This simplification has been made merely for convenience. The third assumption considers debt and equity constant. In the case of the simplified balance sheet of Figure 14–2, the only remaining way for assets to increase as IF increases is through additions to net plant brought about by capital

FIGURE 14–2

Balance Sheet—XYZ Company

Assets	Year 0	Year 1
Total Current Assets (*CA*)	110	130
Net Plant, Start of Period	270	285
Plus: New Capital Assets (*CP*)	30	40
Total	300	325
Less: Depreciation Expense	15	20
Net Plant, End of Period	285	305
Total Assets	395	435

Liabilities		
Total Current Liabilities	60	60
Long-Term Debt	100	100
Equity	235	275
Total Liabilities	395	435

expenditures and by the addition of unspent *IF* to current asset accounts. Thus, our third assumption enables Identity (14–1b) as follows:

$$\Delta \text{ Assets } = \Delta \text{ Liabilities}$$
$$\Delta CA + CP - DP = \Delta RTD \qquad (14\text{–}1b)$$
$$(20) + (40) - (20) = (40)$$

where ΔRTD is the change in accumulated retained earnings. Thus, assumption (*c*) prohibits increases in assets resulting from debt increases or new equity additions. Later we shall relax this assumption and deal explicitly with long-term debt decisions. For now we only note that the effect of relaxing assumption (*c*) does not alter any of our major conclusions, but creates a complicated residual term on the right-hand side of (14–1).

Consider now the left-hand side of equation (14–1). Production costs, administrative costs, interest expense, and tax obligations are all subtracted from sales. Also, preferred dividends are subtracted. The remainder represents the portion of sales revenues that is free from required commitment during a short-run period. This remainder measures funds available internally to the firm on a more-or-less discretionary basis. If the firm's management decided, the entire volume of *IF* could be paid out as dividends. Alternatively, it could all be plowed back into the strategic marketing, product, and plant expansion programs of the firm. In reality, firms normally choose to divide *IF* between dividend use and internal allocation. Indeed, in Chapter 15, we shall discuss rational guidelines for this division process. For now we shall be content with recognizing this flow of *IF* to be deployed in substantial part at management's discretion.

The right-hand side of (14–1) shows the possible allocation of discretionary financial flows. The first three allocational categories—marketing, research and development, and capital investment—represent investment-like programs in which the firm has considerable short-term latitude in the level of its effort. They are discretionary in nature. The fourth category, dividends, is fundamentally a discretionary allocation by management to stockholders, although in some specific cases management policy makes it appear as more of a fixed commitment. Given our three assumptions, the fifth category, change in current assets (ΔCA) is a residual that closes the identity. In other words, funds not spent in the first four allocational categories automatically fall into current asset accounts. During time periods when more discretionary resources are flowing into the firm than are being returned to the external environment by marketing, research, and capital programs, current asset accounts will grow by the difference when assumptions (a) through (c) are met. The reversed is true in the case of total allocations to MK, RD, and CP in excess of discretionary flows, in which case current assets would fall by the difference.

Identity (14–1) should be interpreted as illustrative of a number of different specific similar identities that could be defined to express discretionary sources and allocation of funds for particular firms. For example, in some firms the choice of dividends as a discretionary commitment would better be shown as a fixed use of IF. Such choices depend on the dividend policies and principal objectives of particular firms. Accordingly, the most relevant specific definition of IF can be expected to vary from firm to firm. In some firms, profits or profits-plus-depreciation may be more influential in allocational decisions than the IF variable illustrated, which is kind of net cash flow. Such anticipated interfirm differences should be kept in mind when reviewing the illustrative framework of this chapter.

Finally, IF is not the sum total of funds available for strategic use by management. Funds may be acquired externally in capital markets, either in the form of new debt (ΔDBT) or new equity (ΔEQ), and these funds directly add to the total discretionary pool available. Our earlier assumption (c) ruled out such additions, but we shall later explicitly deal with the role of new debt and equity in our framework. For now, it suffices to recognize that the total pool of discretionary funds, which we call CF, is equal to the sum of internal and external inputs: $CF = IF + \Delta DBT + \Delta EQ$. Then, the effect of assumption (c) is to make $CF = IF$.

INTERDEPENDENCE OF DISCRETIONARY FLOWS

To some degree, virtually every financial commitment made by the firm is undertaken in anticipation of a return or flow of returns over time. Although considering some such input-output relationships in this framework is rather strained and of little value in analysis, for other expenditures the analysis of return versus outlay is of considerable value in the comparison of spending alternatives. For example, the cost to a firm of stock option plans can perhaps be related to an increment of increased executive productivity. The highly indirect nature of such a relationship, however, sharply limits its usefulness in making such decisions. However, when outlays on marketing, research and development, and capital equipment are considered in the same fashion, the result has significant meaning. Marketing programs are undertaken in most corporations with an explicit concern as to the resulting return, even though measuring that expected return is often highly imperfect. The same is true for capital investment programs, where the outlay-return process has been developed in great detail in the capital budgeting literature. Similarly, research and develpment outlays are often evaluated on the basis of whether they at least cover their costs, or "pay their own way."

These three discretionary program categories are of direct concern in our analysis for two reasons. First, as implied above, these outlays are made with the expectation of a return of funds, and they in fact produce discretionary fund flows. Second, the three investment categories of MK, RD, and CP are major recipients of discretionary funds. These two factors imply an interrelationship between the sources of discretionary funds and the uses of those funds. We now consider this interrelationship further.

Returning to (14–1), marketing investments (right-hand side) are obviously undertaken to produce sales (left-hand side). Research and development investments, a second allocation, are made to produce new products, improve existing products, and to generate cost savings in the production process. Product improvements lead to increases in sales and discretionary cash flow. Cost-reducing R&D reduces the required expenditure on the production process for a given sales volume, and has the same final effect on discretionary flows as product improvement. Capital investments affect discretionary flows in at least two ways. A portion of capital investment is made to expand capacity. These outlays generate discretionary flows when the additional capacity is utilized to expand production levels. A second portion of capital investment is undertaken to exploit technological advancements by replacing existing equipment and facilities with more productive. resources. The resulting production cost savings add to discretionary flows.

This discussion illustrates that important interrelationships exist ·between variables on both sides of the basic identity of (14–1) that cause choices made by a firm in allocating its present discretionary financial flows to exert an impact upon the size of its future discretionary financial flows.

SOME CRUCIAL RELATIONSHIPS

Marketing investments are undertaken for a variety of stated reasons by firms, all or most of which are aimed at generating present or future sales revenues. Recent empirical research into the sales effects of marketing has revealed and verified a number of specific properties relating to this relationship, of which two are of interest.[1]

1. A measurable saturation effect is associated with high levels of marketing spending. A study by Lester Telser of advertising spending in the cigarette industry is illustrative. Telser has produced evidence of overspending—i.e., spending too far into this saturation—on the part of one cigarette company for data over the years 1913 to 1960.[2]

2. Current marketing projects exert a continuing, although decaying, effect upon sales in future time periods. This means the total effects of current marketing programs involve an array of returns spaced over time. A study by Vidale and Wolfe has measured this continuing effect and has pointed to the likelihood of a constant sales-decay factor associated with advertising outlays for given firms.[3]

The first of these propositions regarding saturation implies that the marketing sales relationship can be approximated by a curve similar to that of Figure 14–3. In this figure, the point Dm represents the level of marketing expenditures at which diminishing marginal sales returns occur with increased marketing outlays. To the left of Dm, the figure implies a range of increasing sales returns to marketing spending. Such a range is consistent with the notion of a "noise level"—a minimum competitive level of marketing spending below which increased expenditures are increasingly efficient in generating revenue. The second proposition regarding the time distribution of marketing effects is indirectly reflected in Figure 14–3 by the positive intercept of the sales-marketing function, which implies that a portion of current sales is not affected by current marketing expenditures, but is a product of past marketing programs or is related to other nonmarketing variables.[4]

---

[1] For a survey of the literature on the sales effects of advertising through 1964, see Kristian Palda, "Sales Effects of Advertising: A Review of the Literature," *Journal of Advertising Research*, Vol. 4, No. 3, September 1964, pp. 14–16. We assume we may apply the propositions applicable to advertising to marketing in general.

[2] See Lester Telser, "Advertising and Cigarrettes," *Journal of Political Economy*, Vol. 70, October 1962, pp. 471–99. Again, we assume the advertising-sales propositions of this study generally apply to the broader marketing sales propositions.

[3] See M. Vidale and H. Wolfe, "An Operations-Research Study of Sales Response to Advertising," *Operations Research*, Vol. 5, No. 3, June 1957, pp. 370–81.

[4] These "other variables" would comprise the array of factors that position the marketing expenditure-discretionary income function, and would include competitive variables such as market share, as well as variables reflecting growth expectations of the firm and the industry.

FIGURE 14–3

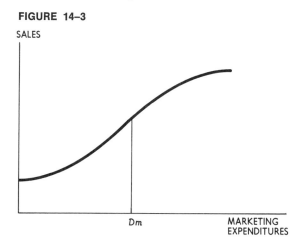

The sales effects of marketing produce a discretionary funds-flow effect of these expenditures. Expression (14–1) indicates that increases in sales generate increases in discretionary funds-flow if other variables on the left-hand side of that expression remain the same. This is a useful starting point. However, it is not reasonable to suppose that all factors do remain the same as increases in sales occur. For example, production costs reduce the discretionary funds-flow effect of sales produced by marketing outlays. The short-run limitations of fixed plant and equipment indicate that increased use of plant assets will be associated with less efficient use of labor resources once normal operating ranges are surpassed. The result is that production costs can be expected to rise at the margin disproportionately as output is increased above normal ranges. These rising marginal production costs, in turn, lower the discretionary cash flow increase associated with a given sales increase. Figure 14–4 depicts this relationship. The figure assumes sales changes and production changes correspond, so that inventories remain essentially constant. Point *A* in the figure represents an initial range of low production over which increases in output and sales bring forth decreases in marginal costs by increasing the efficiency with which labor and other variable inputs are utilized. Over this range, each dollar of sales produces a larger contribution of discretionary financial flows. Once point *A* has been passed, the figure illustrates a range over which marginal costs are approximately constant and increases in marketing spending produce proportional increases in discretionary financial flow. Beyond point *B*, the rise in marginal costs causes the discretionary financial flow to decline as a proportion of sales, and eventually to decline as an absolute amount.

The effect of capital spending programs is ultimately found in the level of production costs required to generate a given output level. Out-

FIGURE 14–4

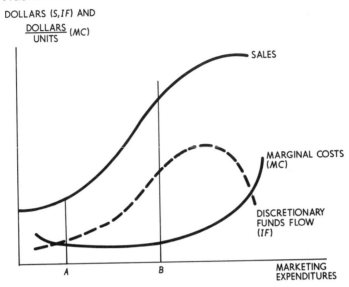

DOLLARS (S, IF) AND

$\dfrac{\text{DOLLARS}}{\text{UNITS}}$ (MC)

SALES

MARGINAL COSTS (MC)

DISCRETIONARY FUNDS FLOW (IF)

A   B

MARKETING EXPENDITURES

lays of a primarily capital-expanding nature should lower production costs in higher ranges of production by adding to plant capacity and thereby shifting the rising-marginal-cost range of output to higher levels of production. The effect on Figure 14–4 of such a change is shown in Figure 14–5 by the shift in *MC* and *IF* to *MC'* and *IF'*. On the other hand, outlays made primarily to replace existing capital goods with technologically advanced goods lower marginal costs and raise the discretionary income flow associated with all specific marketing outlays and

FIGURE 14–5

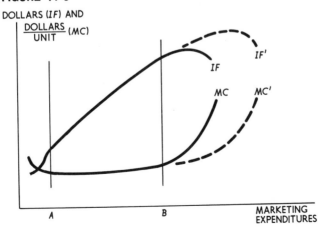

DOLLARS (IF) AND

$\dfrac{\text{DOLLARS}}{\text{UNIT}}$ (MC)

IF'

IF

MC   MC'

A   B

MARKETING EXPENDITURES

sales levels. Such effects are illustrated in Figure 14–6 by a downward shift in the *MC* schedule to *MC'* and an upward shift in *IF* to *IF'*. In addition, both effects result in a given level of marketing expenditures producing more discretionary cash flow. (The *IF* associated with a given

FIGURE 14–6

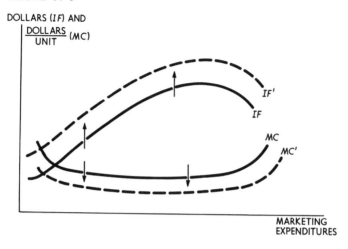

sales increase is greater.) Thus, in addition to the direct cash inflow, capital expenditures enable marketing programs to bring forth greater financial flows.

The effects of research and development programs (R&D) upon this graphical framework are similar to marketing allocations in some respects and similar to capital investment allocations in others. In the first case, R&D programs undertaken to develop new products or improve existing products increase the attractiveness of the firm's array of products and services. Consequently, the effectiveness of the firm's marketing expenditures in producing sales is increased, meaning a given expenditure on marketing produces a higher level of sales and discretionary cash flow. Figure 14–7 shows graphically the effects of successful product development programs in shifting up the discretionary cash flow function from *IF* to *IF'* where a given marketing allocation *Mo* would produce $D' > Do$ discretionary cash flow. In addition, the development of new products may directly lead to increases in sales and *IF* without further marketing programs.

The second primary impact of R&D relates to programs undertaken to find new methods and techniques of production, and to exploit advances in the state of technology in the firm's operations. Outlays for these purposes improve the level of technical efficiency the firm can utilize in its production process. Consequently, these programs lower

FIGURE 14–7

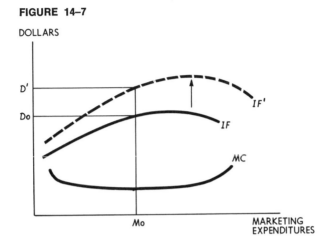

the marginal costs of production in an identical manner as that shown earlier in Figure 14–6.

A DISCRETIONARY FUNDS-FLOW MULTIPLIER

We earlier assumed that the first four categories of expression (14–1), *MK, RD, CP* and *DIV*, normally represent specific management investment plans and commitments while the fifth, change in current assets, is a residual. Small changes in the residual current assets category resulting from changes in discretionary financial flows would not be likely to provoke associated actions by the firm's management. For small changes, current assets would function as a buffer account. But what if changes in residual current assets are substantial? For example, suppose unexpected product market strength produced higher-than-anticipated sales, which increased discretionary funds flow and enlarged current assets significantly. This situation could be expected to affect the firm's allocation decisions in at least two ways. First, the increased financial flows from existing marketing programs causes these expenditures to be more productive than predicted. This can be expected to upgrade management's evaluation of the probable productivity of new marketing expenditures. Accordingly, expected return on new capital investments and new R&D projects may be expected to rise. It is reasonable to assume the firm would be induced by this circumstance to increase its marketing and other investment outlay as long as its current outlay is not at saturated levels. In addition, more current assets are available than required for conduct of the business. The excess liquid assets could readily be used to fund an increase in marketing and other investment programs. The firm is thereby induced by its own increased expectations and by its increased financial flow to engage in a higher level of investment spending in response to a positive increment of discretionary cash flow.[5] We define this behavioral tendency as the firm's cash-flow inducement to spend.

In the particular case of marketing investments, the property now discussed leads to expression (14–2):

$$MK = f(CF, Ex_1) \qquad (14\text{–}2)$$

where marketing expenditures MK are assumed to be a stable and significant function of total internal and external discretionary fund flows, as well as a function of a group of exogenous variables (Ex_1) such as competitive expenditures, general business conditions, and past patterns of marketing expenditure. Such a functional relationship finds statistical support among firms in various industries and for various years. Cross-sectional studies by this author suggest an important empirical relationship between discretionary cash flow and marketing expenditures for a variety of firms.[6] This finding is supported by time-series tests of the same relationships.[7]

Considering the other two discretionary spending categories, similar conclusions result. New capital expenditures may be expected to be undertaken in greater amounts when total discretionary financial flows are enlarged, for the following reasons: enlarged internal discretionary flows increase the cash flow on existing fixed capital and can be expected to produce an increase in expected cash flow on future investment, to the extent that cash flow forecasts are influenced by currently realized results. In addition, enlarged internal discretionary financial flows enable more comfortable internal financing of new capital investment. Finally, external capital acquisition (the ΔDBT part of CF) is often directly tied to new capital investment by mortgages, or by company statements of intent. The inducements of higher expected returns and increased external discretionary funds thereby provide reasons to formulate expression 14–3 as follows:

$$CP = g(CF, Ex_2) \qquad (14\text{–}3)$$

---

[5] Of course, if further expenditures on marketing or other programs were not judged to be minimally productive, this excess discretionary cash flow would likely flow into short-term financial investments.

[6] See J. W. Elliott, "A Comparison of Models of Marketing Expenditures in the Firm," *Quarterly Review of Economics and Business*, Vol. 11, No. 1 (Spring 1971), pp. 53–70, wherein discretionary cash flow was found to be the most important internal determinant of the size of the firm's marketing budget among a number of alternatives considered, once the effect of external influences upon the firm's marketing budget had been taken into account. See also S. Saltzman, "An Econometric Model of a Firm," *Review of Economics and Statistics* (August 1967, Vol. 49, pp. 332–42), in which expenditures were found to be importantly influenced by current sales levels.

[7] See J. W. Elliott, "Forecasting and Analysis of Corporate Financial Performance with An Econometric Model of the Firm," *Journal of Financial and Quantitative Analysis*, Vol. 7, No. 2, (March 1972), pp. 1499–1526.

in which capital expenditures (CP) are a function of total discretionary financial flows as well as an array of exogenous factors (Ex_2) such as cost-of-capital variables and measures of business expectations.

Extensive empirical study has been devoted to the determinants of investment spending in the firm, including considerable attention to relevant financial flow variables. For example, several studies have undertaken to measure the impact of profits upon capital investment, and have produced generally positive although somewhat conflicting results pertaining to the explanatory powers of total profits relative to investment.[8]

Other studies have emphasized the empirical role of gross income or sales measures in the context of accelerator explanations of capital investment fluctuations.[9] These studies have reported empirical results that suggest strong connections between output or sales levels and levels of capital investment. Finally, in all studies of capital investment, a considerable time lag is found between changes in influential variables and changes in investment expenditures. The present analysis will for now abstract from time-lagged relationships in the interests of clarity. However, it should be recognized that the influence of CF on investment is probably subject to a considerable distributed lag in most firms.

Research and development programs directed towards product development can be expected to be affected less by current financial flows than would marketing or capital investment over the short run. This

---

[8] Eisner, for example found profits to be an important explanatory variable in time-series data, but less important in cross-sectional data, a result which he interpreted as showing that most recent past profit performance had more of an impact on investment spending than current profit performance. (R. Eisner, "A Permanent Income Theory for Investment: Some Empirical Explorations," *American Economic Review*, Vol. LVII, June 1967, pp. 363–90.) Jorgenson and Siebert, on the other hand, found less explanatory power attributable to the effect of profits than for other alternatives. (D. Jorgenson and C. Siebert, "A Comparison of Alternative Theories of Corporate Investment," *American Economic Review*, Vol. LVIII, September 1968, pp. 681–712.) However, their results do not stand up to the test of a larger sample and a cross-sectional and time-series framework. See J. W. Elliott, "Theories of Corporate Investment Behavior Revisited," *American Economic Review* (March 1973). Also, the effects of profits upon investment spending has been empirically studied by Kuh with generally positive results. (E. Kuh, *Capital Stock Growth—A Microeconometric Approach*, Amsterdam: North Holland Publishing Company, 1963). Grunfield (Y. Grunfield, "The Determinants of Corporate Investment," in A. C. Harberger, et al., *The Demand for Durable Goods*, 1960, pp. 211–66), and others with generally negative results.

[9] For example, studies by R. Eisner, "Capital Expenditures, Profits, and the Acceleration Principles," *Models of Income Distribution Studies in Income and Wealth*, Vol. 28, Princeton University, 1964, pp. 137–76, and "A Permanent Income Theory for Investment," *American Economic Review*, Vol. 57, June 1967, pp. 363–90, particularly the latter have indicated that sales/output levels, perhaps as proxies for measures of income, are influential in capital expenditures. Also, work by B. G. Hickman, *Investment Demand and U.S. Economic Growth*, Brookings Institute, 1965, and by Kuh, *Capital Stock Growth* have produced positive results for the influence of gross financial flow variables upon investment, primarily sales and output measures.

is due primarily to the long-run staffing and organizational peculiarities associated with mounting and maintaining a continuing competitive program. Such programs typically involve the acquisition of highly specialized expertise through programs of experimentation lasting over several years. This aspect rewards those firms who maintain a high degree of continuity over time in the level of their R&D programs. Nonetheless, specific research projects within the firm's program of research that are of a marginal nature can be expected to be sensitive to financial flow variables. These marginal additions or deletions may be significant enough in particular cases to cause the total to be importantly influenced by variables such as *CF*. Although anticipating wide variation among specific firms, the following relationship analogous to (14–2) and (14–3) may be expected in general:

$$R\&D = b(CF, Ex_3) \qquad (14\text{--}4)$$

where Ex_3 is again a group of exogenous variables such as profits and past R&D expenditures. An empirical cross-sectional study by the author finds statistical support for discretionary funds-flow and a second related funds-flow measure in an equation similar to (14–4), particularly during recessionary years in the economy when liquidity can be presumed to be an evident and pressing problem in firms.[10] The same findings further suggested that the quantitative impact of funds-flow and expectational variables in the firm was relatively minor compared with the influence on R&D levels associated with changes in the firm's market position and changes in competitor's level of R&D outlays.

Other studies of R&D have pointed to the importance of internally generated cash in affecting this spending, thus providing further (albeit indirect) evidence suggesting empirical support for the relevance of expression (14–4).[11]

To this point, we have not introduced specific time relationships into any of our equations merely for convenience in discussion, and not due to an underlying thesis that all relationships are in the "same period." For now we will concentrate on the implications of the relationships outlined over some time period of sufficient length for these relationships to become operative. Expressions (14–2), (14–3), and (14–4) should also

---

[10] See J. W. Elliott, "Funds-Flow vs. Exceptional Theories of Research and Development Spending in the Firm," *Southern Economic Journal*, Vol. 37, No. 4 (April 1971), pp. 409–22.

[11] See, for example, D. Mueller, "The Firm Decision Process: An Econometric Investigation," *Quarterly Journal of Economics*, (February 1967), pp. 71–73, in which depreciation was considered as a liquidity variable and found to play a more important role in recessionary years than in expansionary years; and H. Graboski, "The Determinants of Industrial Research and Development: A Study of the Chemical, Drug, and Petroleum Industries," *Journal of Political Economy*, Vol. 76, (March–April 1968), pp. 295–305, in which significant statistical weighting was attached to the liquidity effect on *R&D* spending in all three industries studied.

be interpreted as proposing that the size of discretionary spending programs is affected by discretionary financial flows only within limits of profitability, a question we shall return to later.

Given the relationships now outlined by (14–2), (14–3), and (14–4), an increment of new discretionary financial flow gives rise to an increase in marketing, capital investment, and possibly research expenditures. From our earlier discussion, we may expect these increased expenditures to result in greater sales and lower production costs, which in turn results in an additional increment of discretionary cash flow. This leads to further increases in marketing, capital investment, and R&D, which increases sales, lower costs, and so forth, as long as successive expenditure increases remain profitable. A multiplier effect associated with discretionary funds is thus evident. We might expect this multiplier to operate in reverse in response to a decline in discretionary cash flow. Management would likely respond to declines in discretionary cash flow by cutting allocations made to discretionary spending categories. This in turn contributes to reducing sales and raising costs, thereby reducing cash flows, which precipitates further downward spending adjustments and so forth.

The cumulative process described is a potentially powerful source of instability in the firm's growth over time, particularly if we focus upon sales as a means of measuring corporate growth. Firms generating growing discretionary flows and reapplying those flows to expenditure categories having high returns can be expected to develop a growth momentum over time. Of course, such momentum could be dampened by unwise use of discretionary flows, i.e., by the allocation of these flows over categories wherein returns were low, or by deterioraton in overall market conditions that would lower returns from existing levels of allocation.

MEASURING FUNDS-FLOW RELATIONSHIPS AND MULTIPLIERS IN FIRMS

Expressions (14–2), (14–3), and (14–4) proposed that discretionary cash flow has an important influence on levels of marketing, capital investment, and research and development programs in firms. Thus usefulness of our resource-allocation framework and the real-world importance of the resulting multiplier effect now identified hinges importantly upon the correctness of that proposal. The author has explored this question in two separate research projects. We now consider some of these results.

A direct test of the statistical importance of discretionary funds-flow in marketing, capital investment, and research and development was obtained in the author's corporate econometric model project discussed in Chapter 13 ("A Model to Analyze and Predict Financial Performance"). In that project, an 11-equation econometric model of the firm was developed and applied to the data of nine corporations that included empirical representations of equations (14–2), (14–3), and (14–4), and enabled measurement of the kind of multiplier now described.[12] Table 14–1 summarizes the results of this analysis with respect to the importance of discretionary funds-flow in explaining strategic expenditures. The entries

TABLE 14–1
Importance of Discretionary Funds-Flow in Strategic Expenditures

Expenditure	*Number firms*	*Firms for which discretionary funds-flow is statistically valuable*
Marketing (14-2)	9	6
Capital Investment (14-3)	9	7
Research and Development (14-4)	6*	4

* Three firms had no research and development programs due to the nature of their business

in Table 14–1 show the number of firms tested and the number for which the discretionary funds-flow variable was statistically valuable. The variable was considered statistically valuable if its measured impact on expenditures was in accord with the proposed behavioral role it is intended to measure *and* if it contributed to the explanation of expenditure levels by resulting in a reduction in the equation's standard error. As seen, substantial if not complete empirical support is found for all three equations regarding proposed funds-flow expenditure relationships.

The funds-flow multiplier associated with this linkage between discretionary funds and strategic expenditures was partially evaluated by the impact on corporate performance of simulated changes in selected exogenous variables. One result of this analysis was the conclusion that the multiplier effect of increases in the money supply in the national economy was slow occuring but ultimately powerful. A similar finding occurred for additions of new equity.

In order to focus more directly on measuring the funds-flow multiplier, the author undertook a separate study employing a greatly aggregated model of financial flows and expenditures designed explicity to represent the framework now discussed in this chapter.[13] This model involved four equations and one identity. The first equation explains real sales as follows:

$$Q = a_1 E + \Sigma_i a_i X_i \qquad (14\text{–}5)$$

---

[12] See expressions (3), (4), and (5) under the discussion of "A Model to Analyze and Predict Financial Performance" in Chapter 13.

[13] See J. W. Elliott, "Funds-Flow Multipliers in Firms: An Econometric Exploration," *Southern Economic Journal* Vol. 39, No. 1 (July 1972), pp. 19–30.

where

Q = real sales, i.e., dollar sales deflated by an index of prices
E = total volume of strategic expenditures on marketing, capital investment, and research and development
X_i = exogenous influences on sales and company performance demand and price variables.

As seen, the E term in (14–5) represents the total volume of discretionary spending, which for simplicity is assumed to have an impact on real sales along with other exogenous variables.

The second equation explains E:

$$E = b_1 CF + \Sigma_i b_i X_i \qquad (14\text{–}6)$$

where

CF = total discretionary cash flow, including internal discretionary funds-flow and net external capital acquired.

Equation (14–6) results if we assume a linear function and if (14–2), (14–3), and (14–4) are added together, i.e., adding marketing, capital investment, and research and development on the left-hand side gives E, while the common dependence on CF and a set of exogenous variables defines the right-hand side.

The next equation explains the production of internal discretionary funds from company operations as follows:

$$IF = c_1 Q + \Sigma_i c_i X_i \qquad (14\text{–}7)$$

where

IF = internal discretionary funds, defined as in our earlier identity (14–1).

In expression (14–7), real sales are seen to be a crucial internal determinant of IF. This expression thus summarizes all the basic behavioral relations that relate sales and IF. In addition, a number of exogenous cost-type influences are presumed to influence the flow of IF.

The fourth equation explains the change in new long-term debt as follows:

$$\Delta DBT = d_1 IF + \Sigma_i d_i X_i \qquad (14\text{–}8)$$

where

$$\Delta DBT = \text{the change in long-term debt.}$$

This expression assumes that a major internal determinant of the amount of new debt is the level of internal discretionary funds-flow, which relates to the firm's financial strength and therefore its debt-capacity. Also, IF may relate to the demand for debt by reflecting the volume of funds available internally.

Finally, our total discretionary cash flow identity discussed earlier completes the model:

$$CF \equiv IF + \Delta DBT + \Delta EQ \qquad (14\text{--}9)$$

where

$$\Delta EQ = \text{new equity funds is assumed exogenous.}$$

This system is seen to be a quantitative representation of the framework we have discussed earlier in this chapter. Thus, real sales (14–5) are influenced by the volume of marketing and other strategic expenditures (14–6), which are influenced by total discretionary cash flows. To complete a circular joint dependence, internal discretionary cash flow (14–7) is influenced by real sales. An additional aspect of this joint dependence is provided by new debt, which adds to total CF, thereby increasing E and real sales, which adds to IF and works an induced influence on new debt.

The specific multiplier associated with this simultaneous framework may be found by substituting equation (14–6) into (14–5), then (14–9) into (14–5), then (14–7) into (14–5), and so forth until the reduced-form expression (Chapter 4) results, giving Q as a function of all the exogenous and predetermined variables. The result of this process is as follows:

$$Q = \frac{1}{1 - (a_1 b_1 c_1)(1 + d_1)} \times f(X_i, \Delta EQ) \qquad (14\text{--}10)$$

in which the term $\left[\dfrac{1}{1 - (a_1 b_1 c_1)(1 + d_1)} \right]$ is a multiplier that operates to magnify the impact of exogenous variables upon real sales and other aspects of financial performance. It is interesting to note that the value of this multiplier is increased by increases in either a_1, b_1, or c_1 as long as:

$$0 \leq (a_1 b_1 c_1)(1 + d_1) \leq 1$$

Since these three coefficients constitute the sales-strategic expenditure (a_1), strategic expenditure-cash-flow (b_1), and internal cash flow-sales (c_1) linkages, this is a perfectly reasonable characteristic, as it amounts to saying that the stronger the simultaneous influences measured by the three coefficients, the bigger the resulting multiplier effect. In addition, if $d_1 > 0$, this implies that greater flows of external funds associate with greater flows of internal discretionary funds so that the two are complementary in magnitude. In these cases, external funds increase the multiplier value, as indicated by the position of the $(1 + d_1)$ term and the result that $(1 + d_1) > 1$. If $d_1 < 0$, just the opposite effect occurs, as internal and external funds are substitutes. In these cases, the value of the multiplier is reduced by the leakages (repayment) of externally borrowed funds associated with positive changes in internal funds.

To obtain quantitative estimates of a multiplier similar to that now discussed, an operational version of our four-equation model was developed. This differed from the present model in two principal ways. First, it dealt with the expected time lags involved in the relationships discussed, such that the coefficients in these time-lagged relationships were measurable. Second, specific exogenous variables were selected for each equation, replacing the X_i and facilitating a more complete statistical explanation of the endogenous variables. For specific details of this operational version, the reader should consult the author's paper cited in footnote 10.

The model was individually fit to the data of six corporations for the period 1948 to 1968. The resulting coefficient estimates enabled calculation of multipliers for each firm. These multipliers show the total impact after one year of changes in each of the exogenous variables. For the operational version of the model, the exogenous variables (X_i) were as follows:

1. Ratio of industry prices to general prices (PR/AP)
2. Index of industry production for firm's industry (IP)
3. New equity funds obtained by firm (ΔEQ)
4. Industry price levels (PR)
5. Debt-equity ratio in previous period (DE_{-1})
6. Ratio of operating profits to fixed charges, average of most recent three years (TIE_n)

Table 14–2 shows the one-year multiplier effects of each of these exogenous variables upon the four endogenous variables in the model. Each of the endogenous variables is measured in millions of dollars. Thus, the entries in the table show millions-of-dollars change for each unit change in the associated exogenous variable.

The PR/AP term in Table 14–2 shows industry price movements relative to the GNP. For firm 6, this term was excluded from the model due to an illogical sign. For firm 3, its impact was confined to the real sales (Q) equation. For the remaining three firms (1,2,5), fluctuations in relative prices exerted an impact not only on sales but on all the endogenous variables. In each of these cases, a relative price rise was found to lower real sales, thus reducing internal discretionary funds flow (IF) and resulting in a decline in the level of strategic expenditures (E). In all three cases, the firms showed a tendency to partially offset the decline in internal funds by expanding new debt, i.e., a positive multiplier was measured in all three cases. Thus, the effect of a price change on total discretionary cash flow CF is in every case less than the initial effect on internal discretionary funds.

For changes in industry demand levels (IP), firms 1 and 3 showed highly insensitive (in fact somewhat counter-cyclical) responses of real sales to industry demand. The remaining three firms showed responses of between 4.5 percent and 7.0 percent of the average sample-period value of real sales for a ten-index-point rise in industry production. In

TABLE 14–2
Multipliers

Firm	Variable	PR/AP^a	IP^b	ΔEQ^c	PR^b	$DE_{-1}{}^a$	$TIE_n{}^a$	Average value of variable
1	Q	−.8114	−.0081	0	0	0	0	21.74
	E	−.0001	−.0000^d	.0297	.0028	−.0029	0	3.40
	IF	−.0049	−.0001	0	.1907	0	0	4.29
	ΔDBT	.0025	.0000^d	.0153	−.0965	−.1001	0	0.40
2	Q	−8.145	1.387	.1192	0	−.0680	0	309.63
	E	−.0240	.0041	.0334	0	−.0191	0	34.44
	IF	−1.093	.1861	.0160	0	−.0091	0	38.23
	ΔDBT	.3605	−.0614	.0059	0	−.5743	0	3.87
3	Q	−12.39	−1.831	1.941	−3.653	−1.087	0	362.96
	E	0	0	.9915	−1.865	−.5549	0	82.02
	IF	0	0	.4729	3.847	−.2647	0	69.66
	ΔDBT	0	0	.7247	−7.981	−.9653	0	34.70
5	Q	−8.957	1.577	.1842	.0564	−.0850	0	225.23
	E	−.6341	1.116	.5468	.1675	−.2522	0	43.63
	IF	−1.749	.3080	.0360	.4620	−.0166	0	46.01
	ΔDBT	.3579	−.0630	.1639	−.0945	−.5369	0	2.67
6	Q	0	3.018	0	0	0	0	432.89
	E	0	.4543	−2.001	.8609	0	0	137.48
	IF	0	.8255	0	1.564	0	0	121.29
	ΔDBT	0	−.4733	−2.551	−.8968	0	0	32.60

[c] The table entry represents millions-of-dollars change in the endogenous variable for each percentage point change in the ratio.

[b] The table entry represents millions-of-dollars change in the endogenous variable for each percentage point change in the index.

[c] The table entry represents millions-of-dollars change in the endogenous variable for each million change in the exogenous variable.

[d] These values are nonzero if carried to six places.

Note: Sample firm number 4 was omitted from these calculations due to unreliable statistical results.

each of these three cases, the real sales impact resulted in: (1) an increase in internal discretionary funds; (2) a reduction in long-term debt; and (3) an increase in strategic expenditures. These results are perfectly consistent with and therefore encouraging to the resource-allocation framework of this chapter. The pattern shows particular strength in the cases of firms 5 and 6, and lesser strength in the case of firm 2.

An infusion of new equity capital (ΔEQ) is seen in Table 14–2 to positively influence strategic expenditures in four of the five cases. This reflects a systematic response of the levels of these strategic programs to total discretionary cash flows, of which new equity is a part. In turn, in three of the four cases where this occurred, real sales rose in response to the rise in strategic expenditures. This produced an increase in internally generated cash flow. In addition, the rise in strategic expenditures created an increased demand for new debt, resulting in an increase in new debt for four of the five firms. In the case of the remaining firm (6), equity and new debt were apparently strong substitutes, so that this firm's response to new equity capital is seen to be a reduction in debt position, which in fact lowers discretionary cash flow and thus reduces strategic expenditures.

In this pattern, it is interesting to note that we have measured a fund-raising effect of new equity capital in all but one case. This is illustrated in Table 14–3 for a 10-million infusion of new equity capital. Columns

TABLE 14–3
Internal Funds Effect

Firm	(1) New equity	(2) New internal discretionary cash	(3) New debt	(4) Total new discretionary cash flow	(5) New strategic expenditures	(6) Ratio of column 5 to column 4
1.....	10	0	0.153	10.153	0.297	.03
2.....	10	0.160	0.059	10.219	0.334	.03
3.....	10	4.729	7.247	21.976	9.915	.45
5.......	10	0.360	1.639	11.999	5.468	.46
6.....	10	0	−25.51	−15.510	−20.010	1.29

2 and 3 show the new internal and external capital that our measurements show associates with the introduction of 10 million in new equity. Column 4 shows the total discretionary cash flow effect, which is larger than the initiating equity change in all cases except firm 6.

In addition, column 5 of Table 14–3 shows the new strategic expenditures that associate with this equity and cash flow change. Column 6 contains the ratio of the change in strategic expenditures to the change in discretionary cash flow, thus representing a kind of cash flow propensity to engage in strategic expenditures. For all firms but one in this table, the observed expenditure propensity is greater than zero but less than one, as expected in every case. This result further suggests support for the specific funds-flow expenditure view of the firm presently under consideration in this chapter.

The observed response to a one-percentage point increase in the lagged debt-equity ratio (DE_{-1}) is seen in Table 14–2 to be consistent in effect among all firms except firm 6, for which this variable was excluded due to its erratic performance. In each of these four cases: (a) a decline in new debt resulted from an increase in the debt-equity ratio, and (b) a decline in strategic expenditures resulted, due to the reduction in discretionary cash flow. For three of these cases, (2,3,5), a decline in real sales and internal funds also resulted from the decline in strategic expenditures.

This result suggests debt-equity relationships may be a kind of bell-wether of corporate accessibility to new debt. But more importantly, it infers that the impact of debt-equity position may be considerably broader than its initial effect, due to the role of new debt in affecting strategic expenditures and the influence of such expenditures on sales.

The findings of the statistical studies now considered in general suggest the particular funds-flow expenditure framework of this chapter finds considerable support empirically among the firms tested. Multipliers calculated for each exogenous variable suggest that firm-level variables such as new equity acquisition and debt-equity relationships work widespread effects on performance of the firm due to their involvement in simultaneous systems of joint dependence. Similarly, industry-level demand and price variables have been found to influence: (a) corporate expenditures on marketing, research and development, and capital investment; and (b) corporate long-term debt decisions as well as corporate sales. These reactions are indicative of the joint nature of the several aspects of corporate financial behavior considered in this study.

The funds-flow framework now outlined invites our attention to prescriptive questions. So far we have only talked of relationships among key economic and financial variables in firms. We have not found cause to consider the objectives of the firm. Neither have we endeavored to prescribe the most reasonable ways in which the corporation can use its discretionary funds for strategic purposes. We have not considered questions such as the optimal level of dividends and new debt. In the next chapter, we shall employ ideas from the framework now developed to seek answers to these questions.

DISCUSSION QUESTIONS

1. What is meant by discretionary funds? How have flows of these funds been described as affecting resource allocation in firms?

2. "The richer the firm, the more profitable investments it can make and the richer it becomes. It's a nasty circle for companies on the outside looking in." Comment.

3. What causes the funds-flow multiplier process described in the chapter? Under what circumstances would this multiplier become virtually nonexistent.

4. The chapter discusses a fund-raising effect of new equity funds. What is this effect?

5. You are a manager of a firm experiencing declines in sales and internal discretionary funds that are placing severe pressures on your marketing, research and development, and capital budgets. In addition, your relations with lending institutions are beginning to deteriorate. Use the framework of this chapter to prescribe a course of action to correct the decline.

Chapter 15

A THEORY OF CORPORATE RESOURCE ALLOCATION

The framework of the previous chapter has laid the groundwork for a consideration of optimal solutions for some of the most crucial economic questions facing the modern firm. Among these questions are:

1. What percentage of the firm's financial resources should be plowed back into its operations, as opposed to being paid out to stockholders?
2. When should the firm seek new external long-term capital—in what amounts and in what form, debt or equity?
3. At what levels should marketing, research and development, and capital investments be undertaken?

The analysis of this chapter provides theoretical guidelines useful in answering these questions in the case of firms whose principal economic objective aligns with that which we shall presently assume. As with all prescriptive-type results, the resulting answers to the three questions now posed do not necessarily make sense for firms whose main economic objective does not correspond with our assumption.

Recognizing that the reasonableness of our assumption about corporate economic objectives largely determines the direct applicability of our prescriptive guidelines, we turn first in our discussion to a consideration of an economic objective we assume to be primary in most modern U.S. corporations.

ON THE FIRM'S PRIMARY ECONOMIC OBJECTIVE

When thinking about reasonable goals to attribute to the producers in a profit-seeking enterprise economic system such as exists in the United States, maximizing profits comes immediately to mind. However, this notion soon becomes unworkably ambiguous when considered against the backdrop of large corporate institutions that supply most of the output of goods and services in the United States. One basic ambiguity is "whose profits." Corporations realize and pay taxes on profits as an entity. The directors and top managers of corporations earn their own personal profits in the form of salaries that are only tied in part to the corporation's profits. Finally, the stockholders in the firm earn their profits in the form of dividends and capital appreciation in the firm's stock. It should be clear that maximizing one of these kinds of profits over a particular time period does not necessarily correspond to maximizing another. So we are left with a choice of profits to maximize. Much of this problem of choice arises from the widely held corporate structure of most large U.S. firms. This structure is accompanied by a separation of legal ownership and operating control in most large firms, thus creating the stockholder group and the management group as separate factors in corporate behavior. A number of statistical studies have been undertaken to attempt to measure the effect of this separation upon corporate performance. Most of the studies find that no important differences in financial performance attach to owner-manager separation.[1] If so, this seems to suggest that the objectives of owners and those of managers may also be more similar than different. We shall accept this premise, and focus our attention on the owner group, we are at least legally more primary than the management group. Owners' profits are maximized by receiving the best combination of dividend payments and capital appreciation. If the interests of the management group align with those of the owner group, management will try to maximize the returns to the stockholders. Specifically, we assume the firm's management tries to maximize the wealth of its stockholders as pertains to the stockholders' holdings of the company's stock. Put slightly differently, this assumption sees the firm as primarily concerned with providing its stockholders with the best overall return on their financial investment. Later we shall have more to say on the implications of this assumption. For now, we turn to a consideration of a related but separate problem arising from the fact that stockholder returns and other important financial flows do not normally occur immediately but are arrayed over time.

TIME DISTRIBUTION OF RETURNS

In the resource allocation framework of the previous chapter it was recognized that the appropriate value for decision making of many finan-

---

[1] See, for example, D. Kamerschen, "The Influence of Ownership and Control on Profit Rates," *American Economic Review*, Vol. 58, June 1968, pp. 432–47, and J. W. Elliott, "Control, Size, Growth and Performance in the Firm," *Journal of Financial and Quantitative Analysis*, Vol. 7, No. 1, (January 1972), pp. 1309–20, who report no significant differences in profit performance between the two groups of firms. A contrary finding that finds a significant difference in return to equity is presented by J. Monson, D. Cooley, and J. Chin, "The Effects of Separation of Ownership and Control on the Performance of the Large Firm," *Quarterly Journal of Economics*, Vol. 82, August 1968, pp. 435–51.

cial flow variables must take into account the time distribution of these flows. We now consider this measure. When thinking of the return from strategic expenditures on marketing, research and development projects, and capital investments, a time-arrayed stream of returns is both logical and expected, as follows:

$$IF_1, IF_2, \ldots , IF_n \qquad (15\text{--}1)$$

where IF_i is the volume of internal discretionary funds and where n represents the firm's planning horizon. This horizon is the furthest point at which the firm is prepared to make projections of returns and costs and thus the longest period over which strategic decisions are planned. Since the components in (15–1) are flows accruing in different time periods, their simple arithmetic sum has little meaning. Instead, evaluation of (15–1) requires that we explicitly recognize that immediate cash-flow receipts are more valuable than distant receipts because of the time value of the funds involved. This situation calls for a discounting process, in order that the value of the time-arrayed returns may be assessed in relation to a common time period. This can be accomplished via discounted present value methods by relating the value of all income flows to the present time period as follows:

$$DSIF = \frac{IF_1}{(1 + r)} + \frac{IF_2}{(1 + r)^2} + \cdots + \frac{IF_n}{(1 + r)^n} \qquad (15\text{--}2)$$

In (15–2), *DSIF* stands for the discounted present value of the stream of internal funds, and r is a rate of discount that represents the current opportunity cost to the firm of using discretionary funds. We shall presently have more to say on this opportunity cost. For now, it suffices to recognize that discounting future proceeds by this rate makes the present value of an array of income flows directly comparable with other present-time flows. For example, the discounted present value of a stream of funds flowing from a marketing project can be compared to the outlay necessary for the marketing program, assuming the cost is incurred entirely in the present time period. Thus, *DSIF* is the discounted present value of discretionary fund flows resulting from a commitment of funds.

Influences on the Present Value of Funds Flows

Expression (15–2) shows that the value of measures such as *DSIF* is determined by two major systems of influence.

1. The value is importantly determined by the projections of funds flow comprising the values of $IF_1 \ldots IF_n$). These projections encompass a large number of factors, including at least the following:
   a) Expected market environment in the n periods ahead—which

determines the expected productivity of new marketing programs, and the expected intensity of use of new machines

b) Anticipated costs and product prices in the n periods ahead—
which determines the discretionary cash throw-off of a given
volume of production

c) Expected strategies of direct competitors—which influences the
productivity of new strategic product-market related outlays

d) The time period n, over which management feels sufficiently
confident of its outlook that it is willing to predict nonzero
values for *IF* components of an income stream.

As this partial list indicates, the projection of *IF* is a broad-gauged
forecasting project that encompasses the basic business expectations
of the firm as well as specific forecasts of particular variables. As
we shall later see, the design of the stockholder-wealth-maximizing
firm's strategy depends importantly on the projection of *IF* values.

2. The opportunity cost r of employing discretionary funds affects the
present value. Expression (15–2) shows that the higher the opportunity cost, the smaller is the discounted present value of a given
stream of returns. This reflects a fundamental property of time-dis-
counted returns—namely that as funds become more costly to employ, a given investment must produce higher income flows to retain
the same present-measured profitability. The reverse is also reasonable. As funds become less costly to employ for strategic purposes,
the required funds-production from a given investment is decreased.

We have now seen that a considerable number of influences on firm
behavior are contained in discounted present value expressions such as
(15–2). The opportunity cost of fund use is of immediate further interest
in our discussion. Although we have now discussed its impact on present
value calculations, a definition of r has not yet been formulated.

THE OPPORTUNITY COST OF REDEPLOYED FUNDS

As with any opportunity cost (see Chapter 1), the opportunity cost
of funds used by the firm to further its own growth and prosperity
is the reward associated with pursuing the next best alternative.

For the corporate context of our discussion, this provokes the question,
"Whose next best alternative, that of the firm's management or that
of the stockholder?" From management's standpoint, the next best alternative to the redeployment of discretionary funds for strategic investment
in the firm's business is likely to be their deployment for the purchase
of interest-bearing or dividend-bearing financial instruments. From the
stockholder's standpoint, the next best alternative to management's internal redeployment of discretionary funds is likely to be the stockholder's

best presently available securities investment opportunity, assuming the firm transferred the discretionary funds to the stockholder via dividends. To unambiguously resolve this "whose cost?" question, we need to consider the relationship between the two costs while keeping in mind our earlier stated assumption that the firm's primary economic goal is to maximize the firm's contribution to stockholder wealth.

We may define one set of conditions in which management's opportunity cost and the stockholder's opportunity cost are the same, thus causing our problem of choice to disappear. That set of conditions is:

1. The stockholder group and the firm's managers have equal access to the same array of possible security investments and other financial investment opportunities. They can both buy or sell the same securities at no transactions costs.

2. The taxation of income earned by the corporation and the taxation of dividends and income earned by stockholders are identical in total for any particular investment opportunity. The effect of this assumption is to make the tax-adjusted return on all investment opportunities the same for both firm and stockholder.

3. Both the stockholder group and the firm's management have the same time horizon in the consideration of investment opportunities.

4. The reaction to risk differences in investment opportunities is the same for the firm's management as it is for the stockholders. Since some possible securities investments carry substantially greater risk of capital loss than others (but also may be expected to carry greater expected earnings), we are herein assuming that the preference for particular risk-expected return combinations is identical.

While the implications of the first three assumptions are apparent, the meaning of the fourth assumption is not so clear. To illustrate the implications of this assumption, consider Figure 15–1, which shows a family of stockholders' risk preference curves. These are indifference curves in that each curve shows risk-expected return combinations that are of equal value in the mind of the stockholder.[2] Thus, curve A shows the extent to which the stockholder is indifferent between higher expected returns and lower expected returns due to his having to assume greater risk in order to obtain the higher expected return. Of course, if risk was identical on two securities, stockholders may be expected

---

[2] Our purpose is not particularly served by a more detailed account at this point. The interested reader should consult one of several recent texts on financial theory for a more explicit discussion. For example, see W. F. Sharpe, *Portfolio Analysis and Capital Markets* (New York: McGraw-Hill, 1970), Harry Markowitz, *Portfolio Selection: Efficient Diversification of Investments* (New York: John Wiley, 1959), or for an introductory treatment, James C. Vanhorne, *Financial Management and Policy* (Englewood Cliffs, N.J.: Prentice-Hall, 1971).

always to prefer higher expected earnings to lower expected earnings.[3] Accordingly, we may reason any point on curve A in Figure 15–1 to be preferred to any point on curve B, and similarly B preferred to C. The argument is simple. Pass a horizontal line through the curves, say at risk level U_A. Then, it is clear that for this level of risk, stockholders would prefer expected return B to expected return C $(R_B > R_C)$ and would prefer R_A to R_B since $(R_A > R_B)$. The same argument can be seen by fixing the expected return, say at R_A, and considering the preference for risk, i.e., U_A preferred to U_B to U_C since $U_A < U_B < U_C$.

The family of curves shown in Figure 15–1 is now seen as expressing

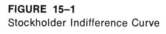

FIGURE 15–1
Stockholder Indifference Curve

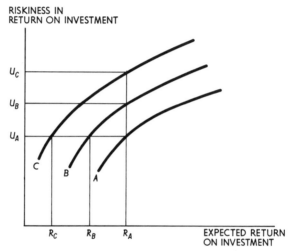

the stockholder's reaction pattern to risk and returns. By assuming (number 4) that the risk-return patterns of stockholders and of the firm's management are the same, we are thus saying that the two families of preference curves are identical.

The conditions now assumed—common investment opportunities, equal tax effects, equal time horizon, and equal risk-return preferences—lead to identical opportunity costs for either management or stockholders. Each group will have the same scenario of opportunities and returns. Their equivalent preferences will thus lead each to select securities with equivalent risk-return properties. Since management's opportunity cost is given by its best alternative investment, this "best alternative" will be equivalent to that of stockholders. Our two opportunity costs merge into one.

---

[3] We are abstracting from arguments about skewness, kurtosis, and higher moments.

However, if these conditions are not met, our conclusion is altered. Both management and stockholders may impose constraints on acceptable additions to their investment holdings. In the case of management, this may come about due to liquidity objectives attached to their investment holdings, while for investors minimum expected earnings may be imposed. Also, in the United States at least, the tax effects are clearly not the same as assumption (2) proposes. Corporate tax rates and individual tax rates differ, and the transfer of funds from the firm to the stockholder in the form of dividends produces an additional tax on the transfer of funds. The result of these tax differences is to make the after-tax fraction of a given before-tax pool of funds different for the firm than for the stockholder. In turn, this suggests that the firm can earn a different return on new funds than the stockholders and still represent an equally profitable after-tax use of funds. Finally, there is little evidence to suggest we might generally expect the risk-return preferences of corporate managers and stockholders to align. The former managerial group is likely to be governed by liquidity and security from capital loss to a greater degree than the latter group. On the other hand, the latter group may prefer different risk-return combinations than the former, due to the more extensive portfolio perspective in which a financial investment opportunity is considered compared to an investment in physical, product-line, and marketing assets.

In this (perhaps more plausible) case where some of our three conditions do not approximate the circumstances at hand, we are returned to a world in which the question of "whose opportunity cost" reappears. Fortunately, having made the round trip we are armed with concepts helpful in choosing an appropriate opportunity cost definition in those circumstances now described where choice is necessary.

One guidepost we may establish concerns the possibility of differing risk-return preference functions for management and stockholders. Our objective of maximizing stockholder wealth indicates we should be singularly concerned with the stockholder's risk-return preferences over those of management in evaluating opportunity costs. A second guidepost concerns the treatment of risk. The returns from redeploying new funds in the firm clearly has a degree of uncertainty attached to it that produces a degree of risk associated with the expected value of the return.

This risk-return character of internally deployed funds by the firm in its business investments is comparable in concept to that discussed earlier associated with security investment alternatives on the part of shareholders. Thus, when deciding to deploy or not to deploy discretionary funds internally, management concerns itself most appropriately with the stockholder group's best alternative available return having the same effect on the risk of stockholders' portfolios as that associated with internally redeployed funds by the firm. Finally, in considering the return on stockholder deployment of company discretionary funds, the tax leakages on the transfer via dividend payments must be taken into account, since stockholders receive only a portion of a given volume of funds. One way this could be taken into account is to consider the dividend tax as adding to the purchase price of the investment if undertaken by the stockholder with dividends. This lowers the effective return on the stockholders' alternative below prevailing market rates.[4]

It should now be clear that *the opportunity cost most appropriate for management decisions on the redeployment of internal funds is the tax-adjusted, best-alternative stockholder return-on-funds invested at the same level of stockholder portfolio risk as that associated with redeployment of funds in the firm.* We shall adopt this definition and hence refer to this opportunity cost as r_{IF}. The value of r_{IF} figures importantly in our discussion of the selection of optimal values for strategic economic questions. We now turn to the first of these questions, beginning with the simplest case of a firm that does no external financing. It is an all-equity, nonlevered (no-debt) firm.

OPTIMAL LEVELS OF STRATEGIC EXPENDITURES: THE ALL-EQUITY CASE

In Chapter 14 we defined and discussed the firm's strategic expenditures (E) as consisting of marketing (MK), research and development (RD), and capital investments (CP), as follows:

$$E = MK + RD + CP$$

We now consider the best overall level of these expenditures for the shareholder-wealth-maximizing firm. For the present, we shall defer consideration as to how a given volume of E should be allocated to MK, RD, and CP, presuming this allocation to be made in the most effective possible way. Later we shall consider this allocation explicitly.

A given expenditure of E associates with a flow of internal discretionary funds. The present value of this flow derives from the firm's opportunity cost of redeployed funds as follows:

$$DSE = \frac{IF_1}{(1 + r)} + \frac{IF_2}{(1 + r)^2} + \cdots + \frac{IF_n}{(1 + r)^n} \qquad (15\text{--}3)$$

where $r = r_{IF}$ is the discount rate.

In the previous chapter the effectiveness of all categories of strategic expenditures in producuing discretionary internal funds was presumed to decline after some point. We now extend those ideas to the discounted present value of flows resulting from an increase in the level of strategic expenditures. More specifically, we expect the discounted present value

---

[4] Funds left in the firm produce earnings and presumably increase the price of the firm's stock. The capital-gains tax on this aspect of return should also be taken into account.

of discretionary fund flows to increase as strategic expenditures increase, but at a declining rate beyond some point. Figure 15–2 shows the idea. In panel (a), the continued expansion of E is seen to produce declining contributions to the total discounted present value of funds flows (DSE)

FIGURE 15–2
Funds-Flow Effects of Strategic Expenditures

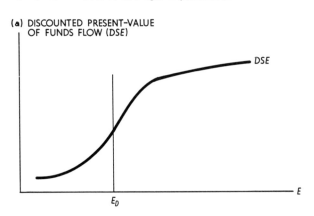

(a) DISCOUNTED PRESENT-VALUE OF FUNDS FLOW (DSE)

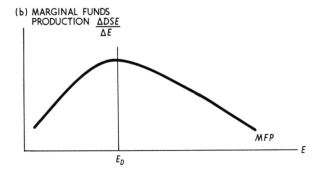

(b) MARGINAL FUNDS PRODUCTION $\frac{\Delta DSE}{\Delta E}$

beyond the point E_D. As indicated in the previous chapter, this expected pattern is due to declining productivity associated with the expansion of marketing and product development programs as well as a declining capital investment opportunity schedule—i.e., declining marginal productivity for new capital investment projects. Panel (b) of Figure 15–2 depicts the pattern of marginal funds production associated with the DSE curve. For convenience we shall refer to this marginal funds production curve as MFP, where

$$MFP = \frac{\Delta DSE}{\Delta E}$$

The MFP curve depicts the pattern of marginal funds production associated with strategic expenditure changes. The MFP curve is the mathematical slope of *DSE*. Accordingly, *MFP* rises when *DSE* is increasing at a growing rate and declines when *DSE* is increasing at a declining rate. Thus, *MFP* shows that the continued enlargement of expenditures beyond E_D results in declining marginal contributions of discounted present-valued funds.

The *MFP* curve now constructed contains the answer to our inquiry as to how far strategic expenditures should be pushed. To make the idea clear at this point, we shall take the easiest case where the optimal value of *E* turns out to be less than available internal discretionary funds-flow, i.e., $(IF > E)$. The numerator of the *MFP* ratio is the present value of discretionary cash inflow added by further expenditure of *E*, (discounted at the opportunity cost of investment funds r_{IF}) while the denominator is the also present-valued measure of the additional discretionary cash outflow required to produce the inflow. Thus, where $MFP > 1$, a change in outflow produces a greater change in present-valued inflow. When $MFP < 1$, an added outlay of discretionary funds produces a smaller addition to the present value of inflows, i.e. $(\Delta E > \Delta DSE)$. This is illustrated by Figure 15–3, panel (a). The point E_0 where expenditures have pushed the *MFP* to 1.0 is the point where

FIGURE 15–3
Optimal Levels of Strategic Expenditures

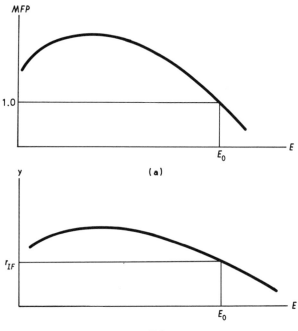

(a)

(b)

all strategic investment opportunities yielding returns above opportunity costs have been undertaken. E_0 is thus the optimal level of strategic expenditures.

Put alternatively but equivalently, when $MFP > 1$, the rate of return on an additional outlay is greater than the all-equity firm's opportunity cost, r_{IF}, and when $MFP < 1$ the marginal rate of return is less than r_{IF}. This can be seen by a reorientation of expression (15–3) as follows:

$$\Delta E = \Delta DSE = \frac{\Delta IF_1}{(1 + y)} + \frac{\Delta IF_2}{(1 + y)^2} + \cdots + \frac{\Delta IF_n}{(1 + y)^n} \quad (15\text{–}4)$$

where y is the marginal internal rate of return on the strategic expenditure and where ΔE, ΔDSE, and ΔIF_i are respectively a change in strategic expenditures, the resulting changes in discounted present-valued fund flows, and internal fund-flows changes for period i. In expression (15–4), we may solve for y by equating ΔE and ΔDSE, i.e., we may find the rate of discount that equates the marginal outflows and inflows of funds. The resulting marginal rate y is the rate of discount necessary for the present value of the returns from an additional strategic expenditure to exactly equal the additional cost required to produce those returns. In other words, if the incremental volume of funds ΔE was deposited in an account earning at a rate y, it would be possible to withdraw ΔIF_1 after period 1, ΔIF_2 after period 2, and so forth, resulting in the account being exactly depleted upon the withdrawal of ΔIF_n after period n. Thus, y is interpretable as a compounded marginal earnings rate associated with the added expenditure ΔE. Accordingly, the internal return y may be directly compared with the all-equity firm's opportunity cost, r_{IF}. When $y > r_{IF}$ the firm is making more productive use of funds at the margin than the stockholder group could, if the funds were transferred as dividends. If $y < r_{IF}$, the firm does better for its stockholders by returning additional funds to the stockholders via dividends. Accordingly, the point where $y = r_{IF}$ corresponds to the optimal level of strategic expenditures, since all profitable opportunities (above-opportunity-cost projects) have been undertaken, and since expenditures have not been pushed to the point where the marginal return is less than the opportunity cost.

This is shown graphically in panel (b) of Figure 15–3. Clearly, this marginal internal rate of return curve is closely related to the MFP curve in panel (a). When the marginal production of funds due to strategic expenditures is growing, it is algebraically necessary that ΔDSE discounted at r_{IF} is increasing faster than ΔE, since $MFP = \dfrac{\Delta DSE}{\Delta E}$. Returning to expression (15–4), it is clear that under these circumstances an increased value of y is required to equate the two. Thus, the MFP

curve and the y curve must rise and fall together. In addition, the point where $MFP = 1$ in panel (a) requires that ΔDSE discounted at r_{IF} equals ΔE. But, since in expression (15–4) we select the rate y that causes ΔDSE discounted at y to equal E, it must be the case that $y = r_{IF}$ at the point where $MFP = 1$.

Accordingly, panel (b) of Figure 15–3 produces the conclusion that if all strategic expenditures yielding returns greater than r_{IF} are undertaken, the result will be a volume of expenditures E_0 where the marginal rate of return y has been pushed to r_{IF}. This is, of course, the identical E_0 as that of panel (a). In the remainder of the chapter, we shall employ the marginal rate-of-return explanation of optimal expenditures rather than the MFP explanation, primarily due to the intuitive familiarity of many readers with rate-of-return concepts.

Stockholder Returns on Reinvested Funds for the All-Equity Firm

Either way our optimizing criterion is expressed, it implies that if the all-equity firm's marginal strategic expenditure opportunities are better than the investment opportunities of the stockholder group, tax effects considered, the firm should engage in increased levels of strategic expenditure as opposed to increased dividend payments. To this, the skeptic may retort, "Where is the advantage to the stockholder in the firm plowing back discretionary funds in its own operations, even if such expenditures are profitable *to the firm?*" Our answer to this question depends on our view of how stockholders in general will react to the results of funds plowed back by the corporation at marginal yields greater than r_{IF}.

Theoretically, there is one circumstance in which stockholder reactions can be expected to be clear-cut. That is the case where investors are perfectly informed and in agreement as to the expected returns from investment in corporate stocks. These returns consist of two elements, a rate of capital gains (r_g) resulting from market changes in the price of the stock, and the rate of dividend yield r_d. Accordingly, the expected total rate of return $E(r_t)$ consists of the sum of the expected capital gains rate and the expected dividend yield:

$$E(r_t) = E(r_g) + E(r_d) \qquad (15–5)$$

In this expression, $E(r_d)$ is largely determined for a particular firm by its dividend policy relative to an investor's purchase price of the stock, while $E(r_g)$ is largely determined by the current market price of its stock relative to an investor's purchase price.

Under conditions where perfect market information is possessed by investors, we would expect to find little if any differences among the total expected return $E(r_t)$ among firms with the same risk characteristics.

Firms that at some point in time are seen by investors as having higher-than-average marginal profitability on the redeployment of funds accordingly have a higher expected return than the average market return on stocks of comparable risk. The demand for these firms' stock increases, causing the price to rise. As the purchase price increases for new investors, the rate of expected dividend yield per dollar newly invested declines for a given dividend flow, and the rate of expected capital gain per dollar newly invested declines for a given expected market price increase. Both these factors decrease the expected return on new investments towards normal market rates of return for the firm's risk class. Equilibrium is restored when the stock price has risen sufficiently that the expected rate of return is equal to the average market return for stocks of comparable risk. The opposite is true for firms seen by investors to have lower-than-average expected yields. The decreased demand for these stocks reduces their price and increases the expected return on investments towards market equilibrium levels.

The result of these market price adjustments in perfect information conditions is to produce equal expected returns on new investment for firms in equivalent risk classes. However, from the standpoint of the existing stockholder, when the firm has a scenario of new strategic expenditures yielding $y > r_{IF}$, the result is an increased expected return on new investments in that company, leading to an increase in the market price of the stock sufficient to reduce the expected return on new investment to market levels. Thus, an existing stockholder will receive his rewards from corporate redeployment of funds in the form of capital gains. If we may set aside tax effects, the amount of capital gain is in proportion to the difference between y and r_{IF} when market information is perfect. That is, tax effects aside, he will wind up receiving the higher return y on new funds rather than his lower opportunity-level of return, r_{IF}.

In the more usual circumstances where market information is not perfect and tax effects are not set aside, we cannot expect a perfectly systematic response by investors to corporate redeployment of funds at $y > r_{IF}$. But an existing stockholder may still expect the market value of his holdings to increase, although by how much we cannot be clear. On the one hand, a marginal return on strategic expenditures greater than the opportunity-cost value generally corresponds to rising expected net profits anticipated by investment analysts. We may expect investors to translate higher expected net profits into higher stock prices. In addition, the firm will have other visible signs of strength when marginal return on investment is greater than opportunity costs. Its marketing programs will be strong in magnitude and of better-than-average productivity. Its product development efforts will be active and unusually rewarding, probably resulting in product innovations found promising to investors. Moreover, it will be expanding its capital facilities—often an investor signal of a growing firm with a promising outlook. In short, the results of better-than-average returns on strategic expenditures can be discerned by prudent investors even in the absence of perfect information, and the picture these results paint suggests a positive impact on stock value.

Thus we conclude that under less-than-perfect market information conditions, the stockholder may expect to make capital gains on funds redeployed by his firm at $y > r_{IF}$. Although we cannot clearly say that these after-tax gains will offset the after-tax value of the forfeited dividends involved, we can envision many circumstances in which this could be expected. Indeed, it is possible to foresee some cases where investors in the company's stock would increase their demand by greater-than-proportionate amounts, thus causing a more than offsetting capital gain. With less-than-perfect information, we expect these results to vary with the speculative characteristic of each firm. Accordingly, in our use of the all-equity firm's opportunity cost r_{IF} as a strategic expenditure cutoff point for less-than-perfect-information conditions, we must attach the provision that investor demand must be expected to react at least proportionately to redeployment of funds at $y > r_{IF}$ returns in order for r_{IF} to remain logical. With this in mind, we now turn to a consideration of strategic expenditure levels in the levered firm.

STRATEGIC EXPENDITURES IN THE LEVERED FIRM

Firms that over time consistently finance a portion of their new investments by debt capital are referred to as financially levered. Moderately levered firms generally do better for their stockholders than if they used no debt. The reason basically is that the financially levered firm can engage in a greater volume of investment projects that contribute to the flow of returns for stockholders than if they employed no debt capital. To see the meaning of this statement, consider a firm that has $100,000 of investment projects it may accept before the marginal return drops to the level of opportunity costs. In addition, for simplicity, assume a constant capital value and a one-year holding period, i.e., the investment is liquidated at the purchase price after one year. This $100,000 will produce $15,000 in pre-tax returns, which gives a pre-tax return of 15 percent to shareholders if the entire $100,000 is an investment of internal funds. Now, assume this firm has only $70,000 available internally, meaning it cannot internally finance all investment projects having returns above its opportunity cost. Furthermore, assume that the average pre-tax return on the first $70,000 of investment projects is $11,900 or 17 percent, while the average pre-tax return on the last $30,000 of the investment is $3,100 or 10.3 percent. The firm may capture this last $3,100 in earnings only by raising external capital of $30,000. Assume this occurs in the form of a one-period term loan at a market cost of 8 percent. The arithmetic of the situation now changes for two reasons fundamental to the impact of leverage.

First, stockholders now realize a greater return on their investment due to the earnings of the borrowed funds working on their behalf. Second, the interest payments on debt are an expense for tax purposes, which shields a portion of the firm's profits from tax liabilities. (We assume a 50% tax rate.) The no-debt and debt pictures are as shown in Table 15–1. The table shows that the acceptance of the last $30,000

TABLE 15–1
Levered and Nonlevered Investments

	No debt	Debt
Total volume of investment	70,000	100,000
Shareholder investment	70,000	70,000
Pre-tax gross return on total investment	11,900	15,000
Interest expense	0	2,400
Pre-tax return	11,900	12,600
Taxes (50%)	5,950	6,300
After-tax return	5,950	6,300
Net rate of return on total investment	8.5%	6.3%
Net rate of return to shareholder	8.5%	9.0%

of investment projects adds $3,100 in pre-tax earnings and creates a cost of $2,400 in interest. This increases pre-tax earnings by the $700 difference between increased revenues and increased costs, and increases after-tax net by $350. While the net return on total investment is decreased by accepting the last $30,000 of investment projects, the leverage effect increases the return to stockholders from 8.5 percent with no debt to 9.0 percent with debt.

The leverage effect now described will in general increase shareholder returns as long as the cost of the funds does not exceed the marginal return associated with their use. However, if the acquisition of external capital is undertaken on too large a scale, the firm may be judged by investors to be more risky than before. In this circumstance, any increased earnings resulting from increased leverage will be accompanied by an increased level of risk, thus making the net resulting impact on stockholder welfare unclear.

The levered firm has additional elements in its opportunity cost of investment funds than the nonlevered firm. In particular, the costs of debt and new equity capital must now be considered in addition to the opportunity costs of internal funds, since these funds intermingle with internal funds in the overall flow of investment funds in the firm. In accounting for these external costs, there is widespread agreement that it is most appropriate to consider a combination of the separate costs of various forms of external financing, as opposed to the approach of trying to associate explicit market costs of particular debt or equity financing operatings to particular investment projects. This latter approach produces particularly myopic investment decisions since the consequences of present financing actions on future capital costs is not taken into account. The most commonly held specific solution to this problem is to weight the individual costs of each financing means by the proportion it constitutes of the firm's normal expected financing mix during the time period of the proposed investment outlay. For example, if a firm normally finances 50 percent of its investments by internal funds at a cost of r_{IF}, 30 percent by debt at a cost of r_D, and 20 percent by new equity at a cost of r_E, then its weighted-average opportunity cost of investment funds r is:

$$r = .5r_{IF} + .3r_D + .2r_E$$

Of course, in any short-run period the firm's flow of investment funds will not necessarily be comprised of stable proportions such as are suggested here. Indeed, the firm will typically raise debt at one point in time, equity at another point in time, and internal funds more or less continuously via operations. But over a period of a year or more, these lumps may be expected to even out for most large firms. Accordingly, a weighted average of individual capital costs such as described by r will normally be an appropriate measure of the marginal cost of capital. Investments that return at least the weighted average measure r in turn return each supplier of capital an amount at least equal to its cost. To illustrate, consider the situation where a firm's pool of capital is financed one-third by debt capital at a cost of 3 percent, one-third by equity at a cost of 12 percent, and one-third by retained earnings at a cost of 6 percent. The weighted-average value of 7 percent can be viewed as a minimum rate of earnings on invested capital that enables equity to be paid 12 percent, debt to be paid 3 percent, and retained earnings to be paid 6 percent. This property rests upon the formulation of weights in the calculation of r which reflect the dollar proportions in which capital is ordinarily supplied for investment purposes by the various factors. If investment funds earn at a rate r, the equity proportion may be thought to have earned at r_E, the internal-funds proportion at r_{IF}, and the debt proportion at r_o, i.e., when the return-on-investment is just equal to the weighted average cost-of-capital, we may think of the earning rate on each component in this average as being equal to its cost.

The weighted-average r measures the comparable opportunity cost for the levered firm that r_{IF} measures for the nonlevered firm. Accordingly, strategic expenditures for the levered firm should be pushed to the point where the marginal return has dropped to the level of r, i.e., optimal levels of strategic expenditures for the levered firm occur where $y = r$.

AN OPTIMAL LEVEL OF NEW EXTERNAL CAPITAL

We have now described the optimal level of corporate startegic expenditures as occurring where the marginal internal return equals the opportunity cost of funds. This rule has made no reference to whether the resulting level of strategic expenditures is less than, equal to, or greater than the firm's available internal discretionary funds. We now consider this relationship in the light of the firm's acquisition of new external capital. Figure 15–4 depicts the situation graphically. Curve A

FIGURE 15–4
External Capital Relationships

DISCOUNTED RETURN (y)

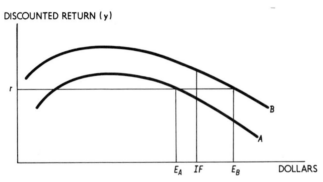

shows the circumstance in which the marginal return on strategic expenditures falls to the opportunity cost level at expenditure level E_A where $E_A < IF$. In this case the firm's production process is generating more discretionary funds than can be profitably put to work in strategic uses. The remainder $(IF - E_A)$ cannot be internally employed at sufficiently high rates to contribute to an increase in stockholder wealth. Curve B shows the contrasting possibility involving marginal returns on strategic expenditures that do not fall to opportunity cost levels until E_B level of strategic expenditures are undertaken, where $E_B > IF$. A situation such as curve B invites acquisition and deployment of external capital to finance the difference $(E_B - IF)$ and thus move to the optimal level of strategic expenditures. Accordingly, we define any positive difference between optimal strategic expenditures and available internal discretionary funds as the optimal level of new external capital.

Specifying the optimal level of new external capital does not indicate in what proportions the firm should seek that capital via debt versus equity channels. We now consider this question.

Debt or Equity

Basically, the cost of the firm of raising debt capital is established by the interplay of the forces of supply and demand in the nation's corporate bond markets and by bank lending conditions. Besides general capital market forces, the cost of debt will be influenced by the risk assessment of the firm on the part of bond investors and bank lenders. A firm that is highly levered is likely to be viewed by lenders as treading on a thin margin of solvency since the impact of possible operating losses upon the firm's equity position can potentially be severe, increasing the chance of bankruptcy. Accordingly, investors and bank lenders would be expected to insist on higher returns on their funds in the perceived riskier case of a firm with a ratio of debt to equity that they consider high.

Besides the impact of market forces and debt-to-equity relationships on the cost of debt, corporate tax rates also have an effect on the net cost of debt to the firm since interest expense is a legal deduction for tax purposes. Specifically, if we define r_D as the market yield on new debt to the firm for a given debt-equity position, the net cost is given by:

$$\text{Net debt costs} = r_D(1 - tx)$$

where tx is the marginal rate of corporate incomes taxes. As a yield statistic, r_D may be viewed as the rate of discount that equates the current price with the future flows of coupon income and capital gains.

The cost of equity capital is the cost of using funds raised by issuing additional ownership shares in the firm. This cost is fundamentally an opportunity cost, which derives from the best available investor alternatives of equivalent risk. Essentially, the wealth-maximizing firm should not employ new equity capital if its net expected return on the capital is not as great as the net expected return of its shareholders on other investment opportunities of equal business and financial risk. To do so would be expected to decrease investors expectations about the firm's future returns relative to those available elsewhere, lead to a decline in the market value of the firm, and thus reduce the wealth position of current stockholders. Accordingly, the expected return on alternative equal-risk investment opportunities constitutes the opportunity cost of equity funds. We thus define the cost of equity r_E as the expected return on representative alternative equal-risk investment opportunities.

This definition is nearly equivalent to that given earlier with respect to the opportunity costs of using internal funds r_{IF}, with the exception of the earlier-mentioned tax adjustment relating to the transfer of funds to the investor via dividends. Apart from tax effects, the firm should not use available internal funds if these funds are less productive than other alternatives available to shareholders at equivalent risk. Thus, with no dividend taxes, the cost of equity and the cost of internal funds are equal.

When taxes are taken into account, the return on company deployment of available internal funds drops below the opportunity cost of investors, i.e., $r_{IF} < r_E$. This is because of the tax leakage that occurs in the form of dividend taxes if the funds are paid by the firm to the shareholder as dividends. Disregarding the investor's transaction costs, the company must earn only a return equal to the best available equal-risk earnings on the after-tax portion of investor dividends to create a position of indifference. Specifically, if we define the marginal rate of shareholder dividend taxation as pt, the opportunity cost of internal funds is given by:

$$r_{IF} = r_E(1 - pt)$$

The costs of debt and of equity have now been described as variables whose values are set in securities markets or by institutional and other lendors. Accordingly, they may both be expected to be influenced by the firm's debt position. It has earlier been pointed out that too much leverage can be expected to lead to higher debt costs for the firm, due essentially to the riskier financial position that investors associate with too much debt. The same is true for the cost of equity. Investors in common stock will normally have alternative investment opportunities that involve both a higher risk and a greater expected return. So, as their perception of the firm's level of risk is increased, the firm's minimum return required to meet opportunity costs is similarly increased, raising r_E.

Normally, the cost of equity may be expected to be larger than the after-tax cost of debt. There are two basic reasons. First, equity capital usually has a significantly larger possibility of capital gains or loss than debt capital. It is accordingly more risky. As such, the expected market return on equity should be larger than for debt to account for risk differences. Secondly, the marginal corporate tax rate is usually significantly nonzero (in the neighborhood of 40 percent or better in the United States), which pushes the net costs of debt down considerably over the market costs.

The patterns of debt and equity costs now discussed are shown graphically in Figure 15–5 and numerically in Table 15–2. In these illustrations, the net cost of debt is shown to be less than the cost of equity for all debt-equity levels. This means that adding lower cost debt to the capital structure of the firm can reduce the total weighted average cost of external capital r_{EF}. In other words, the lower cost debt capital produces a positive leverage effect over an initial range. However, after point A in Figure 15–5 (.30 debt in Table 15–2), the addition of further debt begins to affect shareholder risk assessment, which begins to increase

FIGURE 15–5
Debt and Equity Costs

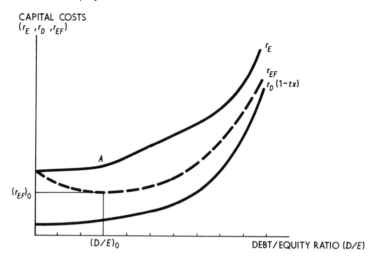

the cost of equity capital. Ultimately (immediately in our illustration) the increase in the equity cost more than offsets the lower but rising debt cost in the weighted calculation of r_{EF} and r_{EF} begins to rise.

Thus, the point $(D/E)_0$ in Figure 15–5 and 3/7 in Table 15–2 represents the proportion of debt for which all the positive advantages of leverage to the shareholder have been realized and no adverse effects

TABLE 15–2
External Funds

	Debt			Equity		
		Cost				*Total*
Proportion	*Before-tax*	*After-tax*		*Proportion*	*Cost*	*after-tax cost*
.00	.050	.025		1.00	.10	.100
.10	.050	.025		.90	.10	.093
.20	.052	.026		.80	.10	.085
.30	.054	.027		.70	.10	.078
.40	.060	.030		.60	.12	.084
.50	.072	.036		.50	.14	.088
.60	.096	.048		.40	.16	.093
.70	.144	.072		.30	.18	.104
.80	.240	.120		.20	.21	.138
.90	.422	.211		.10	.25	.215

Note: Cost of capital at most effective debt/equity ratio (3/7) assuming 50 percent internal, 50 percent external funds and assuming a marginal personal tax rate of 40 percent.

$$r = (.5)(.078) + (.5)(.10)(1 - .4) = .069$$

of leverage have been felt. It is the optimal proportion of debt and equity for the wealth-maximizing firm, producing the lowest cost of external capital $(r_{EF})_0$. Accordingly, we may expect the wealth-maximizing firm to raise the volume of external capital associated with wealth-maximizing investment levels in approximately such optimal proportions over time.

Virtually all firms finance a portion of their investments with internal funds at a cost of r_{IF}. To obtain a measure of the overall cost of capital to the wealth-maximizing firm under this circumstance, our earlier discussion has suggested we must weight the cost of internal funds by the normal proportions that these funds comprise of the firm's total pool of investment funds and weight the *optimal* cost of external funds by the proportion of investment funds they normally comprise. (We assume here the wealth-maximizing firm will move to the optimal point.) Thus, a specific expression for the total cost of capital is:

$$r = w_0 r_{IF} + w_1 (r_{EF})_0$$

where w_0, w_1 are the normal proportions of internal and external funds respectively. This expression is immediately seen to be a more specific version of the weighted-average expression for r considered earlier in the chapter. It is calculated in Table 15–2 for the assumption that $w_0 = w_1 = .5$.

Our previous discussion of the selection of optimal proportions of debt and equity in the external financing mix suggests a parallel argument for the mix of internal vs. external funds. However, at least one important difference prevents such a parallel analysis. Flows of internal funds are a function of sales, labor costs, and other operating expenses that are partially beyond the control of management. Thus, the internal flow of investment funds is as much a result of management decisions on investment projects and operating variables as a cause of these decisions. In addition, internal funds are usually seen as more accessible than external funds and are exhausted before external funds are sought. This makes the proportion of internal/external funds partially a product of the total volume of strategic expenditures, with the proportion of external funds increasing as the volume of strategic expenditures increases beyond the point where $E = IF$. Due to these complexities, we shall not attempt to formulate an optimal internal/external funds proportion, but rely on a reasonably stable proportion of internal and external funds in the investment fund pool over time to enable "normal" weights for r_{IF} and r_{EF} to be defined.

OPTIMAL USE OF STRATEGIC EXPENDITURES

So far, our discussion has identified the optimal level of strategic expenditures and has discussed the optimal acquisition of new external capital in light of this level of expenditure. Earlier we deferred consideration of the specific use of this optimal strategic level. We now consider this matter. To begin, we return to our discussion of the marginal return on the three types of strategic expenditures, marketing (MK), capital investment (CP), and research and development (RD). Our earlier discussion found substantive reasons to suggest the return from continued expansion of each of these programs can be expected to suffer declines, i.e., that in varying degrees, diminishing marginal returns will visit each of these three strategic program areas. If we define y_{MK}, y_{CP}, and y_{RD} as the marginal internal rate of return on additions to marketing, capital, and research and development budgets respectively, we are saying we expect each y to decline after a point. Figure 15–6 illustrates the situation.

FIGURE 15–6
Strategic Expenditure Relationships

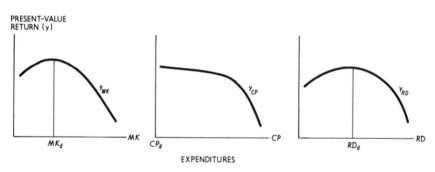

The behavior of y is shown as a function of increased expenditure levels. For the illustrative situation shown, diminishing marginal returns occur at expenditure of MK_d, CP_d, and RD_d. Notice that in this illustration $CP_d = 0$, i.e., diminishing returns to capital investments are hypothetically shown to occur immediately merely to illustrate this possibility. In Figure 15–7, the three marginal returns curves have been superimposed on the same graph. This shows the differences in marginal returns that characterize various expenditure regions. Consider the expenditure level A. If this amount were equally spent on MK, CP, and RD, i.e.:

$$MK_0 = CP_0 = RD_0 = A$$

differing marginal returns would result, as illustrated in Figure 15–7 by the values

$$y_{MK_0} > y_{CP_0} > y_{RD_0}$$

This result makes it clear that the equal expenditure of A on each strategic program is nonoptimal. For if funds are taken from either CP

FIGURE 15–7
Combined Marginal Returns

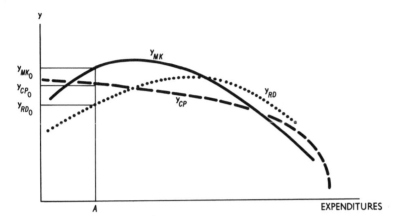

or RD and added to MK, the result will be greater total returns. The reason is that total return will be reduced by y_{CP_0} or y_{RD_0} for a small reduction of funds, and increased by y_{MK_0} for the repositioning of these funds in marketing budgets. Since y_{MK_0} is greater than the other two marginal values, total returns must be increased by the change. This logic continues to hold whenever

$$y_{MK} \neq y_{CP} \neq y_{RD}$$

for when marginal returns are not equal from expenditures on all categories it is possible to increase total returns by shifting funds from low marginal categories to high marginal categories. Thus, the only point where total returns can no longer be increased, i.e., the maximum, is where:

$$y_{MK} = y_{CP} = y_{RD}$$

Applying this equal-marginal rule leads to optimal expenditure combinations for various total expenditure levels. It also enables the total strategic expenditure curve (E) to be derived as a product of optimal combinations of MK, CP, and RD. Figure 15–8 depicts this process. In panel (a) of the figure, the optimal allocation of funds is found by passing a horizontal line through the curves at a particular marginal return. For example, at the point where the marginal return on all expenditure categories is equalized at y_a, expenditures of $MK = MK_a$, $CP = CP_a$, and $RD = 0$ result. Similarly, at the point where the marginal return on all categories is equalized at the lower rate y_b, expenditures of CP_b, MK_b, and RD_b result. In panel (b), the total strategic expenditure (E) curve originally depicted earlier in panel (B) of Figure 15–3 is derived. This derivation comes about by adding together horizontally

FIGURE 15–8
Optimal Strategic Expenditure Combinations

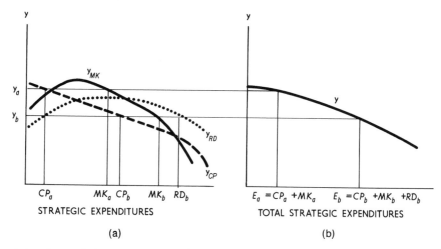

STRATEGIC EXPENDITURES

TOTAL STRATEGIC EXPENDITURES

(a)

(b)

the values of the y_{MK}, y_{CP}, and y_{RD} curves at all levels of y. Thus, at a marginal rate y_a, an optimal allocation involves total expenditures of $E_a = CP_a + MK_a$. Similarly, at y_b, $E_b = CP_b + MK_b + RD_b$ expenditures correspond to optimal allocation of E_b to the three individual strategic expenditure categories.

Figure 15–8 thus shows the optimal selection of *MK*, *CP*, and *RD* expenditure levels and in addition reveals the logic implicit in the construction of the total strategic expenditure curve that appeared earlier in this chapter in connection with our principle of extending E (in optimal proportions) until $y = r$. It is now interesting to note that the level of optimally allocated E where $y = r$ is (by definition of E) equal to the point where

$$y_{MK} = y_{CP} = y_{RD} = y = r$$

In other words, *in an overall shareholder wealth-maximizing position, the marginal internal rate of return from each category of strategic expenditure has been pushed by increased expenditures in that category to the level of the firm's cost of capital.*

ALLOCATION OF STOCKHOLDER DIVIDENDS

Our discussion to this point has provided all the necessary ingredients to determine a level of stockholder dividend allocation consistent with their wealth maximization. The essence of this determination is the view of dividends as a residual allocation category. Earlier, the optimal cutoff point for strategic expenditures was seen to be defined by r. Any funds remaining after the marginal return on strategic expenditures has been pushed to this point cannot be put to use by the firm at earning rates that increase stockholder wealth. These funds should be paid as dividends by the stockholder wealth-maximizing firm, as they will be more productively used by stockholders than by the firm in its own strategic expansion.

The possible situations confronting the firm in this regard are shown in Figure 15–9. Consider first the case of perfect information and markets.

FIGURE 15–9
Dividend-Opportunity Cost Relationships

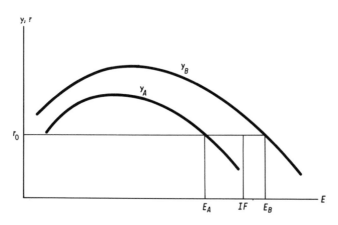

If the firm's cost of capital is r_0 and its marginal return from strategic expenditures is given by curve y_A, the firm exhausts minimum-return opportunities at expenditure level E_A. If internal discretionary funds are given by IF, then the dividend allocation consistent with shareholder wealth maximization is given by $(IF - E_A)$. On the other hand, if curve y_B represents marginal opportunities, then E_B is the optimal level of strategic expenditures, resulting in the acquisition of $(E_B - IF)$ volume of new external capital. For this case, the best dividend allocation is zero for the shareholder wealth-maximizing firm, since available funds may be more profitably employed in the firm's own business than by shareholders in alternative investments.

During times when the marginal return on the firm's new strategic expenditure is rising, we thus expect to find declines in dividend payout for shareholder-wealth maximizing firms *ceteris paribus*, and vice versa for periods when the firm's (not the market's) marginal return is falling.

When information and markets are not perfect, the firm may find it unattractive to follow the optimizing policy just outlined, due to the reaction of investors to the implied instability in dividend payout. Investors may see a dividend reduction as a sign of financial weakness in the firm, rather than an indication that the firm's strategic investment opportunities are expanding. The result may be a short-term decrease in the price of the stock. Perhaps for these reasons, many firms are extremely reluctant to eliminate or cut dividends regardless of the economic circumstances involved. For firms so constrained, dividends may be viewed as consisting of a fixed and a variable portion, where the fixed portion is influenced by past and present dividend levels and the variable portion relates to the model we have outlined. Such a firm would perhaps favor a customary year-end extra as a device to accommodate the fixed and variable portion. Under these policy constraints, the amount of the year-end extra could respond to the relationship between E and IF.

APPLICATIONS OF RESOURCE ALLOCATION THEORY

Our analysis has now dealt with the major resource allocation issues facing the firm, including selecting the best level of strategic expenditures, deciding the best allocation of these expenditures to marketing, research, and capital investment programs, and identifying the level of new external capital and dividend allocations consistent with this alloca-

FIGURE 15–10
Consequence of Easy Money

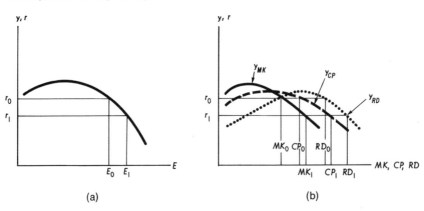

(a)   (b)

tion. At the present time, we see the major application of these results as qualitative in nature and, as with other prescriptive economic principles, basically a tool to aid our reasoning process about these issues. To illustrate this use of our theory, we now consider some examples of questions to which the theory provides qualitative answers.

1. *How should the firm respond to a set of changing aggregate economic conditions that are causing interest rates to fall and money to become more easily available to financial institutions?* Falling interest rates

associated with easy money imply that an increased pursuit of investment opportunities in general is pushing down the return on new
investment opportunities. Accordingly, the cost of capital r may be
decreased unless the money supply change exerts a positive and offsetting effect on expectations of return on new investment. We
ignore this possibility. As Figure 15–10 shows, a decrease in r from r_0

FIGURE 15–11
Impact of Competitive Innovation

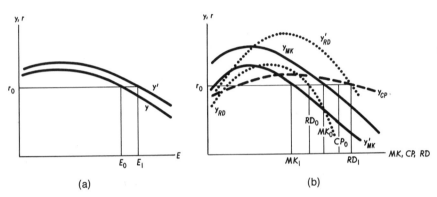

(a)   (b)

to r_1 leads to an increase in strategic expenditures from E_0 to E_1, consisting of an expansion of $(MK_1 - MK_o)$ in marketing programs,
$(CP_1 - CP_o)$ in capital investments, and $(RD_1 - RD_o)$ in research
and development expenditures.[5] Along with these expanding strategic
programs, the firm would be rationally inclined towards smaller dividend allocations, since the larger optimal E implies greater profitability in the internal use of funds relative to the changing opportunity
costs. Also, if $IF < E_1$, the firm would be induced to acquire new
external capital to finance a portion of the expanded strategic opportunities, in proportions corresponding to its optimal debt-equity ratio.
As a result of expanded strategic expenditures, we should also expect
greater flows of sales, profits, and internal discretionary funds, the
latter of which should lead to increased future growth.

2. *How is the firm affected by the introduction of a fundamentally
    superior product innovation by a major competitor?* Although our
    response to this question cannot be unequivocal, it does seem clear
    that the relative attractiveness of our firm's corresponding product
    line is now reduced. This might be expected to increase the produc-
    tivity of new product research efforts, since their returns would rise
    compared to the withering status quo position. Also, the return on
    marketing efforts may be expected to decline as the product becomes

---

[5] Of course, $(E_1 - E_o) = (MK_1 - MK_o + (CP_1 - CP_o) + (RD_1 - RD_o)$.

less saleable relative to competition. Figure 15–11 shows the effects. In panel (b) the marginal returns from RD are shown rising as the curve shifts up from y_{RD} to y_{RD}'. At the same time the marginal returns from marketing fall from y_{MK} to y_{MK}'. The result is a shift in the composition of strategic expenditures towards the now more crucial RD. Specifically, MK drops from MK_o to MK_1 while RD rises from RD_o to RD_1 and CP remains unaffected ($CP_1 = CP_o$). Although it is not clear what would happen to the total E, we have illustrated the case where the fall in MK is not as large as the rise in RD.

3. *What is the impact on the firm of a substantial increase in labor costs that the firm feels it cannot recover in its product markets through higher prices?* The basic impact is to reduce the discretionary funds flow associated with a given level of sales. This would reduce the marginal return from marketing expenditures, as a dollar of additional sales now produces less discretionary cash return. It would also most likely reduce the productivity of new product innovations since the higher costs eat into the net return on new product development. On the other hand, the marginal productivity of new labor-saving capital investments would rise. The overall result should be decreased marketing expenditures, decreased product development-type research and development expenditures, and increased labor-saving capital investments. The impact of these offsetting changes on total E is unclear, as is the effect on new external capital and dividends. However, the decline in marketing and product development expenditures should lead to reduced sales, profits, and flows of internal discretionary funds.

4. *Due to major and abrupt changes in the firm's product market conditions, sales projections and product market assessments are uniformly upgraded. What is the impact on the firm?* Such a change has the effect of increasing the expected return from investments in all strategic programs. Marketing programs now face increased potentials and delayed saturation points. Product improvements and new products face enlivened customer interest, and capital investments are viewed as being operated more intensively with expanded production volume. Due to upward shifts in all three component curves, the marginal return for total discretionary expenditures shifts up as shown in Figure 15–12 from y to y', leading to increased strategic expansion from E_o to E_1. If $E_o < IF < E_1$, this change would lead to the acquisition of ($E_1 - IF$) external capital, reduce dividends (in perfect markets) and associate with increased growth in corporate sales and profits, due to the firm's more aggressive pursuit of its customers, its greater product innovation efforts, and its quickened pace of cost-reducing capital investments.

FIGURE 15–12
Impact of Increased Expectations

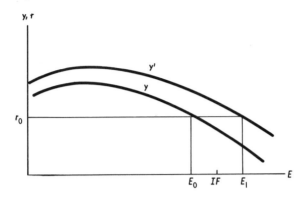

5. *A new law has been established that disallows interest payments by corporations as an expense for income-tax purposes. What is its impact on corporations' financial behavior?* The increase in the net cost of debt would increase the overall cost of capital. In addition, the higher debt cost would decrease the optimal debt-equity ratio and encourage the firm to substitute equity for debt in its capital structure. This substitution and movement to the new optimal debt-equity ratio would partially buffer the rise in the cost of capital. The resulting net increase in the cost of capital would reduce the optimal volume of marketing, research and development, and capital investments. If $IF > E$ after the decrease in E, then an additional result of this law would be an increase in dividends for the wealth-maximizing firm.

DISCUSSION QUESTIONS

1. With respect to the employment of discretionary funds, would you expect the opportunity cost of management to be very different from that of its stockholders in most U.S. corporations? Why or why not?

2. "The major impact of leverage is to cause firms to accept less profitable investments than if they had to use their own money. From an investment standpoint, I would steer clear of levered firms for this reason." Do you agree or disagree? Explain.

3. Consider the circumstance in which shareholders in a firm have a net preference for capital gains over dividends. In other words, if given the choice between a no-dividend stock expected to produce capital gains of 6 percent after taxes and a stock expected to yield 6 percent dividends after taxes but not expected to produce a capital gain, the stockholders will pick the first alternative. As a manager of a wealth-maximizing firm, how does the framework of this chapter suggest you should respond?

4 Do you see any reasons why a firm that has determined its optimal debt-equity ratio to be .60 would not be able to adjust its actual debt-equity ratio towards this figure? Explain.

5. Under what circumstance would the strict wealth-maximizing firm jointly pay dividends and acquire new external capital? Explain.

6. How would a substantial increase in direct labor costs affect the investment, financing, and dividend decisions of the wealth-maximizing firm?

APPENDIX

TABLE A-1

Coefficients of Correlation and t Ratios Significant at the .05 Level (Roman Type) and at the .01 Level (Bold-faced Type) for Varying Degrees of Freedom*

Degrees of freedom	Number of variables 2	3	4	5	6	7	9	13	25	t
1	.997 **1.000**	.999 **1.000**	.999 **1.000**	.999 **1.000**	1.000 **1.000**	1.000 **1.000**	1.000 **1.000**	1.000 **1.000**	1.000 **1.000**	12.706 **63.657**
2	.950 **.990**	.975 **.995**	.983 **.997**	.987 **.998**	.990 **.998**	.992 **.998**	.994 **.999**	.996 **.999**	.998 **1.000**	4.303 **9.925**
3	.878 **.959**	.930 **.976**	.950 **.983**	.961 **.987**	.968 **.990**	.973 **.991**	.979 **.993**	.986 **.995**	.993 **.998**	3.182 **5.841**
4	.811 **.917**	.881 **.949**	.912 **.962**	.930 **.970**	.942 **.975**	.950 **.979**	.961 **.984**	.973 **.989**	.986 **.994**	2.776 **4.604**
5	.754 **.874**	.836 **.917**	.874 **.937**	.898 **.949**	.914 **.957**	.925 **.963**	.941 **.971**	.958 **.980**	.978 **.989**	2.571 **4.032**
6	.707 **.834**	.795 **.886**	.839 **.911**	.867 **.927**	.886 **.938**	.900 **.946**	.920 **.957**	.943 **.969**	.969 **.983**	2.447 **3.707**
7	.666 **.798**	.758 **.855**	.807 **.885**	.838 **.904**	.860 **.918**	.876 **.928**	.900 **.942**	.927 **.958**	.960 **.977**	2.365 **3.499**
8	.632 **.765**	.726 **.827**	.777 **.860**	.811 **.882**	.835 **.898**	.854 **.909**	.880 **.926**	.912 **.946**	.950 **.970**	2.306 **3.355**
9	.602 **.735**	.697 **.800**	.750 **.836**	.786 **.861**	.812 **.878**	.832 **.891**	.861 **.911**	.897 **.934**	.941 **.963**	2.262 **3.250**
10	.576 **.708**	.671 **.776**	.726 **.814**	.763 **.840**	.790 **.859**	.812 **.874**	.843 **.895**	.882 **.922**	.932 **.955**	2.228 **3.169**
11	.553 **.684**	.648 **.753**	.703 **.793**	.741 **.821**	.770 **.841**	.792 **.857**	.826 **.880**	.868 **.910**	.922 **.948**	2.201 **3.106**
12	.532 **.661**	.627 **.732**	.683 **.773**	.722 **.802**	.751 **.824**	.774 **.841**	.809 **.866**	.854 **.898**	.913 **.940**	2.179 **3.055**
13	.514 **.641**	.608 **.712**	.664 **.755**	.703 **.785**	.733 **.807**	.757 **.825**	.794 **.852**	.840 **.886**	.904 **.932**	2.160 **3.012**
14	.497 **.623**	.590 **.694**	.646 **.737**	.686 **.768**	.717 **.792**	.741 **.810**	.779 **.838**	.828 **.875**	.895 **.924**	2.145 **2.977**
15	.482 **.606**	.574 **.677**	.630 **.721**	.670 **.752**	.701 **.776**	.726 **.796**	.765 **.825**	.815 **.864**	.886 **.917**	2.131 **2.947**
16	.468 **.590**	.559 **.662**	.615 **.706**	.655 **.738**	.686 **.762**	.712 **.782**	.751 **.813**	.803 **.853**	.878 **.909**	2.120 **2.921**
17	.456 **.575**	.545 **.647**	.601 **.691**	.641 **.724**	.673 **.749**	.698 **.769**	.738 **.800**	.792 **.842**	.869 **.902**	2.110 **2.898**
18	.444 **.561**	.532 **.633**	.587 **.678**	.628 **.710**	.660 **.736**	.686 **.756**	.726 **.789**	.781 **.832**	.861 **.894**	2.101 **2.878**
19	.433 **.549**	.520 **.620**	.575 **.665**	.615 **.698**	.647 **.723**	.674 **.744**	.714 **.778**	.770 **.822**	.853 **.887**	2.093 **2.861**
20	.423 **.537**	.509 **.608**	.563 **.652**	.604 **.685**	.636 **.712**	.662 **.733**	.703 **.767**	.760 **.812**	.845 **.880**	2.086 **2.845**
21	.413 **.526**	.498 **.596**	.552 **.641**	.592 **.674**	.624 **.700**	.651 **.722**	.693 **.756**	.750 **.803**	.837 **.873**	2.080 **2.831**
22	.404 **.515**	.488 **.585**	.542 **.630**	.582 **.663**	.614 **.690**	.640 **.712**	.682 **.746**	.740 **.794**	.830 **.866**	2.074 **2.819**
23	.396 **.505**	.479 **.574**	.532 **.619**	.572 **.652**	.604 **.679**	.630 **.701**	.673 **.736**	.731 **.785**	.823 **.859**	2.069 **2.807**

* Adapted from Wallace, H. A., and Snedecor, G. W., *Correlation and Machine Calculation*, Iowa Srate Ptess, 1931. by J. P. Guilford *Fnudamental Statistics in Psychology and Education* McGraw-Hill, 1956. Reproduced by permission of authors and publishers.

TABLE A–1 (Continued)

Degrees of freedom	Number of variables									t
	2	3	4	5	6	7	9	13	25	
24	.388 .496	.470 .565	.523 .609	.562 .642	.594 .669	.621 .692	.663 .727	.722 .776	.815 .852	2.064 2.797
25	.381 .487	.462 .555	.514 .600	.553 .633	.585 .660	.612 .682	.654 .718	.714 .768	.808 .846	2.060 2.787
26	.374 .478	.454 .546	.506 .590	.545 .624	.576 .651	.603 .673	.645 .709	.706 .760	.802 .839	2.056 2.779
27	.367 .470	.446 .538	.498 .582	.536 .615	.568 .642	.594 .664	.637 .701	.698 .752	.795 .833	2.052 2.771
28	.361 .463	.439 .530	.490 .573	.529 .606	.560 .634	.586 .656	.629 .692	.690 .744	.788 .827	2.048 2.763
29	.355 .456	.432 .522	.482 .565	.521 .598	.552 .625	.579 .648	.621 .685	.682 .737	.782 .821	2.045 2.756
30	.349 .449	.426 .514	.476 .558	.514 .591	.545 .618	.571 .640	.614 .677	.675 .729	.776 .815	2.042 2.750
35	.325 .418	.397 .481	.445 .523	.482 .556	.512 .582	.538 .605	.580 .642	.642 .696	.746 .786	2.030 2.724
40	.304 .393	.373 .454	.419 .494	.455 .526	.484 .552	.509 .575	.551 .612	.613 .667	.720 .761	2.021 2.704
45	.288 .372	.353 .430	.397 .470	.432 .501	.460 .527	.485 .549	.526 .586	.587 .640	.696 .737	2.014 2.690
50	.273 .354	.336 .410	.379 .449	.412 .479	.440 .504	.464 .526	.504 .562	.565 .617	.674 .715	2.008 2.678
60	.250 .325	.308 .377	.348 .414	.380 .442	.406 .466	.429 .488	.467 .523	.526 .577	.636 .677	2.000 2.660
70	.233 .302	.286 .351	.324 .386	.354 .413	.379 .436	.401 .456	.438 .491	.495 .544	.604 .644	1.994 2.648
80	.217 .283	.269 .330	.304 .362	.332 .389	.356 .411	.377 .431	.413 .464	.469 .516	.576 .615	1.990 2.638
90	.205 .267	.254 .312	.288 .343	.315 .368	.338 .390	.358 .409	.392 .441	.446 .492	.552 .590	1.987 2.632
100	.195 .254	.241 .297	.274 .327	.300 .351	.322 .372	.341 .330	.374 .421	.426 .470	.530 .568	1.984 2.626
125	.174 .228	.216 .266	.246 .294	.269 .316	.290 .335	.307 .352	.338 .381	.387 .428	.485 .521	1.979 2.616
150	.159 .208	.198 .244	.225 .270	.247 .290	.266 .308	.282 .324	.310 .351	.356 .395	.450 .484	1.976 2.609
200	.138 .181	.172 .212	.196 .234	.215 .253	.231 .269	.246 .283	.271 .307	.312 .347	.398 .430	1.972 2.601
300	.113 .148	.141 .174	.160 .192	.176 .208	.190 .221	.202 .233	.223 .253	.258 .287	.332 .359	1.968 2.592
400	.098 .128	.122 .151	.139 .167	.153 .180	.165 .192	.176 .202	.194 .220	.225 .250	.291 .315	1.966 2.588
500	.088 .115	.109 .135	.124 .150	.137 .162	.148 .172	.157 .182	.174 .198	.202 .225	.262 .284	1.965 2.586
1000	.062 .081	.077 .096	.088 .106	.097 .115	.105 .122	.112 .129	.124 .141	.144 .160	.188 .204	1.962 2.581
∞										1.960 2.576

TABLE A–2

The Durbin-Watson of Statistic (Significance poits of d_L and d_U: 5%

n	$k' = 1$		$k' = 2$		$k' = 3$		$k' = 4$		$k' = 5$	
	d_L	d_U	d_L	d_{U}	d_L	d_U	d_L	d_U	d_L	d_U
15	1.08	1.36	0.95	1.54	0.82	1.75	0.69	1.97	0.56	2.21
16	1.10	1.37	0.98	1.54	0.86	1.73	0.74	1.93	0.62	2.15
17	1.13	1.38	1.02	1.54	0.90	1.71	0.78	1.90	0.67	2.10
18	1.16	1.39	1.05	1.53	0.93	1.69	0.82	1.87	0.71	2.06
19	1.18	1.40	1.08	1.53	0.97	1.68	0.86	1.85	0.75	2.02
20	1.20	1.41	1.10	1.54	1.00	1.68	0.90	1.83	0.79	1.99
21	1.22	1.42	1.13	1.54	1.03	1.67	0.93	1.81	0.83	1.96
22	1.24	1.43	1.15	1.54	1.05	1.66	0.96	1.80	0.86	1.94
23	1.26	1.44	1.17	1.54	1.08	1.66	0.99	1.79	0.90	1.92
24	1.27	1.45	1.19	1.55	1.10	1.66	1.01	1.78	0.93	1.90
25	1.29	1.45	1.21	1.55	1.12	1.66	1.04	1.77	0.95	1.89
26	1.30	1.46	1.22	1.55	1.14	1.65	1.06	1.76	0.98	1.88
27	1.32	1.47	1.24	1.56	1.16	1.65	1.08	1.76	1.01	1.86
28	1.33	1.48	1.26	1.56	1.18	1.65	1.10	1.75	1.03	1.85
29	1.34	1.48	1.27	1.56	1.20	1.65	1.12	1.74	1.05	1.84
30	1.35	1.49	1.28	1.57	1.21	1.65	1.14	1.74	1.07	1.83
31	1.36	1.50	1.30	1.57	1.23	1.65	1.16	1.74	1.09	1.83
32	1.37	1.50	1.31	1.57	1.24	1.65	1.18	1.73	1.11	1.82
33	1.38	1.51	1.32	1.58	1.26	1.65	1.19	1.73	1.13	1.81
34	1.39	1.51	1.33	1.58	1.27	1.65	1.21	1.73	1.15	1.81
35	1.40	1.52	1.34	1.58	1.28	1.65	1.22	1.73	1.16	1.80
36	1.41	1.52	1.35	1.59	1.29	1.65	1.24	1.73	1.18	1.80
37	1.42	1.53	1.36	1.59	1.31	1.66	1.25	1.72	1.19	1.80
38	1.43	1.54	1.37	1.59	1.32	1.66	1.26	1.72	1.21	1.79
39	1.43	1.54	1.38	1.60	1.33	1.66	1.27	1.72	1.22	1.79
40	1.44	1.54	1.39	1.60	1.34	1.66	1.29	1.72	1.23	1.79
45	1.48	1.57	1.43	1.62	1.38	1.67	1.34	1.72	1.29	1.78
50	1.50	1.59	1.46	1.63	1.42	1.67	1.38	1.72	1.34	1.77
55	1.53	1.60	1.49	1.64	1.45	1.68	1.41	1.72	1.38	1.77
60	.1.55	1.62	1.51	1.65	1.48	1.69	1.44	1.73	1.41	1.77
65	1.57	1.63	1.54	1.66	1.50	1.70	1.47	1.73	1.44	1.77
70	1.58	1.64	1.55	1.67	1.52	1.70	1.49	1.74	1.46	1.77
75	1.60	1.65	1.57	1.68	1.54	1.71	1.51	1.74	1.49	1.77
80	1.61	1.66	1.59	1.69	1.56	1.72	1.53	1.74	1.51	1.77
85	1.62	1.67	1.60	1.70	1.57	1.72	1.55	1.75	1.52	1.77
90	1.63	1.68	1.61	1.70	1.59	1.73	1.57	1.75	1.54	1.78
95	1.64	1.69	1.62	1.71	1.60	1.73	1.58	1.75	1.56	1.78
100	1.65	1.69	1.63	1.72	1.61	1.74	1.59	1.76	1.57	1.78

Note: k' = number of explanatory variables excluding the constant term.

TABLE A–2 (Continued)
(significance points of d_L and d_U. 2.5%)

n	k' = 1		k' = 2		k' = 3		k' = 4		k' = 5	
	d_L	d_U	d_L	d_U	d_L	d_U	d_L	d_U	d_L	d_U
15	0.95	1.23	0.83	1.40	0.71	1.61	0.59	1.84	0.48	2.09
16	0.98	1.24	0.86	1.40	0.75	1.59	0.64	1.80	0.53	2.03
17	1.01	1.25	0.90	1.40	0.79	1.58	0.68	1.77	0.57	1.98
18	1.03	1.26	0.93	1.40	0.82	1.56	0.72	1.74	0.62	1.93
19	1.06	1.28	0.96	1.41	0.86	1.55	0.76	1.72	0.66	1.90
20	1.08	1.28	0.99	1.41	0.89	1.55	0.79	1.70	0.70	1.87
21	1.10	1.30	1.01	1.41	0.92	1.54	0.83	1.69	0.73	1.84
22	1.12	1.31	1.04	1.42	0.95	1.54	0.86	1.68	0.77	1.82
23	1.14	1.32	1.06	1.42	0.97	1.54	0.89	1.67	0.80	1.80
24	1.16	1.33	1.08	1.43	1.00	1.54	0.91	1.66	0.83	1.79
25	1.18	1.34	1.10	1.43	1.02	1.54	0.94	1.65	0.86	1.77
26	1.19	1.35	1.12	1.44	1.04	1.54	0.96	1.65	0.88	1.76
27	1.21	1.36	1.13	1.44	1.06	1.54	0.99	1.64	0.91	1.75
28	1.22	1.37	1.15	1.45	1.08	1.54	1.01	1.64	0.93	1.74
29	1.24	1.38	1.17	1.45	1.10	1.54	1.03	1.63	0.96	1.73
30	1.25	1.38	1.18	1.46	1.12	1.54	1.05	1.63	0.98	1.73
31	1.26	1.39	1.20	1.47	1.13	1.55	1.07	1.63	1.00	1.72
32	1.27	1.40	1.21	1.47	1.15	1.55	1.08	1.63	1.02	1.71
33	1.28	1.41	1.22	1.48	1.16	1.55	1.10	1.63	1.04	1.71
34	1.29	1.41	1.24	1.48	1.17	1.55	1.12	1.63	1.06	1.70
35	1.30	1.42	1.25	1.48	1.19	1.55	1.13	1.63	1.07	1.70
36	1.31	1.43	1.26	1.49	1.20	1.56	1.15	1.63	1.09	1.70
37	1.32	1.43	1.27	1.49	1.21	1.56	1.16	1.62	1.10	1.70
38	1.33	1.44	1.28	1.50	1.23	1.56	1.17	1.62	1.12	1.70
39	1.34	1.44	1.29	1.50	1.24	1.56	1.19	1.63	1.13	1.69
40	1.35	1.45	1.30	1.51	1.25	1.57	1.20	1.63	1.15	1.69
45	1.39	1.48	1.34	1.53	1.30	1.58	1.25	1.63	1.21	1.69
50	1.42	1.50	1.38	1.54	1.34	1.59	1.30	1.64	1.26	1.69
55	1.45	1.52	1.41	1.56	1.37	1.60	1.33	1.64	1.30	1.69
60	1.47	1.54	1.44	1.57	1.40	1.61	1.37	1.65	1.33	1.69
65	1.49	1.55	1.46	1.59	1.43	1.62	1.40	1.66	1.36	1.69
70	1.51	1.57	1.48	1.60	1.45	1.63	1.42	1.66	1.39	1.70
75	1.53	1.58	1.50	1.61	1.47	1.64	1.45	1.67	1.42	1.70
80	1.54	1.59	1.52	1.62	1.49	1.65	1.47	1.67	1.44	1.70
85	1.56	1.60	1.53	1.63	1.51	1.65	1.49	1.68	1.46	1.71
90	1.57	1.61	1.55	1.64	1.53	1.66	1.50	1.69	1.48	1.71
95	1.58	1.62	1.56	1.65	1.54	1.67	1.52	1.69	1.50	1.71
100	1.59	1.63	1.57	1.65	1.55	1.67	1.53	1.70	1.51	1.72

TABLE A–2 (Concluded)
(significance points of d_L and d_U: 1%)

n	k' = 1		k' = 2		k' = 3		k' = 4		k' = 5	
	d_L	d_U	d_L	d_U	d_L	d_U	d_L	d_U	d_L	d_U
15	0.81	1.07	0.70	1.25	0.59	1.46	0.49	1.70	0.39	1.96
16	0.84	1.09	0.74	1.25	0.63	1.44	0.53	1.66	0.44	1.90
17	0.87	1.10	0.77	1.25	0.67	1.43	0.57	1.63	0.48	1.85
18	0.90	1.12	0.80	1.26	0.71	1.42	0.61	1.60	0.52	1.80
19	0.93	1.13	0.83	1.26	0.74	1.41	0.65	1.58	0.56	1.77
20	0.95	1.15	0.86	1.27	0.77	1.41	0.68	1.57	0.60	1.74
21	0.97	1.16	0.89	1.27	0.80	1.41	0.72	1.55	0.63	1.71
22	1.00	1.17	0.91	1.28	0.83	1.40	0.75	1.54	0.66	1.69
23	1.02	1.19	0.94	1.29	0.86	1.40	0.77	1.53	0.70	1.67
24	1.04	1.20	0.96	1.30	0.88	1.41	0.80	1.53	0.72	1.66
25	1.05	1.21	0.98	1.30	0.90	1.41	0.83	1.52	0.75	1.65
26	1.07	1.22	1.00	1.31	0.93	1.41	0.85	1.52	0.78	1.64
27	1.09	1.23	1.02	1.32	0.95	1.41	0.88	1.51	0.81	1.63
28	1.10	1.24	1.04	1.32	0.97	1.41	0.90	1.51	0.83	1.62
29	1.12	1.25	1.05	1.33	0.99	1.42	0.92	1.51	0.85	1.61
30	1.13	1.26	1.07	1.34	1.01	1.42	0.94	1.51	0.88	1.61
31	1.15	1.27	1.08	1.34	1.02	1.42	0.96	1.51	0.90	1.60
32	1.16	1.28	1.10	1.35	1.04	1.43	0.98	1.51	0.92	1.60
33	1.17	1.29	1.11	1.36	1.05	1.43	1.00	1.51	0.94	1.59
34	1.18	1.30	1.13	1.36	1.07	1.43	1.01	1.51	0.95	1.59
35	1.19	1.31	1.14	1.37	1.08	1.44	1.03	1.51	0.97	1.59
36	1.21	1.32	1.15	1.38	1.10	1.44	1.04	1.51	0.99	1.59
37	1.22	1.32	1.16	1.38	1.11	1.45	1.06	1.51	1.00	1.59
38	1.23	1.33	1.18	1.39	1.12	1.45	1.07	1.52	1.02	1.58
39	1.24	1.34	1.19	1.39	1.14	1.45	1.09	1.52	1.03	1.58
40	1.25	1.34	1.20	1.40	1.15	1.46	1.10	1.52	1.05	1.58
45	1.29	1.38	1.24	1.42	1.20	1.48	1.16	1.53	1.11	1.58
50	1.32	1.40	1.28	1.45	1.24	1.49	1.20	1.54	1.16	1.59
55	1.36	1.43	1.32	1.47	1.28	1.51	1.25	1.55	1.21	1.59
60	1.38	1.45	1.35	1.48	1.32	1.52	1.28	1.56	1.25	1.60
65	1.41	1.47	1.38	1.50	1.35	1.53	1.31	1.57	1.28	1.61
70	1.43	1.49	1.40	1.52	1.37	1.55	1.34	1.58	1.31	1.61
75	1.45	1.50	1.42	1.53	1.39	1.56	1.37	1.59	1.34	1.62
80	1.47	1.52	1.44	1.54	1.42	1.57	1.39	1.60	1.36	1.62
85	1.48	1.53	1.46	1.55	1.43	1.58	1.41	1.60	1.39	1.63
90	1.50	1.54	1.47	1.56	1.45	1.59	1.43	1.61	1.41	1.64
95	1.51	1.55	1.49	1.57	1.47	1.60	1.45	1.62	1.42	1.64
100	1.52	1.56	1.50	1.58	1.48	1.60	1.46	1.63	1.44	1.65

TABLE A–3

Table of Areas under an F Distribution*

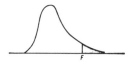

n_1 = degrees of freedom for numerator

n_2 = degrees of freedom for denominator

n_2	1	2	3	4	5	6	7	8	9	10	11	12
1	161	200	216	225	230	234	237	239	241	242	243	244
	4,052	**4,999**	**5,403**	**5,625**	**5,764**	**5,859**	**5,928**	**5,981**	**6,022**	**6,056**	**6,082**	**6,106**
2	18.51	19.00	19.16	19.25	19.30	19.33	19.36	19.37	19.38	19.39	19.40	19.41
	98.49	**99.01**	**99.17**	**99.25**	**99.30**	**99.33**	**99.34**	**99.36**	**99.38**	**99.40**	**99.41**	**99.42**
3	10.13	9.55	9.28	9.12	9.01	8.94	8.88	8.84	8.81	8.78	8.76	8.74
	34.12	**30.81**	**29.46**	**28.71**	**28.24**	**27.91**	**27.67**	**27.49**	**27.34**	**27.23**	**27.13**	**27.05**
4	7.71	6.94	6.59	6.39	6.26	6.16	6.09	6.04	6.00	5.96	5.93	5.91
	21.20	**18.00**	**16.69**	**15.98**	**15.52**	**15.21**	**14.98**	**14.80**	**14.66**	**14.54**	**14.45**	**14.37**
5	6.61	5.79	5.41	5.19	5.05	4.95	4.88	4.82	4.78	4.74	4.70	4.68
	16.26	**13.27**	**12.06**	**11.39**	**10.97**	**10.67**	**10.45**	**10.27**	**10.15**	**10.05**	**9.96**	**9.89**
6	5.99	5.14	4.76	4.53	4.39	4.28	4.21	4.15	4.10	4.06	4.03	4.00
	13.74	**10.92**	**9.78**	**9.15**	**8.75**	**8.47**	**8.26**	**8.10**	**7.98**	**7.87**	**7.79**	**7.72**
7	5.59	4.74	4.35	4.12	3.97	3.87	3.79	3.73	3.68	3.63	3.60	3.57
	12.25	**9.55**	**8.45**	**7.85**	**7.46**	**7.19**	**7.00**	**6.84**	**6.71**	**6.62**	**6.54**	**6.47**
8	5.32	4.46	4.07	3.84	3.69	3.58	3.50	3.44	3.39	3.34	3.31	3.28
	11.26	**8.65**	**7.59**	**7.01**	**6.63**	**6.37**	**6.19**	**6.03**	**5.91**	**5.82**	**5.74**	**5.67**
9	5.12	4.26	3.86	3.63	3.48	3.37	3.29	3.23	3.18	3.13	3.10	3.07
	10.56	**8.02**	**6.99**	**6.42**	**6.06**	**5.80**	**5.62**	**5.47**	**5.35**	**5.26**	**5.18**	**5.11**
10	4.96	4.10	3.71	3.48	3.33	3.22	3.14	3.07	3.02	2.97	2.94	2.91
	10.04	**7.56**	**6.55**	**5.99**	**5.64**	**5.39**	**5.21**	**5.06**	**4.95**	**4.85**	**4.78**	**4.71**
11	4.84	3.98	3.59	3.36	3.20	3 09	3.01	2.95	2.90	2.86	2.82	2.79
	9.65	**7.20**	**6.22**	**5.67**	**5.32**	**5.07**	**4.88**	**4.74**	**4.63**	**4.54**	**4.46**	**4.40**
12	4.75	3.88	3.49	3.26	3.11	3.00	2.92	2.85	2.80	2.76	2.72	2.69
	9.33	**6.93**	**5.95**	**5.41**	**5.06**	**4.82**	**4.65**	**4.50**	**4.39**	**4.30**	**4.22**	**4.16**
13	4.67	3.80	3.41	3.18	3.02	2.92	2.84	2.77	2.72	2.67	2.63	2.60
	9.07	**6.70**	**5.74**	**5.20**	**4.86**	**4.62**	**4.44**	**4.30**	**4.19**	**4.10**	**4.02**	**3.96**
14	4.60	3.74	3.34	3.11	2.96	2.85	2.77	2.70	2.65	2.60	2.56	2.53
	8.86	**6.51**	**5.56**	**5.03**	**4.69**	**4.46**	**4.28**	**4.14**	**4.03**	**3.94**	**3.86**	**3.80**
15	4.54	3.68	3.29	3.06	2.90	2.79	2.70	2.64	2.59	2.55	2.51	2.48
	8.68	**6.36**	**5.42**	**4.89**	**4.56**	**4.32**	**4.14**	**4.00**	**3.89**	**3.80**	**3.73**	**3.67**
16	4.49	3.63	3.24	3.01	2.85	2.74	2.66	2.59	2.54	2.49	2.45	2.42
	8.53	**6.23**	**5.29**	**4.77**	**4.44**	**4.20**	**4.03**	**3.89**	**3.78**	**3.69**	**3.61**	**3.55**
17	4.45	3.59	3.20	2.96	2.81	2.70	2.62	2.55	2.50	2.45	2.41	2.38
	8.40	**6.11**	**5.18**	**4.67**	**4.34**	**4.10**	**3.93**	**3.79**	**3.68**	**3.59**	**3.52**	**3.45**
18	4.41	3.55	3.16	2.93	2.77	2.66	2.58	2.51	2.46	2.41	2.37	2.34
	8.28	**6.01**	**5.09**	**4.58**	**4.25**	**4.01**	**3.85**	**3.71**	**3.60**	**3.51**	**3.44**	**3.37**
19	4.38	3.52	3.13	2.90	2.74	2.63	2.55	2.48	2.43	2.38	2.34	2.31
	8.18	**5.93**	**5.01**	**4.50**	**4.17**	**3.94**	**3.77**	**3.63**	**3.52**	**3.43**	**3.36**	**3.30**
20	4.35	3.49	3.10	2.87	2.71	2.60	2.52	2.45	2.40	2.35	2.31	2.28
	8.10	**5.85**	**4.94**	**4.43**	**4.10**	**3.87**	**3.71**	**3.56**	**3.45**	**3.37**	**3.30**	**3.23**
21	4.32	3.47	3.07	2.84	2.68	2.57	2.49	2.42	2.37	2.32	2.28	2.25
	8.02	**5.78**	**4.87**	**4.37**	**4.04**	**3.81**	**3.65**	**3.51**	**3.40**	**3.31**	**3.24**	**3.17**
22	4.30	3.44	3.05	2.82	2.66	2.55	2.47	2.40	2.35	2.30	2.26	2.23
	7.94	**5.72**	**4.82**	**4.31**	**3.99**	**3.76**	**3.59**	**3.45**	**3.35**	**3.26**	**3.18**	**3.12**
23	4.28	3.42	3.03	2.80	2.64	2.53	2.45	2.38	2.32	2.28	2.24	2.20
	7.88	**5.66**	**4.76**	**4.26**	**3.94**	**3.71**	**3.54**	**3.41**	**3.30**	**3.21**	**3.14**	**3.07**
24	4.26	3.40	3.01	2.78	2.62	2.51	2.43	2.36	2.30	2.26	2.22	2.18
	7.82	**5.61**	**4.72**	**4.22**	**3.90**	**3.67**	**3.50**	**3.36**	**3.25**	**3.17**	**3.09**	**3.03**
25	4.24	3.38	2.99	2.76	2.60	2.49	2.41	2.34	2.28	2.24	2.20	2.16
	7.77	**5.57**	**4.68**	**4.18**	**3.86**	**3.63**	**3.46**	**3.32**	**3.21**	**3.13**	**3.05**	**2.99**
26	4.22	3.37	2.98	2.74	2.59	2.47	2.39	2.32	2.27	2.22	2.18	2.15
	7.72	**5.53**	**4.64**	**4.14**	**3.82**	**3.59**	**3.42**	**3.29**	**3.17**	**3.09**	**3.02**	**2.96**

* Reproduced by permission from *Statistical Methods*, 5th ed., by George W. Snedecor, ©1956 by the Iowa State University Press. For given values of degrees of freedom, n_2 for the numerator and n_2 for the denominator, the entries in the table indicate the corresponding values of F for areas in the right tail of the distribution. The value of F indicating that 5% of the total area is in the right tail printed in light type; the value of F indicating that 1% of the total area is in the right tail printed in bold type. The areas are shown in the illustration above. For example, given $n_1 = 4$ and $n_2 = 9$, the values of F is 3.63 when 5% of the total area is in the right tail of the distribution.

TABLE A–3 (Continued)

$n_1 =$ degrees of freedom for numerator

$n_2 =$ degrees of freedom for denominator

	14	16	20	24	30	40	50	75	100	200	500	∞
1	245 **6,142**	246 **6,169**	248 **6,208**	249 **6,234**	250 **6,258**	251 **6,286**	252 **6,302**	253 **6,323**	253 **6,334**	254 **6,352**	254 **6,361**	254 **6,366**
2	19.42 **99.43**	19.43 **99.44**	19.44 **99.45**	19.45 **99.46**	19.46 **99.47**	19.47 **99.48**	19.47 **99.48**	19.48 **99.49**	19.49 **99.49**	19.49 **99.49**	19.50 **99.50**	19.50 **99.50**
3	8.71 **26.92**	8.69 **26.83**	8.66 **26.69**	8.64 **26.60**	8.62 **26.50**	8.60 **26.41**	8.58 **26.35**	8.57 **26.27**	8.56 **26.23**	8.54 **26.18**	8.54 **26.14**	8.53 **26.12**
4	5.87 **14.24**	5.84 **14.15**	5.80 **14.02**	5.77 **13.93**	5.74 **13.83**	5.71 **13.74**	5.70 **13.69**	5.68 **13.61**	5.66 **13.57**	5.65 **13.52**	5.64 **13.48**	5.63 **13.46**
5	4.64 **9.77**	4.60 **9.68**	4.56 **9.55**	4.53 **9.47**	4.50 **9.38**	4.46 **9.29**	4.44 **9.24**	4.42 **9.17**	4.40 **9.13**	4.38 **9.07**	4.37 **9.04**	4.36 **9.02**
6	3.96 **7.60**	3.92 **7.52**	3.87 **7.39**	3.84 **7.31**	3.81 **7.23**	3.77 **7.14**	3.75 **7.09**	3.72 **7.02**	3.71 **6.99**	3.69 **6.94**	3.68 **6.90**	3.67 **6.88**
7	3.52 **6.35**	3.49 **6.27**	3.44 **6.15**	3.41 **6.07**	3.38 **5.98**	3.34 **5.90**	3.32 **5.85**	3.29 **5.78**	3.28 **5.75**	3.25 **5.70**	3.24 **5.67**	3.23 **5.65**
8	3.23 **5.56**	3.20 **5.48**	3.15 **5.36**	3.12 **5.28**	3.08 **5.20**	3.05 **5.11**	3.03 **5.06**	3.00 **5.00**	2.98 **4.96**	2.96 **4.91**	2.94 **4.88**	2.93 **4.86**
9	3.02 **5.00**	2.98 **4.92**	2.93 **4.80**	2.90 **4.73**	2.86 **4.64**	2.82 **4.56**	2.80 **4.51**	2.77 **4.45**	2.76 **4.41**	2.73 **4.36**	2.72 **4.33**	2.71 **4.31**
10	2.86 **4.60**	2.82 **4.52**	2.77 **4.41**	2.74 **4.33**	2.70 **4.25**	2.67 **4.17**	2.64 **4.12**	2.61 **4.05**	2.59 **4.01**	2.56 **3.96**	2.55 **3.93**	2.54 **3.91**
11	2.74 **4.29**	2.70 **4.21**	2.65 **4.10**	2.61 **4.02**	2.57 **3.94**	2.53 **3.86**	2.50 **3.80**	2.47 **3.74**	2.45 **3.70**	2.42 **3.66**	2.41 **3.62**	2.40 **3.60**
12	2.64 **4.05**	2.60 **3.98**	2.54 **3.86**	2.50 **3.78**	2.46 **3.70**	2.42 **3.61**	2.40 **3.56**	2.36 **3.49**	2.35 **3.46**	2.32 **3.41**	2.31 **3.38**	2.30 **3.36**
13	2.55 **3.85**	2.51 **3.78**	2.46 **3.67**	2.42 **3.59**	2.38 **3.51**	2.34 **3.42**	2.32 **3.37**	2.28 **3.30**	2.26 **3.27**	2.24 **3.21**	2.22 **3.18**	2.21 **3.16**
14	2.48 **3.70**	2.44 **3.62**	2.39 **3.51**	2.35 **3.43**	2.31 **3.34**	2.27 **3.26**	2.24 **3.21**	2.21 **3.14**	2.19 **3.11**	2.16 **3.06**	2.14 **3.02**	2.13 **3.00**
15	2.43 **3.56**	2.39 **3.48**	2.33 **3.36**	2.29 **3.29**	2.25 **3.20**	2.21 **3.12**	2.18 **3.07**	2.15 **3.00**	2.12 **2.97**	2.10 **2.92**	2.08 **2.89**	2.07 **2.87**
16	2.37 **3.45**	2.33 **3.37**	2.28 **3.25**	2.24 **3.18**	2.20 **3.10**	2.16 **3.01**	2.13 **2.96**	2.09 **2.89**	2.07 **2.86**	2.04 **2.80**	2.02 **2.77**	2.01 **2.75**
17	2.33 **3.35**	2.29 **3.27**	2.23 **3.16**	2.19 **3.08**	2.15 **3.00**	2.11 **2.92**	2.08 **2.86**	2.04 **2.79**	2.02 **2.76**	1.99 **2.70**	1.97 **2.67**	1.96 **2.65**
18	2.29 **3.27**	2.25 **3.19**	2.19 **3.07**	2.15 **3.00**	2.11 **2.91**	2.07 **2.83**	2.04 **2.78**	2.00 **2.71**	1.98 **2.68**	1.95 **2.62**	1.93 **2.59**	1.92 **2.57**
19	2.26 **3.19**	2.21 **3.12**	2.15 **3.00**	2.11 **2.92**	2.07 **2.84**	2.02 **2.76**	2.00 **2.70**	1.96 **2.63**	1.94 **2.60**	1.91 **2.54**	1.90 **2.51**	1.88 **2.49**
20	2.23 **3.13**	2.18 **3.05**	2.12 **2.94**	2.08 **2.86**	2.04 **2.77**	1.99 **2.69**	1.96 **2.63**	1.92 **2.56**	1.90 **2.53**	1.87 **2.47**	1.85 **2.44**	1.84 **2.42**
21	2.20 **3.07**	2.15 **2.99**	2.09 **2.88**	2.05 **2.80**	2.00 **2.72**	1.96 **2.63**	1.93 **2.58**	1.89 **2.51**	1.87 **2.47**	1.84 **2.42**	1.82 **2.38**	1.81 **2.36**
22	2.18 **3.02**	2.13 **2.94**	2.07 **2.83**	2.03 **2.75**	1.98 **2.67**	1.93 **2.58**	1.91 **2.53**	1.87 **2.46**	1.84 **2.42**	1.81 **2.37**	1.80 **2.33**	1.78 **2.31**
23	2.14 **2.97**	2.10 **2.89**	2.04 **2.78**	2.00 **2.70**	1.96 **2.62**	1.91 **2.53**	1.88 **2.48**	1.84 **2.41**	1.82 **2.37**	1.79 **2.32**	1.77 **2.28**	1.76 **2.26**
24	2.13 **2.93**	2.09 **2.85**	2.02 **2.74**	1.98 **2.66**	1.94 **2.58**	1.89 **2.49**	1.86 **2.44**	1.82 **2.36**	1.80 **2.33**	1.76 **2.27**	1.74 **2.23**	1.73 **2.21**
25	2.11 **2.89**	2.06 **2.81**	2.00 **2.70**	1.96 **2.62**	1.92 **2.54**	1.87 **2.45**	1.84 **2.40**	1.80 **2.32**	1.77 **2.29**	1.74 **2.23**	1.72 **2.19**	1.71 **2.17**
26	2.10 **2.86**	2.05 **2.77**	1.99 **2.66**	1.95 **2.58**	1.90 **2.50**	1.85 **2.41**	1.82 **2.36**	1.78 **2.28**	1.76 **2.25**	1.72 **2.19**	1.70 **2.15**	1.69 **2.13**

TABLE A–3 (Continued)

n_1 = degrees of freedom for numerator

n_2 = degrees of freedom for denominator

n_2	1	2	3	4	5	6	7	8	9	10	11	12
27	4.21 / 7.68	3.35 / 5.49	2.96 / 4.60	2.73 / 4.11	2.57 / 3.79	2.46 / 3.56	2.37 / 3.39	2.30 / 3.26	2.25 / 3.14	2.20 / 3.06	2.16 / 2.98	2.13 / 2.93
28	4.20 / 7.64	3.34 / 5.45	2.95 / 4.57	2.71 / 4.07	2.56 / 3.76	2.44 / 3.53	2.36 / 3.36	2.29 / 3.23	2.24 / 3.11	2.19 / 3.03	2.15 / 2.95	2.12 / 2.90
29	4.18 / 7.60	3.33 / 5.42	2.93 / 4.54	2.70 / 4.04	2.54 / 3.73	2.43 / 3.50	2.35 / 3.33	2.28 / 3.20	2.22 / 3.08	2.18 / 3.00	2.14 / 2.92	2.10 / 2.87
30	4.17 / 7.56	3.32 / 5.39	2.92 / 4.51	2.69 / 4.02	2.53 / 3.70	2.42 / 3.47	2.34 / 3.30	2.27 / 3.17	2.21 / 3.06	2.16 / 2.98	2.12 / 2.90	2.09 / 2.84
32	4.15 / 7.50	3.30 / 5.34	2.90 / 4.46	2.67 / 3.97	2.51 / 3.66	2.40 / 3.42	2.32 / 3.25	2.25 / 3.12	2.19 / 3.01	2.14 / 2.94	2.10 / 2.86	2.07 / 2.80
34	4.13 / 7.44	3.28 / 5.29	2.88 / 4.42	2.65 / 3.93	2.49 / 3.61	2.38 / 3.38	2.30 / 3.21	2.23 / 3.08	2.17 / 2.97	2.12 / 2.89	2.08 / 2.82	2.05 / 2.76
36	4.11 / 7.39	3.26 / 5.25	2.86 / 4.38	2.63 / 3.89	2.48 / 3.58	2.36 / 3.35	2.28 / 3.18	2.21 / 3.04	2.15 / 2.94	2.10 / 2.86	2.06 / 2.78	2.03 / 2.72
38	4.10 / 7.35	3.25 / 5.21	2.85 / 4.34	2.62 / 3.86	2.46 / 3.54	2.35 / 3.32	2.26 / 3.15	2.19 / 3.02	2.14 / 2.91	2.09 / 2.82	2.05 / 2.75	2.02 / 2.69
40	4.08 / 7.31	3.23 / 5.18	2.84 / 4.31	2.61 / 3.83	2.45 / 3.51	2.34 / 3.29	2.25 / 3.12	2.18 / 2.99	2.12 / 2.88	2.07 / 2.80	2.04 / 2.73	2.00 / 2.66
42	4.07 / 7.27	3.22 / 5.15	2.83 / 4.29	2.59 / 3.80	2.44 / 3.49	2.32 / 3.26	2.24 / 3.10	2.17 / 2.96	2.11 / 2.86	2.06 / 2.77	2.02 / 2.70	1.99 / 2.64
44	4.06 / 7.24	3.21 / 5.12	2.82 / 4.26	2.58 / 3.78	2.43 / 3.46	2.31 / 3.24	2.23 / 3.07	2.16 / 2.94	2.10 / 2.84	2.05 / 2.75	2.01 / 2.68	1.98 / 2.62
46	4.05 / 7.21	3.20 / 5.10	2.81 / 4.24	2.57 / 3.76	2.42 / 3.44	2.30 / 3.22	2.22 / 3.05	2.14 / 2.92	2.09 / 2.82	2.04 / 2.73	2.00 / 2.66	1.97 / 2.60
48	4.04 / 7.19	3.19 / 5.08	2.80 / 4.22	2.56 / 3.74	2.41 / 3.42	2.30 / 3.20	2.21 / 3.04	2.14 / 2.90	2.08 / 2.80	2.03 / 2.71	1.99 / 2.64	1.96 / 2.58
50	4.03 / 7.17	3.18 / 5.06	2.79 / 4.20	2.56 / 3.72	2.40 / 3.41	2.29 / 3.18	2.20 / 3.02	2.13 / 2.88	2.07 / 2.78	2.02 / 2.70	1.98 / 2.62	1.95 / 2.56
55	4.02 / 7.12	3.17 / 5.01	2.78 / 4.16	2.54 / 3.68	2.38 / 3.37	2.27 / 3.15	2.18 / 2.98	2.11 / 2.85	2.05 / 2.75	2.00 / 2.66	1.97 / 2.59	1.93 / 2.53
60	4.00 / 7.08	3.15 / 4.98	2.76 / 4.13	2.52 / 3.65	2.37 / 3.34	2.25 / 3.12	2.17 / 2.95	2.10 / 2.82	2.04 / 2.72	1.99 / 2.63	1.95 / 2.56	1.92 / 2.50
65	3.99 / 7.04	3.14 / 4.95	2.75 / 4.10	2.51 / 3.62	2.36 / 3.31	2.24 / 3.09	2.15 / 2.93	2.08 / 2.79	2.02 / 2.70	1.98 / 2.61	1.94 / 2.54	1.90 / 2.47
70	3.98 / 7.01	3.13 / 4.92	2.74 / 4.08	2.50 / 3.60	2.35 / 3.29	2.23 / 3.07	2.14 / 2.91	2.07 / 2.77	2.01 / 2.67	1.97 / 2.59	1.93 / 2.51	1.89 / 2.45
80	3.96 / 6.96	3.11 / 4.88	2.72 / 4.04	2.48 / 3.56	2.33 / 3.25	2.21 / 3.04	2.12 / 2.87	2.05 / 2.74	1.99 / 2.64	1.95 / 2.55	1.91 / 2.48	1.88 / 2.41
100	3.94 / 6.90	3.09 / 4.82	2.70 / 3.98	2.46 / 3.51	2.30 / 3.20	2.19 / 2.99	2.10 / 2.82	2.03 / 2.69	1.97 / 2.59	1.92 / 2.51	1.88 / 2.43	1.85 / 2.36
125	3.92 / 6.84	3.07 / 4.78	2.68 / 3.94	2.44 / 3.47	2.29 / 3.17	2.17 / 2.95	2.08 / 2.79	2.01 / 2.65	1.95 / 2.56	1.90 / 2.47	1.86 / 2.40	1.83 / 2.33
150	3.91 / 6.81	3.06 / 4.75	2.67 / 3.91	2.43 / 3.44	2.27 / 3.14	2.16 / 2.92	2.07 / 2.76	2.00 / 2.62	1.94 / 2.53	1.89 / 2.44	1.85 / 2.37	1.82 / 2.30
200	3.89 / 6.76	3.04 / 4.71	2.65 / 3.88	2.41 / 3.41	2.26 / 3.11	2.14 / 2.90	2.05 / 2.73	1.98 / 2.60	1.92 / 2.50	1.87 / 2.41	1.83 / 2.34	1.80 / 2.28
400	3.86 / 6.70	3.02 / 4.66	2.62 / 3.83	2.39 / 3.36	2.23 / 3.06	2.12 / 2.85	2.03 / 2.69	1.96 / 2.55	1.90 / 2.46	1.85 / 2.37	1.81 / 2.29	1.78 / 2.23
1,000	3.85 / 6.66	3.00 / 4.62	2.61 / 3.80	2.38 / 3.34	2.22 / 3.04	2.10 / 2.82	2.02 / 2.66	1.95 / 2.53	1.89 / 2.43	1.84 / 2.34	1.80 / 2.26	1.76 / 2.20
∞	3.84 / 6.64	2.99 / 4.60	2.60 / 3.78	2.37 / 3.32	2.21 / 3.02	2.09 / 2.80	2.01 / 2.64	1.94 / 2.51	1.88 / 2.41	1.83 / 2.32	1.79 / 2.24	1.75 / 2.18

TABLE A–3 (*Concluded*)

n_1 = degrees of freedom for numerator

n_2 = degrees of freedom for denominator

	14	16	20	24	30	40	50	75	100	200	500	∞
27	2.08 **2.83**	2.03 **2.74**	1.97 **2.63**	1.93 **2.55**	1.88 **2.47**	1.84 **2.38**	1.80 **2.33**	1.76 **2.25**	1.74 **2.21**	1.71 **2.16**	1.68 **2.12**	1.67 **2.10**
28	2.06 **2.80**	2.02 **2.71**	1.96 **2.60**	1.91 **2.52**	1.87 **2.44**	1.81 **2.35**	1.78 **2.30**	1.75 **2.22**	1.72 **2.18**	1.69 **2.13**	1.67 **2.09**	1.65 **2.06**
29	2.05 **2.77**	2.00 **2.68**	1.94 **2.57**	1.90 **2.49**	1.85 **2.41**	1.80 **2.32**	1.77 **2.27**	1.73 **2.19**	1.71 **2.15**	1.68 **2.10**	1.65 **2.06**	1.64 **2.03**
30	2.04 **2.74**	1.99 **2.66**	1.93 **2.55**	1.89 **2.47**	1.84 **2.38**	1.79 **2.29**	1.76 **2.24**	1.72 **2.16**	1.69 **2.13**	1.66 **2.07**	1.64 **2.03**	1.62 **2.01**
32	2.02 **2.70**	1.97 **2.62**	1.91 **2.51**	1.86 **2.42**	1.82 **2.34**	1.76 **2.25**	1.74 **2.20**	1.69 **2.12**	1.67 **2.08**	1.64 **2.02**	1.61 **1.98**	1.59 **1.96**
34	2.00 **2.66**	1.95 **2.58**	1.89 **2.47**	1.84 **2.38**	1.80 **2.30**	1.74 **2.21**	1.71 **2.15**	1.67 **2.08**	1.64 **2.04**	1.61 **1.98**	1.59 **1.94**	1.57 **1.91**
36	1.98 **2.62**	1.93 **2.54**	1.87 **2.43**	1.82 **2.35**	1.78 **2.26**	1.72 **2.17**	1.69 **2.12**	1.65 **2.04**	1.62 **2.00**	1.59 **1.94**	1.56 **1.90**	1.55 **1.87**
38	1.96 **2.59**	1.92 **2.51**	1.85 **2.40**	1.80 **2.32**	1.76 **2.22**	1.71 **2.14**	1.67 **2.08**	1.63 **2.00**	1.60 **1.97**	1.57 **1.90**	1.54 **1.86**	1.53 **1.84**
40	1.95 **2.56**	1.90 **2.49**	1.84 **2.37**	1.79 **2.29**	1.74 **2.20**	1.69 **2.11**	1.66 **2.05**	1.61 **1.97**	1.59 **1.94**	1.55 **1.88**	1.53 **1.84**	1.51 **1.81**
42	1.94 **2.54**	1.89 **2.46**	1.82 **2.35**	1.78 **2.26**	1.73 **2.17**	1.68 **2.08**	1.64 **2.02**	1.60 **1.94**	1.57 **1.91**	1.54 **1.85**	1.51 **1.80**	1.49 **1.78**
44	1.92 **2.52**	1.88 **2.44**	1.81 **2.32**	1.76 **2.24**	1.72 **2.15**	1.66 **2.06**	1.63 **2.00**	1.58 **1.92**	1.56 **1.88**	1.52 **1.82**	1.50 **1.78**	1.48 **1.75**
46	1.91 **2.50**	1.87 **2.42**	1.80 **2.30**	1.75 **2.22**	1.71 **2.13**	1.65 **2.04**	1.62 **1.98**	1.57 **1.90**	1.54 **1.86**	1.51 **1.80**	1.48 **1.76**	1.46 **1.72**
48	1.90 **2.48**	1.86 **2.40**	1.79 **2.28**	1.74 **2.20**	1.70 **2.11**	1.64 **2.02**	1.61 **1.96**	1.56 **1.88**	1.53 **1.84**	1.50 **1.78**	1.47 **1.73**	1.45 **1.70**
50	1.90 **2.46**	1.85 **2.39**	1.78 **2.26**	1.74 **2.18**	1.69 **2.10**	1.63 **2.00**	1.60 **1.94**	1.55 **1.86**	1.52 **1.82**	1.48 **1.76**	1.46 **1.71**	1.44 **1.68**
55	1.88 **2.43**	1.83 **2.35**	1.76 **2.23**	1.72 **2.15**	1.67 **2.06**	1.61 **1.96**	1.58 **1.90**	1.52 **1.82**	1.50 **1.78**	1.46 **1.71**	1.43 **1.66**	1.41 **1.64**
60	1.86 **2.40**	1.81 **2.32**	1.75 **2.20**	1.70 **2.12**	1.65 **2.03**	1.59 **1.93**	1.56 **1.87**	1.50 **1.79**	1.48 **1.74**	1.44 **1.68**	1.41 **1.63**	1.39 **1.60**
65	1.85 **2.37**	1.80 **2.30**	1.73 **2.18**	1.68 **2.09**	1.63 **2.00**	1.57 **1.90**	1.54 **1.84**	1.49 **1.76**	1.46 **1.71**	1.42 **1.64**	1.39 **1.60**	1.37 **1.56**
70	1.84 **2.35**	1.79 **2.28**	1.72 **2.15**	1.67 **2.07**	1.62 **1.98**	1.56 **1.88**	1.53 **1.82**	1.47 **1.74**	1.45 **1.69**	1.40 **1.62**	1.37 **1.56**	1.35 **1.53**
80	1.82 **2.32**	1.77 **2.24**	1.70 **2.11**	1.65 **2.03**	1.60 **1.94**	1.54 **1.84**	1.51 **1.78**	1.45 **1.70**	1.42 **1.65**	1.38 **1.57**	1.35 **1.52**	1.32 **1.49**
100	1.79 **2.26**	1.75 **2.19**	1.68 **2.06**	1.63 **1.98**	1.57 **1.89**	1.51 **1.79**	1.48 **1.73**	1.42 **1.64**	1.39 **1.59**	1.34 **1.51**	1.30 **1.46**	1.28 **1.43**
125	1.77 **2.23**	1.72 **2.15**	1.65 **2.03**	1.60 **1.94**	1.55 **1.85**	1.49 **1.75**	1.45 **1.68**	1.39 **1.59**	1.36 **1.54**	1.31 **1.46**	1.27 **1.40**	1.25 **1.37**
150	1.76 **2.20**	1.71 **2.12**	1.64 **2.00**	1.59 **1.91**	1.54 **1.83**	1.47 **1.72**	1.44 **1.66**	1.37 **1.56**	1.34 **1.51**	1.29 **1.43**	1.25 **1.37**	1.22 **1.33**
200	1.74 **2.17**	1.69 **2.09**	1.62 **1.97**	1.57 **1.88**	1.52 **1.79**	1.45 **1.69**	1.42 **1.62**	1.35 **1.53**	1.32 **1.48**	1.26 **1.39**	1.22 **1.33**	1.19 **1.25**
400	1.72 **2.12**	1.67 **2.04**	1.60 **1.92**	1.54 **1.84**	1.49 **1.74**	1.42 **1.64**	1.38 **1.57**	1.32 **1.47**	1.28 **1.42**	1.22 **1.32**	1.16 **1.24**	1.13 **1.19**
1,000	1.70 **2.09**	1.65 **2.01**	1.58 **1.89**	1.53 **1.81**	1.47 **1.71**	1.41 **1.61**	1.36 **1.54**	1.30 **1.44**	1.26 **1.38**	1.19 **1.28**	1.13 **1.19**	1.08 **1.11**
∞	1.69 **2.07**	1.64 **1.99**	1.57 **1.87**	1.52 **1.79**	1.46 **1.69**	1.40 **1.59**	1.35 **1.52**	1.28 **1.41**	1.24 **1.36**	1.17 **1.25**	1.11 **1.15**	1.00 **1.00**

Index

INDEX